HURON COUNTY LIBR
P9-CTP-858
R BRANCH LIBRAR
Due
HURON COUNTY LIBRARY
2 008 1533399 2

MUTUAL HOSTAGES

Patricia E. Roy
J.L. Granatstein
Masako Iino
Hiroko Takamura

MUTUAL HOSTAGES

Canadians and Japanese during the Second World War

UNIVERSITY OF TORONTO PRESS
Toronto Buffalo London

University of Toronto Press
Toronto Buffalo London
Printed in Canada
ISBN 0–8020–5774–8

Printed on acid-free paper

Canadian Cataloguing in Publication Data

Main entry under title:

Mutual hostages

Includes bibliographical references.
ISBN 0-8020-5774-8
1. Japanese Canadians–Evacuation and relocation, 1942–1945.* 2. Canada–Politics and government–1935–1948.* 3. World War, 1939–1945–Prisoners and prisons, Japanese. 4. World War, 1939–1945–Prisoners and prisons, Canadian. 5. World War, 1939–1945–Evacuation of civilians–Japan. 6. Canadians–Japan–History. 7. Japan–Politics and government–1926–1945. I. Roy, Patricia, 1939– .

FC106.J3M88 1990 940.53'1771 C90-093527-8
F1035.J3M88 1990

In memory of Genji Okubo and Nobuya Bamba
and for Yuko Ohara,
founders of Canadian studies in Japan

Contents

Preface

Mutual Hostages is an attempt to re-examine the subject of Japanese and Canadians during the Second World War. Initially, the authors, two Canadian historians and two Japanese historians of Canada, planned to make this a comparative study of Canada and Japan. Although we have drawn on a wide range of English and Japanese manuscript and printed sources in Canada, the United States, and Japan, we have been unable to make our story truly comparative. Before and during the Second World War, Canada did not loom large in the Japanese consciousness, and the pertinent records of the Imperial Japanese government which escaped destruction in August and September 1945 are thin. Even so, we have been able to include more on Japanese policy towards Canada and Canadians than can be found elsewhere. Most of the relevant records of the Canadian government have survived and are available to researchers, despite the occasional vagaries of Ottawa's Access to Information and Privacy acts. Thus, this book concentrates on Ottawa's actions and policies and their effects on the Japanese in Canada.

Our object in writing this book has been the historian's traditional task: to set out what happened and to try to determine the reasons. We have sought to explain, not to condone or condemn. We have several major themes. Both wartime Canada and Japan looked on the Japanese and Canadians under their control as mutual hostages. There is evidence that Japan viewed interned civilians and prisoners of war in this way and, though its treatment of POWs was sometimes appalling, it tempered its policies as a result. Ottawa always acted towards Japanese Canadians with the clear understanding that any harsh action could endanger Canadians in Japan. This is not to suggest that the Canadian and Japanese governments' treatment of their hostages was equivalent; it was not. But there were similarities as well as differences, and these need to be made clear.

We also set out to try to determine what the Canadian and Japanese governments and peoples knew and, more importantly, what they believed about each other. In Canada, Ottawa had little detailed information on the Japanese-Canadian community and much of what it had was contradictory. Similarly, Canadian military officials had contradictory information and conflicting opinions about the possibility of a Japanese attack on Canada's Pacific coast. In short, the Canadian government acted largely out of ignorance and in response to public fear. In Japan, the Imperial government and the public had only modest interest in and knowledge of the Japanese in Canada. And, given Japanese military law and custom, only passing awareness of the actions and practices of prison camp commanders.

A third theme is the mixture of loyalties uncovered in our research. Some Japanese Canadians knew exactly where their loyalties lay and never wavered. Two extreme examples illustrate the point. Both Thomas Shoyama and Kanao Inouye were North American-born *Nisei* from the BC interior city of Kamloops. Shoyama graduated from the University of British Columbia, edited the *New Canadian*, the newspaper founded before the war for Japanese Canadians, worked for equality for his people, fought for the right to join the Canadian army, and eventually rose to high positions in the Canadian public service. Inouye, in contrast, went to Japan with his mother and became an interpreter with the *Kempeitai*, the Japanese secret service. To Canadian soldiers captured at Hong Kong, Inouye became known as the 'Kamloops Kid,' a vicious and terrifying interrogator responsible for several deaths and countless beatings. He was executed for his crimes after V-J Day. Many Japanese-born *Issei* and *Nisei*, however, found that choosing sides was not easy, as the emotional turmoil surrounding the repatriation question in 1945 and 1946 demonstrates. For *Nisei*, their dilemma was complicated by Ottawa's largely ignoring their status as Canadian citizens.

To a lesser extent, some Canadian missionaries in Japan also found their affections divided between their parishioners and students and their homeland. Only prisoners of war were in no doubt about their loyalties; their situation left them little need to reflect. In Canada, the public was far from united in its attitude to Japanese Canadians, as debates over their fate reveal. Even in British Columbia, where hostility to the Japanese was high, there were always at least a few voices calling for just treatment for the Japanese in Canada.

Perhaps because Canada was only a minor player in the Pacific war, little has been written about the more than 2000 Canadians who spent the war in uncomfortable captivity in Japanese hands. A small array of official and popular histories of the brief and disastrous Hong Kong campaign have been published, along with regimental histories of the units involved and a useful collection of edited interviews with former POWs by Daniel Dancocks, but historians have ignored Canadian missionaries and civilians interned in Japan.

In contrast, there is a growing and varied literature on the Japanese Canadians during the Second World War. Forrest LaViolette's sociological study, *The Canadian Japanese in World War II*,[1] was published soon after the peace and lacked access to primary sources. Similarly, though Ken Adachi's study of the Japanese in Canada is comprehensive, he employed little archival material.[2] Peter Ward, in *White Canada Forever*,[3] made good use of the available material but his short book essentially concludes with the evacuation of 1942. Before writing *The Politics of Racism*,[4] Ann Sunahara exploited the archival sources and interviewed many participants, but she tends to see issues in black and white and to ignore the shades of grey that often cloud history.

In recent years, some Japanese Canadians have published their own accounts. Joy Kogawa's powerful and popular novel *Obasan*[5] has had great emotional impact. Much of it is based on the letters and memoirs of Muriel Kitagawa, whose writings have been posthumously published as *This Is My Own*.[6] Less well known is *Within the Barbed Wire Fence*, a memoir by Takeo Nakano, who spent fourteen months at the Angler, Ontario, internment camp.[7] A scattered sampling of memoirs can also be found in the oral history compiled by journalist Barry Broadfoot in *Years of Sorrow, Years of Shame*.[8] Although scholars in Japan have studied aspects of the Japanese experience in Canada and some individuals have published memoirs of their time in Canada, virtually none of these works deals with the wartime experiences of Japanese Canadians.

We know that ours is an emotional subject, especially in Canada where the Japanese Canadians' long campaign for redress of the wrongs of war has kept the issue in the public conscience. We wrote this book with the intention of examining the events of the war years as dispassionately as possible and trying to explain them in the context of their times. Fingers can easily be pointed at historical actors, blame can readily be affixed on politicians and generals, but that would do little to help today's Canadians and Japanese understand the wartime actions of their compatriots and governments.

Understanding the past is hard at the best of times. After examining the evidence, we are convinced that no simple answers can satisfactorily explain the events of the war years. Only by accepting the complexity of motivation, only by understanding the context and attitudes of a half century ago, can the truth be found. That we have tried to do.

Acknowledgments

The Social Sciences and Humanities Research Council of Canada funded this work and allowed all four of us to travel to distant archives. The Ontario Arts Council also helped. We are most grateful for this assistance.

We have, as so often before, been assisted by archivists in Canada and in Japan. Special thanks are due to the National Archives of Canada, the British Columbia Archives and Records Service, the British Columbia Legislative Library, the University of British Columbia Special Collections, the City of Vancouver Archives, the Directorate of History, National Defence Headquarters, and the Department of External Affairs. In Japan, the Foreign Relations Archives and the Institute of Defence Archives were most cooperative.

Special assistance has been provided by Greg Johnson and Sylvie Beaudreau, who helped us with research, by Professor Peter Mitchell, who kindly read one particular chapter and prevented innumerable errors of interpretation, and by the secretarial staff of the history department of the University of Victoria. Gerald Hallowell, Mary McDougall Maude, and Rosemary Shipton were most understanding and perceptive editors. Our thanks to them all.

Abbreviations

BCARS	British Columbia Archives and Records Service
BCSC	British Columbia Security Commission Records, NA
BSC	British Security Coordination
CEP	Office of the Custodian of Enemy Property Records, NA
CVA	City of Vancouver Archives
CWC	Cabinet War Committee Records, Privy Council Records, NA
DCER	*Documents on Canadian External Relations*
DEA	Department of External Affairs Records, NA
DHist	Directorate of History, Department of National Defence, Records
DImm	Department of Immigration Records, NA
DLab	Department of Labour Records, NA
DND	Department of National Defence Records, NA
EAR	Department of External Affairs Records held at the department, Ottawa
GK	Gaimushō Kiroku: Documents of the Diplomatic Record Archives, Ministry of Foreign Affairs, Tokyo
HCD	House of Commons, *Debates*
IMP	Ian Mackenzie Papers, NA
JCCA	Japanese Canadian Citizens' Association Records, NA
KD	Mackenzie King Diary, NA
NA	National Archives of Canada, Ottawa
NC	*New Canadian*
NGB	*Japanese Diplomatic Documents*
NMEG	Nisei Mass Evacuation Group
PJBD	Permanent Joint Board on Defence
PCO	Privy Council Office Records, NA

PP	Premiers' Papers, BCARS
RCAF	Royal Canadian Air Force
RCMP	Royal Canadian Mounted Police Records, NA
RCN	Royal Canadian Navy
UBC	University of British Columbia Special Collections, Vancouver
UCA	United Church Archives, Toronto
USNA	United States National Archives, Washington
WLMK	Mackenzie King Papers, NA
WLP	Wilfrid Laurier Papers, NA

MUTUAL HOSTAGES

One

The Imin *and Canadians*

In 1877 Manzo Nagano, a nineteen-year-old sailor, stayed ashore when his ship left New Westminster, British Columbia, to return to Asia. The energetic Nagano, who may have been the only Japanese in Canada for about fifteen years, first earned his living fishing for salmon and longshoring.[1] He returned to Japan for a time, travelled to the United States, and finally settled in Victoria in 1892, where he established a shop selling Japanese products and later branched out into the salmon-exporting business. Soon he brought a woman from Japan to be his wife and opened a hotel. Nagano's industry was characteristic of the Japanese who came to Canada in later years, but Caucasians in British Columbia paid scant attention to his varied activities. Like this first *imin*, the Japanese who came later enjoyed economic successes but, unlike him, they were conspicuous by their numbers and their concentration in particular areas. They were visible targets of economic jealousy and racial fears.

As a ship jumper, Nagano violated Japan's maritime law and its policy of discouraging emigration. Japan wanted potential emigrants, particularly members of the former Samurai class, to colonize the northern island of Hokkaido, to raise foodstuffs, and to help check Russia's southern expansion. Emigration seemed to do little to ease population pressures at home[2] and, despite individual remittances and the claims of advocates of emigration, emigrants' earnings added little to the domestic economy.[3]

Although its interest in the well-being of its subjects who did go abroad was minimal,[4] the Meiji government (1868–1912) was determined to gain Western respect for both Japan and the Japanese. Based on its experience with contract labourers in Hawaii, it drew up an Emigration Protection Ordinance in 1896. The law emphasized government control over the emigration process and the operations of private emigration companies, but its aim was primarily to avoid any impression abroad of a 'disorganized and unregulated emigration' that would hurt 'Japan's image as a modern nation.'[5] In fact, it laid out only minimum guidelines and allowed the privately owned emigration companies to recruit emigrants and help them on their way.[6] About three-quarters of all emigrants in the last years of the Meiji era left through the auspices of such companies. The companies flourished especially in the southwestern prefectures from which successful emigrants had earlier gone and were, of course, more interested in profits than in the fate of their clients.

The government's only contribution to the *imin* in Canada was 'protection' through its consulates, the first of which was established in Vancouver in 1889.[7] As Japanese citizens abroad, the emigrants had to turn to the consulate to secure passports, certificates of Canadian residency, the papers needed to bring family members to Canada, and documents relating to family matters such as births, deaths, marriages, divorces, adoptions, and inheritances. The consuls, from a higher social class than most of their countrymen in Canada, seldom comprehended the problems of the *imin.*[8] Nevertheless, the consuls were almost the only people on whom the *imin* could rely in their strange new land.

The consuls, however, did try to develop a favourable image of their countrymen, especially after a Vancouver newspaper remarked that 'the lower class Japanese are by no means ... desirable settlers ... They stand in a wholly different position from that occupied by the intelligent Japanese of the middle and higher classes.'[9] The consul in Vancouver shamefully reported to Tokyo that arriving immigrants had a 'grotesque' appearance and were from the lowest class of labourers.[10] In the hope of making Japanese immigrants more acceptable in a province that had been antagonistic to the Chinese since they first arrived in 1858, the consulate in Vancouver repeatedly proclaimed that the Japanese, unlike the Chinese, were 'highly civilized,' 'clean and frugal,' 'set up families,' 'opened churches,' and wore the same kind of clothing and ate the same kind of food as Canadians. In short, said the consulate, the Japanese were good citizens who helped develop the country.[11]

Ironically, the good qualities the consul attributed to his countrymen made the Japanese seem more formidable competitors than the Chinese. Moreover, the dependence of the *imin* on the consul roused suspicions in the white community that Japan exercised a firm control over her people abroad and did not allow them to surrender their Japanese citizenship and loyalties.

The consul, in fact, saw his primary role as maintaining good relations with the Canadian government, not helping migrants with their problems, a point underscored by the establishment in 1902 of a consulate general in Montreal, where there were few, if any, *imin*, and its relocation to Ottawa two years later. Japan expected her emigrants to keep quiet, cause no difficulties, and attract no untoward attention. Only when anti-Japanese sentiments in Canada and the United States came to Tokyo's attention did Japan pay serious attention to the problems of emigrants.

Most early migrants to Canada came from southwestern Honshu, the main island, and especially from the depressed prefectures of Shiga, Wakayama, Hiroshima, Kumamoto, and Fukuoka.[12] Koto in Shiga Prefecture was typical of such once prosperous villages. Repeated floods had reduced its rice production, and cheap imports had harmed its cotton industry.[13] The single most important source of *imin* in British Columbia, however, was Mio in Wakayama Prefecture. One of its residents, Gihei Kudo, a poor carpenter, stowed away on a freighter and arrived in British Columbia in 1887. Impressed by the salmon-fishing opportunities on the Fraser River, he encouraged so many of his fellow villagers, whose local fisheries and trading economy were in distress, to join him in the new world that Mio village became popularly known in Japan as 'America village.'[14] In fact, many immigrants to Canada had intended to go to the United States but stayed when their ship docked first at a Canadian port. Others made little distinction between Canada and the United States, calling the two North American nations by the generic name, 'America.' Even in the 1890s, Canada had an identity problem abroad!

About two-thirds of the emigrants to Canada in the Meiji era were peasants, but there were also craftsmen, such as carpenters, and even a few ex-Samurai.[15] Emigrants normally did not come from the poorest classes because they needed a substantial sum of money to pay their passage, passport charges, and other fees.[16] Until at least 1908 about 80 per cent of the *imin* were single males.[17] Often, they were second or younger sons who could not inherit land but who, unlike their eldest brothers, had neither responsibilities for continuing the family line nor special legal rights.[18] In Canada, even contract labourers could expect to earn four to five times the going rate in Japan.[19] Conditions were often unsatisfactory but stories of the successful and the advertisements of emigration companies encouraged emigration.

Most migrants were *dekasegi* or sojourners who planned to work abroad temporarily before returning home in triumph. They worked mainly in the resource industries of fishing, mining, and lumbering and in railroad construction and maintenance. Individuals changed jobs frequently, but the concentration of the Japanese in a few industries made them conspicuous and seem more numerous than they actually were.

Although the *dekasegi* tradition was that they return home, the growth of the Japanese population in Canada suggests that many did not. Some were clearly such failures that they were too embarrassed to return; others began to consider Canada as home, especially after bringing wives from Japan and raising Canadian-born children for whom they saw a bright future. An obvious sign of commitment was the purchase of land. In 1906 Jiro Inoue became the first Japanese landowner in Canada when he bought property in the Fraser Valley at Haney and began to grow strawberries. Finding the business profitable and encountering less discrimination in agriculture than in other occupations, he encouraged others to join him through articles in Japanese newspapers. Because he was one of the few Japanese settlers in the district who could speak English, he became a community leader and, in 1919, the first president of their Haney Agricultural Association. He remained in Haney as the respected pioneer of Japanese settlement until his death in 1931.

Though many immigrants firmly established themselves and their families in Canada, others maintained close ties with Japan, even sending their children home for their education. In some cases, families in economic difficulties thought little of asking relatives to look after their children. Those working in isolated mining or lumbering camps knew the limitations of local schools; some wanted their children to acquire Japanese culture;[20] and still others wanted their children to escape the resentment that British Columbia whites directed at the Japanese people.

In British Columbia, employers had welcomed Japanese immigrants as a source of cheap and efficient labour. Their white employees, however, objected to Japanese competition for jobs and, with the province's racists, sought to restrict Japanese immigration and employment opportunities. As a federal royal commission concluded in 1902, the consensus in the province was that the Japanese

> do not and cannot assimilate with white people, and that while in some respects they are more desirable than the Chinese, in that they adopt more readily our habits of life and spend more of their earnings in the country, yet in all that goes to make for the permanent settlement of the country they are quite as serious a menace as the Chinese and keener competitors against the working man, and as they have more energy, push and independence, more dangerous in this regard than the Chinese.[21]

The provincial government was receptive to such ideas, particularly since it did not have to worry about any political repercussions from the Japanese whom it had quietly disfranchised in 1895. Disfranchisement was tantamount to a denial of full civic rights, since inclusion on the provincial voters' list was often a prerequisite for voting in federal elections, for membership in certain professional organizations, and for the receipt of certain kinds of licenses.

Because only those Japanese who had become naturalized British subjects might have expected to vote, the government of Japan does not appear to have protested the denial of these basic civil rights to its former subjects.[22] Japan, however, was keen to avoid embarrassment caused by legislation directed against Japanese subjects in general. Thus, in 1897, the consul successfully protested provincial government attempts to reserve employment in the mining and transportation industries for whites and to prevent the 'unrestricted immigration of Japanese.' In objecting to British Columbia's labour laws, Japan had a sound argument. Japan and Great Britain had signed a Treaty of Commerce and Navigation in 1894 which allowed the citizens of each country 'full liberty to enter, travel or reside in any part of the dominions and possessions of the other contracting party.' Since Canada was then a dominion of Great Britain with no independence in her foreign policy, Tokyo had an effective lever. And, while the Liberal government of Sir Wilfrid Laurier did not want to alienate people in British Columbia, it was unwilling to cause complications between Tokyo and London or do anything that might retard the development of Canadian trade with Japan.[23]

Japan was also keen to develop trade. Thus, in 1897, the consul suggested that Japan would be willing to restrict emigration provided it was done by mutual regulation.[24] Nothing seems to have developed from this proposal, but in the summer of 1899 Tokyo tried to forestall any anti-Japanese immigration legislation on the part of British Columbia by announcing a voluntary ban on emigration to Canada. British Columbians were not impressed, especially after an influx of Japanese immigrants in 1900. The provincial legislature began passing its own immigration acts, the so-called Natal acts which required immigrants, if challenged, to demonstrate a knowledge of English. That the Japanese were the main targets was clear; as one provincial newspaper noted, having British Columbia 'over-run by Japanese is [not] in the best interests of the British Empire.'[25]

Such vehement attacks and the inability of the new arrivals to find work led the consul in Vancouver to urge the *Gaimushō*, the Ministry of Foreign Affairs, to limit emigration. Tokyo agreed, but its declaration was so ambiguous that British Columbians were uncertain whether the maximum number of emigrants was to be 120 or 5000 per year! Meanwhile the consul informed the governments in Ottawa and Victoria that Japan had voluntarily decided to ban emigration to Canada completely, effective 30 July 1900. British Columbians were delighted,[26] especially when only six immigrants arrived in 1900–1 and none in the next three years.

Nevertheless, British Columbians, who were also concerned about Chinese immigration, continued to protest the idea of unrestricted Asian immigration, particularly after the federal government bowed to diplomatic pressure from Japan and regularly disallowed the Natal acts which the legislature passed almost annually from 1900 to 1908. Partly as a means of assuaging British Columbians, the federal government in 1900 had appointed a royal commission to investigate Chinese and Japanese immigration. A Vancouver lawyer, probably hired by the consul, reminded the commissioners of Britain's policy of an 'open door,' referred to trade prospects, and suggested that Japan would discuss immigration problems as 'one of the great nations.'[27]

Such propaganda was partly effective. Although British Columbians did not change their opinion about the Japanese in their midst, they keenly followed the Russo-Japanese War, 1902–5, and joined the local Japanese community in celebrating victories and raising funds for war relief. Freed from the immediate pressure of new immigrants, they welcomed the renewal of the Anglo-Japanese Treaty of Commerce and Navigation in 1905 and the visits of General Kuroki and Prince Fushimi, who came separately in the spring of 1907.

Japan's success in the war made her expansionist. As one influential journal noted, 'our expansive energy, now bursting out after a long period of waiting should not be channeled only in the direction of Asia, but should cover the whole of mankind.'[28] Some serious scholars began advocating expansion and emigration; the government of Japan evidently shared this view.[29]

Thus, once Canada adhered to the Anglo-Japanese Treaty of Commerce and Navigation in 1906, Tokyo sought to relax her voluntary emigration restrictions. Before doing so, the Foreign Ministry had Consul Kishiro Morikawa in Vancouver prepare a long report on the situation in British Columbia. Morikawa warned that the anti-Japanese movement in California was 'reaching its peak and the irrational arguments of anti-Japanese agitators [were] being reported in the Vancouver morning and evening newspapers, spurring anti-Japanese sentiments here.' He advised that if emigration restrictions were relaxed, only a 'small number at a time' should be permitted to come.[30] From Ottawa, Consul-General Tatsugoro Nosse agreed that mass immigration would upset 'the balance of supply and demand of labour' and stimulate vehement opposition against Japanese immigration.[31]

Despite such admonitions, 5571 Japanese immigrants arrived at BC ports in the first six months of 1907. Rumours abounded, including one that the Grand Trunk Pacific Railway was planning to import thousands of workers. British Columbians talked about a 'systematic scheme' to flood the market with cheap labour and protested that the Japanese were a 'menace to the country' who could easily dispossess the small white population.[32]

In the summer of 1907 an Asiatic Exclusion League appeared in Vancouver. Modelled on similar bodies on the west coast of the United States, it was locally organized and had the support of prominent local politicians. Surprisingly, it had trouble recruiting members. To draw attention to itself, it organized a parade and rally in downtown Vancouver on 7 September 1907. About 5000 men, some carrying banners with such slogans as 'Stand for a White Canada,' marched towards the City Hall where the Asiatic Exclusion League had organized a meeting featuring local speakers and some visiting Americans. Reporters estimated that as many as 25,000 people had gathered around City Hall on an unusually hot and muggy evening. Inside, the audience was orderly; outside, the same speakers addressed the volatile overflow crowd. When someone threw a brick through a store window, the banner-waving mob pressed towards the nearby Chinese and Japanese quarters. Initially, the city police could not cope 'with the mass of struggling, cursing, shouting humanity.' 'Little Tokyo,' the Japanese quarter, had a little warning of the riot and its residents were able to dispel the mob. Eventually, after arresting some men for rioting and disorderly conduct, the city police persuaded the rest to go home.[33] Many windows were broken but, fortunately, there were no serious injuries and no loss of life.

Almost before the last of the rioters had gone to bed, reporters were sending news of the riot around the world. Vancouver residents, who wanted to present an image of law and order to attract white immigrants and investors, wrongly accused American agitators of fomenting the riot. Because of Canada's adherence to various Anglo-Japanese treaties of commerce and navigation, the federal government was seriously embarrassed and immediately sent William Lyon Mackenzie King, the deputy minister of labour, to Vancouver to receive and investigate claims and to pay for actual property damages. King accepted $9000 worth of damage claims from the Japanese community. In the course of his investigation he also determined that Japanese boarding-house keepers and employment agencies were responsible for much of the recent influx of immigrants. Privately, King believed that Japan had increased the number of passports issued for Canada and he suggested that because of Japan's desire to become a great power in the Pacific it was natural that 'her statesmen should have an eye on the western coast of North America.' His report vaguely hinted at possible collusion between the government of Japan and the immigration companies. Although King admitted that Japan could not control her subjects once they left her shores, he insisted that to retain friendly relations between the two countries there should be 'effective restriction of the number of Japanese who shall be admitted to Canada each year.'[34]

The *Gaimushō* perceived the Vancouver riot as 'a thunderbolt from a clear sky' and as an 'unprecedented incident.'[35] The shock was especially great because Canada's adhesion to the Anglo-Japanese Treaty of Commerce and Navigation in 1906 had seemed to herald good relations between Japan and Canada. Ottawa's prompt apologies for the riot, comments in the Vancouver press that the riot was a 'disgrace,' and the offer of compensation for damage to Japanese-owned property helped soothe Japanese concerns. The commissioner of the Bureau of Commerce of Japan, the experienced diplomat Kikujiro Ishii, recommended an amicable and informal settlement of the incident because of the 'constant and unfailing friendly attitude' of Canada.[36] Similarly, the consul in Vancouver, while noting that Canadians deeply regretted the incident, warned that the Canadian people were 'not pleased with the influx of alien immigrants' and wanted to keep theirs as a 'white man's country.' He urged his government to act to prevent any recurrence of trouble, but at the same time he insisted that Japanese people had a legal right to enter Canada and live there under the terms of the Anglo-Japanese Treaty. The *Gaimushō* recognized that the plight of the *imin* in British Columbia was no longer a local matter but 'an important problem concerning the principles of the nation.'[37]

Soon after the riot, Ottawa decided to appease British Columbia by sending the minister of labour, Rodolphe Lemieux to Japan to discuss immigration problems. The *Gaimushō,* aware that Lemieux's 'actual expectation' was 'to restrict the entry of Japanese immigrants' and not simply to 'calm hostile public opinion,' was not pleased by Ottawa's request that it receive Lemieux. Because he had to consider his own public opinion, Ishii told Laurier that Japan 'could not make any binding agreement' to restrict emigration. Moreover, he argued that by adhering to the Anglo-Japanese Treaty, Canada had surrendered her right to restrict immigration. Laurier angrily replied that Japanese diplomats had misled Canada into believing that their government would honour existing restrictions on emigration, and he threatened to denounce the treaty if it were shown 'that the Japanese government was willfully violating it.' But Laurier was also a realist. Rhetorically, he asked, 'Is it not infinitely better in view of trade relations with Japan and of Japan being an ally of Great Britain, that the restrictions which we desire should be imposed not by act of Parliament but by voluntary action of the Japanese government itself?'[38]

Tokyo agreed that refusing to discuss immigration restrictions might lead to a worse situation – namely, the election of the Conservative party; it was so vehement in its opposition to Japanese immigration that it might denounce the treaty and incidentally cause substantial commercial losses. Recognizing that Lemieux's mission enabled Ottawa to respond to demands for restrictions on immigration without causing a loss of face for Japan, the *Gaimushō* accepted it and offered 'assurance that emigration from Japan would be restricted in some form or other.'[39] Also influential was Britain's declining enthusiasm for the Anglo-Japanese Alliance of 1902.[40] To avoid irritating Britain further, Tokyo accepted Canada's proposal to negotiate restrictions on emigration.[41] The resulting Gentlemen's Agreement of 1908, commonly called the Lemieux Agreement in both Canada and Japan, specified numerical restrictions; later that year, a Gentlemen's Agreement with the United States also significantly restricted the number of emigrants to that country.

The Lemieux Agreement obliged Japan to issue no more than 400 passports annually to labourers and domestic servants, even though that figure did not appear in the document.[42] Foreign Minister Hayashi accepted the necessity of encouraging Japanese immigration along 'the lines of least resistance,'[43] stressed industrial and commercial expansion, and accepted the agreement for the sake of trade prospects which could be seriously compromised by anti-Japanese sentiment in Canada.

That sentiment was real. Prime Minister Laurier feared that, despite the strict limitation on Japanese immigration, the secret nature of the details of the agreement would upset British Columbians, who were 'full of the idea their province is to be, as a result of a deep plot and design to be taken possession of by a quiet, persistent and systematic Japanese invasion.'[44] Only with some difficulty did Lemieux persuade Laurier, the cabinet, and the BC members of parliament to accept the agreement. Liberals were satisfied, but some Conservatives predicted a Japanese takeover. However, an order-in-council, later confirmed by an amendment to the Immigration Act, which required all immigrants to come to Canada direct from their country of origin effectively shut off immigration via Hawaii. Closing this loophole in the new Japanese emigration policy reduced political agitation against the Japanese in Canada.

British Columbians, however, had noticed an influx of immigrants direct from Japan early in 1908; they suggested that Japan was not honouring the agreement. Canada investigated possible abuses in Japan and warned Count Hayashi against any abrogation of the agreement. Through the consul general in Ottawa, Japan knew that the feeling was 'quite unfavourable' and that the Laurier government was disappointed because of the slow growth of trade and the opportunity for attack which the 'unexpected difficulty' over immigration was giving to the opposition Conservatives.[45]

In fact, Japan was honouring the agreement. According to Japanese emigration statistics, the number of emigrants going to Canada fell sharply from 7601 in the 1907 fiscal year to 858 in 1908. Most of those who entered in 1908 had secured passports before the agreement came into effect or were the wives and children of Japanese already established in Canada. Many of the women were 'picture brides' who had met their husbands through mail-order matrimonial agencies in Japan, married them at proxy ceremonies, and then left Japan to see their husbands for the first time in Canada.[46] Indeed, the year 1908 really marked the beginning of Japanese family life in Canada and the end of immigration as the major source of growth in the Japanese population in Canada.

As the number of Japanese immigrants arriving on Canadian shores declined, the immigration question received less attention in Canada. In the 1911 federal election, the Conservatives under Robert Borden defeated the Liberals under Laurier, but even in British Columbia Japanese immigration was scarcely mentioned.

In 1913, a year of serious economic depression in British Columbia, the immigration question reappeared. In part, British Columbians were infected by propaganda from Californians, who were agitating for what became that state's Alien Land Laws which denied Japanese immigrants the right to buy land. Premier Richard McBride returned from a visit to California and pressed for an absolute prohibition of immigration from Asia in order to preserve 'Canada's national life.'[47] The main stimulus to renewed discussion of Japanese immigration, however, was the pending renewal of the Anglo-Japanese Treaty of Commerce and Navigation. British Columbians had long resented the fact that Japan, not Canada, controlled immigration; thus, the Borden government sought assurances that the treaty would not interfere with Canada's taking over control. The *Gaimushō*, intending to 'continue the existing line of policy,' considered such assurances unnecessary; but again Japan yielded and accepted 'almost the whole of the Canadian proposal.' Tokyo decided it was better to give Canada what it sought rather than to face the abrogation of the treaty and the possible loss of its ability to intervene on behalf of Japanese nationals in British Columbia. If Canada emulated

California and imposed truly restrictive laws on land ownership or fishing licences, for example, the Japanese in Canada would have little opportunity to earn a living. But, in accepting the Canadian position, the *Gaimushō* emphasized that existing Canadian immigration laws should apply to all countries, including Britain. The restrictions on Japanese immigration, it maintained, were agreed to only by the 'voluntary resolution of the Japanese government.'[48]

Those Canadians who wished to go to Japan apparently faced no difficulties in gaining admission. From the 1870s on, there were always some Canadians in Japan, but their numbers were few. Indeed, in 1938 the Canadian legation knew of only 575, and that number included individuals in Formosa, Korea, and Manchuria.[49] A few represented Canadian transportation, timber, trading, and insurance companies; most were Christian missionaries, chiefly from the United Church of Canada (before 1925, Methodist) and certain Roman Catholic orders. The Presbyterians and Anglicans had a smaller presence.

The missionaries were best known for the educational work which they used to contact possible recruits for Christianity. The Reverend Dan Norman, a Methodist who served in Nagano from 1902 to 1934, for example, early 'established a night school for teaching English to students, which was well attended and the means of reaching many who later became Christians.'[50] Others, such as the Quebec-based Roman Catholic Sisters of the Holy Names of Jesus and Mary, established private schools. Their high school for girls, opened in Kagoshima in 1934, employed Japanese teachers to prepare students for the government examinations while the sisters taught such 'extras' as English, French, music, European typewriting, and domestic arts.[51]

Hugh L. Keenleyside, who served in the Canadian legation in Tokyo during much of the 1930s, recalls that 'most of the church groups from Canada were industrious concerned people who were strongly committed to their work. Moreover, most of them interpreted their duties as including the promotion of the *spirit* of Christianity rather than just an accumulation of converts.'[52] He refers particularly to missionaries who did social work in the slums of Tokyo, to Dr Caroline Macdonald, the first president of the YWCA in Tokyo, and to Emma R. Kaufman, who took over much of the YWCA work after Macdonald's death.

The missionaries and social workers maintained ties with their sponsoring organizations and families in Canada and, after the Canadian legation was established in 1929, with Canadian diplomats in Tokyo. Yet, with the notable exception of the Canadian Academy in Kobe, a high school established by the Methodist church in 1913 to prepare the children of their missionaries and other foreigners for the matriculation examinations of the University of Toronto, many of the missionaries seem to have regarded themselves as Christians of a particular denomination first and as Canadians second. As Canadian social scientist Charles J. Woodsworth noted in 1938, 'Canadian influence cannot be entirely separated from missionary endeavour as a whole.'[53] This is explained by the supranational organization of most of the churches and especially by the desire of all denominations to create an indigenous Japanese church of their particular persuasion. A good example is the *Kwansei Gakuin*, a large mission school. American Episcopalians started it in 1889; Canadian Methodists joined them in 1910. Later it became a Japanese institution and the Japanese government recognized it as a university in 1932. Similarly, when the Sisters of the Holy Name were recalled to Canada in 1940, they consoled themselves with the thought that their work would be in the hands of a congregation of Japanese sisters. In sum, although individual Canadian missionaries might spend their entire working lives in Japan and some, such as the Reverend Dan Norman, saw their children continue the work, the churches themselves did not perceive their workers as permanent settlers of Japan.

During the Great War of 1914–18, Japan and the British Empire were allies. Thus, despite the annual entry of a few hundred *imin*, the agitation against them virtually disappeared as British Columbians focused their attention on the battlefields of France and Flanders. With the coming of peace, hostility to Japan and, especially, to the Japanese in Canada began anew. During the war, many Japanese in British Columbia had taken advantage of the demand for fishery products and the availability of bargain-priced land to extend their economic activities. The general postwar economic slump and severe unemployment drew attention to their expansion and aroused jealousies, particularly among veterans' organizations. Then, the resumption of normal trans-Pacific shipping brought a large influx of Chinese and Japanese, many of whom were actually earlier immigrants returning from routine visits home that had been prolonged by the war and the depression of 1912–16.

Peace also aroused Japanophobia when Japan tried to secure recognition of the principle of racial equality in the Treaty of Versailles.[54] Similarly, British Columbians opposed the renewal of the Anglo-Japanese Alliance under the misapprehension that it referred to immigration. The provincial government and various bodies such as the Retail Merchants' Association and the Native Sons of British Columbia pressed Conservative Prime Minister

Arthur Meighen to insure that any renewal of the alliance protect Canada's right 'to restrict Japanese immigration in the interest of a white British Columbia.' In response, the Canadian Japanese Association, which acted as a social, political, economic, and educational society for all Japanese Canadians, objected to its members being 'numbered among the undesirable elements of the population,' and recalled the Gentlemen's Agreement, Japan's assistance to the British Empire during the war, and the peaceful and law-abiding nature of the Japanese in Canada. In any event, Meighen opposed the alliance primarily because the United States opposed it and Britain favoured a broader arrangement for Pacific security which would include the United States. Ultimately, the Washington Agreement on Naval Disarmament replaced the alliance.[55]

The primary concern of British Columbians, as always, was to limit Japanese and other Asian immigration. During the federal election campaign of 1921, Liberal and Conservative candidates tried to outdo each other in proclaiming the effectiveness of their parties' Asian exclusion programs. Most propagandists called for general exclusion of Asians; a few singled out the Japanese. For example, John Nelson, a Vancouver journalist, told readers of a national magazine that the Japanese were the chief problem because of their high birth rate, their 'independence and initiative in industrial development,' their 'racial pride and national self-consciousness,' and 'their insistence on racial equality and political rights.'[56]

The Conservatives won the majority of British Columbia's seats but, nationally, the Liberals under Mackenzie King won sufficient seats to form a minority government. The new prime minister was well acquainted with the Asian question, having investigated damage claims after the 1907 Vancouver riot. As prime minister, he responded to rumours of Japanese evading the Gentlemen's Agreement by jumping ship, being smuggled in through the Queen Charlotte Islands, or using documents of earlier immigrants who had returned to Japan by alerting immigration officers and informing Consul General Ohta that Canada was considering registering all Asians on the Pacific Coast 'as a means of keeping track of [the] number in this country & silencing & answering agitation as to numbers coming in.'[57] King also warned Ohta that unless Canada could control immigration from Japan she might have to end the Gentlemen's Agreement and possibly denounce the Anglo-Japanese trade treaty. Noting Japan's anxiety to protect its 'dignity and legitimate standing,' Ohta replied that Japan did not contemplate allowing more than 150 household servants and agricultural labourers to emigrate to Canada each year.[58] This answer was not fully satisfactory since only about 30 per cent of the immigrants were servants or agricultural labourers and, as the Department of Immigration noted, 'so-called agriculturalists' did not always remain on the farm and were often the forerunners of wives and families.

Indeed, one of the chief concerns of British Columbians was not a question of immigration but the Japanese 'baby boom.' In 1921 the overall birth rate in the province was 20.1 per thousand; among Japanese it was 36.8.[59] High birth rates are not unusual among first-generation immigrants but the Japanese situation was unique because of the relatively high proportion of women of child-bearing age in the population. Many of them were picture brides who were exempt from the provisions of the Lemieux Agreement until Japan accepted minor revisions of it in 1923.

Minor revisions, however, did not stop the clamour in British Columbia for more extensive restrictions on Japanese immigration, particularly after the United States banned Japanese immigration in 1924. As King later observed, 'the action of the United States in doing away in 1924 with the Gentlemen's Agreement of 1907 and adopting a policy of complete exclusion of Japanese immigrants' led to 'much pressure for drastic action by Canada.'[60] Thus, in the spring of 1925, the prime minister complained to Consul General Matsunaga that Japan was evading 'the spirit of the Lemieux Agreement' because overall immigration from Japan had not declined and the number of women and children had increased. Because British Columbians were exerting great political pressure, King warned that Canada might have to legislate against Japanese immigration.[61]

Shortly after the 1925 election, which left King clinging to power, Baron K. Matsui, the Japanese ambassador to the United Kingdom, passed through Ottawa where King told him that admitting wives and children of future immigrants would give 'rise to [the] view that colonization of our Pacific coast was [the] real aim of Japan.' When BC politicians persistently called for exclusionary legislation, King encouraged Japan to accept a new agreement quickly. Negotiations, however, proceeded slowly. Finally, early in 1928, King informed Baron Tomii, Japan's consul general, that Canada wanted to admit only a total of 150 agricultural labourers, domestic servants, clergy, and women and children, though arrangements might be made individually for 'special clerks of high grade.' In addition, the new Canadian legation in Tokyo would issue visas. When Japan dallied over details, Canada threatened to regulate the number itself. Finally, Tokyo agreed to the 150 limit, provided a ceiling of seventy-five female immigrants was not publicized, and to an end to the picture-bride system. The arrangement was 'really better' than King had anticipated because it avoided 'exclusion & on all else (save these few) we have everything in our own hands.'[62] The *Gaimushō* was also satisfied.

The restrictions were draconian but, as in 1907, preserved Japan's national dignity.[63]

Yet, even as the new Gentlemen's Agreement was being concluded, the situation was changing. Japan's population was increasing rapidly and food shortages loomed. Manchuria and Mongolia were obvious targets of public attention, and Chiang Kai-shek's national unification campaign and nationalistic xenophobia stimulated Tokyo to assert its 'special rights and interests' in those mainland territories. Advocates of a tougher policy in Tokyo cited the revised Lemieux Agreement and the American Immigration Act of 1924 in justifying their hard line that Asian peoples should be united against 'white imperialism.'[64] The first steps on the road to war in Asia had been taken; by 1931, after the Manchurian incident, Japan had forcefully established a puppet regime in Manchukuo.

It was in this increasingly volatile situation that Canada established its first legation in Tokyo in 1929. Promoting trade was a major consideration,[65] but King was also concerned about immigration. As he told a Vancouver audience in November 1929, the Japanese immigration question had to be resolved by 'good will,' not 'force.'[66]

In fact, the revised Gentlemen's Agreement and the onset of Depression in late 1929 reduced the number of Japanese arrivals in Canada from between 400 and 500 per year in the late 1920s to about 100 per year or less in the 1930s (see Tables 1 and 2), a number which included wives and children of Canadian citizens who, as Canadian nationals, were not covered by the agreement. The sharp decline in numbers virtually ended Japanese immigration as a political issue in British Columbia. Even the conviction of Fred Yoshi, the former interpreter of the Department of Immigration, for conspiring to violate immigration laws and publicity surrounding the deportation of several illegal immigrants aroused no public clamour.[67]

Japan's moves in Asia towards establishing her Greater East Asia Co-prosperity Sphere in the 1930s had not been entirely unnoticed in Canada, but Canada's preoccupation with domestic problems created by the Depression meant they were not headline news. Even British Columbians paid little attention to Japan and the Japanese, although the Chinese in the province boycotted Japanese goods and distributed propaganda to draw attention to their side of the Sino-Japanese War which had begun in earnest in 1937. Late that year, Archdeacon F.G. Scott of Quebec City told Toronto reporters that Japanese naval officers, disguised as fishermen, lived on the BC coast. In an increasingly tense international situation, this hoary rumour revived British Columbians' old fears and allegations of widespread illegal Japanese

TABLE 1
Japanese Emigrants to Canada: Japanese Government Data

Year	Number	Year	Number
1891	181	1917	1,226
1892	112	1918	1,780
1893	1,135	1919	1,764
1894	774	1920	1,371
1895	454	1921	1,163
1896	549	1922	1,022
1897	206	1923	684
1898	1,151	1924	1,103
1899	1,726	1925	979
1900	2,710	1926	1,009
1901	–	1927	1,062
1902	35	1928	1,050
1903	178	1929	430
1904	159	1930	137
1905	196	1931	106
1906	442	1932	98
1907	2,753	1933	91
1908	601	1934	105
1909	281	1935	57
1910	538	1936	82
1911	820	1937	109
1912	1,025		
1913	1,270		
1914	1,284		
1915	778		
1916	1,055		

SOURCE: *Statistics on Overseas Migration*, Department of Overseas Affairs, Tokyo 1937

immigration. Veterans' organizations, boards of trade, and provincial politicians demanded an investigation. Officials in Ottawa claimed the estimated 400 illegal Japanese immigrants in the country were too few to worry about, but their political superior, Prime Minister King, wanted action. Thus, the civil servants recommended squelching rumours and calming the public by creating a 'flying squad' of RCMP members and interpreters to check information on the spot, and by inviting citizens to present evidence of Asian

TABLE 2
Japanese Immigrants to Canada: Canadian Government Data

Year	Number	Year	Number
1900–01	6	1921	481
1901–02	–	1922	395
1902–03	–	1923	404
1903–04	–	1924	510
1904–05	354	1925	424
1905–06	1,922	1926	443
1906–07	2,042	1927	511
1907–08	7,601	1928	535
1908	858	1929	179
1909	244	1930	217
1910	420	1931	174
1911	727	1932	119
1912	675	1933	106
1913	886	1934	125
1914	681	1935	70
1915	380	1936	103
1916	553	1937	146
1917	887	1938	57
1918	1,036	1939	44
1919	892	1940	43
1920	525	1941	4

*Fiscal years from 1900–1 to 1907–8
SOURCE: Canada, Division of Immigration, Department of Manpower and Immigration; Department of Citizenship and Immigration

and other illegal immigrants to a board of review which would organize the search for illegal immigrants. The board's chairman, Hugh Keenleyside, was exceptionally well qualified for the task; he had been raised and educated in British Columbia and had recently returned to the Department of External Affairs in Ottawa from a posting at the Tokyo legation.

The board secured 'excellent' publicity in British Columbia but received so little specific information that its interim report tentatively concluded 'that the great majority of those politicians, editorial writers and others who had been most voluble in spreading the impression that orientals were entering Canada illegally in large numbers were making those assertions

Vancouver *Daily Province*, 22 February 1938

without any facts – or even second-hand knowledge of the facts.' All told, only about 100 suspected illegal immigrants were named, and of these only nineteen were Japanese.[68]

Paradoxically, the board stimulated anti-Japanese opinion in British Columbia rather than easing it. The Vancouver *Sun*, for example, noted that, although the board had found few illegal immigrants, it called for greater vigilance by police and immigration officials. The Gentlemen's Agreement, the *Sun* concluded, 'was only kept on a gentlemanly basis by erecting what practically amounts to a barbed wire fence to keep hordes of would-be violators out.'[69] Adding insult, in British Columbia's view, was Ottawa's failure to act on any of the board's recommendations.

Allegations of illegal immigration were but one part of the story. General antipathy to Japanese immigration and to the Japanese in Canada had been increasing in the late 1930s as a result of Japan's aggressive policies in Asia, controversy over the desire of *Nisei* for enfranchisement, and jealousy over the apparently low unemployment rate among Asians in British Columbia and their apparent success in agriculture and in small retail and service businesses in the coastal cities. In Vancouver, Alderman Halford D. Wilson, who had been elected to City Council at the age of twenty-nine in 1934 and who made municipal politics a full-time career, was making a name for himself by demanding that the number of business licences issued to Asians in the city be limited. Wilson's father, the Rev. G.H. Wilson, an Anglican clergyman, had spoken at the Asiatic Exclusion League meeting which preceded the 1907 Vancouver riot. The younger Wilson expanded his father's sermon into a full-scale anti-Japanese crusade as he added campaigns against Japanese language schools and the possible presence of fifth-columnists to his litany of objections to the Japanese in Vancouver.

Wilson was but one of many BC politicians agitating against the Japanese. Early in 1938, A.W. Neill (Independent MP for Comox-Alberni) drew Ottawa's attention to the broader immigration question by introducing a Japanese exclusion bill. British Columbians welcomed the bill as a means of checking sinister Japanese motives, halting 'intolerable' interference with white retailers, fruit growers, and fishermen, and preserving British Columbia as 'a white country.' Members of parliament rehashed traditional complaints against the Japanese but restrained their oratory after the prime minister privately warned some British Columbia members that extreme anti-Japanese statements could embarrass Great Britain. Nonetheless, King hoped the debate would show Japan 'in what difficulties we are placed' and that a grateful Japan would thank his government for defeating the bill halting anti-British demonstrations in Tokyo.[70]

With the defeat of the exclusionary bill, British Columbians renewed their complaints about Japanese immigration. Spurred on by this support, Neill sought to achieve his ends by introducing a variation of the old Natal Act to bar unwanted immigrants through a language test. But once again the Canadian government feared offending Japan. The Department of External Affairs warned that Neill's bill might contravene the Anglo-Japanese Treaty of 1911 and would certainly break faith with the 1928 revision of the Gentlemen's Agreement. Moreover, they observed it would be ineffective. The Japanese population of British Columbia was growing mainly through natural increase and many Japanese knew English. The King government easily killed Neill's bill.[71]

Yet in the spring of 1938 no one in the Canadian government, either elected officials or civil servants, questioned the need to do something to satisfy British Columbia's demands for a halt to Japanese immigration. Officials considered a number of schemes, none of which was fully satisfactory. The plan which most appealed to King was a form of reciprocal agreements whereby Canada and Asian nations would ban permanent immigration to each other. Since it would apply equally to citizens of Canada and of Asia, it would in theory cause no loss of 'face' to either party. In fact, it would not be equal. Few Canadians were likely to emigrate to Asia. Canada had never restricted the admission of visiting Asian traders, diplomats, and missionaries and had always been keen to protect the right of her traders, diplomats, and missionaries to go to Asia. Baron Tomii, the Japanese minister in Ottawa, correctly interpreted the proposed reciprocal agreement to mean an end to all Japanese immigration to Canada. After communicating with Tokyo, Tomii warned that even initiating negotiations for such a plan would 'give rise to considerable ill feelings in Japan' and reflect poorly on Japan, which had honoured the Gentlemen's Agreement. Indeed, he warned that Japan would construe any Canadian exclusionary measure 'as something done by the [British] Empire itself.'[72]

Meanwhile, to assuage opinion in British Columbia, representatives of the federal departments concerned set up an Interdepartmental Committee to study 'the general problem of Orientals in Canada' with special reference to the Japanese in British Columbia. The committee defined two problems: the future of Oriental immigration and the status of Orientals already in Canada. Because the Japanese population in British Columbia was increasing and because of Asian competition in the market place, the committee recommended ending Oriental immigration, even though this would require the termination or radical revision of the Gentlemen's Agreement.[73] Continued pressure from British Columbia and from national bodies such as the 1938

Conservative national convention persuaded the Canadian government to do something.

When Baron Tomii and former Consul General Matsunaga made a social visit to Prime Minister King in August 1938, King said he hoped Japan would voluntarily halt emigration to Canada rather than risk an exclusionary measure. At the same time, King managed to cut short a parliamentary debate on Japanese immigration and to modify a Conservative resolution for the abrogation of the Gentlemen's Agreement. He also reminded the Liberal premier of British Columbia, T.D. Pattullo, that exclusionary legislation would embarrass Britain in its relations with Japan. In fact, after making inquiries through the Canadian legation in Tokyo, King concluded that an exclusion act would simply help Japan maintain a closed door in China.[74]

The outbreak of the European war in September 1939 increasingly drew Ottawa's attention across the Atlantic, but did not end the anti-Japanese campaign in British Columbia. During the 1940 federal election, for example, Howard Green, the incumbent Conservative member for Vancouver South, promised that, if elected, his party would cancel the Gentlemen's Agreement. Groups such as the Vancouver Junior Board of Trade and the Native Sons of British Columbia also advocated the abrogation of the Gentlemen's Agreement. Its most vocal critic, Alderman Wilson, extended his campaign against Asian competition in business to include claims of illegal Japanese immigrants and possible Japanese subversives. The disastrous situation of the Allies in Europe in the spring and summer of 1940, and reports of quislings in Norway and Nazi collaborators everywhere, strengthened his charges. Thus, Wilson, who had drawn the ire of Japanese consular officials for 'derogatory statements made against the Japanese-Canadians and Japanese residents in British Columbia,' persuaded Vancouver City Council to call for limits on the rights and privileges of foreign nationals equal to those imposed by their homeland on Canadian nationals, for a federal survey of all aliens, and for the deportation of illegal entrants. Although Wilson mentioned Germans and other European enemy aliens, his prime targets were the Japanese.[75] Council passed the resolution unanimously but some members, including Mayor L.J. Telford, recognized the possible diplomatic consequences of denying new trade licences to Japanese.

Like the Japanese consul, some members of the council and the press realized that the Japanese community consisted of Japanese nationals, naturalized *Issei*, and the *Nisei* or Canadian-born who were Canadian citizens and proud of it. The Vancouver *Province*, observing that the Japanese question was a domestic rather than an alien problem, suggested ending the Gentlemen's Agreement and deporting illegal immigrants in order to 'establish a basis for dealing wisely with the Japanese in British Columbia.' 'Whatever the path of wisdom may be, it cannot lead to persecution of people who entered the country legally, who are here in large numbers – most of them born here,' counselled Vancouver's leading newspaper.[76] The Japanese question in British Columbia was still very much an international matter but it was also, as the *Province* suggested, a domestic problem concerning all Canadians and especially those whose ancestral land was, unfortunately, preparing for war.

Indeed, Japan was beginning to pay closer attention to the *imin.* In part this reflected the serious possibility of war with the United States and Britain; in part it revealed a growing sense of confidence and the realization that Japan's voluntary acceptance of restrictions had inevitably hurt national dignity; and it also demonstrated pride in the great achievements of the Yamato race.

In November 1940 the Department of Overseas Affairs and the *Gaimushō* jointly invited some 1500 Japanese from Manchuria, Southeast Asia, and North and South America to Tokyo to celebrate the birth of the nation, the 2600th anniversary of Emperor Jimmu's ascension in 640 BC. They hoped to exchange opinion on overseas development; to bring overseas Japanese up to date on conditions in their homeland; to spread propaganda about the Sino-Japanese War; and to inspire the overseas Japanese with the purposes of the new expansionist order in East Asia and the nationalist feelings of Japan.[77] For the *Issei* delegates from Canada, reading papers, seeing military installations and tourist sights, and receiving awards from the government were thrilling events with great symbolic meaning. At last, Tokyo had acknowledged them. Like their American counterparts, they were deeply moved. One delegate from Canada, Eikichi Kagetsu, told the conference that his compatriots struggled against the harshest and most wicked kinds of exclusion and suppression, with a burning love for their own country, Japan.[78] This dual loyalty, harmless as it may have seemed to the North American Japanese at the Tokyo Conference, would soon be viewed in a very different light.

Two

The Approach of War in the Pacific

Although Japan was always intent on preserving its prestige, it could tolerate restrictions on emigration to North America because its main expansionary interests were always focused in Asia. Indeed, Japan had had substantial interest in China, Taiwan, and Korea since the late nineteenth century and, by taking advantage of the military and political weakness of China and Russia in a succession of wars, Japan had increasingly strengthened its economic and military control over Manchuria. By the 1920s, Manchuria was little more than a satellite of Tokyo, and the Imperial government made it a national policy to encourage settlement there. Between 1910 and 1930 the Japanese population in Manchuria increased by 150,000, but even that figure was substantially less than the expectations in Tokyo.[1]

Manchuria and Mongolia, officials in Tokyo agreed, were 'closely related to our survival in defense as well as economic terms.'[2] This 'lifeline theory' dominated Japanese thinking in the 1920s and 1930s, especially as the nation continued to suffer from overpopulation and a shortage of food. Given that North America no longer offered an outlet for surplus population, Japan came to believe that it had to ensure its resources and markets abroad as the foundation for 'national survival.'[3]

By the late 1920s, therefore, when the Soviet Union, which bordered Manchuria, began to be perceived as a major threat, the Imperial government reinforced the military forces it stationed there. (Japan had stationed troops in the Soviet Union's Siberian territories from 1918 to 1922 as part of the anti-Bolshevik Allied intervention, and these had long looked attractive to Japan as fields for expansion.) Inevitably this reinforcement led to clumsy schemes to install a pro-Japanese government in China, allegedly to foster defence cooperation against the Soviets, and by September 1931, after a staged attack on the tracks of the Manchurian Railway, to the outbreak of serious fighting between the Japanese and Chinese armies. In Tokyo, government and military authorities viewed the Manchurian incident as a natural struggle between a slowly awakening China and Japan's national policy, and there was little doubt, especially in the army, that Manchuria had to be brought completely under Tokyo's control.[4] On 1 March 1932 the army, having established its hold over virtually all of Manchuria, proclaimed the establishment of Manchukuo, openly a puppet state.

Japanese actions in Manchuria aroused substantial, if ineffectual, criticism at the League of Nations in Geneva, and Japan left the world organization in 1932.[5] In China, nationalist and anti-Japanese sentiment increased, and the Japanese army responded by ruthlessly tightening its grip on areas under its control. By November 1936, at the same time as Japan joined Italy and Germany in the Anti-Comintern Pact directed at the Soviet Union, army forces in northern China had been reinforced substantially, further increasing tension. The next year the first open hostilities occurred at the Marco Polo Bridge near Beijing. The government in Tokyo, essentially unable to control the army, hoped to confine the fighting to northern China, but the war spread rapidly.[6]

Japanese public opinion quickly focused on the 'Chinese attack' that had plunged the Imperial army into the quagmire of war in China. The newspapers that had hitherto criticized army policies now largely ceased to do so, and the comforts sent to the troops and contributions raised for the War Ministry increased rapidly.[7] And, as international criticism of Japan increased, especially after such appalling incidents as the 'rape of Nanking' in 1937 when its army slaughtered some 200,000 Chinese civilians, defensive nationalism in Japan grew. Ill-informed about the situation, increasingly feeling beleaguered in a white-dominated world that made no effort to hide its racist attitudes towards Asians, most people in Japan believed their country to be the victim of aggression in China, not the aggressor.

At the same time, the Soviet Union remained a feared opponent, especially after Russian troops had mauled the probing Imperial forces in the bloody battle of Changkufeng Hill on the Manchukuo – Outer Mongolia border in the summer of 1938 and again the next year on the Khalkin Gol. The Japanese army quickly developed a healthy respect for the tenacity and military skill of the Soviets (led by a little-known general named Zhukov) and that might have played some part in the Imperial Headquarters' decision to turn elsewhere for expansion. The Western powers became the focus of popular hostility, and the Imperial navy, in particular, concentrated on the United States as its potential enemy.

Japanese hostility to the United States in fact had grown apace with the hostility shown to Japanese immigrants in California, and it reached a climax after the naval limitation negotiations early in the 1920s and the passage of a restrictive American Immigration Act in 1924. So intense was the feeling that there were calls in Japan for war, and the armed forces began to study the problems and possibilities involved in such a conflict. Not coincidentally, American strategists simultaneously were updating the 'Orange' Plan that was premised on war between the two countries.

The first Japanese war plans in the 1920s called for the bombing of United States navy ships at their Asian bases and the occupation of Guam and the Philippines in an attempt to prevent any American advance into the western Pacific.[8] But by 1934, as tension increased in the wake of the Manchurian incident, the Japanese navy revised its preparations and planning for war. The focus remained the same, but the picture was not good: the planners estimated that, in a war between the two countries, Japan lacked the strength for a long and drawn-out struggle. As a result, Japan decided to abrogate the naval limitation treaties put in place by the Washington Conference of 1921 and to expand its fleet as rapidly as possible.[9]

By 1936 Japanese planners saw Britain as a potential enemy as well.[10] Anti-British sentiment had been building in the navy since the dissolution of the Anglo-Japanese alliance in 1922, and Britain's strengthening of defences in Hong Kong and Singapore after the Manchurian crisis also drew unfavourable notice. Moreover, there was a sharp reaction among Imperial navy officers to the restrictive London Naval Treaty of 1930.[11] But if hostility was there, it may have been less than was directed at the United States.[12] The long history of friendly relations with Britain and the all-too-practical concerns about fighting a war with Britain and the United States at the same time dampened the sparks.

When Japan defined its defence policy in 1936, it listed Britain only as a potential enemy, while citing the United States and the Soviet Union as major threats. Japan's basic policy, stated to be the establishment of Japan as the leader in East Asia by eliminating 'white pressure,' obliged the army and navy to have sufficient strength. If war came, the government and the military authorities assumed it would be short, and long-range plans were not set out. If Britain and Japan were to go to war, Japan's first aim was to seize British bases in East Asia and to defeat the main British fleet if it ventured into the Pacific.[13]

The outbreak of the Sino-Japanese War in 1937 changed the way Britain was viewed in Japan. As army casualties mounted, the perception grew that Britain and the United States were supporting China's resistance. The war was soon seen not only as a war with China, but as one between 'rising nations represented by Japan and the existing powers represented by England.'[14] Tension escalated when the Western powers rejected Japan's plans in 1938 for a 'New Order in East Asia' under Japanese hegemony. A Japanese army blockade at Tientsin, a Chinese treaty port to which Britain had a concessionary interest, also added heat to the situation. In July 1939 anti-British sentiment reached its peak when 65,000 people paraded to the British embassy in Tokyo to demand that Britain surrender its concession at Tientsin and withdraw from East Asia.[15]

The Russo-German Pact of August 1939 and the European war that began in September 1939 altered Japanese plans and ambitions, forcing the Tokyo government to consider the Sino-Japanese war in the context of the changed world strategic situation. Assuming that Western support for the Chinese Nationalists led by Chiang Kai-shek might decline after the Nazi triumphs of April, May, and June 1940, the army hoped to end the war in China with a quick victory and to force Britain, France, and the Netherlands from their Asian colonies. The aim was the creation of a Greater East Asia Co-Prosperity Sphere that would guarantee Japan the raw materials and room for expansion it needed. In September 1940 Japan concluded a Tripartite Alliance with Germany and Italy, binding itself to enter the European war on the side of its partners should the United States go to war in support of Britain.

By the end of 1940, therefore, the stage was set for the expansion of the European war into the Second World War. The Imperial Japanese army and navy prepared plans to seize Indochina, Thailand, Burma, Malaya, and the Netherlands East Indies. The admirals and generals could not know whether such a move would oblige Britain and the United States to combine to resist. The army focused on operations against Britain as the major enemy, on the assumption that the United States would be committed to the European theatre. The navy, in contrast, viewed the Americans as the most dangerous threat and believed that Britain and the United States would cooperate in a war against Japan; the navy emphasized that operations against the United States should take priority over southward operations because of the certainty that war in Southeast Asia would provoke a war over the whole Pacific.

The internal disputes were not resolved until news of the meeting at Argentia, Newfoundland, in August 1941 between U.S. President Franklin Delano Roosevelt and British Prime Minister Winston Churchill persuaded the Imperial Headquarters that that this was 'an outward declaration of American participation in the war.' Subsequently, an Imperial Conference on 6 September decided to complete the plans for war. Japan would not hesitate to fight Britain, the United States, and the Netherlands. The plans were to be drawn up for simultaneous assaults on the American fleet at Pearl Harbor and on American and British possessions from Hong Kong to Malaya to the Philippines.[16]

While the United States and, to a slightly lesser extent, Britain inevitably bore the brunt of the Japanese public's opprobrium and drew the attention of the Japanese military, Canada attracted its own small share of interest. The exchange of ministers and the establishment of legations in 1929 had indicated that both countries considered trade with the other to be important.[17] For the Japanese, however, the position of Canada was complicated, figuring as it did in both Anglo-Japanese and Japanese-American relations. To the Imperial navy, Canada was an inseparable part of the American land mass rather than a part of the British Commonwealth. But early in the Manchurian crisis Canada had almost seemed a 'friend' to the public. Though the general response in Canada had in fact been highly critical of Japanese policy, the one opinion Tokyo noticed favourably was the 'highly pro-Japanese' speech delivered in December 1932 at Geneva by Secretary of State C.H. Cahan, the Canadian spokesman at the Geneva session. Strikingly, Cahan had rejected the advice of the head of Canada's Permanent Mission to the League and violated his instructions from Ottawa, which were to support China's case to the limit. Instead, he offered only a few words of comfort at the end of an extraordinarily pro-Japanese statement.[18] As a result, an embarrassed Department of External Affairs was warmly thanked by the Japanese minister in Ottawa.[19]

But opinion could alter quickly and, in 1935, a vicious trade war erupted when Canada charged that Japan was dumping goods. Claiming that she was being discriminated against, Japan slapped a 50 per cent surtax on Canadian imports. The government of R.B. Bennett, with an election imminent, quickly retaliated with a surtax of its own, and all the while dispatches from Tokyo to Ottawa spoke of an 'Active newspaper campaign ... directed against Canada.' As might have been expected, the Japanese press defended their country's position, one newspaper noting that 'The trade balance between Japan and Canada is as if Canada bought one-yen articles from Japan and sold her six-yen articles. To such a good customer, however, Canada not only did not send gifts but imposed tariffs.' Another newspaper in Osaka argued that Canada not only failed to show good faith but 'counterattacked Japan's demand for trade negotiations.'[20] The war of words ended only after the Liberals under Mackenzie King took power in October and reached a compromise that took effect on 1 January 1936.[21] Bitter as the controversy became in the Tokyo press, however, no one had suggested war against Canada.

Nor did anyone suggest drastic action against Canada when public opinion there became aroused by Japanese actions in Manchuria and China or by the resurgence in 'Yellow Peril' scare campaigns in British Columbia in the 1930s. Although these movements and attitudes in Canada, and especially in British Columbia, were minutely reported to Tokyo by the legation in Ottawa and the consulate in Vancouver,[22] the Imperial government scarcely bothered to lodge protests with the Department of External Affairs.

For its part, Ottawa officially contemplated the denunciation of the country's trade agreement with Japan. In the summer of 1939 such a move had initially been considered in response to a British request,[23] and two years later Canada was again looking at denunciation of the treaty as a step, one official noted, 'which should be taken in the event of further Japanese aggression.'[24] But there were difficulties here, not least that Canada's trade with Japan had always been small. In 1902 exports to Japan had amounted only to $293,277, while imports were $1.5 million, largely in silk and tea. Three decades later, in 1931, exports were just under $19 million while imports were only $3.46 million. And in 1941, Canada-Japan trade had been drastically reduced to $1.5 million in exports and $2.3 million in imports thanks to the cessation of exports of strategic materials.[25] All that Canada was shipping to Japan of any consequence by 1941 was wheat and pulp logs, and export permits were required for virtually every other commodity. Still, the denunciation of the commercial treaty was possible, even though, as Norman Robertson, the undersecretary of state for external affairs, told the American minister to Canada, 'denunciation itself should not be interpreted as a form of reprisal. Our feeling was that, with changing conditions, the treaty itself would become inapplicable and that it might be better to get rid of it.'[26] That action quickly followed. Canada emulated Britain and the United States in freezing Japanese assets, and Ottawa also offered notice of intention to terminate the 1911 Treaty of Commerce and Navigation.[27] Trade between Canada and Japan had ended.

As the nations of the Pacific hesitated on the verge of war, no one could claim that Canada had been a major player in the events that had led Britain, Japan, and the United States to the brink. For Japan, Canada was an independent nation when trade was discussed, a member of the British Commonwealth when international questions were being considered, and part and parcel of America in terms of defence. To Japan, Canada was thus an inextricable part of the British Empire and the North Atlantic Triangle.

As all three nations in that triangle were simultaneously Pacific powers as well, it was all too clear by 1941 that if Japan went to war with Britain or the United States, Canada too would become an enemy. The military strength that Canada could bring to a war in the Pacific did not trouble Japan unduly.

For most of the twentieth century, the Canadian armed forces had been concerned with the weaknesses of Canada's defence posture on the west coast. Although Britain and Japan were allied after 1902, some uneasiness about Japan was nonetheless apparent.[28] 'Japan,' said one BC newspaper in 1904, 'is a new unfathomed force with a future hard to read.'[29] As early as 1908, in fact, Canadian officers were expressing fears about the numbers of Japanese living in British Columbia. 'The Japanese in British Columbia are very numerous,' Colonel Willoughby Gwatkin, a future chief of the general staff wrote. 'The great majority have served in the Japanese Army. They are in possession of arms and ammunition. In a military sense, they are organized; and they are in close touch with their own Foreign Office.'[30] There was little evidence to support those allegations, but that scarcely mattered because Gwatkin's comments faithfully reflected views already widespread on the coast where there was anger at Japanese economic competition, especially in the fisheries, and at continued (if limited) immigration from Japan. The Colonial Defence Committee, a subcommittee of the Committee of Imperial Defence in London, also warned in 1911 that a raid by Japanese cruisers on the Pacific coast of Canada was possible in the event that Japan became hostile to Britain.[31] Not even Japan's loyal and valuable cooperation at Britain's side during the First World War – when the Imperial Japanese navy patrolled the North Pacific and for more than a year stationed an officer at Esquimalt, BC[32] – eased the concerns. In 1919 a flurry of military intelligence reports suggested that Japanese were buying strategic properties and had a large network of agents in the province. In May the naval staff in Ottawa concluded darkly that 'Japan is the enemy,'[33] although this view was probably more related to the fledgling Canadian navy's desire to secure both a fleet and a major base on the Pacific coast than to a genuine military assessment.

Negative attitudes strengthened during the 1920s. In 1921 the commissioner of the Royal Canadian Mounted Police called for the creation of an intelligence system to investigate the potential for espionage among Japanese Canadians.[34] Army officers studying Canada's defence expressed concerns about Japan's growing influence by noting that war with 'the yellow races might very well mean the invasion of our Pacific provinces.' That prospect inevitably drew attention to the Japanese in British Columbia who, army officers maintained, 'live and group in little colonies expanding like fungus driving out the European.'[35] If that reasoning was simple racism of the worst sort, however widely it was shared by BC civilians, the military exercised what influence it had – admittedly little – to support Canada's encouraging of the abrogation of the Anglo-Japanese Alliance. In the Pacific, America was the champion of Western civilization, and the alliance held out the fearful prospect that, when and if Japan and the United States went to war, Canada as a British dominion might find itself obliged to fight on the wrong side – and subject to American invasion.[36] By 1922 the Anglo-Japanese alliance was history. The United States was friendly, and Japan was now a potential enemy. Moreover, Admiralty studies prepared for the 1923 Imperial Conference pointed alarmingly to the exposed nature of Canada's seaborne commerce on the west coast in the event of war with Japan.[37] As Brigadier A.G.L. McNaughton wrote to a staff officer at army headquarters in British Columbia in 1929, 'Remember George, keep your eyes on the Pacific. You can't trust those Japanese.'[38] That summed up the military view.

The marked change in Japan's international policies and the ascendancy of the military after 1931 increased concerns about the west coast. Atrocities such as those in Nanking in late 1937 drew the horrified attention of the world. One United Church missionary in Tokyo said that at first he could scarcely credit the 'stories of rape and looting we heard then, I could not bring myself to believe that these nice Japanese boys that we know so well could do the things told of them.' Unfortunately, he concluded, the stories he had heard in letters from his compatriots in China were true.[39] Because there were many Canadian missionaries in China, including some who were killed in the fighting there and others whose missions were devastated, the Canadian public followed events with interest and concern.

In the circumstances, it was inevitable that the Canadian military would grow more concerned about the links between the Japanese Canadians and Japan. As early as 1932, Naval Service Headquarters in Ottawa asked that files be maintained on 'persons of Japanese nationality who pursue occupations of a seafaring nature,' including their general attitude, behaviour, and political views.[40] General McNaughton, now chief of the general staff at Army Headquarters in Ottawa, also remained deeply concerned by the threat to the west coast. A distinguished artillery officer in the Great War and a scientist with important discoveries to his credit, McNaughton was also very skilled at playing the political balancing game that was necessary if the Canadian armed forces were to survive the cutbacks of the Depression. In a memorandum in February 1933 he suggested that in the event of a war between Japan and the United States, Canada's first responsibility was 'the maintenance of our neutrality,' something that required 'considerable Naval and Air Forces ... The first action required is the patrol and supervision of our territorial waters on the Pacific Coast and for this Naval craft and Flying Boats are required.'[41]

McNaughton also seized the occasion of a visit to Ottawa in 1934 by the secretary of Britain's Committee of Imperial Defence, Sir Maurice Hankey, to remind London of Canada's precarious position on the Pacific coast. Any effort by London to improve relations with Tokyo would damage relations with Washington and, Hankey noted, 'if we estrange the United States we shall estrange many people in Canada.'[42]

The Liberal government of Mackenzie King that came to power in the fall of 1935 gradually took some interest in the country's Pacific defences. However, the King administration was not one to take a forward position in foreign affairs. The prime minister feared the impact of another world war for the destruction it was sure to bring and for the strains it was bound to place on Canada's fragile unity. King could never forget the conscription crisis of 1917 which had split the French Canadians in Quebec from their English-speaking countrymen, and his policy throughout the 1930s was to refrain from commitments and to minimize the attention that foreign affairs received in Parliament. 'Parliament will decide,' the prime minister said repeatedly when asked what Canada's policy would be in the event of war. So it would, but in the meantime Parliament talked of other questions.

If his overall policy was to keep Canada's head in the sand, King nonetheless favoured a gradual improvement in Canada's military preparedness and defences. When the Liberals returned to power in 1935, they found Canada's armed forces in a wretched condition. The army, for example, had no tanks or armoured cars, almost no trucks, limited numbers of steel helmets, and only a few gas respirators. The air force and the navy were in similar states of decay. The armed forces quickly prepared their case for the new government and in September 1936 presented a major paper, 'An Appreciation of the Defence Problems Confronting Canada, with Recommendations for the Development of the Armed Forces.' The military chiefs considered that 'The possibility of a major world war is becoming more apparent' in Europe and Asia. The chiefs, undoubtedly influenced by gloomy British staff papers from the Committee of Imperial Defence that foresaw trouble with Japan in 1936 or 1937,[43] looked with particular attention to the west coast and the prospect of a war between Japan and the United States in which Canada would be neutral. In such circumstances, 'the indented and sparsely settled coast of British Columbia provides an admirable area from which Japanese submarines, and even surface craft, can develop raids against U.S. sea communications and Pacific Coast ports.' The planners also feared that war between Britain and Japan would mean 'the liability of direct attack on Canada by Japan becom[ing] a matter requiring urgent consideration.' Landings by Japanese troops on the coast as well as air and naval attack were possibilities.

To protect the country adequately, the army, navy, and air force maintained, they needed $200 million over the next five years, a very large sum at a time of economic depression when the total annual budget of the federal government was around a half billion dollars a year.[44] The forces, not unexpectedly, did not get nearly all the money they asked for, but they did get a $10 million increase over the budget of three years before – $36 million in all for 1937–8. As important, the armed forces were given their priorities:

1 Fortification of Pacific Coast prior to Atlantic Coast.
2 Development of the air force in priority to navy and, so far as possible, the navy in priority to the militia [army].[45]

In short, the government of Canada had decided that the most serious threats to Canada itself came from across the Pacific Ocean. A staff paper estimated that a Japanese attack 'would take the form of raids, designed to effect as much moral and material damage as possible, on Canadian ports and other coastal objectives, with [the] object of disrupting Trans-Pacific trade and diverting a disproportionate amount of our effort from the main theatre,' Europe.[46]

Thus even while the main priority was the Pacific coast, the military clearly had its eyes on Europe. By 1938, as Hitler's demands on Czechoslovakia and Poland escalated and as Britain and France desperately sought to appease Germany and avert war, the military chiefs in Ottawa gave the government a 'Review of Canada's Position With Respect to Defence' which noted that 'the centre of gravity of danger' had shifted 'from the Pacific to the Atlantic Coast.'[47] Even so, the fixed defences on the Pacific coast had already been strengthened. By 1939 coastal defences were in place or under construction at Esquimalt, Vancouver, and Prince Rupert,[48] and the planned expansion of the navy was almost completed. The air force had selected sites for airfields and amphibious airplane bases along the coast to make reconnaissance to sea practical and to enable counter-attacks against seaborne raiders. Geography made the air force (and to some extent the navy) the key player in the defence of British Columbia, and as early as 1938 a separate Western Air Command had been created, responsible for 'all phases of air action in the defence of the Western Canadian coast line and waters.'[49] The military's estimated 'form and scale of air attack' on British Columbia in the event of war with Japan was, in July 1938, 'Occasional medium attacks. Definite risk of torpedo, bomb, or gas attack. Maximum of twelve aircraft from enemy cruisers, armed merchant vessels or improvised carriers.'[50]

The military noted the continuing deficiencies – there remained too few modern shore batteries and almost no anti-aircraft weaponry and the Royal Canadian Air Force still had almost no up-to-date aircraft of any type. The RCAF was especially weak on the Pacific where the Western Air Command had only two permanent and three auxiliary squadrons by September 1939. Even that sounded grander than the reality – just eight serviceable aircraft, all obsolescent.[51] But it was a beginning, and it is significant, especially given Canada's traditional tilt towards Europe, that the fixed defences on the British Columbia shore had been pressed ahead far quicker than those on the Atlantic Coast, perhaps because Prime Minister King feared what Japan might do.[52]

Thus as Canada readied itself to go to war against Germany at Britain's side in September 1939, the armed forces were better prepared than they had been a few years before. But that improvement was only a matter of degree. At the outbreak of war, the Royal Canadian Navy consisted of eight destroyers, only four of which were modern, and five minesweepers. The RCN's total strength was only 191 officers and 1799 ratings. The Royal Canadian Air Force had eight squadrons and 270 aircraft, but only thirty-seven could be described as modern. The RCAF had 298 officers and 2750 men in its ranks. The army, with 4261 permanent force officers and men, was still poorly equipped despite the progress since 1937. There were only four anti-aircraft guns in Canada, only two light tanks, and only five mortars. The reserve forces in all three services were, of course, substantially less well equipped. In other words, if ever a nation was not ready for war, it was Canada.

That unreadiness also extended to Canada's defence relations with the United States. The two North American nations had cooperated with each other as allies after America's entry into the First World War in the spring of 1917, but with the peace all military cooperation had ceased. Until 1931, in fact, the basic Canadian defence plan had been premised on the idea of war with the United States.[53] Not until 1937 were there any stirrings of interest in joint defence on either side of the border, and the major reason for that interest lay in President Roosevelt's concern about the defencelessness of North America against attacks from the sea. In 1936 he had publicly alluded to the security of North America: 'Our closest neighbors are good neighbors. If there are remoter nations that wish us not good but ill, they know that we are strong; they know that we can and will defend ourselves and defend our neighborhood.'[54] Mackenzie King read the text of this speech and wrote in his diary that 'Roosevelt ... has spoken of looking after this continent.' It was a warning not to Hitler and Mussolini, the prime minister believed, but to Japan. 'He senses danger there.'[55] The next year, Roosevelt and King met in Washington on one of King's periodic visits and tentatively discussed defence questions.[56] That was the beginning.

The Canadian government had already seen signs that Roosevelt wanted to look after the continent. When word of American plans to construct air bases along the border between the two countries reached Ottawa in late April 1935, one alarmed General Staff paper noted that 'If Canada is unprepared to defend her neutrality in the event of a Pacific war in which the United States is engaged ... it is as clear as can be that the Americans will not hesitate for one moment to occupy our country in order to deny potential bases to their enemy.'[57] In a similar vein, Roosevelt had likely sent a small tremor through Mackenzie King in July 1936 when he replied to the question 'What would the United States do if Japan attacked British Columbia[?]' by saying, 'Of course, we would go in and help to prevent her getting a foot hold.' Such a pledge was at once reassuring and frightening to Ottawa.[58]

The Americans had earlier sounded out Ottawa on the prospect of a north-south highway through Canada to Alaska, a possibility that frightened McNaughton's successor as chief of the general staff, Major-General E.C. Ashton, who fretted that it would be 'a strong military inducement to the U.S.A. to ignore our neutral rights on the crisis [of a Japan-U.S. war] arising.'[59]

Roosevelt continued to worry about the lack of overland access to Alaska. In September 1937 he visited Victoria, BC, where he found Premier Duff Pattullo generally interested in the defence of the west coast and in the possibility of a road to Alaska. To Roosevelt, quite correctly, 'the British Columbia coast had to be regarded in reality as a link between the United States and Alaska.'[60] To Pattullo, a land route through his province to Alaska was good politics, a useful way of combatting Depression unemployment. But to some Canadians, notably Bruce Hutchison of the Vancouver *Sun*, 'An American financed highway could be nothing less than a military highway, which, by tying us to American foreign policy would, forever, prevent our being masters in our house.'[61] The American president would pursue the idea once the war with Japan began in December 1941 and the Alaska Highway indeed would be a military road.

In December 1937 the American minister to Canada raised the question of continental defence with Colonel H.D.G. Crerar, the director of military operations and intelligence at National Defence Headquarters. Subsequently, senior officers of the two countries met between 18 and 20 January 1938.[62] 'We were to give and to receive all information desired by either party,' Ashton wrote afterwards, 'but we were to make no commitments.'[63]

Neither side was well prepared for the discussions. Significantly, the major topic was not the east but the west coast, and particularly the defence position of the Straits of Juan de Fuca for which both countries shared responsibility. After they outlined their armaments in the area, the Americans asked for details of the Canadian defences 'and the probable size of the forces, particularly naval and air, which could be assembled.' The chief of staff of the U.S. army maintained that his forces were 'prepared to extend their defensive operations to cover the Pacific Coast from the United States-Canadian border to the Canadian-Alaskan border line,' and asked for information on landing fields. For his part, Admiral W.D. Leahy, the chief of U.S. naval operations, said that the defence of the British Columbia coast was 'a very minor problem' in a war that pitted the navies 'of the United States plus the British Empire versus Japan.' The cautious Canadian officers then offered a brief civics lesson on Canada's relationship with the British Empire, and on the necessity of avoiding 'any overt act which might affect Canadian neutrality and thereby react on other portions of the British Empire.'[64]

The officers then considered the possible scale of a Japanese attack on the coast, generally dismissing the prospect of raids and heavy naval attacks, but all being concerned about air attack, especially from aircraft carriers. Admiral Leahy 'did not consider the Japanese would attempt a landing in the Aleutian Islands or in Alaska ...' but would 'probably use Canadian harbours or territorial waters as bases for submarines and aircraft carriers.' On another subject, General Malin Craig, the U.S. army chief of staff, 'impressed the necessity of immediately interning all Japanese on an emergency arising,' Ashton reported, 'and said they had them all listed and located.'[65]

The meeting was a start, a hesitant and cautious one, to be sure, towards defence cooperation.[66] It was also a portent of action to come. Other meetings followed in April and November 1938, and again much of the discussion centered on Pacific Coast defences.[67] At the November meeting, in fact, Craig repeated his warning that the Japanese in British Columbia had a 'network of wireless reaching from British Columbia to Japan.'[68]

The most significant public move in the delicate dance towards defence cooperation came in August 1938 when Roosevelt came to Kingston, Ontario, to dedicate a new bridge spanning the St Lawrence River and linking the two countries. The people of the United States, the president said, 'will not stand idly by if domination of Canadian soil is threatened by any other empire.' Mackenzie King reciprocated the president's gesture two days later: 'We, too, have our obligations as a good friendly neighbour, and one of these is to see that, at our own instance, our country is made as immune from attack or possible invasion as we can reasonably be expected to make it, and that, should the occasion ever arise, enemy forces should not be able to pursue their way either by land, sea or air, to the United States across Canadian territory.' Roosevelt made his position even clearer in November 1938, by indicating that the United States stood ready to guarantee the entire Western Hemisphere against attack.[69]

The United States remained neutral when Canada went to war against Germany on 10 September 1939, and the American Neutrality Act limited the effective military aid that Roosevelt might have wished to extend to the Allies. After the fall of France in May and June 1940, the British Commonwealth stood alone against Hitler and Mussolini. From being a slightly reluctant partner in the second great war of the twentieth century, Canada after June 1940 suddenly became Britain's ranking ally. Ten million Canadians geared themselves up for the long struggle and rushed every ship, aircraft, and soldier able to fight to Britain. That effort left Canada virtually defenceless, without guaranteeing England against a German invasion.

In the circumstances, the Canadian government had to assure the security of Canada as best it could, and that meant seeking a formal military arrangement with the still-neutral United States. Canada's choices were few. If the country hung back and rejected an alliance with the Americans, the United States would simply have to act to protect its security, regardless of Canadian concerns, if North America were attacked. 'It is a reasonable assumption,' Hugh Keenleyside wrote in the summer of 1940, 'that the United States will expect, and if necessary demand, Canadian assistance in the defence of this continent ... Concrete steps such as the construction of the Alaskan Highway, the defensive development of the Pacific Coast ... these are lines along which Washington is likely to require Canadian co-operation.'[70]

By mid-August 1940 the world balance of power had changed almost completely and Mackenzie King was ready to respond to a request from Roosevelt to meet at Ogdensburg, New York. The two leaders talked over the situation and agreed to establish the Permanent Joint Board on Defence with a mandate to study common defence problems. The PJBD was an important step, primarily because it guaranteed Canada's military security and because it allowed Canada to continue giving the maximum possible assistance to the struggle against Germany. Equally important, the PJBD was a signal that Canada had switched from Britain to the United States as its imperial protector.

The board turned to its task quickly and, as befitted the war situation, most of its early recommendations concerned the joint defence of the Atlantic coastal region. But by November 1940, as the tense diplomatic situation between Japan and the United States and Britain continued, the PJBD began to look at the defence of the Pacific coast. In that month, the board recommended the construction of landing fields in Canada to facilitate air communication between Alaska and the United States and the construction of an airfield at Ucluelet on the west coast of Vancouver Island.[71]

Most important, the PJBD had recommended in August 1940 that the two countries prepare a joint plan for the defence of the continent. This 'Joint Canadian–United States Basic Defence Plan – 1940,' ready by October, was designed to defend against 'direct attack by European and/or Asiatic Powers.' On the Pacific coast, the planners specified two joint tasks: the defence of the coast and the protection of vital sea communications. The planners expected Japanese raids on the west coast and 'large scale sabotage and "fifth column" activities in Canada and the United States.' Mutual support was to be provided as necessary.[72] Another plan, Basic Defence Plan No. 2, was also in preparation, looking to American strategic direction of all forces in British Columbia.[73] In addition, the commanders and staffs of the American and Canadian armies on the west coast met and began to work together.[74]

There were still serious weaknesses in equipment and numbers of personnel in the Canadian forces on the coast, but, despite the work of the PJBD, planners at National Defence Headquarters in Ottawa discounted the possibility of an attack by Japan and kept their attention fixed on the war in Europe. The chief of the general staff had told the Cabinet War Committee in July 1940 that he had no fear of attack in the Pacific, and he agreed to keep troops in British Columbia only 'on account of the numbers of Japanese there.'[75] As a result, by early 1941, the army had only six indifferently trained battalions of infantry (or under 5000 men) in British Columbia, the RCAF had four weak operational squadrons, and naval defences were weaker still.[76] As late as November 1941 this complacency remained unaltered. In a military appreciation prepared that month, the chiefs of staff concluded that Japan was likely to launch only 'hit and run' raids, and they expected the United States navy to protect Canada's coastal communications. Their only concern was the lack of anti-aircraft guns on the coast.[77] Bad as it was, the Canadian military situation on the Pacific was much better than it had been two years earlier. Most importantly, before the beginning of the war with Japan, the two North American nations had begun coordinating their forces on the west coast.

The political and military events in North America had not passed unnoticed in Tokyo. President Roosevelt's August 1938 speech in Kingston led the Japanese press to watch closely the relations between Roosevelt and King and the developing military relations between the two countries. The Ogdensburg Agreement of August 1940 and the Hyde Park Declaration of April 1941 that tied the North American economies together provoked *Tokyo Asahi* to note that 'The United States has subjected Canada to her economic rule; unlike Latin America, Canada has become resigned to this situation. It is clear that the United States, taking advantage of the war, aims to establish hegemony in North America in the name of the Monroe Doctrine and joint defence.' The article concluded, correctly enough, by observing that Canada 'has not entered the war in national unity in the Japanese sense.'[78] Another newspaper, published in Osaka, observed that the establishment of the Permanent Joint Board on Defence 'was nothing but Canada's military subordination to the United States.'[79]

There was a certain shrewdness in these views, and an uncanny similarity to later nationalist views in Canada! *Tokyo Asahi* also was correct when it noted that the PJBD would help to draw Britain and the United States closer together, thus marking a first step towards bringing the United States into the European war. The Tokyo newspaper's correspondent in Ottawa had clearly picked up the gossip in the Canadian capital.[80] This same reporter commented in September 1940 on the buildup of the Royal Canadian Air Force as a 'rear base' essential to British planning, and focused on the way Canadian factories were assembling American parts into weapons destined for Britain. This, he wrote, proved that Canada, Britain, and the United States had a triangular relationship. Another article continued this theme: 'It is common knowledge that the United States, Canada, and Britain are destined to maintain triangular relations by history, trade and defence. The fact that Canada as a British Dominion has just entered a defence alliance with the United States lays the groundwork for the United States to enter the war.'[81]

Britain and France had declared war on Germany on 3 September 1939. A week later, Canada's Parliament also decided on war, a decision greeted with little enthusiasm anywhere in the country. For the second time in a quarter-century an anxious, troubled Canada was at war because of the policies and actions of its Mother Country – and Germany.

The government in September 1939 was better prepared than its predecessor had been in August 1914. A standing interdepartmental committee on emergency legislation had been created by the cabinet in March 1938 to examine and report on legislation that might be required in time of war, and in July 1938 the committee reported with a series of recommendations that eventually became the Defence of Canada Regulations.[82] The War Measures Act, passed by Parliament in 1914 and revised in 1927, remained on the statute books, giving the government enormous and sweeping powers to act with dispatch, to censor the press, intern enemy aliens, confiscate property, and curtail the liberties of Canadians: 'The Governor in Council,' the act stated, 'shall have power to do and authorise such acts and things, and to make from time to time such orders and regulations, as he may ... deem necessary or advisable for the security, defence, peace, order, and welfare of Canada.'[83]

The act was proclaimed in force on the morning of 1 September 1939, the cabinet declaring the existence of a state of 'apprehended war' as of and from 25 August. Under the act the armed forces were placed on alert and specified militia and reserve units were called out for active service. On 3 September the same act was used to proclaim the Defence of Canada Regulations in force.

Under the authority of the War Measures Act, the government quickly suppressed Nazi groups operating in Canada. Indeed, the RCMP had prepared a sweeping program for 'suppressing subversive activities,' including the immediate outlawing of all Nazi, fascist, and communist organizations, all foreign-language political groups of fascist or communist affiliation, the suppression of the English-language communist press and of the Nazi, fascist, and communist foreign-language press, and the seizure of the assets and records of all such organizations, including those in consular archives.[84]

This extraordinary proposal was squelched by the departments of Justice and External Affairs; instead, a small committee with a representative from each of those departments and the RCMP met to go over the lists of suspected subversives. The communists were excluded for the time being, the Italians were let alone so long as Italy remained neutral, but a list was prepared for the arrest of 325 Germans, sixty of whom were naturalized citizens. Arrests began on 3 September under the authority of the Defence of Canada Regulations which empowered the minister of justice to intern 'any particular person' who might be 'acting in any matter prejudicial to the public safety or the safety of the State.'[85]

Eventually communists were also interned, as were Italians after the Mussolini government entered the war against Britain and France in June 1940. By January 1941 763 Germans had been arrested and, after appeals were heard by a government review committee, 127 released; 586 Italians were interned and 105 released; and 87 communists were arrested and 5 released. In addition, 28 domestic fascists were interned.[86] The most notable internee was the mayor of Montreal, Camilien Houde, who had urged his French-Canadian compatriots not to cooperate with the National Registration of August 1940. It is fair to add, as Ramsay Cook has noted, that 'the King government, in taking the steps that it did to protect the internal security of the country, had the support of the vast majority of the Canadian people.'[87]

This was the harsh context in which the question of the Japanese Canadians must be considered. There was little tolerance evident anywhere in Canada at a time of war, and particularly when the war was proceeding so disastrously for the Allies. People were fearful, worried, and unready to trust the actions of those living among them who spoke a different language or merely looked different.

Japanese Canadians had of course perceived the increased hostility directed against them. The *Tairiku Nippō* of Vancouver, for example, reported that vandals had removed the principal image of the Buddha from the 'Canada Shrine' atop a North Shore mountain, that arsonists were believed to be active in the city's Little Tokyo, and that at least one community member had been assaulted.[88] Such incidents were seldom reported in the Japanese press. In October 1940, however, after the Vancouver City Council demanded that Japanese-language schools be closed, the *Asahi*, a large circulation national newspaper published in Tokyo, headed the story 'Anti-Japanese Feelings in Canada Becoming More Conspicuous.' The imminence of war, *Asahi* said, had put Japanese Canadians under heavy pressure.[89]

The fear of attacks against Japanese Canadians had troubled Ottawa for some time and not least Hugh Keenleyside of the Department of External Affairs. Raised in British Columbia, equipped with the historical perspective provided by a PHD earned at Clark University, with his perceptions sharpened by seven years in the legation in Tokyo, and no bigot, Keenleyside had warned in March 1938 that 'riotous incidents' could occur if Parliament did nothing to appease opposition to Japanese immigration.[90] On 1 October 1940, in the atmosphere troubled by Vancouver Alderman Halford Wilson's diatribes, the BC attorney-general, Gordon Wismer, called a meeting of police and military officials to discuss the danger posed by the presence of Japanese in the province. There was no agreement on that, but those present forecast 'trouble by mobs against Japanese should war be declared' and feared their ability to contain it.[91] Subsequently, Mackenzie King noted that the increase in anti-Japanese agitation and the existence of groups threatening direct action 'showed that the local internal danger was greater than any immediate threat from without.'[92]

Still, there was a threat from without, and it is clear that the government hoped to be able to follow as moderate a course as possible in its dealings with the Japanese Canadians should war occur. One issue, for example, was the question of military service for Japanese Canadians. Alderman Wilson expressed one concern: 'the establishment along Canada's Pacific Coast of large numbers of highly trained soldiers who are Japanese is to court eventual trouble and possible disaster.'[93] Wismer voiced the major worry of politicians in the province, however, when he said, 'if these men are called upon to perform the duties of citizens and bear arms for Canada, it will be impossible to resist the argument that they are entitled to the franchise.' His premier agreed.[94] On 1 October 1940 the Cabinet War Committee decided to accede to British Columbia's request and, underscoring the racist aspect of the question, to exempt Japanese- and Chinese-Canadian citizens from military training under the National Resources Mobilization Act which had put conscription for home service into effect. As King explained, he had supported the representations from British Columbia because 'the danger of the whole Oriental problem' made it essential to give every consideration to the wishes and judgment of the provincial government.[95] When Keenleyside protested,[96] the Cabinet War Committee stayed its decision and appointed a Special Committee on Orientals on 1 October 1940 'to investigate the position of persons of Japanese and Chinese racial origin, who are resident in British Columbia, and to report upon the problem ... of internal security and with particular reference to the question of military training.'[97] Keenleyside was appointed one of the committee's three members.

The committee heard testimony and conducted quiet investigations in Ottawa and British Columbia in October and November and delivered its findings on 2 December 1940. Its report noted that there was substantial suspicion of the Japanese Canadians 'and a feeling that their racial solidarity was likely in an emergency to override their loyalty to Canada and produce subversive or otherwise dangerous activities.' But the report stated bluntly, 'No concrete evidence was adduced in support of this sentiment,' and charges against individuals or groups of Japanese 'proved in every instance upon further examination to arise from unsubstantiated rumour and hearsay.' That, the committee added, did not prove that no such acts had been committed or would not be committed in the future. Though they could find no hard evidence to justify it, Keenleyside and his colleagues had to admit that the suspicion was real. This they attributed to economic motives and to 'racial prejudice [which] is an important element in producing dislike and mistrust of the Japanese.'

The committee claimed that there was less danger to the state from the Japanese Canadians than from 'the animosity of white Canadians' to the Japanese, and the members suggested a series of steps to calm public fears and to reduce mistrust and anxiety. Among them were a voluntary new registration of Japanese Canadians (who had been registered along with all other Canadians in the National Registration in the summer of 1940) and the need to impress upon the responsible leaders in the Japanese-Canadian community 'that the wrongful act of a single Japanese would, even in present circumstances, and *a fortiori* if the international situation were to deteriorate further, imperil the lives and property of *all* Japanese, whether loyal or otherwise.'

The committee then returned to the original question of military training and, because of its concerns that trouble in the armed forces between Japanese and other Canadians might spread to the civilian community, recommended 'most reluctantly and not unanimously' that 'Canadians of Japanese race should not be given military training.'[98]

Some senior officers in the army clearly had worried over the effects of mixing white and Asian soldiers together. Brigadier C.V. Stockwell, commanding Military District No. 11 which included all of British Columbia, while agreeing that the presence of a few Orientals in a training camp would pose no difficulty, nonetheless warned that 'it would be very lowering to the prestige of the white race if they were to become the menials of the coloured races.'[99] In the circumstances, the government accepted the recommendations of the Special Committee on Orientals about military service and announced them early in 1941. (Chinese Canadians were also barred from enlisting.) Neither the objections of the *New Canadian*, the *Nisei* newspaper in British Columbia, nor the Japanese minister to Canada swayed the decision.[100] The efforts of individual Japanese Canadians to enlist in the armed forces were now routinely rebuffed.[101]

At the beginning of January 1941, following one of the recommendations of the special committee, the federal government created a standing committee to 'assist the Government by overseeing the execution of such recommendations of the Special Committee on Orientals in British Columbia as the Government may from time to time refer to it for action, and by keeping the Government constantly informed ... as to the oriental situation in that Province.' Under the chairmanship of Mayor F.J. Hume of New Westminster, the committee's first task was to organize the re-registration of the Japanese Canadians in cooperation with the RCMP and the Japanese community. Despite internal divisions over the government's selection of Japanese members of a liaison committee, and despite a widespread belief that the committee was too cooperative with the RCMP, the re-registration proceeded smoothly.[102] The Japanese Canadians also demonstrated their loyalty in other ways. In October 1941, at a conference sponsored by the Canadian Japanese Association, various groups agreed to promote 'Canada's prosperity as well as future development of the Japanese community in Canada' and urged their members to support the Canadian government. Similarly, the Fraser Valley Japanese Farmers' Association pressed members to assist the war effort. The community bought $42,000 in Victory Bonds and canned salmon which was sent to Britain.[103]

Meanwhile, bureaucrats in Ottawa had continued to 'Discuss Measures To Be Taken In The Event Of War With Japan.' At the meeting on 25 July 1941 Keenleyside 'said that it was understood by the departments concerned that there was not going to be any general internment of Japanese nationals,' most of whom, the RCMP representative repeated, 'are considered loyal.'[104] A subcommittee was assigned to consider the matter further. Its report, dated just three days later, recommended to the cabinet that Japanese Canadians be treated exactly the same as Germans and Italians, something it immediately violated by recommending that the voluntary registration then nearly complete be made obligatory. 'As regards internment,' by which the subcommittee meant incarceration under guard, the Defence of Canada Regulations provided 'ample powers both before and after the commencement of a state of war' to intern Japanese nationals and Japanese Canadians who were British subjects. 'There is also power under Regulation 21 to restrict the activities of any persons, e.g. fishermen, without interning them.' The recommendations concluded that the internment of some individuals might be necessary, 'but it is anticipated that the bulk of the Japanese population in Canada can continue its normal activities.'[105]

The committee report had not dealt expressly with fishing vessels owned by Japanese Canadians. In August the naval officer commanding on the Pacific coast, Commander W.J.R. Beech, requested that in the event of war, the vessels should be rounded up and their crews interned.[106] Keenleyside replied that 'If the vessels are in fact Japanese owned and registered ships [ie, owned in Japan or by citizens of Japan residing in Canada] then his plan requires no comment.' But if the commander meant fishing ships owned by Canadian residents, then Beech's plan was 'of course, wholly impossible. I would suggest that the matter should be cleared up by definite instructions to the Officer Commanding that the proposals outlined in his memorandum under reference are applicable only to vessels owned and operated by Japanese *nationals.*' The navy agreed that only boats owned and operated by Japanese nationals would be seized in the event of war. 'Vessels owned and operated by British subjects of Japanese origin will only be interfered with where there are positive grounds for suspicion, comparable to those which would justify the internment of a British subject of Japanese origin.'[107] After Pearl Harbor, the prewar good intentions disappeared. The Cabinet War Committee soon accepted the recommendations of the committee. In the circumstances of 1941, they were relatively liberal.

Indeed, given the evidence in the possession of the government, the recommendations were most surprisingly liberal, as we shall see. As early as February 1940 the Canadian government had intercepted telegrams *en clair* from the Foreign Office in Tokyo to the consulate in Vancouver that expressed the *Gaimushō*'s concern about the fate of Japanese in North America if 'present relations ... turn to the worst. In such an event,' Tokyo said, 'confinement (internment?) would be most unpleasant.'[108] Japan's concern was understandable, but that concern had not prevented Tokyo from taking actions that were certain to cause difficulties for Japanese and Japanese Canadians living on the west coast.

At the first and second meetings of the chief of staff of the U.S. army and the Canadian chief of the general staff in 1938, the American general had raised the necessity, in his view, of interning Japanese Americans immediately on the outbreak of war with Japan. That was not a new idea to the Canadians.

For years, British Columbians had worried about the activities of Japanese living on the coast. Regularly, reports appeared of spying by 'Japanese naval officers in the guise of fishermen,'[109] rumours that Japanese Canadians were drilling with arms,[110] and concerns about the propaganda efforts and possibly subversive activities of the Japanese consul in Vancouver.[111] 'It has yet to be proven,' said the naval staff officer (intelligence) at Esquimalt in 1937, 'that a Canadian born Japanese is other than a Japanese national. Many of them return to Japan for schooling, and possibly military service.'[112] In 1933 *Maclean's* published an article on 'The Oriental Threat' that led to questions in Parliament and further sensationalist press stories.[113] These fears were fed by paranoia, but there was just enough in the open and secret actions of Japan and Japanese Canadians during the 1930s to keep them at the boil.

For example, in 1932 the Japanese navy had secretly dispatched two intelligence officers to the west coast of North America where both operated under the control of the military attaché at the embassy in Washington. One, based in San Francisco, had the task of watching American fleet activities;

the second, stationed in Seattle, was to gather information on the north Pacific coast, and especially Alaska and the Aleutian Islands, by using Japanese-Canadian and Japanese-American fishermen. He sought information on weather conditions from these fishermen and from the crews of fishing boats operating out of Japan.[114] These officers controlled spies as part of their efforts to gather information on American military capacity, and they also negotiated with *Issei* and *Nisei* civilians in San Francisco, Los Angeles, and Seattle in an effort to persuade them to operate radios in the event of war.[115] These efforts had only limited success: the Imperial navy had no clear idea of American defences in the Aleutians or weather conditions in the area when plans were made for the occupation of Attu and Kiska in late 1942.[116] The officers stationed in North America did, however, inform Tokyo of the impressive technology available to the Americans.[117] No material has been discovered to indicate to what extent, if at all, the Japanese navy was interested in Canada's defence posture.[118]

There were, however, some propaganda activities in British Columbia. Once Japan invaded northern China in 1937, the Imperial authorities vigorously fostered support for the war in China at home and abroad.[119] This included the dissemination of propaganda about Japan's civilizing mission in China, activity in which the consulate in Vancouver and *Issei* and *Nisei* Japanese Canadians took part, most notably through the wide distribution of a pamphlet by the Canadian Japanese Association, 'Sino-Japanese Conflict Elucidated.' That pamphlet, published 'in the interests of truth, to meet unfair and untrue propaganda,' was anything but unbiased.[120] There were also fund-raising campaigns to gather money for the war effort, comforts for the troops, medical supplies, and even tin foil. Again *Issei* and *Nisei* groups in British Columbia participated, and the Japanese war minister, Seishiro Itagaki, gratefully thanked the Canadian Japanese Association which had organized the collections.[121]

Such propaganda work backfired. Japan's actions in China were widely condemned in Canada. Even those whites who were generally supportive of Japanese-Canadian claims to equality criticized the pro-Japan campaign. Boycotts of Japanese goods seriously affected sales and decreased the number of Japanese freighters calling at Canadian ports. Many Chinese Canadians refused to conduct any business with their Japanese neighbours and, together with a variety of pacifist organizations, pressed Ottawa to prohibit the export of strategic materials to Japan.[122]

Early in 1937 an intelligence officer at Esquimalt reported that major financial concerns in Japan, probably with at least the moral support of their government, were increasingly exploiting British Columbia's forest, copper, and iron ore resources.[123] The armed forces and RCMP watched the situation, especially since many timber and mining properties were strategically located. Similarly, they worried that the thousands of Japanese nationals in British Columbia lived near harbours, railways, bridges, and power plants 'in a position to cause serious trouble' in case of war.[124] Though Mackenzie King feared imposing any economic sanctions on Japan, the government eventually moved towards such a ban, and it also deliberately delayed naming a new minister to Japan in 1940 and in the summer of 1941 as an overt expression of its displeasure with Japanese policy.[125] So strong was the Canadian opposition to Japan's war that some *Nisei* began publishing the *New Canadian*, in part to combat 'this vociferous anti-Japanese feeling' that had, its founder Edward Ouchi said later, caused Japanese businessmen to suffer.[126]

While they may have been imprudent, there was nothing remotely improper in the Japanese-Canadian activities. Other ethnic groups in Canada had acted similarly in the past and would do so again in the future. Inevitably, however, as Japan grew more aggressive and as the prospect of war between the Western powers and Japan increased, these innocent actions of Japanese Canadians began to appear very different both to the public and to the military. Not even the generous *Issei* and *Nisei* donations to Canadian war-bond campaigns – so they 'might make their future somewhat brighter,' as a Japanese-language paper described it[127] – eased suspicions in the white community.

Paradoxically, the weaknesses of Canada's intelligence and security apparatus may have contributed to the growing fears. The RCMP and the armed forces' intelligence branches were extraordinarily weak in general and especially so in that they had almost no officers able to speak and read Japanese. In March 1939, for example, there was only one trained Japanese interpreter in the three armed services.[128] As a result, the Canadian government had very little factual information available on the Japanese Canadians and almost no hard information on who likely troublemakers or spies might be. The RCMP was responsible for internal security generally, assisted as necessary by the military. But the police, as late as mid-1941, had only three persons with responsibilities for collecting intelligence on and among the 23,000 Japanese Canadians: a sergeant who did not speak Japanese, a constable who did, and a civilian interpreter. The armed forces by this date still had only a handful of men responsible for intelligence as it related to Japan and Japanese Canadians. For the navy, a lieutenant-commander was in charge of west coast intelligence and, while he was 'greatly interested in the Japanese problem generally,' he did not speak Japanese and had other duties. The RCAF had two intelligence officers on the coast, again with other duties, but both spoke Japanese and one, at least, could read it to some extent. Neither of the two army officers, responsible for all intelligence questions in British Columbia spoke Japanese. In addition, the BC Provincial Police had four officers working in the Japanese-Canadian community. Cooperation between the various intelligence organizations was hampered by RCMP regulations forbidding the police to share reports without specific permission from their Ottawa headquarters. Even so, a West Coast Intelligence Committee had been set up to coordinate information. Finally, the British intelligence services had some representation on the west coast, apparently reporting to William Stephenson's British Security Coordination in New York.[129]

Moreover, as one RCAF intelligence officer surveying the situation on the coast noted, it was almost impossible to get 'proof' of espionage or subversive activity

> because (a) the Japanese keep themselves very much to themselves; (b) they live to a great extent in isolated communities; (c) few white men speak Japanese and few Japanese will talk freely to a white man; (d) the Japanese are naturally law-abiding; and also realize they will suffer if any individual Japanese irresponsibly jeopardizes the community; (e) espionage and subversive activity is largely carried on by a few key Japanese working under the Consul ... (f) it is difficult to draw the line between Japanese nationalistic propaganda and organisation and seduction of H[is]. M[ajesty].'s subjects from their allegiance.[130]

Some other Canadian intelligence-gathering efforts should be mentioned. As early as the beginning of 1940 the Canadian government was successfully intercepting some Japanese diplomatic wireless communications sent *en clair*, using as its base a wireless intercept station at Rockcliffe in Ottawa,[131] but the armed forces faced serious difficulties in finding suitable translators able to handle the material.[132] In December the Department of Transport's radio monitoring service on the west coast began to intercept Japanese news broadcasts, a useful source of information, while the Royal Canadian Navy's wireless intercept stations in western Canada provided additional information.[133] And just after Pearl Harbor, the British government asked the Canadian government's Examination Unit, a secret agency established by the Departments of External Affairs and National Defence in the spring of 1941 under the sheltering wing of the National Research Council, to intensify decoding work on intercepted Japanese diplomatic and military wireless traffic.[134] In November 1941 the army had begun to construct a major wireless interception station on the Pacific coast. The station came into use in April 1942.[135]

As the manuscript history of the Examination Unit notes, the translation difficulties continued. The unit's 'Joint Discrimination Unit,' working on Japanese diplomatic codes and low grade military ciphers, as well as Vichy French traffic from Indochina, was severely hampered by a shortage of Japanese translators. In August 1942 a Mr and Mrs T.L. Colton were hired: 'It was hoped that Mrs. Colton, who was very well educated in Japanese but could not handle translation into English, might be able to explain the contents of messages to her husband who could then write them out in English. This system,' the unit chronicler wrote drily, 'did not prove very satisfactory.'[136]

In this atmosphere of improvisation and amateurism, one fact stands out: the Canadian government knew little about Japanese plans for war or about the attitudes of members of the Japanese-Canadian community. As Hugh Keenleyside, who had publicly sympathized with the *Nisei* campaign for the same civil rights as other Canadians, told his friend H.F. Angus in June 1940, 'If Japan should enter the war against us ... there would certainly be danger of subversive activities on the part of some elements in the Japanese community. The police are not in a position to ferret out the dangerous Japanese as they have done with the Germans and Italians; they have lines on a few Japanese who might be expected to take part in attempts at sabotage,' he continued. 'But that would not really solve the problem.'[137] In other words, in the opinion of someone in a position to know, one who understood and sympathized with the Japanese Canadians, the intelligence information being gathered on the coast was strictly limited. The officers involved were too few in number and were largely baffled by the impenetrability of the Japanese language and by the tendency of Japanese Canadians to keep to themselves and not to trust whites except for those lawyers and merchants with whom they had worked for years.

The simple truth is that the RCMP and the military were extremely unsophisticated in their general intelligence work. The mounted police remained so fixated on the idea of tracing communists and blocking Red subversion that their efforts in Nazi and fascist circles in the late 1930s, to say nothing of the Japanese Canadians, were desultory.[138] The armed forces were so limited in manpower and so underfunded before the war as to be virtually paralysed.[139] As a result, the intelligence reports – now available to historians – swing wildly between expressions of real danger from Japanese Canadians to equally confident assertions that all but a handful in the community were law abiding and loyal to Canada. 'As a result of their numbers and their scattered villages at all points along the coast, directly under the control of the Japanese Government through their consul at Vancouver,' the RCAF's intelligence officer at Victoria, BC, wrote in June 1940, 'a serious situation could arise immediately upon the outbreak of hostilities.'[140] The RCN's staff officer (intelligence) at Esquimalt took a similar view in 1937: 'The fact that there are a large number of Japanese fishermen operating in British Columbia waters ... and having a thorough and practical knowledge of the Coast, is in itself a matter of some concern to the Naval authorities.'[141]

In contrast, the deputy minister of national defence, Gen. L.R. LaFlèche, noted that his department had heard of 'few if any cases' of illegal activity by Japanese on the Pacific coast, though they had been inquisitive and had a thorough knowledge of the waters as a result of their fishing activities. He thought the 'military development of Canada had not been such as to attract espionage efforts on the part of foreign powers.'[142] The RCMP tended to agree. 'No fear of sabotage need be expected from the Japanese in Canada,' said Assistant Commissioner Frederick J. Mead, a specialist in communism and subversion, who boasted that he had blocked communist attempts to organize Japanese-Canadian fishermen in the 1930s. His statement was 'broad,' he admitted, but 'at the same time I know it to be true.'[143] Mead's primary source appears to have been Etsuji Morii, a notorious underworld figure and *padrone* who had substantial influence with *Issei.* He was mistrusted by many *Nisei,* however, perhaps because of his influence with the RCMP, but also because he was thought to be blackmailing members of the community.[144]

The fairest thing that can be said almost a half century after the fact is that the RCMP and military intelligence had uncovered little hard information about possible subversion within the Japanese-Canadian community, if indeed the potential for any existed, because they lacked the necessary resources and competence. Moreover, much of the RCMP's information came from sources that were regarded with suspicion by many within the community. As important, the civil authorities in British Columbia did not accept the RCMP's calm assessment. Attorney-General Wismer wrote to Ottawa in October 1940 that, while he had 'the greatest respect for Mead and hesitated to disagree with him,' nonetheless 'every law enforcement agency in this province, including ... the military officials charged with local internal security, are unanimous that a grave menace exists.'[145]

The implications of the different assessments of the situation and the undoubted weaknesses in intelligence in British Columbia were serious. Because there were as many disquieting reports as those that demonstrated loyalty to Canada, because those in authority admitted honestly that it was very difficult indeed to find out what was going on among the Japanese Canadians, there was a tendency to suspect the worst and to feel that only drastic actions could deal with the feared threat. One intelligence officer summed it up: 'No one knows' if the Japanese Canadians were loyal, 'but no one would take a chance on Japanese loyalty.'[146]

Not wishing to take a chance – that was generally the view of the armed forces. As early as 1938, significantly after the U.S. army chief of staff had first expressed himself in favour of widespread internment, National Defence planners had indicated worry about the possibility of wartime sabotage and recommended that Japanese Canadians not be permitted to purchase land near strategic areas.[147] In July 1940 the Joint Services Committee, Pacific Coast, the committee that united the three service commanders in British Columbia, prepared plans to prevent Japanese already in British Columbia from sabotaging military and civilian installations. Yet so limited were their resources that they feared preventive action might provoke open hostility with which they could not cope. Though the RCMP's Mead expected little or no danger from the Japanese Canadians in the event of war, the provincial police were far less certain, and the director of the RCMP Criminal Investigation branch in Vancouver secretly recommended that steps be taken to investigate Japanese-Canadian fishermen, many of whom, he believed, had served in the Imperial Japanese navy.[148] Similarly, the Joint Canadian–United States Basic Defence Plan, drawn up in October 1940, warned of 'large scale sabotage' and 'increased fifth column' activities in both countries.[149] By mid-1941 the Joint Services Committee had recommended that 'the Japanese population residing in the vicinity of the Royal Canadian Air Force Advanced Base at Ucluelet should, in the event of an emergency, be evacuated for reasons of security. It was felt,' the report said, 'that similar steps should be taken in connection with Japanese residents near other important defence areas, and particularly those established near air bases.'[150] Two months later the committee also called for the coordination of any action against Japanese Canadians with the United States government.[151]

The view in Ottawa, however, was ordinarily less alarmist. Nevertheless, some in the Department of National Defence agreed with their colleagues in British Columbia. For example, when in 1938 the Interdepartmental Committee on Orientals looked at, among other matters, internal security, LaFlèche told the civil servants on the committee that 'there seems to be little reason for any assurance as to the peaceful behaviour of even Canadian nationals of Japanese origin at a time when racial feelings will be aroused.' He felt that it was possible, and even likely, that 'action will be required ...

to restrain the activities and, consequently, the liberties of such Canadian nationals of Japanese origin whose sympathies may be deemed hostile to this country.'[152]

The next year many of the same civil servants met again in the Interdepartmental Committee on the Treatment of Aliens and Alien Property. As a result of this work, preparations were made for interning enemy aliens in the event of war. The Department of National Defence, which was responsible for setting up and manning the internment camps, began to plan for the task. In British Columbia, for example, the estimates of aliens in the province amounted to 7732, including 4724 Japanese, 1405 Germans, and 1603 Italians; of those, 25 per cent of the Italians and Germans and 100 per cent of the Japanese were deemed to require internment.[153] The committee had concluded that 'If the enemy should be an Asiatic power, it might be necessary in that contingency, to recommend the internment of nearly all enemy nationals, since it is recognized that public feeling in that section of Canada on the part of Canadian citizens and other Asiatics might render this course necessary, not alone to avoid the danger of espionage and sabotage, but also for the protection of the person and property of enemy aliens.'[154] In September 1941 the Joint Services Committee, Pacific Coast, considered the same question and concluded that in case of war with Japan, it would be necessary 'to arrest and intern' certain Japanese nationals and Canadians, to evacuate Japanese Canadians from important defence areas, and to round up the fishing fleet. The committee also observed, most perceptively and most unusually for military officers, that discrimination against Japanese Canadians could alienate 'the loyalty of what might otherwise be a loyal and useful section of the community.'[155] If evacuation did become necessary, however, the chief of the general staff did not want it to be the army's responsibility. General Harry Crerar noted on 14 August 1941 that the RCMP should be responsible for that unpleasant chore.[156]

The various government committees had recognized two sides of a related problem: how to differentiate between persons of Japanese racial origin who were Canadian citizens and those who were Japanese nationals. That question was to trouble the government in the years ahead. How could the Japanese Canadians be protected – even if they were completely loyal? Ideally, the state should use whatever police and military protection was necessary to ensure the safety of peaceful citizens and resident aliens. Ideally. But if Canada and Japan were at war, there would be serious practical difficulties in using the armed forces for this duty. All the militia units and many of the few trained troops in British Columbia were citizens of that province who likely shared the suspicions and prejudices of their neighbours.

The federal government could provide security for the Japanese Canadians, but only at the very real risk of serious political disruptions and possible breakdowns in military discipline.

Moreover, the simple truth is that espionage and sabotage were genuine possibilities. On 28 February 1941 Canada's high commissioner in London, Vincent Massey, had reported in great alarm to Ottawa that 'reliable information of a most secret character' had revealed that 'official Japanese circles' were taking great interest in the British Columbia coast. 'Reference is also made to large number of Japanese settled in British Columbia and on western coast of United States, who are all said to have their duties,' a peculiarly ominous phrase.[157] That telegram was discussed in the Cabinet War Committee,[158] but it was almost instantly discounted, the minister of national defence (naval services), Angus L. Macdonald, saying that there was 'little danger of serious attack by Japan' on the coast.[159] That comment seemed to end the discussion, and the records provide no evidence to suggest that precautions were stepped up.

The Massey telegram, however, was soundly based on information from American sources, likely conveyed by Sumner Welles, the undersecretary of state, to Lord Halifax, the British ambassador in Washington, and then passed to Whitehall from whence it reached Massey.[160] From 1940 on, the American military had been reading Japanese cipher telegrams in an operation under the code-name 'Magic.' Yet there were great difficulties in deciphering the highest-level Japanese diplomatic code, 'Purple,' and it was not until January 1941 that the military code-breakers in Washington solved the puzzle. (By the spring of that year, as the situation in the Far East worsened and as the two great English-speaking countries began to plan for eventual American entry into the war against Hitler, Britain and the United States began to pool their intelligence, thus giving the United Kingdom access to the fruits of the Magic operation.)[161]

Magic produced a treasure-trove of political and strategic information, including some telegrams that bore directly on the *Issei* and *Nisei* living in North America. Soon after cracking the Purple code, the decryption team in Washington deciphered an important two-part telegram, dated 30 January 1941, from the Foreign Office in Tokyo to the embassy in Washington, which gave the *Gaimushō*'s orders to its officials in the United States and Canada to de-emphasize propaganda and to step up intelligence gathering. Special reference was made to 'utilization of our "Second Generations" [*Nisei*] and our resident nationals' and to the need for utmost caution so as not to bring persecution down on their heads. Those telegrams had been copied to Ottawa and Vancouver as 'minister's Orders' – instructions, in other words, to be carried out in Canada just as in the United States. The Americans also intercepted a telegram of 15 February 1941, from the Foreign Office to the embassy in Washington, specifying 'the information we particularly desire with regard to intelligence involving U.S. and Canada,' that concerning the strengthening of Pacific Coast defences. The consulate in Vancouver had been advised on 14 February to pay special attention to paragraph 10 of the message to Washington: 'General outlooks on Alaska and the Aleutian Islands, with particular stress on items involving plane movements and shipment of military supplies to those localities.'[162] The telegrams intercepted on 30 January and 14 and 15 February clearly formed the basis for Massey's dispatch to Ottawa.

The Magic documents also make clear that at least as early as 1939, intelligence and counter-intelligence work was carried on from the Vancouver consulate, exactly as it was in the United States, throughout the Western Hemisphere, and in Southeast Asia.[163] How much, if anything the Canadian government knew of this, beyond the suspicions of military intelligence officers and the information conveyed in the Massey telegram, remains indeterminate.[164]

The Vancouver consulate's success or lack of it in carrying out the 'minister's Orders' to recruit *Nisei* and Japanese nationals for espionage purposes also remains unknown, since the Magic documents do not appear to report espionage results and the records in Japan seem to have been destroyed in August and September 1945. We should not forget, however, that the consulate's officials had some powerful arguments to use in recruiting. Most, if not all, of the Japanese Canadians had relatives in Japan, and virtually all the Japanese nationals did. The Tokyo regime, it must also be recalled, was a harsh dictatorship with its own very effective secret police, the *Kempeitai*, not a benign democracy unwilling to use pressure tactics to secure its ends. Threats of punishment of family in the old country would be hard for anyone to resist. All countries gather information on friendly or potentially hostile powers through their diplomatic officials and military attachés, of course, but not all countries try to recruit spies for this purpose. Among those that do, dictatorships have weapons that democracies do not.

In these circumstances, the benign attitude taken by the Canadian government and the police to the information received from the high commission in London before Pearl Harbor can only be described as careless and foolhardy. The cabinet's attention was on the war in Europe, where all of Canada's military and economic efforts were concentrated. Neither the military's intelligence branches nor the RCMP could be classed as effective, and their capacity for gathering and interpreting information on activities of the Japanese consulate and of Japanese Canadians was minimal. Indeed, one official in the Prime Minister's Office even complained about the RCMP's 'total lack of the capacity, education and training required for real intelligence work.'[165]

The Japanese Canadians unfortunately would pay a heavy part of the price for the weaknesses in Canada's intelligence and security apparatus. On 7 December 1941 Japanese carrier-launched aircraft struck at the great American naval and air bases at Pearl Harbor on Oahu in the Hawaiian Islands. The United States navy's own carriers were at sea, but its battleships were caught at anchor. The destruction wrought by the carrier aircraft reversed the balance of power in the Pacific Ocean and for a time appeared to put the west coast of North America at risk. Canada declared war on Japan the day of the surprise attack, and the RCMP moved at once to arrest Japanese Canadians suspected of serving the interests of Imperial Japan. More action would follow, all too often ill-informed and motivated by a combination of fear and prejudice.

Three

Beyond the Help of Their Government: Canadians in Hong Kong, Japan, and Japanese-Occupied Territories

On 7 December 1941 Canadian troops suddenly were fighting in an unlikely part of the world – Hong Kong. The Pacific theatre was not a natural arena of action for the Eurocentric Canadian government and its armed forces, but in the fall of 1941 almost 2000 Canadian soldiers had been sent to help defend the Crown Colony.[1] At the same time, there were Canadian civilians living in occupied China and Korea and in Japan. Most of these civilians had gone to Asia to proselytize on behalf of their God and their church. Both soldiers and civilians found themselves caught up in events beyond their control and far beyond the aid of their government.

For more than a half century, Canadian Protestant churches and Roman Catholic orders had been sending missionaries and priests to China and Korea to seek converts, to teach, and to offer medical care. The United Church of Canada was present in large numbers in the late 1930s, many of its missionaries working in the recently Japanese-occupied territory of Honan in northern China. 'Why did we not evacuate?' John Mathieson, one of the missionaries, wrote in a letter to friends in Canada in December 1937. He then quoted the British consul general at Hankow in answer: 'I understand that the majority of the active members of the Honan Mission intend to remain at their posts. [They] feel it as much their moral duty to remain with their congregations and pupils as the doctors feel it theirs to remain with the sick and wounded. This attitude is not fanaticism,' the consul concluded, 'but their considered Christian resolution.'

The considered decision to remain exposed the Honan missionaries to great personal danger. The Japanese army, Mathieson wrote, 'had gained entrance to the city and the Rising Sun flag floated over the city walls. "Mopping up" operations included the killing of several hundred civilians [unjustly described as] plainclothes soldiers.'[2] Wounded Chinese soldiers, even those under care in mission hospitals, were routinely shot.[3]

French-Canadian Jesuits were also present in substantial numbers in Honan. There were thirty-one priests and brothers at Suchow (with a further twenty-one in Beijing and Shanghai) ministering to 54,000 Chinese Christians. The arrival of the Japanese armies altered everything, one priest wrote of relations with the Chinese. Before, 'we went to them'; after, the Chinese 'came to us.' The local Chinese flocked to the missions, seeking refuge from Japanese bombings and escape from the depredations of the occupying armies. At Suchow, after the capture of the city, there were 2000 refugees living at the Jesuit compound.

According to some reports, the Japanese military initially were impressed at the care provided by the Jesuits, but once the commander realized that the Jesuits were Canadians and hence British subjects, and not French citizens as he had first believed, the situation rapidly worsened. Refugees were ordered out of the compound and, in 1939, Japanese soldiers shot and killed one brother and wounded another, apparently inadvertently. The British embassy in Shanghai doubted the shootings were unintentional since the Jesuits had been 'wearing the large white hats customarily – and almost exclusively – worn by missionaries.'[4] Despite that incident, however, the Jesuits ordinarily seem to have been better treated than the United Church missionaries; perhaps this was because the anti-communist and largely anti-Kuomintang Jesuits seemed generally sympathetic to the Japanese, ostensibly battling communism in their war on Chiang Kai-shek's China. One priest (the same one wounded in the shooting incident) even wrote a book, *The Japanese Soul*, and dedicated it to the local commandant.[5]

But by the spring of 1939 as the invaders grew more exasperated at the Chinese people's continued resistance and widespread refusal to cooperate, at the stiffening diplomatic positions of the Western powers, and perhaps at the increasingly vociferous pro-Chinese North American fund-raising and relief efforts launched by the churches,[6] the Japanese army stepped up its harassment of missionaries. In Honan, the United Church bore the brunt. Some Canadian missionaries were jailed on trumped up charges and their Chinese mission employees were beaten by military police.[7] There were officially sponsored anti-British demonstrations that included the Canadians whose missions always flew the Union Jack. The Japanese also tried to dissuade Chinese students and the sick from using mission facilities. In October the Japanese army insisted on billetting troops in the Honan mission compound and forced its closure by the end of that month.[8] Other missions faced a similar fate.[9] Still others were damaged in the continuing battles of the Sino-Japanese war, and more than twenty instances were documented of the bombing of mission properties by the Japanese air force.[10] A study prepared in Ottawa by Hugh Keenleyside observed that while there had been few attacks on Canadian missionaries in 1937 and 1938, by September 1939 there had been fifteen.[11] That suggested a concerted campaign. And the Canadian government, disturbed by the treatment of its nationals and particularly by the death of four from Japanese military actions, began for the first time to consider whether or not it should recommend that Canadians abandon the Chinese interior.[12]

The Japanese pressure on the missions was difficult enough. More painful still was the inability of the missionaries to do anything to alleviate the suffering of the Chinese. The atrocities in Nanking in December 1937 were much the worst perpetrated by the Japanese army, the toll of dead being estimated at over 200,000. The slaughter astonished and horrified missionaries – and all who heard of it.[13]

By early 1941, as the relations between Japan, Britain, and the United States plunged deeper into crisis, Ottawa again became deeply troubled about the fate of Canadian missionaries in Asia. Two medical missionaries had been arrested at Kaishu, Korea, in August 1940 and given 'vindictive fines' for trivial offences. The British consul general at Keijo had described the proceedings as a 'frame-up,' but there was almost nothing he – or anyone in Ottawa – could do to protect the missionaries.[14] In February 1941, as a result, the acting undersecretary of state for external affairs, Norman Robertson, met with United Church representatives in Ottawa only to be told that almost all their missionaries refused to seek safety. 'While we naturally admire, and would like to commend, the spirit actuating ... their decision against evacuation, we must again bring strongly to your attention the dangers which are inherent in this stand,' Robertson wrote.[15] Only a few missionaries and some of their family members left in response to Ottawa's pleas, and there were additional arrests as war neared.[16] In essence, the Canadian government could do nothing to protect its nationals in China where it had no diplomatic representation. The fate of the missionaries was in their own hands – and that of the Japanese army.

If Ottawa was powerless to assist missionaries in China and Korea, it was almost so in Japan where it did have a legation and diplomatic representation. For some time before the outbreak of war, conditions in Japan had been less than favourable for Canadian, British, and American missionaries living, teaching, and preaching there. Japan had become increasingly nationalistic and militaristic since the 1920s, and the pervasive influence of the *Kempeitai*, the secret police, was everywhere. Then, too, Japan had always been a closed society, racially distinct and conscious of its divine mission and superiority. Thus the Japanese were normally suspicious of foreigners, and the tensions in the Pacific had increased that suspicion. Finally, the Japanese were naturally and understandably concerned about missionaries, preaching an alien gospel and trying, through conversions, to alter an ancient system of beliefs and way of life.

The inevitable result was that white teachers and missionaries became subject to increasing state surveillance. One United Church missionary teacher at Kwansei Gakuin University in Nishinomiya reported in December 1939 that his mail to Canada was censored, and he lamented the arrest of a colleague for distributing seditious literature – 'the book on the Japanese Terror in China.'[17] Another missionary at the same university noted early in 1941 that

> It is not comfortable to be continuously living under surveillance, to have spotters in your class, to have to weigh every word, to restrict your movements to certain recognized routes, to be daily in fear of some trumped-up charge of espionage or the danger of infringement of some unreasonable and utterly ridiculous economic law, to be unable to purchase nourishing and necessary foods, to know that people are paid to concoct malicious misrepresentations, and so on, to say nothing of such little annoyances as having your correspondence held up indefinitely and frequently not delivered at all.[18]

In the circumstances, that any Canadians remained in Japan was a tribute, in the case of the missionaries, to their religious zeal and Christian concern, if not to their good sense. Certainly their government wanted them to return to Canada, as it did their co-religionists in China and Korea. In October 1940 the Department of External Affairs tried to persuade the United Church and a number of Roman Catholic orders to withdraw their missionaries from Japan or, alternatively, to concentrate them near Tokyo where 'extrication in case of crisis would be less doubtful.'[19] At least one order of nuns, the Montreal-based Sisters of the Holy Names of Jesus and Mary, had already ordered its members home – 'an answer to their ardent prayers,' the sisters called it.[20] The Canadian chargé in Tokyo, E. d'Arcy McGreer, talked with remaining missionaries in a number of centres but had little success in persuading any to return to Canada. 'My impression,' he reported to Ottawa after conversations with Dominican and Franciscan nuns and priests, 'is that if Japanese do not force them to leave, the majority would prefer to remain even after hostilities break out.'[21] One aged Japanophile United Church missionary, Agnes Coates, decided to stay in Japan, she wrote to her children in Canada, because 'some of us can do considerable in the interests of peace – or rather the prevention of war.'[22] The naiveté was touching.

Whether or not it was Japanese government policy to force out foreigners, the tactics employed had that effect. McGreer reported in January 1941 that 'Canadians as a whole have not been greatly molested if one discounts the usual Japanese inquisitiveness and distrust toward foreigners in general.' He then recounted two cases, one of a Sulpician held for several days for questioning and another of a Dominican detained for at least a week in Hokkaido. In neither case did the priests' superiors ask the Canadian government to assist, something that troubled Ottawa. 'How far we can go,' Robertson wrote to McGreer, 'without prejudicing the prestige of the Canadian government by failing to defend Canadian nationals who have been unjustly treated is a question that cannot easily be decided.'[23]

Shortly, however, the legation in Tokyo had to intervene when in December 1940 a Dominican, Father Marcel Fournier, faced 'sex charges involving a Japanese boy.' By May 1941 the *Gaimushō* claimed, in addition, that there was 'concrete evidence of his having been engaged in espionage and that the sex charges [were then] of secondary importance.' To compound the problem, the Japanese government based its 'utterly fantastic' case 'on a letter McGreer is alleged to have written [Fournier], asking him to procure military secrets.' As tensions between Japan and Canada increased and the Fournier affair escalated through the summer of 1941, McGreer informed the minister for foreign affairs in Tokyo that no new Canadian minister to Japan would be appointed until Fournier was released and the allegations against him withdrawn. Tokyo was not cowed by Ottawa's feeble threat, and Fournier was found guilty and sentenced to five-years imprisonment (subsequently reduced to three years on appeal). Happily, no reference was made to McGreer in the trial judgment. Even so, Ottawa believed the 'forged letter had a considerable effect on the mind of the Judge.'[24]

Trumped up as it appeared to be, the Fournier case increased Ottawa's concerns about its nationals, as did the steady deterioration in relations between Japan and both Britain and the United States.[25] Only a few United Church missionaries left in response to Ottawa's repeated urgings, and the efforts to persuade Roman Catholic clergy to leave were even less successful.[26] Meanwhile, the harassment of Canadian missionaries continued.[27]

So exasperated was Ottawa by the Fournier case and other arrests of Canadians in Japanese-controlled China and in Korea that in October 1941 the Department of External Affairs seriously contemplated following the

British precedent of retaliatory arrests of Japanese citizens in Canada.[28] But there were problems. Retaliatory measures could lead Tokyo to raise difficulties 'over the evacuation of Canadian nationals from Japan or occupied territory, if things turn to the worse in the Far East.' Moreover, the arrest of prominent Japanese nationals 'might impress unfavourably the Japanese population in British Columbia, at the precise time when their cooperation is most needed.' The suggestion, in the circumstances, was to ask the RCMP 'to submit the names of some Japanese who are at present under observation ... This selection should leave "nisei" out of the picture.'[29] Keenleyside, to whom this memorandum came, did not even wait to ask the RCMP's advice. The very next day he advised Robertson that 'While it might be possible to find Japanese nationals in British Columbia against whom some meagre suspicion exists, there is certainly no Japanese national at large in that Province or elsewhere in Canada against whom any really convincing case can be made out.' His recommendation, therefore, downplayed the effectiveness of any possible retaliation, and none took place.[30]

The clergymen and missionary women in Japan had decided to stay of their own free will. But the soldiers of the two Canadian regiments sent to Hong Kong in the fall of 1941 were not given any choice.

The British chiefs of staff in August 1940 had declared the Crown Colony of Hong Kong to be virtually indefensible, and they had recognized that the colony and its defenders could be neither reinforced nor relieved in the event of war with Japan. 'Hong Kong,' they said in a memorandum that was sent to the Canadian chiefs of staff, 'is not vital and the garrison could not long withstand Japanese attack ... In the event of war, therefore, Hong Kong must be regarded as an outpost and held as long as possible.' Militarily, the appreciation concluded in the unsparing style ordinarily favoured in such documents, 'our position in the Far East would be stronger without this unsatisfactory commitment.'[31] A few months later, the governor of the Crown Colony actually recommended removing the garrison entirely 'in order to avoid the slaughter of civilians and the destruction of property which would follow a Japanese attack,'[32] but London turned down that sensible advice. Nevertheless, Churchill also rejected insistent requests from the British high command in the Far East to increase the size of the garrison, explaining early in 1941 that 'If Japan goes to war with us there is not the slightest chance of holding Hong Kong or relieving it. It is most unwise to increase the loss we shall suffer there.'[33] Churchill added that 'we must avoid frittering away our resources on untenable positions.'[34]

But the sound judgments of the chiefs and Churchill were eventually overridden, in part because the retiring British commander of troops in China, the Canadian-born Major-General A.E. Grasett, passed through Canada on his way home in August 1941. Grasett thought the Crown Colony could be defended against the Japanese army which he, like so many British and American officers, considered to be inferior in training, equipment, and leadership to white or white-led forces. 'They fought well against third-rate Chinese,' Grasett argued, 'but they had yet to meet first class troops such as his battalions, which would give them a bloody nose.' Moreover, Grasett was convinced that Japan was bluffing and believed the bluff should be called.[35] In discussions with General H.D.G. Crerar, the chief of the Canadian general staff, Grasett had argued that 'the addition of two or more battalions to the forces then at Hong Kong would render the garrison strong enough to withstand for an extensive period of siege an attack by such forces as the Japanese could bring to bear against it.' When he returned to London, Grasett suggested that Canada could supply those battalions, and the British chiefs of staff, apparently now convinced, reversed their position and recommended that Churchill approach the Canadian government. 'A small reinforcement of one or two battalions would increase the strength of the garrison out of all proportion to the actual numbers involved,' the chiefs now argued. It would 'have a very great moral effect in the whole of the Far East.'

The British prime minister duly changed course and, accepting the advice of his military staff, asked Ottawa for one or two battalions. 'There have been signs of a certain weakening in attitude of Japan towards United States and ourselves,' the Dominions Office telegram to Canada of 19 September said.[36]

In Ottawa, London's request came before the Cabinet War Committee on 23 September and was deferred pending the advice of the army. General Crerar indicated the next day that it was possible to provide two battalions 'without reducing the strength of our Coast Defence garrisons and without further mobilization.' By 27 September Ottawa had made the fateful decision, and two days later London was so advised.

As C.P. Stacey, the official historian of the Canadian army in the Second World War, has noted and as has been pointed out before in this volume, in 1941 Canada had no intelligence organization, either military or civilian, capable of making an adequate assessment of the situation in the Far East: 'essentially, Ottawa depended upon London for such information. Nor was any military appreciation requested of or prepared by the Canadian General Staff as to the situation of Hong Kong in the event of war with Japan.'[37] The decision to send troops to Hong Kong, therefore, was made in ignorance, and the history of the army's intelligence operations notes that the Canadian troops 'were not provided, as they should have been, with adequate, accurate information on their opponent.'[38] Had the information to prepare a proper military appreciation been available, and had it followed the line of the British paper of August 1940, the government might have held back.

But in the political circumstances of the day in Canada, with opposition critics and important newspapers across English Canada charging that recruits for the armed forces were lacking and that conscription was necessary if Canada was to fight a 'total war,' rejecting a direct British request for troops could have been enormously damaging if word of it leaked out. The government of Mackenzie King was caught between a rock and a hard place, and the Hong Kong decision, in the circumstances, was inevitable.

By the end of September, Crerar had decided which units to send. He wanted 'efficient, well-trained battalions capable of upholding the credit of the Dominion in any circumstances,' and he recommended the Royal Rifles,[39] a unit recruited from the Quebec City area, and the Winnipeg Grenadiers, an infantry battalion whose members came from the Manitoba capital and its surrounding area. Both battalions had spent their war service on garrison duty, one in Newfoundland and the other in Jamaica, and Crerar believed that 'The duties which they carried out there were not in many respects unlike the task which awaits the units to be sent to Hong Kong.' That was a gross misjudgment. As Crerar later told a royal commission set up to investigate the Hong Kong disaster, 'Information at my disposal during the latter part of September, 1941 indicated that the outbreak of hostilities with Japan was not imminent and that time would, in all probability, be available to carry out adequate and possibly extensive training of Canadian forces at Hong Kong after their arrival.'[40]

The government compounded its mistake on 11 October when London asked that the Canadian commitment be expanded to include a brigade headquarters and various specialists. Ottawa agreed, and Crerar recommended that Colonel J.K. Lawson, an experienced Permanent Force officer, should be given the command with the rank of brigadier.

The two battalions in fact were not quite the 'well-trained' units that General Crerar had claimed – and likely believed. Their experience with their weapons was scanty, shortages of arms and ammunition had hampered their work on the rifle ranges, their field training was limited, and the Winnipeg battalion in particular had taken fifteen new officers and a substantial number of men on strength just before embarking. 'The two battalions.' Stacey noted, 'had clearly not reached that advanced state of training which one would wish troops to attain before being sent against the enemy.' Moreover, the battalions had no preparation for service in semi-tropical Hong

Kong. Presumably the assumption was that the battalions would have time in Hong Kong to become accustomed to the climate.

Nonetheless, on 27 October the battalions and the brigade headquarters boarded the *Awatea*, a British transport, and the HMCS *Prince Robert*, an armed merchant cruiser, and sailed that night. In all, ninety-six officers and 1877 men left Canada for Hong Kong. Unfortunately, none of the 212 vehicles that were to accompany the force was loaded on the *Awatea*, although there was space available for some twenty vehicles. The motor transport was put aboard an American ship on 4 November, which sailed by way of Honolulu and Manila, and did not reach the Philippine capital until 12 December, after war had begun. The Canadian vehicles were turned over to the American forces that were vainly attempting to defend the Philippines.

The Hong Kong force reached the Crown Colony on 16 November. The Canadian troops marched through the streets to their quarters at Sham Shui Po camp. The officers soon attended a briefing on the Japanese army and were told that there were only 5000 troops in the vicinity, ill-equipped, with little artillery, unused to night fighting, and supported by obsolete aircraft flown by myopic pilots incapable of dive-bombing attacks.[41] Some of the private soldiers had sounder instincts. 'The minute I got off the boat in Hong Kong,' one Canadian soldier recalled with a clarity that was certainly sharpened by hindsight, 'I realized that if the Japanese attacked they'd wipe us out. "We've got no air force, no navy, no place to go," I told my pals ... My pals laughed. "We won't have to worry, Wilf. It's them that will be running away." '[42]

The Japanese army was not to run away from Hong Kong. Indeed, the Crown Colony was viewed by the Imperial Headquarters as a festering sore, the major route through which Chiang Kai-shek's Nationalist armies received the war supplies that permitted them to continue their resistance.[43] Estimates were that war materiel shipped through Hong Kong amounted to as much as 6000 tons a month. Chiang's government openly maintained offices in the British colony, and there was weekly air service to Chungking, the Nationalist capital.[44] The British colony was thus a natural focus of Japanese attention.

As early as the end of 1939, therefore, Imperial Headquarters in Tokyo and the staffs of the army in China began secret efforts to stir up anti-British plots among Chinese in Hong Kong. Simultaneously, a Chinese volunteer force was formed in Canton, ready to intervene in the event that anti-British riots broke out in the colony.[45] In fact, there was divided counsel on how to proceed to take Hong Kong. Some military officers insisted on using the pretext of anti-British riots as an excuse for intervention; others preferred an attack by Imperial forces, arguing that such an attack would not result in a general war with Britain.[46] Caution won out, however, and in July 1940 Imperial Headquarters decided that Hong Kong should be seized only in the context of a general war with Britain.[47]

Orders to prepare for the attack on the Crown Colony came on 6 November 1941. The intention, to strike at the same time as Japanese forces fell upon British Malaya, was to launch an assault on Hong Kong Island immediately after the New Territories and Kowloon were seized. On that basis, the army and navy completed their planning on 30 November.[48] The plan called for air strikes on the Royal Air Force's base and an attack on the Gin Drinkers' Line, the mainland defences on Kowloon. The air force, while not bombing indiscriminately and attempting to preserve bridges and wharves to permit their later use, would strike every identifiable military position on the island. Artillery was also to be positioned on the Kowloon shore immediately it was taken in order to soften up British defences. At the same time, efforts to stir up revolt among Chinese and Indians – and to encourage the assassination of British officials and officers – were stepped up.

Japanese intelligence on British preparations was effective. The Japanese army had learned that the British now intended to defend the colony vigorously, a reversal of the earlier policy. Estimates of the troops available to the British commander were 3000–4000 British soldiers, 3000–4000 Indian soldiers, and 1000 Chinese. In addition, one intelligence report noted, 'Canadian troops had arrived in the middle of November. Their strength is 1000–2000, and these men are not excellent in character.'[49]

The two Canadian infantry battalions and a brigade headquarters had indeed arrived in Hong Kong on 16 November 1941. 'We climbed mountains all day long,' one private of the Royal Rifles of Canada had written in his diary on 21 November, 'and we are shown the many posts for which soon we shall be fighting for our own lives.'[50] The men barely had time to accustom themselves to the subtropical climate before Japan's powerful armies fell upon the Crown Colony at 3:40 AM on 8 December 1941 Hong Kong time. The Crown Colony's garrison had no air cover (the five obsolete aircraft flown by the Royal Air Force were destroyed on the first day of fighting exactly as the Japanese attackers had planned), insufficient artillery, mortars, and ammunition, and far too few trucks. Soon there were shortages of food, water, and medicine.

The British planners who had considered the defences of Hong Kong had persuaded themselves that the Japanese army would easily be handled by good white or white-led troops. They also believed the stereotypical view that Japanese soldiers had difficulty operating at night, something almost instantly disproven when the Gin Drinkers' Line, ill-planned and scarcely completed, was largely overrun with ease. The steep hills of the New Territories, now an extraordinary forest of high-rise buildings stretching from Kowloon almost to the border with China but then only lightly populated, the indented bays, and the limited number of roads that channeled any attacking force should have enabled a commander of even limited competence to mount time-consuming blocking operations before the main defensive works were reached. But, secure in their prejudices, the British had done little and their mainland defences fell quickly. The attackers never forfeited the moral ascendency gained by this first victory, and the morale of the defenders and of the European and Chinese population of Hong Kong could not recover.

Curiously, the Japanese army had expected the colony to surrender after the debacle on the mainland, and there was some surprise at the governor's refusal to order arms to be laid down.[51] Forced to continue the battle, the Japanese army launched its amphibious assault on Hong Kong island on 18 December, rapidly establishing itself ashore in force with the aid of Chinese fifth columnists and local Japanese who cut the wire entanglements on the beaches, sabotaged vehicles, and sniped at the defenders.[52] The Canadian battalions, dispersed and often under British command that was not always competent, soon found themselves engaged in hand-to-hand combat against heavy odds. 'The officers of the new Brigade Staff,' the war diary of the Royal Rifles recorded on 11 December, even before the Japanese had launched their assault on Hong Kong Island, 'were in a highly nervous state and apparently very tired.'[53] 'The whole thing was disorganized confusion,' a private of the Winnipeg Grenadiers recalled. 'Nobody was prepared for it. There was no communication. We didn't have transportation. You carried everything on your back.'[54] For a week, the Canadian troops took part in a succession of hopeless counter-attacks against superior forces and grim defensive actions against well-equipped and heavily supported Japanese units. On 19 December Brigadier Lawson, the Canadians' commander, was killed when his brigade headquarters defending the critical Wong Nei Chong gap in the centre of the island was overrun. Lawson had told General Maltby, the island's commander, that he was 'going outside to fight it out' with a pistol in each hand. The Canadians had resisted fiercely, one Japanese account noting that 'a narrow path was soon filled with a line of Japanese casualties.' In all, about 600 Japanese soldiers were killed or wounded in this three-day assault on the Canadian position.[55] A Japanese colonel later said that 'We wrapped up [Lawson's] body in the blanket of Lt. Okada, o.c. No. 9 Company, which had captured the position. I ordered the temporary burial of the officer on the battleground on which he had died so heroically.'[56]

That was almost the only chivalry shown by the Japanese. When the defenders, their position completely hopeless and with no prospect of either evacuation or reinforcement, surrendered on Christmas Day, the Japanese reported the capture of 1689 Canadians, 5072 British, 3829 Indians, and 189 Chinese soldiers. Japanese casualties in all were 2096, including 683 dead.[57] Perhaps that higher than anticipated toll was responsible for the orgy of rape and brutality that preceded and followed the capitulation.

One Canadian nursing sister wrote that just before the surrender the 'Japanese took the hospital,' St Stephen's College at Stanley. 'The two M[edical] O[fficer]s tried to stop them from entering the hospital by showing them the Red Cross and telling them there were only wounded there, but it didn't do any good. They were both killed ... The Japanese troops went wild – bayonetted patients in their beds. [Nursing] Sisters and 4 [female volunteer aides] were raped and then they killed three of the [volunteers].'[58] Forty male captives, patients and orderlies, were locked in a storeroom at the hospital. Every half hour Japanese troops took two or three at random and killed them. Four Royal Rifles soldiers were then taken out. 'The Japanese,' one account of the day said, 'made the four stand by while soldiers cut out one man's tongue and chopped off another man's ears. "Go to Fort Stanley and tell your officers what you have seen," the Japanese commander told the four. "Hong Kong must surrender or else all prisoners will be killed in this manner." '[59] The chaplain of the Royal Rifles, Captain James Barnett, was also held in this storeroom. After the war he testified before the Tokyo War Crimes trials about his experiences there, about the killing of 'fifteen to twenty wounded men' in their hospital beds and the rape of nurses at the hospital.[60] At another hospital, however, or so one Hong Kong escapee reported, 'the kindest and most considerate treatment was accorded by the Japanese Commander who did everything in his power to be friendly and courteous.' The difference in treatment, he added, 'depended entirely upon the character of the Commanding Officers in charge,'[61] something that held true for virtually all prisoners of war and civilian internees in the Far East.

Moreover, Japan had not ratified the 1929 Geneva Convention on the treatment of prisoners of war; the army and navy had opposed it, arguing that favourable treatment for POWs would weaken military discipline. Nonetheless, once Japan was advised that Britain, Canada, and other dominions intended to apply the Geneva rules to Japanese prisoners, Tokyo stated that it too would observe its provisions for both civil and military prisoners.[62] Unfortunately, the Japanese army did not formally recognize a soldier as a prisoner of war until he had reached a POW camp. In other words, as the chief delegate of the International Red Cross in the Far East noted, 'From the time a man was captured to the time when he entered a *formal* prisoner of war camp there were no regulations regarding his treatment, and before 1943 there were no regulations for formal camps.'[63] One Japanese academic, Junpei Shinobu, writing in 1942, observed that a 'POW is not a guest,' and that POWs were not entitled to favourable treatment, although the provisions of the Geneva Convention must be respected. Shinobu added that military operations could make it necessary to abandon humanitarian treatment – if, for example, there was no way to feed or intern prisoners and it was dangerous to free them, then 'under the rules of belligerency it could be justifiable to kill them ... Favourable treatment in such a case would not be of benefit but of harm' to Japan.[64] Moreover, as the Japanese wartime prime minister, General Hideki Tojo, stated at his war crimes trial, 'It is the Japanese custom for a commander of an expeditionary army in the field to be given a mission in the performance of which he is not subject to specific orders from Tokyo, but has considerable autonomy. This can mean that under the Japanese method of warfare such atrocities were expected to occur, or were at least permitted, and that the Government was not concerned to prevent them.'[65] Japanese soldiers had been trained to believe that capture was worse than death – 'Never live in shame as an imprisoned captive,' their orders went – and they took a dark view of white soldiers who surrendered when a position could no longer be held. General Yamashita, one of the Imperial army's most successful commanders, expressed just this view when he inspected British POWs in Singapore. 'Serves you right,' he said. 'I wish to send them to Japan to work in the coal mines, but it would waste shipping space.'[66] Prisoners of war, in other words, were at the mercy of their captors.

Not only soldiers but Japanese civilians also sometimes believed that capture was shameful. One 1942 magazine article argued that the Geneva Convention 'provided too favourable treatment for POWs' and to abide by it would 'spoil our captives.' The provisions on food and tobacco, for example, 'made no difference between prisoners of war and guests.' In the west, the article noted, 'nothing was more honourable than capture for soldiers who had fought their utmost.' That was not true in Japan: 'we have been taught since childhood that we should choose to kill ourselves by biting off our own tongue rather than to be captured.'[67] The Japanese newspapers added that white POWs lacked patriotism and had low morale. *Tokyo Asahi* reported that prisoners worried about their wives and children, not the fates of their own countries, and one report jeered at the words of an American POW who had asked 'When can I go home? I was reluctantly drafted into the army. My girl friend is waiting for me.'[68] Japan's warrior code of *bushido* viewed such considerations as those of weaklings, not soldiers.

In such circumstances, mercy was often in short supply. A corporal of the Royal Rifles remembered being marched away after the surrender. 'We went by different groups of our fellas that had been bayonetted. They were tied up in groups of six to ten and butchered.'[69] A private in the Grenadiers remembered that 'they were pretty rough on us. They tied our hands together with barbed wire. A lot of the boys that fell and couldn't walk because they were wounded so badly, they were cut loose and bayonetted right there. They didn't believe in taking too many prisoners,' he said.[70] That seemed to be so, for Captain Barnett testified at the war crimes trials that Lieutenant Honda, the camp commandant of North Point Camp, said that 'his orders were all prisoners must die.'[71]

Fortunately, that order must have been countermanded. The atrocities against prisoners were horrific, but not universal. Most Canadian and British soldiers who surrendered were not physically abused, though tales of the killings at the hospital and the abuses witnessed by many of the captured terrified all the survivors. One American assessment later was that most atrocities against captured soldiers came in the first months of war 'when the Japanese were drunk with triumph and thought that they had virtually won the war already.'[72]

The last message from Hong Kong to reach Canada arrived in Ottawa after the surrender: 'Situation critical. Canadian troops part prisoners residue engaged casualties heavy ... Troops have done magnificent work spirit excellent.' It was all true, especially the reference to the heavy casualties. The Canadians had suffered severely in the fighting – twenty-three officers and 267 other ranks killed, twenty-eight officers and 465 other ranks wounded, a high percentage of the 1973 Canadians at Hong Kong. The brief battle was over; the long captivity was to begin.

The Canadian prisoners of war were initially held in temporary camps with others captured at Hong Kong. In late January 1942 the Japanese concentrated all the Canadian captives at North Point Camp and shifted British prisoners to Shamshuipo camp. The Canadians' camp had been built by the Hong Kong government in 1939 to house Chinese refugees. During the fighting, it had been seriously damaged, and later the Japanese army had stabled horses there. As a result, insects, lice, and flies abounded in the huge piles of manure and garbage just outside the wire.[73]

The International Red Cross visited North Point on 3 July 1942 and reported that the accommodation was crowded, especially the hospital. But the men were said to look well. 'Have own bakery and well-equipped Dental

Clinic ... Commanding Officer states that they are being well treated and that they could not complain about the food.'[74]

In fact, that report was either incorrect or made while the Red Cross delegate was wearing rose-coloured spectacles. Rations were in appallingly short supply and the accommodations provided the POWs were completely inadequate, particularly in the first four months after the capture of Hong Kong. Even the Japanese admitted this.[75] During the first months of captivity, the daily food intake was less than 900 calories per soldier, totally insufficient for men averaging 170 pounds. From July to November 1942 a reduction in rations as collective punishment for an escape attempt led to semi-starvation. By the end of the war 195 Canadian POWs had died in the Hong Kong camp.[76] One report from the Canadian minister in China to Ottawa, received in July 1943 through 'most secret underground channels' from Lt-Col. J.H. Price, the commanding officer of the Royal Rifles and the senior Canadian officer surviving, noted that the men were in poor shape. But Price added, 'Since last December health of men has improved due to Red Cross food which is sufficient to prevent further deterioration but not to build up. Present supplies will last to September when return to purely Japanese diet will probably cause increase of disease and death.'[77] A U.S. Joint Chiefs of Staff paper a few months later noted that conditions in POW camps 'could scarcely be much worse and unless conditions are improved, few American prisoners will survive.'[78]

A detailed interrogation of a New Zealand naval officer who had escaped from captivity in Hong Kong in July 1944 provided more information in terms of the caloric intake prisoners received. British camp doctors had prepared a report for the Japanese camp commandants in an effort to get increased rations, and the escapee provided details. The medical officers had argued that, in October 1942, POWS received 2338 calories a day and, in November 1942, 2395, figures that seem improbably high against later estimates of 900 calories per day.[79] If those figures were correct, it is difficult to account for the diary kept by Rifleman D.L.W. Welsh of the Royal Rifles, a diary devoted entirely to food:

April 1, 1942. Breakfast – Had rice, syrup, one bun and black tea. Dinner – Had rice patties, bread and cold water. Supper – Had rice, Chinese sauce, bread and black tea.

May 1, 1942. Breakfast – Had rice, brown sugar, one bun and black tea. Dinner – Had two buns and black tea. Supper – Had rice, one egg plant and cold water.

Welsh's diary continued in this vein until 5 October 1942, when he died.[80] If those were the good conditions and the high caloric intake, a year later conditions had worsened and food value had fallen to 2032 calories a day in October 1943 and 1869 a day in November, or so calculations had it.[81]

Operating with different attitudes to standards of diet, hygiene, and the treatment of their own soldiers, the Japanese military was not impressed by complaints about the treatment and status of POWS. The POWS and their governments at home seemed to expect that the Japanese would recognize that whites were 'different' and entitled to better treatment and food than the Japanese military provided for its own troops. That was not forthcoming, nor could it have been expected. What might have been provided, however, what ought to have been provided, was enough food to prevent starvation and enough medicine to allow the effective treatment of the sick. The Japanese army failed to meet this standard, something to which prisoners of war were entitled under the Geneva Convention.

In the circumstances, with food so scarce and so deficient in vitamins, the health of the Canadian POWS rapidly deteriorated. As a result, medicines were in critically short supply. Other than the stocks held in the Bowen Road hospital and the small amounts saved from the infantry battalions' stocks, there were almost none. Within weeks of the capture of Hong Kong, dysentery swept the POW camps and men died, including the commanding officer of the Winnipeg Grenadiers. Beriberi, pellagra, parasitic infections, and diphtheria also developed quickly, the latter reaching epidemic proportions and killing fifty men in early 1942. Only a small quantity of anti-diphtheria serum was available on the black market and the Japanese provided little more.[82]

So grim was the medical situation by mid-1943 that secret reports received in London estimated that only 40 per cent of the Canadians were now 'fit for fatigues.' Even that dreadful state of affairs was stated to be an improvement over the situation six months before.[83]

Since the Japanese made POWS work, the health of the prisoners ought to have concerned them. But since the POWS were supposed to be paid for their work in accordance with the Geneva Convention, it may be that money was being siphoned off. According to the Japanese army's pay regulation for POWS, the Japanese were to pay commissioned officer POWS a salary equivalent to that paid Japanese officers of equal rank, while not paying POWS of other ranks; after paying for their own food, the officers contributed most of the remainder of this money to a fund to buy food and medicines, often on the black market, for their men. Fit men who were put to work by the Japanese, initially on extending the runways at Hong Kong's Kai Tak airfield, were paid a pittance – .15 yen for NCOS and .1 yen for other ranks.[86] By contrast, Japanese day labourers in 1939 received 1.97 yen per day.

Captain Barnett of the Royal Rifles testified later that sick men on stretchers were also sent out on work parties. 'Even though they could not work, the numbers had to be made up,' he said. 'The men would be called at four o'clock in the morning, and although work did not start actually until nine o'clock in the morning, the intervening hours were spent in counting out the men and getting them sorted out and transferred to the place of work.'[85]

The medical, food, and labour conditions at North Point were bad enough, but the Canadian POWs also suffered from the special attention of Kanao Inouye, the 'Kamloops Kid.' Inouye served as an 'honorary corporal' and interpreter at Shamshuipo camp and later for the *Kempeitai* in Hong Kong. Born in 1916 at Kamloops, BC, Inouye had lived in Canada until 1935, when he had returned to Japan.[86] 'When I was back in Canada and going to school,' Inouye told one Royal Rifles corporal, 'they called me "slant eyes" and "yellow" and all the names you could think of. I've got you SOBS now where I want you. You're going to pay for it.' And they did. Three Canadian POWs reportedly died as a direct result of the interpreter's malice; others, notably two officers of the Winnipeg Grenadiers, were subjected to 'severe and brutal public beating[s].'[87] 'He was a sadist, no question about it,' the corporal recalled. 'He was so evil against the white man, against the Canadians, particularly.'

At the end of the war, the Kamloops Kid was charged as a war criminal with twenty-seven counts of overt cruelty, presumably the soundest cases from the more than 200 affidavits filed about his activities.[88] His case involved a number of difficult legal questions about jurisdiction, and for a time it seemed possible that, 'having regard to the cowardly and treacherous nature of his conduct and to the feelings of the Canadians to whom he directed his attentions,' as an External Affairs officer put it to his minister,[89] he might be tried in Canada for offences under the Treachery Act. The cabinet considered this question in May 1946 and decided that Inouye instead should be brought to justice at a war crimes tribunal in Hong Kong. Probably, although the records are not entirely clear, 'the possible effects' on 'the internal political situation here, having special regard to the deportation, etc., of persons of Japanese race' helped persuade the cabinet to minimize publicity by holding the trial in the Far East.[90] The case duly proceeded but, after Inouye's defence counsel pointed out that he was a Canadian citizen, he was retried by the civilian courts in Hong Kong for treason, found guilty, and executed on 25 August 1947.[91]

Among other war crimes to which Canadian POWs were subjected was the murder or execution of four soldiers of the Winnipeg Grenadiers, Sergeant John Payne, Lieutenant-Corporal George Berzenski, and Privates John Adams and Percy Ellis, after a failed escape attempt on 20 August 1942. The Japanese claimed that the men had been shot and killed during the escape, but other POWS heard no firing, and rumours persisted that the men had been seen alive in Stanley Prison and tortured.[92] The officers responsible and other Japanese, most of whom were soldiers ranging in rank from private to major-general, were among the ten men prosecuted by Major G.B. Puddicombe of the Canadian army in war crimes trials also held at Hong Kong.[93] All but one were found guilty and sentenced to terms ranging from two years' imprisonment to death. Two officers, Colonel Tokunaga and Captain Saito, the commanding officer and medical officer in charge of the camps in the Hong Kong area, were held responsible for the deaths of more than a hundred Canadians and sentenced to be hanged. But the sentences were commuted by the acting general officer commanding at Hong Kong, a British officer, to life imprisonment and twenty years, respectively, a decision that angered the Canadian military authorities.[94]

For the Canadians, the viciousness that had been directed at them by the Kamloops Kid was unusual, largely because American and British POWS, not Canadians, were ordinarily singled out for especially severe treatment by the guards. 'They did not dislike us, or hate us,' a private of the Royal Rifles said. 'If you were American you got the worst treatment. The British got the next worst.'[95] Whatever their rank on the hate list, the Canadian POWS at Hong Kong paid heavily for their government's too easy acquiescence to London's request for reinforcements for the Crown Colony.

Four

The Decision to Evacuate

The Canadians in Hong Kong were the victims of military atrocities; the Japanese in Canada were the victims of civilian paranoia. In the first days after Pearl Harbor, 7 December 1941, inadequate air-raid precautions and confusion about blackout restrictions compounded the jitters of coastal British Columbians as they rushed to buy building paper to cover up windows. Businesses closed early, night shifts at war plants were cancelled, and radio stations went off the air at 5:30 PM to insure that neither lights nor radio beams would aid attacking Japanese bombers. The mayor of Victoria announced, 'The Japanese are reported off the Aleutian Islands. We expect them here at any time. The situation is very grave.' In Vancouver, the *Province* described the picture as 'ominous and disquieting.'[1] After three days the strict blackout was lifted, but people knew it could be reimposed at any time.

While air-raid precautions were the immediate local concern, officials in Ottawa worried about protecting loyal residents of Japanese racial origin from the mob violence and demonstrations they had long feared.[2] Indeed, as recently as 4 December a Vancouver newspaper had observed, 'if we were fighting Japan it would be too much to expect that every Japanese in British Columbia would be on our side ... It would not be so much the danger of sabotage or of subversive activity ... The real danger would arise from hot-headed minorities, amongst the Japanese and amongst ourselves, whose talk and actions could easily set a match to a dynamite-laden situation.'[3] Well aware of such possibilities, the RCMP and the provincial police immediately followed prearranged plans and began interning approximately forty Japanese nationals whom they suspected of having subversive intentions. The Royal Canadian Navy began rounding up the fishing boats operated by Japanese Canadians. And, at the request of the Standing Committee on

Oriental Affairs, the Japanese Canadians voluntarily closed their Japanese-language schools and newspapers after the RCMP advised them that their continued existence might cause disturbances 'by overenthusiastic or irresponsible Occidentals.' To the Japanese Canadians, the closing of their newspapers and language schools were 'the sharpest pinches.'[4]

Although the Canadian government had little accurate knowledge of the loyalties of members of the Japanese-Canadian community, it did not act without suspicions. Few white British Columbians were aware of what the three Japanese-language newspapers, the *Tairiku Nippō* (Continental News), *Canada Nichi Nichi Shimbun* (Canada Daily News), or *Nikkan Minshū* (People's Daily), had printed in the months before Pearl Harbor. The staples of all three were gossip, sensation, fiction, and reports on the anti-Japanese movement in British Columbia, but they also fostered nationalistic feelings by featuring Japan's military activities in China on their front pages. Whites had also suspected the language schools. In January 1941, for example, Tsutae Sato, the principal of the Vancouver Language School, defended his school from attacks by such japanophobes as Alderman Wilson by assuring the mayor of Vancouver that 'above everything else ... our institutions are NOT Japanese in spirit. The aim of our schools is and has been since the inception of the first school in 1906 to inculcate fine and true Canadian citizenship among our pupils.' Yet some schools used textbooks approved by the Ministry of Education of Japan, which also supplied teachers.[5]

Fishermen, however, were the chief targets of widespread public suspicion that their true loyalties lay with Japan and that some of them were actually Japanese naval officers in disguise. The fishermen had tried hard to establish their loyalty to Canada. Their spokesmen at Steveston, the main fishing community, volunteered their boats for coast defence and, on 11 December, the Northern British Columbia Residential Fishermen's Association, a Japanese group at Prince Rupert, unanimously affirmed their loyalty as Canadian citizens and offered themselves 'for any service which Canada may desire of us.' None of the fishermen, all of whom were Canadian nationals by birth or naturalization, was arrested; instead, their fleet was impounded. The fishermen were not surprised and remained so confident in the Canadian government that, after the unfamiliarity of new RCN recruits with small boats and tidal rivers led to the sinking of more than seventy vessels at their moorings, the Japanese Fishermen's Union executive agreed not to make any claims since the damage was accidental and they expected the government would make it good.[6]

The RCMP had not anticipated any immediate hardship for the fishermen because winter was normally a slack season, but the impounding procedure severely tried all fishermen, especially those on the Skeena River. The navy had ordered Skeena fishermen aboard their 1300 boats, but did not tell them where it was going to take them. Thus, they had inadequate water and food for a three-day 'voyage in hell' through rough seas to the Fraser River. The fishermen had to accept the impoundment and subsequent distress-price sale of their boats because they wanted to cooperate and they needed the money.[7]

Except for the fishermen, internees, teachers, and journalists, the majority of the Japanese Canadians were free to continue in their ordinary work during the first three months of the war. These controls on the most 'suspected' of the Japanese briefly served their purpose of making the white community feel more secure. During December, British Columbians generally heeded the advice of the commissioner of the RCMP and of the local press to keep calm and to recognize that the majority of the Japanese Canadians were loyal to Canada and that the police and armed forces were dealing with the handful who might not be. Moreover, despite previous complaints about inadequate defences, they apparently accepted the statement of Lieutenant-General Kenneth Stuart, the vice-chief of the general staff, that Pacific coast defences were 'capable of coping with any probable attack we have to face.'[8]

Yet there were disquieting problems. Japanese Canadians had been shocked by Pearl Harbor. Some may have been comforted by Consul Ichiro Kawasaki's assurance the previous summer that Britain and Japan would not fight each other. Few could imagine that Japan would start a war in such a manner. Many could not convince themselves it had really happened.[9] Nevertheless, they quickly proclaimed their 'unswerving' and 'unflinching' loyalty to Canada. As early as 12 December the *New Canadian* reaffirmed that the Japanese Canadians would support Canada's war effort. The white public, which seldom distinguished between Japanese who were Canadian citizens and those who were nationals of Japan, was not convinced. Japan's consul in Vancouver said he expected 'the great majority' of Japanese in British Columbia would 'remain loyal to Canada,' but he was hardly a disinterested observer. It was widely reported that Masakuo Fuchioka, a resident of Winfield, near Kelowna, had been fined $100 under the Defence of Canada Regulations for saying that 'Pretty soon this will all be Japan.' Even more ominous was the sensational allegation of Frank Knox, the United States secretary of the navy, that 'with the possible exception of Norway,' the Japanese in Hawaii had done 'the most effective fifth column work of the entire war.'[9]

Initially, Caucasians expressed their doubts about the loyalty of the Japanese Canadians in private communications to Ottawa. A Vancouver school principal, for example, wrote to the prime minister: 'the Japanese who are living in British Columbia, all along the Coast are not thinking nor working for Canada ... they are a sly race of people ... [and] ... not to be trusted ... I noted two of them on the streets of Vancouver today with joyful and mirthful expressions on their faces ... The most arrogant race on the face of the earth when their country is having success.' More significantly, some government officials on the coast felt the same way. Air Commodore L.F. Stevenson violated military protocol by writing directly to Air Force Headquarters to recommend moving 'all male Axis aliens between 16 and 50 years' from the coast and interning them or keeping them under close surveillance. 'Japanese sympathies,' he claimed, were 'towards Japan' and would 'increase as restrictions mature, earnings consequently decrease, personal incidents occur and they awaken to the realization of the success Japan has won and may yet win.' Security, he concluded, 'cannot rest on [the] precarious discernment between those who would actively support Japan and those who might at present be apathetic.' Similarly, Major-General R.O. Alexander, commanding on the Pacific Coast, urged the internment of Japanese males of military age. However, he was more fearful of white violence against them than he was of sabotage. G.W. McPherson, who had recently arrived in Vancouver to represent the custodian of enemy property and to administer property seized from enemy aliens, also reported mounting 'anti-Japanese' feeling as whites became disturbed about fifth-column activity. McPherson himself felt 'that if the worst comes and an invasion is attempted, we will find hundreds of the Japanese regardless of their nationality helping the invaders – as I would do myself in Japan.'[10]

Publicly, representatives of the armed forces, the RCMP, and the Standing Committee on Orientals tried to maintain calm by issuing a press release declaring that 'adequate measures' had been taken to prevent any fifth-column 'treachery.' Unfortunately, the press somewhat garbled the release. The *Province,* usually a model of responsibility, for example, commented editorially that although it was unwise and illogical to resent the Japanese in British Columbia, two-thirds of whom were Canadian-born and educated, it was difficult to forget fifth-column activities at Pearl Harbor and in Thailand and Malaya.[11]

The government also imposed a modest form of censorship to control rumours and speculation about fifth-column activity. The Canadian Broadcasting Corporation advised radio stations not to broadcast any suspicions of disloyalty but to relay any such reports to the police. Newspapers, however, were not so limited. In an editorial, the Victoria *Colonist* agreed that the authorities probably had prevented fifth-column work, but it published letters demanding 'that immediate action be taken to gather up all Japanese in the province ... so that there will be no chance of our being "taken off guard" by any fifth column activity.' The press also reported calls such as that of Lieutenant Alan Chambers, MP (Nanaimo, Liberal) for the 'total exclusion of Japanese from any activity, including the preparation of food, in which they could commit sabotage and the detention of males of military age who might be under Tokyo's orders.' Thus, groups such as the Victoria Kiwanis Club charged it was impossible to distinguish 'between the loyal and disloyal, especially when one is dealing with a people who have given ample demonstration of their treachery and deceit,' and demanded the internment of 'the entire Japanese population of British Columbia' in a place 'where it would be impossible for them to engage in fifth column activity.'[12]

By 29 December there was sufficient anti-Japanese hysteria that the Chiefs of Staff Committee in Ottawa advised the Cabinet War Committee that they, police, and local authorities 'were concerned less at the possibility of subversive activity by Japanese than at the danger of serious anti-Japanese outbreaks.' Indeed, the next day, Major-General R.O. Alexander, commanding on the Pacific Coast, wrote to the chief of the general staff:

> The situation with regard to the Japanese resident, in British Columbia is assuming a serious aspect. Public feeling is becoming very insistent, especially in Vancouver, that local Japanese should be either interned or removed from the coast. Letters are being written continually to the press and I am being bombarded by individuals, both calm and hysterical, demanding that something should be done. I have been informed that certain sections of the public in Vancouver propose to hold public demonstrations and street parades against the Japanese in the near future unless official action is taken. If these are held, they might lead to very serious inter-racial clashes involving considerable damage, bloodshed and possibly fatal casualties.

Thus, he arranged to have troops ready to go into the Powell Street area of Vancouver and to Steveston to protect Japanese residents should that be necessary, but he believed it was 'impossible to give protection to scattered elements' even though he realized that Japan might use any action against 'local Japanese' as an excuse 'to deal harshly with our own prisoners.'[13]

Commissioner C.H. Hill of the RCMP also informed his superiors that the Japanese in Vancouver were being loyal and cooperative, but 'the Occidental population here feels they have reason to fear the Japanese, and the Military authorities ... admit that in the event of attack here, they would be unable to handle the large number of local Japanese should those Japanese assist the enemy.' The Standing Committee on Orientals which oversaw the situation in British Columbia feared both 'rising public opinion' and the 'potential menace to our security' posed by the male Japanese. It 'strongly' recommended removing all male Japanese between the ages of eighteen and forty-five from the coast.[14] Its immediate worry were the unemployed Japanese – both fishermen and those who had been dismissed from other jobs because of their race – who had gone mainly to Vancouver and New Westminster.

It was in these circumstances that the prime minister called the standing committee and representatives of the provincial government to meet in Ottawa on 8 January to consider the problems of the fishermen as well as the overall situation. No one, of course, thought of inviting any Japanese. This meeting, the prime minister hoped, would 'result in the formulation of a definite policy with respect to Canadian Japanese and Japanese nationals in Canada which all concerned can cooperate in implementing.'[15]

As members of the standing committee travelled eastward, the mail arriving in Ottawa carried more warnings of possible violence if the government did not take 'drastic action' or if there was 'bad news' from the Pacific. Mayor J.W. Cornett of Vancouver explained to Minister of Justice Louis St Laurent that 'ambitious politicians' had fanned some of the anti-Japanese feeling, but 'a good many serious thinking citizens have sensed a potential danger here as Japan's ambitions grew and war approached.' Major-General E.C. Ashton, a former chief of the general staff who had retired to Victoria, told Minister of Defence J.L. Ralston, 'I have consulted men who know the Japanese, and it is possible that they could raise a force of six or seven thousand trained fighting men. This is a real fifth column, many have held commissions.' Ashton excluded the Canadian-born Japanese from his suspicions, but others were less trusting. Although H.T. Matson, the publisher of the *Colonist*, claimed his paper was not taking much of an editorial stand since 'it would not require much to detonate an actual physical explosion against the local Japanese,' his editors declared that 'it would be the height of folly to leave free and untrammeled in a vital defence zone those who, though friendly enough on the surface, may in fact be enemy aliens under orders to create mischief as and where they can.' Though admitting that many were loyal to Canada, the *Colonist* asserted that, until their loyalty could be determined, 'all Japanese must rest under some degree of suspicion.'[16] So widespread were doubts about loyalties that many observers recommended removing all Japanese Canadians from the coast 'for their own protection.' For example, when the University of British Columbia ordered Japanese-Canadian members of the Canadian Officers' Training Corps to turn in their uniforms, President L.S. Klinck explained, 'it's for their own protection as well as ours.

Feeling runs high down in the business section and Japanese in uniform would be an unfortunate sight.'[17]

As the coastal press speculated on what the federal government would do, the Conference on Japanese Matters met in Ottawa on 8 and 9 January 1942. Chaired by Ian Mackenzie, it was attended by J.E. Michaud, the federal minister of fisheries; J.T. Thorson, the minister of national war services; G.S. Pearson, the provincial secretary and minister of labour for British Columbia; the members of the standing committee; and representatives of the Department of External Affairs, the RCMP, the British Columbia Provincial Police, and the armed forces. Most of those present were past or present residents of British Columbia, but they did not think alike.

Ian Mackenzie chaired the meeting. Born in Scotland and educated there as a lawyer, he had migrated to Vancouver in 1914, went overseas with the Seaforth Highlanders of Vancouver, and, on his return, became president of the Vancouver branch of the Great War Veterans' Association. In the last role he had campaigned, unsuccessfully at the time, for the enfranchisement of Japanese veterans of the Canadian Expeditionary Force. From 1920 to 1930 Mackenzie served as a Liberal MLA for Vancouver but transferred his political activities to Ottawa after being elected for Vancouver-Centre in 1930. On his return to office in 1935, King appointed Mackenzie minister of national defence. But Mackenzie was a man *manqué;* as war was declared, King transferred him to the less prestigious and less demanding portfolio of pensions and national health. Mackenzie, however, was the only British Columbia representative in the cabinet and, as such, acted as a major conduit through which many ideas from his adopted province reached the prime minister.

Mackenzie opened the meeting by explaining that, unlike other enemy aliens, the Japanese were 'concentrated in one province in proximity to a theatre of war' and had shown no strong opposition to the present government of Japan. He noted the widespread belief that 'Japanese loyalties are racial rather than national'; observed the 'intense economic jealousy of the Japanese,' including 'a wish in some quarters to appropriate their property'; and recalled that the Japanese, like the Chinese and East Indians, already faced political and economic disabilities. Finally, he remarked that Canada had no long-range policy with respect to the future of its Japanese population. Following Mackenzie, Hugh Keenleyside set out the Department of External Affairs position that, insofar as policy was compatible with defence considerations, Canadians of Japanese race should receive 'just and decent treatment.' The conference seemingly had no difficulty agreeing that national defence was the primary consideration; that Japanese in Canada should be treated 'with justice and consideration'; and that the 'full force of the law' should be invoked to prevent anti-Japanese demonstrations, to protect the Japanese Canadians, and to avoid any situation which might give Japan an excuse to retaliate against Canadians under its control. The conference also accepted such practical defence measures as keeping persons of Japanese origin out of the coastal fisheries, controlling the sale of gasoline and blasting powder, maintaining surveillance of Japanese nationals, and prohibiting them from possessing or using short-wave radios, radio transmitters, and cameras.[18]

In fact, the meeting was a stormy one because officials and politicians based in Ottawa were generally less suspicious of the Japanese Canadians and less fearful of attack than their counterparts with recent experience at the coast. This division of opinion had already been apparent within the Department of National Defence. Despite the devastating losses suffered by the United States navy at Pearl Harbor, the chiefs of staff believed that geography precluded a major invasion, though they conceded Japan might attempt to 'harass' the west coast with a seaborne air attack, naval bombardment, or both. They did order an additional ship and several squadrons of aircraft to the coast and agreed to send light anti-aircraft guns there as soon as they were available, but the Canadian chiefs disputed the British and American suggestion that Japan might risk its naval superiority by attacking the west coast of North America. In sum, the chiefs of staff in Ottawa were prepared to accept 'temporary weakness on the West Coast' since geography seemed to ensure that only hit-and-run raids were likely.[19]

However, like the American officers on the Permanent Joint Board on Defence, all three Canadian commanders on the west coast were 'very frightened' by the prospect of invasion or, more likely, carrier attacks on west-coast naval bases. British officers in London also feared suicide raids on the coast and warned of the 'unfortunate' psychologial effects of air raids if there were only weak defences. They continued to warn of carrier-borne attacks and the possibility of a 'small scale destructive raid.' Indeed, when the superior of a French-Canadian missionary order inquired about the wisdom of sending two nuns to Victoria, the Department of External Affairs advised that, although a 'hit-and-run' raid was unlikely, bombing raids were possible and the coast was 'a war zone.'[20]

Canadian defences on the west coast were indeed weak. The RCN ships in the Pacific were too few and too lightly armed; the RCAF lacked airfields, aircraft, and trained crews or anti-aircraft guns to protect them.[21] West-coast commanders thought the RCN could possibly counter an attack by a merchant raider or with small surface or submarine vessels, but they knew their forces could not cope with attacks by larger vessels or airborne raids nor prevent sabotage. At the meeting of the Joint Service Committee, Pacific Coast, on 9 January 1942, as the Ottawa conference was meeting, they recommended removing 'all male Japanese and other enemy aliens between the ages of 16 and 50' from coastal areas to reduce the likelihood of sabotage.[22]

While the west-coast commanders were expressing these views, their superiors in Ottawa could not believe that unarmed Japanese Canadians, 80 per cent of whom were Canadian nationals, could 'jeopardize Canadian defence in the event of a bombardment.' They requested substantiation of this opinion.[23] Representatives of the RCMP had similarly told the Conference on Japanese Matters that they had no concerns about the Japanese in British Columbia. When they heard this, 'all hell broke loose' among the BC delegates who had gone to Ottawa 'breathing fire.' The British Columbians declared that 'no Japanese could be trusted,' and all must 'be driven out of their jobs in British Columbia' and interned. Escott Reid of the Department of External Affairs later recalled how 'they spoke of the Japanese-Canadians in the way that the Nazis would have spoken about Jewish-Germans.' Hugh Keenleyside remembered the 'almost vitriolic manner' in which George Pearson, a family friend, denounced him for being 'uninterested in the fate of the people living in great danger' in British Columbia. Although the majority at the meeting decided that the compulsory movement of 'all persons of Japanese racial origin (or at least all males between 18 and 45)' was neither necessary nor wise, they suggested accepting the offers of Japanese Canadians to perform 'any service to Canada in the present crisis which the government may desire of us' and organizing a Civilian Corps to allow them to work on projects of national value.[24]

Responding to the demands of Pearson and Hume and reflecting his own ideas, Mackenzie prepared a minority report recommending that because of the difficulty of 'satisfying the residents of British Columbia that there is no need to fear subversive activities on the part of Japanese nationals,' able-bodied male Japanese nationals must be removed from the coast, provided with suitable employment, and, where circumstances permitted, be joined by their families. In presenting this minority report, Mackenzie had trump cards. Not only had members of the standing committee refused to leave Ottawa until their case was heard, but he warned that, 'unless we take immediate action, our white people may resort to unwise tactics in Vancouver.'[25] The cabinet accepted Mackenzie's advice to remove 'as soon as possible' those Japanese male nationals of military age who did not have an RCMP permit to remain in a 'protected area.'[26]

A press release was the government's only written record of its policy.

Issued on 14 January, it reiterated the primacy of national defence, the desire to treat persons of Japanese racial origin justly, and the need to maintain 'a calm and reasonable attitude among Canadian citizens generally.' At the specific request of the prime minister, it warned against any anti-Japanese action or demonstration which might give Japan an excuse to mistreat Canadians in its hands. Specifically, the government announced the immobilization of the Japanese fishing fleet, restrictions on the purchase of gasoline and explosives and the use of radios and cameras, and plans to organize a Civilian Corps and to provide employment for male enemy aliens. Buried in the announcement was the news that steps were being taken to remove enemy aliens without RCMP permits from the protected area which was yet to be defined.[27]

At the coast there was general satisfaction because everybody seems to have interpreted the announcement as they wished. The *Province*, for example, described it as an effective means of preventing possible fifth-column activity and praised the government for putting 'a premium on Canadian citizenship,' a point which the *New Canadian*, the newspaper voice of the *Nisei*, heartily endorsed. The Victoria *Times* welcomed the policy of protecting British Columbia against 'Nipponese nationals' who might have subversive intentions. The *Sun* gloated that the federal government had heeded its editorial advice and implied that all Japanese would be leaving the coast. Indeed, the general public seldom distinguished between Japanese and Canadian nationals. Thus, even Alderman Wilson, who had been trying to organize a mass meeting to demand that all Japanese be moved from the coast, declared that if the coast were declared a protected area, 'anti-Japanese talk' would stop.[28]

When the BC Liberal members of parliament returned to Ottawa after the Christmas recess, they too indicated their expectation that all able-bodied male Japanese would be removed from the coast. Through Mackenzie, they warned that without a full and frank discussion between all the BC members and officials of the Department of External Affairs there could be an unpleasant discussion in Parliament.[29] Though no such meeting seems to have taken place, the members temporarily held their fire.

When coastal residents saw no evidence of any Japanese moving, they rapidly lost patience. In the legislature, Attorney-General R.L. Maitland said he did not 'feel safe while the Japanese are on the coast' and warned that the danger of attack and fifth-column activities were much greater than anyone in Ottawa realized. Federal officials in British Columbia sent similar warnings

'Strategic Withdrawal to Prepared Positions'

—Les Callan in Toronto Star

Vancouver Sun, 21 January 1942

to their superiors. J.H. McVety, the superintendent of the Pacific region of the Unemployment Insurance Commission wrote:

> In certain quarters there is always a smouldering hatred of Orientals, particularly Japanese, and if this city or any of the Coast area were to be bombed and lives lost, I think that the vengeance of the population would be taken out on Japanese regardless of the category to which they belong. I have heard certain threats and rumours along this line already. In such a contingency it might become necessary for us to provide troops to protect Japanese from our own people. If the males are removed, the natural chivalry of our people, I think, would prevent attacks on the Japanese women and children.

Similarly, Major H.C. Bray, intelligence officer in Pacific Command, observed 'considerable discontent and resentment among the white population at the apparent inaction' of the government and the loss of the 'good effect' of the announcement of 14 January.[30]

Apart from reports of delays and cancellation of a plan to employ Japanese nationals in an Ontario lumber camp, there was little more news about the movement of the Japanese Canadians. Almost every day, however, headlines depicted Japan's forces swarming through Southeast Asia, capturing Hong Kong, Manila, the Dutch East Indies, a host of other Allied possessions, and rapidly advancing towards Singapore. British Columbians felt vulnerable from the outside as well as within.

Widespread concern about a Japanese attack on British Columbia reappeared in late January. The public was unaware of the demands of the Pacific coast commanders that male Japanese nationals be removed, at least from such vulnerable points as Ucluelet, Prince Rupert, the Skeena River, the Queen Charlotte Islands, and Quatsino Sound. Indeed, as the military situation deteriorated, the commanders demanded the removal of all persons of Japanese racial origin from these areas. Eventually, the chiefs of staff referred the matter to the Cabinet War Committee.[31]

The cabinet was also aware of mounting public demands in British Columbia for stronger defence measures. Howard Green, MP (Vancouver South, Conservative), told Parliament that, in seven weeks, Japan had gained control of the Pacific Ocean. He predicted that sooner or later British Columbia would be bombed, and quoted from the *Japan Times and Advertiser* that 'it was within the realm of probability "that the armed forces of this country [Japan] will land on the American continent." ' The Canadian forces on the west coast, Green complained, were so inadequately equipped that some reserve army members lacked rifles. Moreover, Green, like many others, had

Vancouver *Daily Province*, 12 February 1942

lost faith in the generals, suggesting that in case of invasion they 'would make another of their strategic retreats with the remnants of our forces to the mountains, leaving the people on the coast to their fate.'[32] A few days later, Thomas Reid (New Westminster, Liberal) observed: 'so many optimistic reports have been made by high military men and authorities, which later events showed were certainly not justified, that people to-day can hardly be blamed for being rather sceptical.'[33]

The BC public regarded such observations with foreboding, presuming that members of parliament had access to full information. The provincial legislature and the Vancouver City Council demanded assurances from the federal government that the coast was properly defended.[34] The Vancouver *Sun* insisted that Ottawa do something. As Singapore was falling in early February, the *Sun*'s respected political reporter, Bruce Hutchison, began a series of articles from Ottawa outlining the inadequacies of Pacific coast defences, the efforts of the British Columbia members of parliament to improve them, and the conflict between civilian and military authorities over the need to strengthen them. 'Nero supplies the music. The Japanese will supply the background, the flames, and the sound effect in Vancouver,' Hutchison predicted. Drawing on Hutchison's report, a front-page editorial in the *Sun* declared, 'The success of Japanese forces in controlling a large part of the Pacific basin suddenly increases the danger of the Canadian Pacific Coast.'[35] The fall of Singapore and President Roosevelt's statement that the United States could not defend Alaska increased the jitters at the coast. The mayor of Victoria wired the prime minister: 'Unanimous opinion that enemy action will develop against this coast and people alarmed at lack of defence precautions and complacent attitude of your government.' Victory Loan advertisements exploited such fears by showing Japan holding power over Canada.[36]

The deteriorating military situation, the continued presence of male Japanese nationals at the coast, and stories of Japanese in British Columbia 'exulting' or 'gloating over the victories of their countrymen' increased the clamour for removal. Those who a short time earlier might have been satisfied with the removal only of able-bodied male Japanese nationals now called for the removal of all Japanese from the coast, if not from the province as a whole. 'We did try to steady public opinion,' W.C. Nichols, the publisher of the *Province* told Keenleyside, but a week later the *Province* remarked that 'a concern about the disposition of our local Japanese is an essential part of our general disposition of defence.'[37]

In Vancouver, the city council, which had been resisting Aldermen Wilson's pressures, now called for 'speedier action' in removing the Japanese

Another Thing That 'Couldn't Happen'

Victoria Daily Times, 17 February 1942

Victoria Daily Times, 17 February 1942

from defence areas in order to provide 'greater security.' Such a move, the council declared, 'will allay fear of Vancouver citizens generally and will be in the best interests of the Japanese resident here.' A week later, the council passed a stronger resolution describing the presence of approximately 25,000 Japanese as 'a potential reservoir of voluntary aid to our enemy, Japan in the event of raids or an invasion,' and imploring Ottawa 'to remove all residents of Japanese racial origin to areas of Canada well-removed from the Pacific Coast.' The Victoria City Council also warned of 'the menace of allowing persons of enemy races to live in any place that may be open to attack' and of the 'unrest and grave apprehension' this was causing. Victoria circulated its petition throughout the province; other cities and municipalities endorsed it and sent copies to Ottawa.[38]

Service clubs, veterans' organizations, boards of trade, the Provincial Council of Women, and other groups and individuals dispatched similar resolutions. Many letter writers and telegram senders were frightened men and women who doubted the loyalty of the local Japanese population. As one Vancouver resident reminded the prime minister, fifth-column activity in Norway, Hawaii, and the Malay states had contributed to military disaster. Since the Japanese in Canada had been treated as an inferior people, he wondered if 'even the most peace-loving and well-disposed Japanese can resist the feeling of pride in belonging to a conquering race ... ? Even if eighty-five per cent of the Japanese should remain loyal there is still danger. A few hundred determined men ... could completely immobilize the defences of Vancouver.'[39]

But it was not just ordinary folk who had such fears. Lieutenant-Governor W.C. Woodward, who had been talking to 'the senior officers of the Canadian Forces here,' wrote a three-page epistle explaining that he had 'rarely felt so keenly about the impending danger as I do about the Japanese on this coast being allowed to live in our midst.' J.A. Paton, MLA (Point Grey, Coalition [Conservative]), envisioned British Columbia 'as the meat in a Japanese sandwich, with landing parties in front and "quislings, fifth columnists and enemy aliens" in the rear.' T.W.S. Parsons, the commissioner of the provincial police, confidentially advised Attorney-General Maitland that 'with these people neither Canadian birth nor naturalization guarantees good faith ... [It is] something to remember in the case of invasion or planned sabotage.' Publicly, Maitland declared that all Japanese were dangerous and called for their removal from strategic areas. Given that local leaders were frightened, warnings about 'a popular outburst of feeling' which could have regrettable repercussions both for the Japanese in Canada and the Canadians in Japanese hands were prudent.[40]

Opportunities for such 'popular outbursts' of feeling increased as groups in several coastal cities planned demonstrations to demand the removal of all Japanese from the coast. In Victoria, a self-appointed Provisional Citizens Committee was arranging a mass meeting; in Vancouver, the United Commercial Travellers invited representatives of approximately sixty groups, including veterans' associations, fraternal lodges, the Imperial Order Daughters of the Empire, and munitions workers, to discuss methods of 'impressing upon Ottawa the necessity for immediate action in removing British Columbia's entire Japanese population east of the Rockies.' At the meeting, Alderman Wilson, the featured speaker, declared that even second-generation Japanese Canadians were loyal to Japan. In the Fraser Valley, Reeve S. Mussallem of Maple Ridge claimed that the 'Japanese [had been] hostile since Singapore' and asked for immediate action to avoid 'riot and bloodshed.'[41]

Prime Minister King, who remembered that the Vancouver riots of 1907 had followed a mass meeting of the Asiatic Exclusion League, recognized the danger. He admitted in his diary on 19 February that his government had been slow to act and that moving the Japanese, especially those who were Canadian-born or naturalized, would be difficult: 'Public prejudice is so strong in British Columbia that it is going to be difficult to control the situation.' Moreover, he recognized that riots might have serious effects on Canadian prisoners of war in the Far East. On 20 February, he told the Cabinet War Committee that Canada should send more troops to 'help quiet the feeling' there.[42]

The federal government had made a feeble attempt to mollify BC opinion by announcing its plans to move males of military age from the coast, but the prime minister had never taken the people into his confidence. If he did so, the *Province* suggested, we might 'make allowances for unavoidable setbacks' and 'delicate diplomatic considerations' if we knew that the government recognized our 'dangerous situation and is proceeding with all possible haste to meet it.' St Laurent did remind Vancouver City Council that male Japanese Canadians were being moved as a precautionary measure only and advised that because of fear of reprisals against Canadians in Japanese hands, Canada had to make proper arrangements for their reception inland. The CBC presented a public-affairs program on the loyalty of the Canadian-born Japanese to Canada, but the broadcast on 17 February simply irritated British Columbians.[43]

By late February, British Columbians were adamant in their demands for protection from the Japanese in their midst. In Ottawa, eight MPs, including six Liberals, one Conservative, and A.W. Neill, an Independent, sent the prime minister a manifesto. They demanded the removal of all persons of

Japanese origin from the protected area (recently defined as the coast and approximately 100 miles inland); the extension of restrictions on the ownership of radios, cameras, motor vehicles, and the like to Canadian nationals of Japanese origin; the imposition of a dusk-to-dawn curfew on all persons of Japanese origin; and a prohibition on their acquisition of land. In British Columbia, Victory Bond salesmen reported that people were saving their money to provide for air-raid protection or were refusing to buy to protest inaction on moving the Japanese.[44]

Indeed, the Victory Loan campaign provided a vehicle for protest. On 20 February, over 800 people attended a Victory Loan luncheon sponsored by the Vancouver Board of Trade and the Canadian Club where Dr Hu Shih, the Chinese ambassador to Washington, was the featured speaker. They unanimously supported a resolution complaining that the BC coast was 'in imminent danger [of] attack by enemy armed forces,' that 'no effective measures' had been taken to relieve the 'menace to security' posed by the 'presence of enemy aliens,' and that the 'matter is hourly becoming more alarming to civil authorities[,] business officials and to population generally.' The resolution urged immediate evacuation of 'all enemy aliens and all people of Japanese origin from defence areas of Pacific Coast.' Among those at the luncheon were members of a recently self-appointed Citizens Defence Committee which included such prominent figures as P.A. Woodward and Victor Spencer, department store owners; A.E. Jukes, a stockbroker; Austin Taylor, an industrialist; B.O. Moxon, the president of the Vancouver Board of Trade; J.A. Clark, a lawyer, infantry brigadier in the First World War, and former Conservative MP; Birt Showler of the Vancouver Trades and Labour Council; Harold Winch and Grant MacNeill, CCF MLAS; and Mrs F.J. Ralston, a Coalition (Conservative) MLA. It was, in short, a fairly representative group of Vancouver's business, labour, and political elite. The committee set up an office in the prestigious Marine Building and asked 'all loyal organizations' to hold 'emergency meetings' to demand the removal of all Japanese from key points designated by the military and publicly announce plans to evacuate 'all Japanese from coast area.' The committee hoped to impress the government by constitutional means. Its members had come together because they feared 'unfortunate incidents' might follow the mass meeting on the downtown Cambie Street grounds that The Flying Column, an old alarmist group, was planning to hold on 4 March. The Rotary Club and the Labour Council endorsed the resolution almost immediately; so too did the BC Command of the Canadian Legion which circulated the resolution to all of its branches in British Columbia.[45] Within days, copies of the resolution were arriving in Ottawa.

In Victoria, the Kinsmen Club, a service club, invited representatives of other groups to organize a Citizens' Civil Defence Committee which warned that 'the feeling of the people of BC is rapidly becoming uncontrollable and will undoubtedly lead to violence' if all Japanese were not removed from the coast and other vital areas. To back up their demands, the committee proposed to boycott individual Japanese and their businesses and to call members of parliament 'to the bar of public opinion.' The latter idea probably inspired the Victoria City Council to call for the resignation of Ian Mackenzie, BC's representative in the federal cabinet. In Victoria, as in Vancouver, another group was making similar demands but using less constitutional means. Some members of the Canadian Legion, styling themselves the Immediate Action Committee, distributed a leaflet headed 'News Flashes After We Are Dead.' In a covering letter they urged people to look at the sketch at its side, where, through flaming orange colouring, could be seen an 'evil Japanese face and hands ... menacingly regarding any and all of our coast cities and the foundation of their community life and even their means of escape.' The scene showed blown-up bridges, broken utility lines, and blazing docks and petroleum depots. This message concluded with a demand for the immediate removal of Japanese 'of all ages and all sexes' from the Pacific coast. This committee's plan to hold a mass meeting on 1 March led the Victoria Chamber of Commerce to urge Ottawa to place all Japanese on Vancouver Island under guard until they could be removed.[46] It feared 'irrevocable steps being taken subsequent to such a mass meeting.'

The situation in British Columbia was alarming. By telephone, Premier John Hart told Mackenzie that feeling was 'simply aflame.' Mackenzie advised St Laurent that 'I greatly fear *disorder* ... unless all able-bodied males of Japanese origin are immediately evacuated.'[47] Mackenzie was preaching to the converted. St Laurent had publicly expressed his sympathy with British Columbians who wanted all Japanese removed from the coast, though he had some concerns about the Canadian-born. Prime Minister King 'spoke more or less freely about the Japanese situation' at the secret session of Parliament on 24 February and 'the need to be very much on our guard.' Exactly what he said remains unknown, but a memorandum prepared for the secret session by the armed forces had provided him with some evidence. The Joint Service Committee, Pacific Coast, wanted reinforcements to help calm public opinion. Moreover, the chiefs of staff, while still claiming that an invasion was impractical, now conceded that Japan might stage raids 'to damage important undertakings and to cause alarm and despondency' as well as 'to contain North American forces in America.'[48] J.L. Ralston told the secret session that he accepted this advice and would do more to improve the defences of British Columbia.[49]

The cabinet, however, had made an even more significant decision to calm British Columbians. On 24 February, the same day as the secret session, it amended the Defence of Canada Regulations to empower the minister of justice 'to take any required security measures with regard to any person in the protected area.' The meaning of this seemingly vague statement was clear: all Japanese, no matter their citizenship, age, or sex, would be removed from the protected area.[50] Although the evidence of coordination between Canadian and American decisions on the fate of their Japanese residents is scanty, there seems no doubt that Canadian officials were well aware of U.S. policy. Even before Pearl Harbor, the Permanent Joint Board on Defence had discussed the types of action that might be necessary in the event of war. After Japan's surprise attack, there were further consultations in Ottawa and Washington. No one in Ottawa was surprised, therefore, when, on 20 February, the U.S. government announced that a day earlier President Roosevelt had authorized the secretary of war or his designate to remove any or all persons from specified military areas.[51]

Coastal residents reacted with restrained satisfaction to the news that Canada would move all of her Japanese residents inland. As the *Colonist* declared, from past experience there was no evidence 'that the Government will not go on changing its mind and toying with a situation in which it has so far only accomplished meagre results.' Thus, municipal councils, service clubs, boards of trade, Canadian Legion branches, and the like continued to demand the immediate removal of the Japanese from the coast. Other groups suspended their agitation. Those organizing mass meetings in Vancouver and Kelowna cancelled their plans; in Victoria, the Immediate Action Committee lost support. At its meeting in Beacon Hill Park on 1 March, speakers such as Brigadier J. Sutherland Brown, the long retired director of military operations and intelligence, declared that, 'if Japanese forces arrived here, they would be greeted by the children of local Japanese waving flags of the Rising Sun.' The mainly middle-aged and elderly crowd remained 'orderly and undemonstrative.' On the same day, an overflow crowd at Mission in the Fraser Valley heard Alderman Wilson declare that some *Nisei* had 'admitted sympathy for Japan's aspirations in the Far East,' but contented itself with calling for expeditious action to remove the Japanese.[52]

For the Japanese Canadians, the publication of PC 1486 which ordered their removal from the coast and the related orders which authorized the RCMP to search without warrant, to enforce a dusk-to-dawn curfew, and to confiscate automobiles, radios, cameras, and firearms 'shook the very foundation of the Japanese Canadian community and left it reeling from a deep sense of betrayal.'[53] Many *Issei* viewed the evacuation order with resignation – 'it can't be helped. It's war time.' In Japan, their fate generated limited interest. During February and March the *Asahi* published several brief articles about the curfew, the eastward movement of fishermen, lumbermen, and others who expected they would be forced to move, and, without comment, listed the names of internees. Not until 23 and 24 March, a month after the event, was there a report in a column, 'World War II and Overseas,' that Canada, like the United States, had ordered its Japanese to move.[54]

In Canada, those *Nisei* who had expected 'a distinction would be drawn between those who are aliens and those who are citizens' were angered by the decision of their government to force them to move. One *Nisei* asked 'Why not come right out and tell us to quit? That would be easier to take; after all, the war is a war, and I am quite ready to realize that these measures are necessary. But why not be honest about it. This squeezing us isn't British!' For others, the evacuation order was presumably a relief. One, for example, had told a white Victory Loan canvasser: 'If the Can-Japs are loyal, then invasion means death to them by the Japanese. If a mob goes mad with the arrival of a few parachute troops – then the Can-Japs will be killed because of their racial faces – and no distinction is possible in a fight. Therefore – it is better to move out.'[55]

In the short run, the policy prevented anti-Japanese disturbances, even though British Columbians continued to worry about a Japanese attack if not an invasion. So fretful were many British Columbians that the attempt of General A.G.L. McNaughton, Canada's commander in Great Britain, to reassure them that any Japanese raid on Canada's west coast would be designed only as a local diversion revived concerns about the lack of preparedness.[56] Bruce Hutchison wrote that the defence of the British Columbia coast was 'being deliberately minimized as part of an overall strategy.'[57] The statement of his fellow *Sun* columnist, Alan Morley, that defence officials had 'convinced themselves that they cannot defend Canada's Pacific coast' so angered military authorities that the crown charged the *Sun* with violating the Defence of Canada Regulations.[58] Such comments had their impact. Lieutenant-Governor W.C. Woodward told the New Westminster Board of Trade that he expected British Columbia would be bombed within six months. In Parliament, Howard Green painted a scenario in which Japanese invaders bayoneted prisoners and raped and murdered women.[59]

Ottawa responded to this agitation by forming a unified Pacific Command under Major-General R.O. Alexander and, more significantly, by creating two mobile divisions for use on both coasts. To the *Sun*, this was 'vindication'; to the *Province*, the news had more psychological than military value but was welcome.[60] A few days later, J.L. Ralston, the minister of national defence, and C.G. Power, the minister of national defence (air), inspected Pacific coast defences. Ralston told the press he was not wholly satisfied, had ordered some 'on the spot' changes, and would continue 'plugging along just as fast' as he could to improve the situation. This pacified the press, which insisted that British Columbia was not asking for 'some fantastic guarantee of immunity against attack, bloodshed, or even property damage,' but would be satisfied with 'a sturdy effort' to protect the coast.[61]

The dispatch of additional forces to British Columbia eased civilian fears without resolving the worries of west-coast commanders.[62] The military at Prince Rupert warned that their ability to defend the port was 'entirely inadequate,' even though American heavy artillery had been brought to the area; the Joint Service Committee, Pacific Coast, prepared an appreciation on 1 April 1942 which noted that 'developments in other theatres of war might bring about a set of circumstances which would make it possible for the enemy to launch attacks' on British Columbia 'on a scale hitherto considered highly improbable.'[63]

Under the pressure of events, Canada slowly strengthened its Pacific defences. Since December the army had been moving more troops to British Columbia, and by late June there were nineteen battalions of infantry in the province.[64] The RCAF had begun building new airfields in northern British Columbia and, after some prodding from President Roosevelt, on Vancouver Island.[65] The RCN expanded its bases at Esquimalt and Prince Rupert, but neither project was complete before the danger of attack passed in early 1943.

During the spring and summer of 1942 there was good reason to fear an attack. At the beginning of June, the Japanese launched 'their main endeavor, a twin offensive against the Aleutians, Operation AL, and against the western Hawaiian Islands, Operation MI.'[66] As part of this plan, they attacked Dutch Harbor, Alaska, from the air on 3 June and occupied Kiska and Attu in the Aleutian Islands four days later. These successes in the Aleutians suggested Japan might seek a base in the Queen Charlotte Islands from which aircraft could easily strike the Canadian and American mainlands.[67] Closer to the centres of population, submarines shelled Santa Barbara, California, and points in Oregon, and on 20 June 1942 Estevan Point on Vancouver Island. A submarine also sank two ships at the entrance to the Straits of Juan de Fuca. Prime Minister King feared an attack on British Columbia;[68] he did not know that Japan was readying two plans for the invasion of Hawaii and eventual strikes from there against the North American mainland.[69]

In late September 1942 the chief of the general staff, General Kenneth Stuart, assured the Cabinet War Committee that he saw 'no reason to fear any invasion from the Pacific Coast at the present time,' the same reassuring advice that the Ottawa military had provided both before and after Pearl Harbor. But two months later, the Combined Chiefs of Staff, the highest Allied military authority, determined that while 'carrier-borne air attacks and sporadic naval bombardment' were the most probable form of attack, the possibilities of 'a small scale destructive raid cannot be ignored.' For the chiefs, that implied 'a force comprising 10/15 fast merchant ships carrying up to two brigades.' Not until August 1943 did the Combined Chiefs declare a serious attack on the west coast 'very unlikely.' By that time, in fact, the situation had turned in the Allies' favour. The Battle of Midway in June 1942 had checked the Imperial Japanese navy and aborted Operation MI. The landings in the Aleutians forced the Americans to deploy substantial forces in Alaska, but in May 1943 they retook Attu in a bloody fight. In July, Canadian and American troops occupied Kiska, from which the Japanese had withdrawn under cover of persistent fog.[70] That month, the Joint Service Committee, Pacific Coast, reported that both the armed forces and civilians confidently believed the Allies were on the offensive.[71] Indeed, the situation so improved that late in 1943 the RCAF transferred several squadrons from British Columbia to Britain.[72]

Defending the west coast undoubtedly used resources that Canada might have profitably employed elsewhere.[73] But hindsight is always 20/20, and had Japan chosen to do so, its forces probably could have launched raids on Canada and the United States. Had such raids occurred, no one knows what the Japanese Canadians might have done or what other Canadians would have done to them.

Certainly the decision of the Canadian government in February 1942 to remove all Japanese Canadians from the coast did ease civilian tensions. In early March, despite fears that the revelations about atrocities committed by Japanese forces at Hong Kong might lead white British Columbians to vent their anger on local Japanese, British Columbians were quiet. While the press referred to 'unspeakable atrocities,' even the Vancouver *Sun* counselled that 'because the Japanese have made beasts of themselves, [it] is all the more reason why our treatment of Japanese in Canada should be completely exemplary of the rights and principles expected of a Christian country.'[74]

Nevertheless, coastal British Columbians were impatient when the British Columbia Security Commission, the federal agency established in late February to supervise the evacuation, seemed slow to move Japanese even from such vulnerable locations as Prince Rupert and around hydroelectric dams in the Fraser Valley. The beginning of the evacuation from Vancouver Island in early March temporarily reduced anti-Japanese agitation.[75] Yet, within weeks the Vancouver Island press was complaining that the movement seemed to have halted and that the continued presence of the Japanese could 'spell the difference between freedom and slavery for Canada.'[76]

Most of the evacuees from Vancouver Island and upcoast points were first removed to Hastings Park in Vancouver. Rumours that Japanese women and children might be confined there throughout the war created local concern. A labour newspaper, the *Federationist,* expressed fears for their safety if Japanese forces invaded Australia and committed atrocities. Wilson and another alderman who were worried about the possibility of disease caused by the crowded conditions warned of 'undesirable occurrences' if the Japanese were not quickly removed from Hastings Park. Even after Wilson left the city to join his regiment, the city council protested the continued presence of Japanese in the city. It was angered to learn in August that 172 Japanese businesses were still operating and, arguing that the BCSC had failed, urged that the military take over the evacuation.[77]

In Ottawa, the British Columbia members of parliament privately protested the dilatoriness of the BCSC. Indeed, Mackenzie warned of the danger of mass meetings if the government did not act quickly. When the members repeated these warnings in Parliament, the *Province* suggested they were out of touch with British Columbia if they believed there was any possibility 'of anti-Japanese riots in Vancouver or the turning of British Columbia into another Hong Kong.' The authorities, the *Province* declared, had the matter well in hand and the BCSC was doing a sensible and humane job in spite of a lack of cooperation from potential reception areas. Indeed, by the end of September a few hospital patients and the handful of Japanese married to Caucasians were the only Japanese in Vancouver. By that time, too, the military situation of the Allies in the Pacific had improved, and Mackenzie King accepted the arguments of the chief of the general staff that there was no longer any reason to fear an invasion of the Pacific coast.[78]

In the eyes of the General Staff, the threat of invasion had always been slight. Their west-coast commanders, like their American counterparts and the west-coast public and politicians, however, had feared an invasion or at least coastal raids, and had been uncertain of the loyalty of all Japanese Canadians. As the *Sun* explained almost a year after Ottawa decided to evacuate the Japanese:

Very satisfactory it is that the authorities have removed from our midst all possible chances that Japanese in Canada could assist threatening invaders. Thousands of

HOW DO YOU TELL A JAP FROM A JAP?

Vancouver Sun, 1 June 1943

people of Japanese blood who might have been altogether innocent of fifth column intentions have been necessarily inconvenienced in the evacuation from the British Columbia coast, but nobody could separate the sheep from the goats. We are in a war and the only safety lies in our adopting the totalitarian methods of the totalitarian countries of our enemies. Neither they, nor their apologists in Eastern Canada, should complain of our activity in this regard.

The occasion for this comment was the statement of G.E. Trueman, the Department of Labour's Japanese placement officer in Toronto, that 'the reason for [the] mass evacuation of Japanese from Pacific coastal areas was not because of the Japanese but because of the white residents.' The statement hit so close to the mark that it incensed many British Columbians. The Vancouver press described it as 'foolish' or 'nonsense' and claimed that 'mass hysteria' existed only in Trueman's imagination. Thomas Reid, MP, called it 'an insult to every person in the province,' and the council of the Vancouver Board of Trade declared its 'strong resentment.' Ian Mackenzie agreed.[79]

The human memory can be short. While no one in British Columbia in February 1942 could be absolutely certain that Japan would not attack the coast or that no Japanese Canadian would engage in fifth-column activity or sabotage, no one in Ottawa could be certain that the civilian population, or even individual members of the armed forces or local police, might not take out long-standing antipathies by physically attacking Japanese Canadians or their property. Canada could not guarantee the safety of Japanese Canadians and that, as Mackenzie King recorded when he was deciding to evacuate all, would have had 'repercussions in the Far East against our own prisoners.'[80] The Japanese Canadians, including those who were Canadian nationals by birth or naturalization, effectively became hostages for Canadians in Japanese hands.

Five

In Temporary Quarters: The Experiences of the Evacuees

When the government of Canada announced that all Japanese would be moved inland, it had little idea what to do next about this evacuation. As an official in the Department of External Affairs informed the prime minister, the government had made little visible progress in removing enemy aliens from the coast or in establishing a Civilian Labour Corps. It could not expect the Japanese to leave the coast on their own initiative, especially since communities outside the protected area were likely to resent them and deny them employment. Believing 'it would be cruel and ineffective to stand on a negative policy of deporting persons of Japanese origin from the protected area and allowing them to fend for themselves,' this official recommended that the movement 'be organized and controlled from beginning to end' and that the government maintain the Japanese until suitable employment could be found. He urged haste and suggested the army was best equipped to move them. The Department of National Defence, though willing to assist with administration, housing, and food services, was overburdened with its immediate responsibilities for the defence of the Pacific coast. Similarly, the RCMP, pleading a shortage of manpower, refused to accept full responsibility. Since neither agency would take on the task of administering the evacuees, on 27 February the Cabinet War Committee unanimously accepted the prime minister's recommendation to set up a special agency. This became the British Columbia Security Commission (BCSC), which supervised the evacuation and arranged resettlement.[1]

The BCSC consisted of a chairman, Austin C. Taylor, a prominent BC industrialist, and his assistant commissioners, F.J. Mead and John Shirras of the RCMP and British Columbia Provincial Police, respectively. An advisory board of twenty British Columbians served more as window dressing than as a policy-making body. Although the BCSC had considerable autonomy, it kept in regular contact with other government agencies and departments, notably the RCMP and the Department of External Affairs, and reported to the Department of Labour. Once the evacuation was complete and resettlement begun, the government formally dissolved the BCSC on 5 February 1943 and assigned its duties to the Department of Labour. Though the BCSC no longer existed legally, Japanese Canadians continued to regard it as the government agency supervising them, and indeed the Department of Labour kept the same staff and even the same stationery.

Soon after its formation in March 1942, the BCSC appointed an administrative staff in Vancouver to supervise the evacuation, housing, welfare, and resettlement programs. The BCSC initially housed evacuees from outside Greater Vancouver in that city's Hastings Park. From there, evacuees left for temporary placements inland. Initially, able-bodied men had little choice: they could leave their families and go to road camps or face internment. Some families stayed together by accepting work on prairie sugar-beet farms; a few families moved independently, and some established self-supporting communities. Most Japanese, however, spent at least part of the war years in the government-run interior housing settlements.

The BCSC communicated with its charges through the *New Canadian*, the *Nisei* newspaper which it 'virtually' took over, subsidized by about $500 per month, and distributed free to all evacuees in order to keep families and friends in touch with each other, to dispel opposition and fears caused by unfounded rumours, and 'to educate the Japanese to the Commission's point of view with regard to various aspects of the evacuation,' thereby securing voluntary cooperation rather than forcing large-scale and expensive internment. To serve *Issei*, whose Japanese-language papers were no longer published, the *New Canadian* became bilingual. Because of their 'unique position,' Thomas Shoyama and the other editors of the paper felt themselves 'hedged about both with self-imposed and other restrictions' that prevented them from expressing opinions as freely as the *Nisei* press in the United States.[2] Nevertheless, they continued to work with the government.

Doing its best to treat the Japanese fairly was the hallmark of BCSC policy. In his first public statement as chairman, Taylor urged the BC public to be cooperative, patient, considerate, and humane in their treatment of the Japanese. '[F]or our own protection,' he declared, 'we have unavoidably brought sorrow to many thousands of people,' but he warned that the Japanese must be treated 'as well as we expect our Canadian soldiers and civilian internees to be treated in Japanese-occupied territory in the Far East.'[3] Indeed, throughout the whole evacuation and resettlement process, the Canadians in Japanese hands were the hostages who guaranteed at

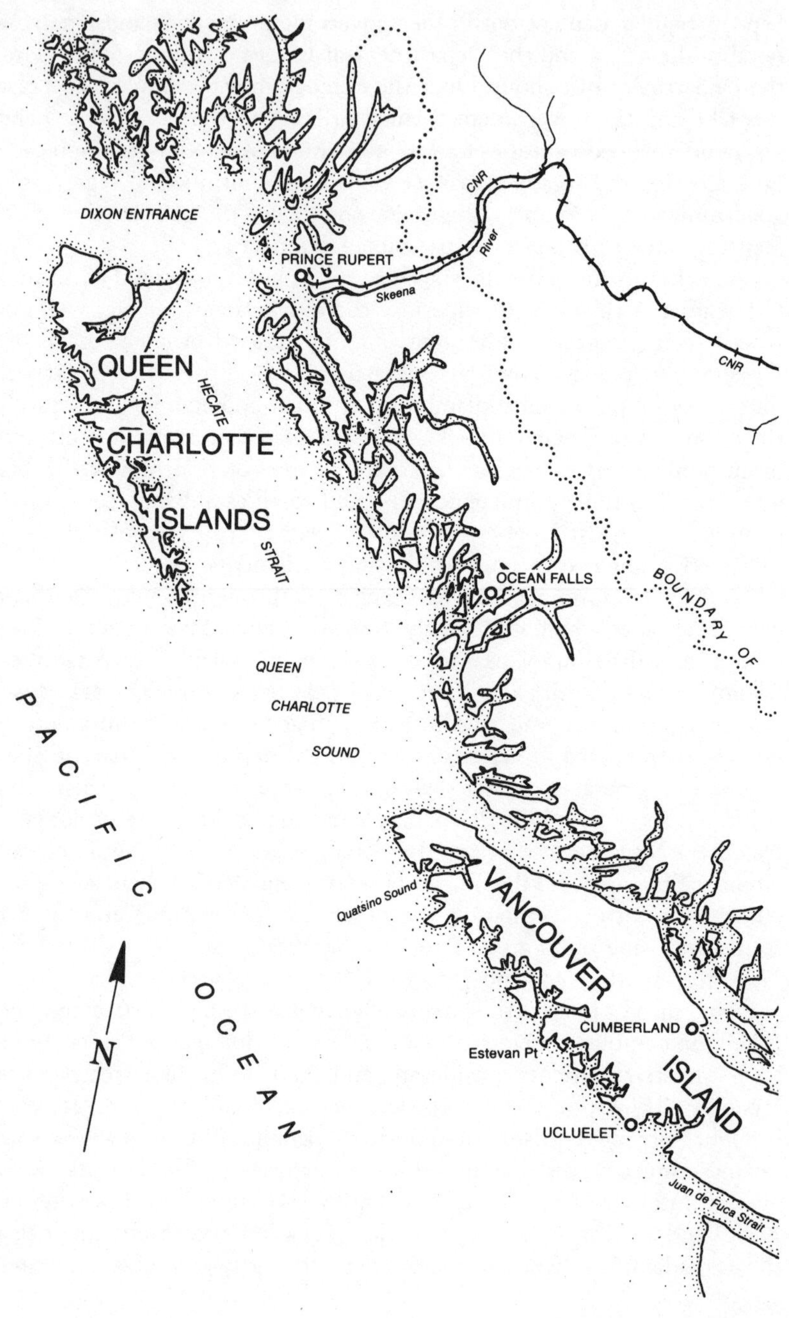
DIXON ENTRANCE
PRINCE RUPERT
CNR
Skeena
River
CNR
QUEEN
CHARLOTTE
ISLANDS
HECATE
STRAIT
OCEAN FALLS
BOUNDARY OF
QUEEN
CHARLOTTE
SOUND
PACIFIC
OCEAN
N
Quatsino Sound
VANCOUVER
ISLAND
CUMBERLAND
Estevan Pt
UCLUELET
Juan de Fuca Strait

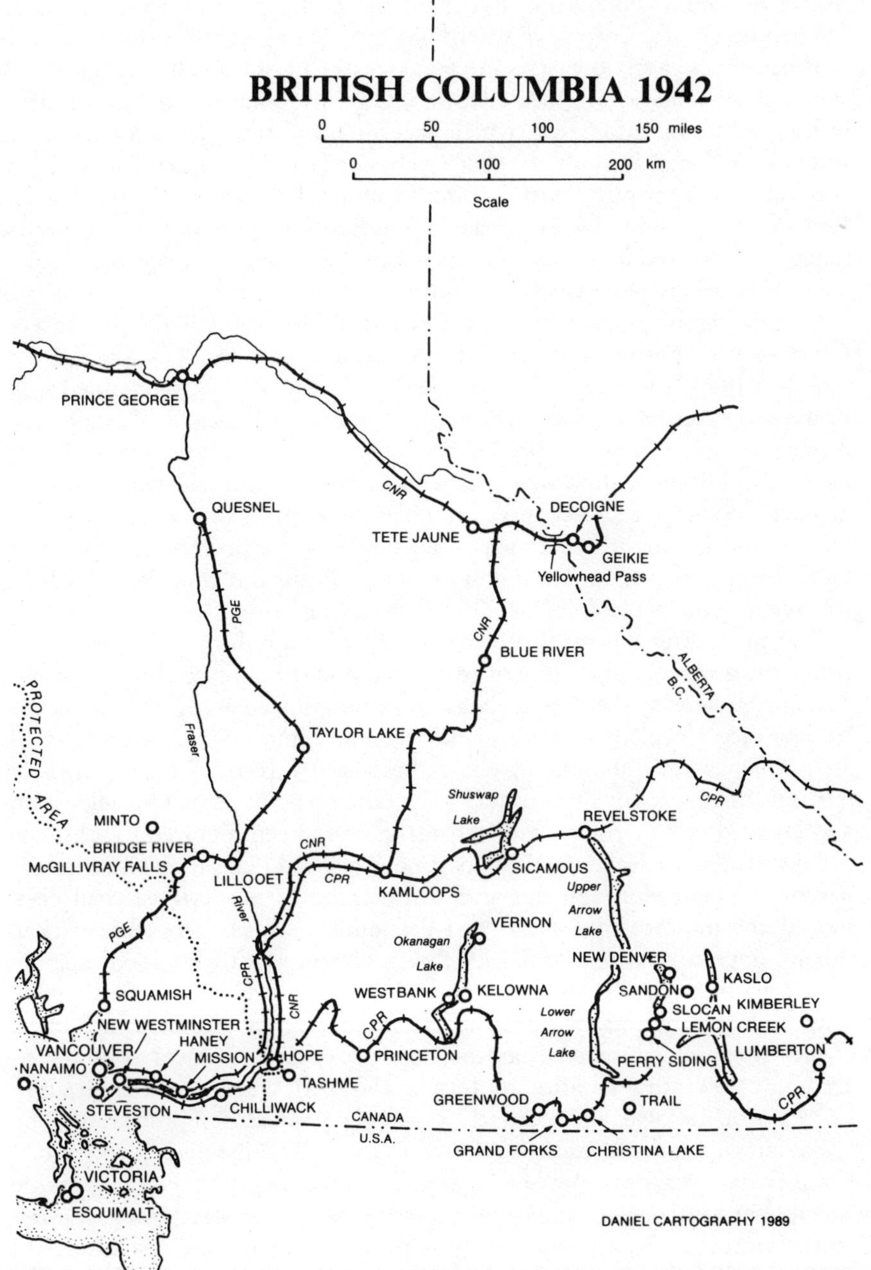
BRITISH COLUMBIA 1942
0 50 100 150 miles
0 100 200 km
Scale
PRINCE GEORGE
QUESNEL
PGE
Fraser
CNR
TETE JAUNE
DECOIGNE
GEIKIE
Yellowhead Pass
BLUE RIVER
ALBERTA
B.C.
TAYLOR LAKE
PROTECTED AREA
MINTO
BRIDGE RIVER
McGILLIVRAY FALLS
LILLOOET
River
CPR
KAMLOOPS
Shuswap Lake
SICAMOUS
REVELSTOKE
Upper Arrow Lake
VERNON
Okanagan Lake
NEW DENVER
SANDON
KASLO
SLOCAN
KIMBERLEY
LEMON CREEK
LUMBERTON
PERRY SIDING
Lower Arrow Lake
WESTBANK
KELOWNA
PRINCETON
SQUAMISH
NEW WESTMINSTER
VANCOUVER
HANEY
MISSION
HOPE
TASHME
NANAIMO
STEVESTON
CHILLIWACK
CANADA
U.S.A.
GREENWOOD
TRAIL
GRAND FORKS
CHRISTINA LAKE
VICTORIA
ESQUIMALT
DANIEL CARTOGRAPHY 1989

least a minimum standard of living for those of Japanese race in Canada. Unfortunately, the reverse did not hold true.

Because of her anxiety to secure good treatment of Canadian prisoners of war and missionaries in Asia, Canada invited the International Committee of the Red Cross, and Spain, which was the protecting power for Japanese interests in Canada, to observe her treatment of the Japanese. Throughout the war years, Spanish consular officials and E.L. Maag, the International Red Cross representative in Canada, periodically inspected Japanese settlements and received written communications. Generally, they accepted Canada's explanations of particular circumstances.

Canada insisted, however, that the responsibility of the Red Cross and of the protecting power extended only to Japanese nationals. Canada did not strictly enforce this policy with the Red Cross but always maintained it in dealing with Spain. This posed difficulties since many individuals appearing on their own behalf or as representatives of their communities claimed dual nationality. Because they were warned of unspecified consequences if they contacted Spanish representatives and had their names recorded, few Canadian nationals sought the advice or assistance of the protecting power.[4] In fact, during the later repatriation program, officials did check to see which Canadian nationals had contacted the protecting power.

The protecting power also acted as the conduit through which Japan complained about the treatment of her nationals. Significantly, one of her first objections was that Canada was discriminating against Japanese on the basis of race, since other enemy aliens were not removed from the restricted area. This was an embarrassing charge because it was true. Fearing reprisals against Canadians, the Department of External Affairs denied the allegation and claimed that Germans and Italians had also been required to leave the protected area. In any case, the department insisted that 'in accord with the practice of belligerents in this and all other wars,' the Japanese had been moved for military, not racial and economic reasons. This explanation, though not entirely in accord with the facts, temporarily satisfied Japan.

In October 1942, however, Japan accused Canada of committing 'an unprecedented outrage of humanity' by depriving 'all Japanese in Canada of their means of subsistence on [the] pretense of establishment of protected areas,' by separating families, by forcing the aged, women, and children to live 'in wild desolate places,' and by leaving property 'unprotected.' The Canadian government readily admitted individual hardships but contended it was doing everything possible to adjust 'legitimate grievances,' to provide 'suitable and congenial' employment, and, where necessary, financial assistance. Moreover, by the time the complaint was received, Canada could report that families had been reunited and were settled not in 'wild and desolate places' but in 'fertile and beautiful districts.' Japan made similar allegations in domestic publications, but diplomatically accepted Canada's explanation without comment. In fact, she could do no more for her nationals in Canada than Canada could do for her nationals in Japan.[5]

As the first step in the evacuation procedure, about 4000 Japanese Canadians who resided in northern British Columbia, on the Queen Charlotte Islands, and on Vancouver Island were rounded up in a clearing station or assembly centre in Vancouver's Hastings Park Exhibition Grounds. Some families had only two or three hours to close their homes and leave. Residents of Vancouver, the last to be evacuated, had more time to dispose of their property but even those who had several months to prepare could only take 150 pounds per adult and 75 pounds per child, the normal baggage allowance permitted by the railways.

Many families sold almost all their belongings at firesale prices. Every day, one *Issei* recollected, hordes of Chinese and Indians came looking for a good buy. Advertisements in the *New Canadian* proclaimed: 'I will pay spot cash for your business if you want to sell your business quick' or 'We buy radios, washers, refrigerators.' Other entrepreneurs advertised storage services and 'evacuees supplies' such as tents. Some families equated selling their precious possessions at bargain prices with a loss of self-respect. One family, being moved by ship to Vancouver, wanted to take their piano. At the pier, a government official forced them to put it to auction. Rather than take an insultingly small offer of $15.00, they shoved the piano into the sea. Money was not what they wanted.[6]

Some families stored possessions with white friends or in locked buildings nominally under the supervision of the federal government's custodian of enemy property. The custodian had recognized that many were exploiting 'the plight of the Japanese' to buy property cheaply, but he did little to secure property. The Japanese minister of the Congregational church at Ocean Falls, one of the last to be moved from that north coastal town, witnessed 'a strange weird scene of many white people as well as Indians streaming into emptied houses and taking out things ... that might be useful for them.' In July 1942 a director of the Fraser River Fishermen's Union returned to Steveston to settle the union's remaining business. His voice choking with emotion, he told how he found the ashes of the dead among the broken pieces of glass in the yard of the Buddhist church. Evacuees, thinking the church would be a safe place, had left the urns, normally kept in household altars, there. To treasure hunters, the urns and their ornate boxes must have seemed worth stealing. The custodian's comment, 'Too bad,' could not soothe feelings, commented one *Issei.* The Japanese felt acutely betrayed. Even those who entrusted their businesses and property to non-Japanese lawyers soon realized they could not rely on anyone. The loss of property would remain a bitter memory.[7]

The first evacuees entered Hastings Park on 16 March 1942; the last left on 30 September 1942. All told, about 8000 Japanese passed through the park and many Japanese residents of Vancouver visited. Inhabitants of Hastings Park could get weekly passes to the city and, to avoid congestion on the crowded public transport system, the BCSC arranged special buses between the park and Powell Street, the heart of Vancouver's Japanese quarter.

Despite this limited freedom, life at Hastings Park was unpleasant, indeed humiliating. The Department of National Defence had simply adapted the livestock barn for human use by setting up double decker cots in dormitories, one for the men, and one for women and children. Later, a partition was built to separate teenage boys from the drinking and gambling which seemed endemic in the men's quarters and beyond the control of the RCMP and the BCSC. Not only was there a lack of privacy but the place was most unsanitary. Smells of livestock lingered; attempts to clean the floors merely disturbed the maggots; and toilet facilities were limited. Only after women complained did the BCSC provide such basics as partitions between the latrines. Most families got some privacy by hanging blankets or clothing from wires strung between the beds.[8]

Food was served in mess halls organized by the Department of National Defence at the cost of less than ten cents per meal. Residents made no official complaints but there was at least one sit-down strike and many long remembered the monotony of the menus and the absence of Japanese-style food. The BCSC, however, congratulated itself for giving residents of Hastings Park 'many valuable lessons in food values.' Despite several outbreaks of diarrhoea, the main health concerns that residents presented to the Spanish consul and the Red Cross were the proximity of the tuberculosis ward to the general hospital, the lack of a resident doctor to treat sudden illnesses and maternity cases, and the high cost of medicine. Although the BCSC was keen to satisfy the protecting power, it did not consider these grievances to be well founded.[9]

Most health services as well as maintenance, kitchen, and clerical duties were provided by paid Japanese workers under the general supervision of the BCSC's own staff. In addition, forty-five Japanese veterans of the Canadian Expeditionary Force of the First World War acted as guards. Wages for all were minimal. One maintenance worker recalled being paid fifteen cents per hour to look after the public baths.[10] Nevertheless, some *Nisei* resented the fact that Japanese nationals were getting such jobs.

To liaise with the Japanese community, the BCSC appointed a committee of three *Issei:* Etsuji Morii, Arthur Nishiguchi, and Ippei Nishio. Morii became so unpopular among his supposed constituents that another self-appointed representative committee suggested that general 'discontent rose to a near riot.' Some members of the BCSC had doubts about Morii, who allegedly advised Japanese to evade evacuation orders, accepted money in return for promises to secure the deferment of individual evacuation orders, and belonged to a subversive Japanese society. Despite these reports, demands from naturalized Canadians that Morii not be given any position where he could control them, and the knowledge that some Japanese Canadians distrusted Morii, Commissioner Mead regarded Morii as 'most co-operative.'[11]

Thus, the BCSC only slowly acceded to pressure from *Nisei* and agreed to consult other bona fide groups such as a *Nisei* subcommittee to the Advisory Board on Welfare. This committee was already planning cultural, social, and recreational programs, including special classes for women in English, home economics, and civics, musical and dramatic concerts, athletic activities, and a library. Young children, however, were denied access to a nearby swimming pool when neighbours complained.

Both the United and Anglican churches which had long operated kindergartens for Japanese children transferred their workers to Hastings Park. To provide schooling for older children, the BCSC borrowed W.S. McRae from the Vancouver School Board and instructed him to organize education and recreation, 'provided it didn't cost the Commission any money.'[12] While the BCSC wanted to provide a good elementary education, economy was a guiding principle. With the help of Hideko Hyodo, the only *Nisei* with experience teaching in the BC public-school system, and Gwen Suttie, a United Church worker who had taught high school in Japan, he organized volunteer student teachers from among the residents of Hastings Park to provide classes for over 600 children in grades one to seven. Grade eight students were enrolled in correspondence courses. The Reverend W.H.H. Norman, who had spent some years in Japan, and Albert Takemoto supervised five Japanese assistants who taught high-school classes.

Despite the difficult conditions, residents of Hastings Park generally cooperated with the BCSC. Indeed, the author of the BCSC's report on the first seven months of its activities concluded almost romantically:

> The story of those days in Hastings Park will never be fully recorded. The exacting hours of labour, the realization of playing a part in the conformation of Canadian

History, the closeness of the picture to the observer, left all who viewed it with only kaleidoscopic images imprinted on their memories. The pathos and humour, the simple joys, the heart-breaking discouragements suffered by reluctant inmates awaiting dispersement to an unknown future, may have sown the seed in the heart and brain of some Canadian born Japanese which will come to fruition in later years in the literary expression of this tale of the evacuation of a saddened people, but no present record of this exodus from Hastings Park should be allowed to stand without comment on the willing adaptability and reasonable attitude displayed on the part of the Japanese in general.[13]

Three years later, when children in the interior housing settlements wrote autobiographies as a school exercise in composition, many recollected the 'terrible' life at Hastings Park. Since then, several *Nisei* have published memoirs, but all were Vancouver residents who only occasionally visited Hastings Park. Yet, even fleeting experiences of the stench were remembered. Almost thirty years later, for example, Shizuye Takashima described Hastings Park as the 'hell-hole my Sunday school teacher spoke of with such earnestness.'[14]

The husbands, fathers, and adult brothers of many of the residents of Hastings Park had already departed for the road camps of the interior. This scheme had been devised at the Ottawa Conference on Japanese Problems in January 1942. It was not a new idea; both the BC and federal governments had used road camps to get unemployed men out of the cities during the Depression. The scheme was not satisfactory then, especially to the inmates; it was also unsatisfactory to most Japanese.

When British Columbians urged that all Japanese males of military age, no matter what their citizenship, be removed from the coast, the Department of External Affairs warned that enemy aliens should not be interned but placed in special camps under 'modified discipline' pending assimilation into economic activities outside the defence area. The department feared creating a situation in which Japan 'would be justified in drafting our people and our allies' into labour battalions or military formations. As a sop to British Columbia, Canada ordered Japanese nationals and other enemy aliens to leave the protected area and offered them work on road construction and accommodation 'in camps without necessarily being interned but being under surveillance.'[15] At the same time, the Ottawa Conference proposed a voluntary corps of Japanese Canadians. In coastal British Columbia, the press generally welcomed the news that enemy aliens would be moved from defence areas and readily admitted the necessity of treating the Japanese justly lest Japan retaliate against Canadians in her hands.

Although there was no shortage of possible road projects, the federal government moved slowly as it debated the financing and administration of the scheme with provincial governments and contemplated the relationship of the plan to the provision of normal employment for the Japanese. Finally, the federal Department of Labour accepted responsibility for the camps and had the RCMP instruct Japanese nationals to leave the protected area by 1 April 1942 and to go either to the camps or to jobs they found for themselves. Meanwhile, the plan for a civilian labour corps bogged down in administrative problems.

In anticipation, a few *Issei* accepted the advice of Etsuji Morii that if they cooperated and went to road camps, the remaining Japanese could remain safely where they were. Such cooperation was short-lived. In mid-February, probably to demonstrate their desire to stay together, to protest the evacuation policy, to express their resentment of other provinces' refusing to accept them, and possibly to reflect their confidence in Japan's eventual success, some Japanese nationals refused to accept road work. At least one *Issei* changed his mind when he determined he had been 'tricked' into volunteering. Infuriated, he refused to go, even though he would face great difficulties as a *Gambari* or resister. Another *Issei* remembered how, when ordered to report to RCMP headquarters, he entered a room alone. Without giving him time to read them, the officers told him he would be sent to an internment camp if he refused to sign the documents before him. When he asked about their meaning, they gave him a few words of explanation which made little sense. He 'had no choice,' he emphasized in his memoirs, 'literally "signing with his eyes closed." ' He was then ordered to leave on the seven o'clock train that night. Later, a fellow labourer who argued with a supervisor was told they had come to work 'voluntarily.' For the first time they learned they were 'volunteers!'[16]

The Japanese government, which correctly denied forcing any Canadian civilians to do compulsory labour, complained that men had been forced to 'volunteer' for road camps at the point of a pistol, but offered no specific evidence. More realistically, Japan charged that men had been interned for refusing to do compulsory labour. Canada replied that men had been interned only for refusing to obey evacuation orders or for having a generally hostile attitude. In fact, Canada had cut rations of able-bodied Japanese who refused to work and had interned others who quit work. The Department of External Affairs, revealing a class rather than a racial bias, believed the difference in social levels between the Japanese in Canada, who were 'largely manual workers,' and the Canadian civilians in Japanese territory, who were 'largely persons with income or salaried personnel,' made the situations different.[17]

Because of delays in setting up the road camps, Canada had not pressed Japanese nationals to leave before 1 April 1942. These delays contributed to mounting demands for the removal of all Japanese from the coast.[18] The decision to remove all Japanese meant extending the road-camp program to include *Nisei* and quietly abandoning the Civilian Labour Corps. By mid-March the BCSC expected to place over 4000 men on three major projects: Yellowhead to Blue River, which employed many single Japanese nationals; Hope to Princeton, which employed both single and married Japanese nationals; and Revelstoke to Sicamous, which employed Canadian-born single men. The BCSC also planned work between Prince George and Tête Jaune Cache and in northern Ontario. This division of workers by national status was one of the few instances in which the BCSC recognized such distinctions.

The camps provided useful but temporary work. By late June 1942, 2233 men were employed; by the end of October, only 986 remained. The numbers continued to decline so that by 1 July 1944 only 367 men were still engaged in road work.[19] As the statistics indicate, the camps were not a success.

American and Canadian military officers and the RCMP complained that camps near transcontinental railway lines offered opportunities for sabotage.[20] For security reasons, the BCSC refused to change its policy requiring men to have a permit to leave the camp areas despite the workers' protest to the Spanish consul about their lack of freedom. Indeed, as Kenzie Tanaka, the former vice-president of the Japanese Canadian Citizens League, explained from Red Pass Junction, all the men could see ahead was 'hard work which looms in their minds as lifeless drudgery.' A provincial government engineer, who was more concerned about the road near Blue River than the people building it, claimed that many Japanese nationals were unwilling to cooperate in part because their leaders believed 'that Hirohito was coming out of the fight top dog' and regarded the road as a military project designed 'to assist in decimating their kin in Japan.' However, he concluded there was insufficient evidence to intern any of them.[21]

Men refused to work for a variety of reasons, sometimes trivial ones. At Solsqua, they would not work because their breakfast hotcakes were not hot; at another camp, they disobeyed bedtime 'lights out' orders because they disliked the foreman. In some cases the RCMP found that men accused of loafing were former clerks and storekeepers who had neither proper tools nor the skills to use them. In a few instances, no one would work with chronic loafers whose removal generally improved morale. Indeed, some agitators seem to have been interned because they refused compulsory labour. One such individual complained of inadequate and irregular pay, leaky tents, the lack of workmen's compensation in case of injury, the absence of recreational facilities, and the feeling of being 'a prisoner.' He told the RCMP, 'If I cannot go somewhere with my family I would rather be interned.' Throughout the spring of 1942 the complaints were so numerous that the Department of Mines and Resources, which briefly ran the camps, suggested the newspapers ignore complaints implying that workers were 'badly treated' and publicize how well they were cared for. Such information would 'do no harm to our men who are in Japanese prison camps.'[22]

Though spartan, living conditions were comparable to those usually prevailing in temporary construction camps and the food was similarly good. The *New Canadian*, in urging men to go to the camps, reported that the meals were adequate and that stoves were supplied. A naturalized Canadian, Ryuichi Yoshida, lived in a tent near Revelstoke but got more food than he could eat. Takeo Ujo Nakano recalled how 'the good food' served at his camp near Yellowhead 'did much psychologically to alleviate the emotional hardship of the time.' The Canadian government wanted to treat Japanese nationals fairly for humane considerations and 'to secure for our people in the hands of the Japanese similar standards of comfort.' Yet, at the same time, the BCSC feared feeding Japanese crews 'on a better scale than our own soldiers receive in any Military camp' lest it arouse public criticism.[23]

The *Nisei*, many of whom were justly sensitive about their Canadian birth and citizenship, made the strongest protests against going to the road camps. About 150 of them were offended when the police accidentally issued them an evacuation notice headed 'Notice to Enemy Aliens.' Some *Nisei* resented that Japanese nationals had not yet been moved or had got positions with the BCSC while Canadian-born and naturalized Canadians were being sent away. Yet, some *Nisei* had ties with Japan. Late in March, 135 *Nisei* who refused to go to the road camps sought the advice of Vice-Consul Ogawa who was still functioning in Vancouver. Ogawa, aware of the diplomatic proprieties, merely advised them that as an official of the Japanese government he was 'not in a position to tell the *Nisei* what to do. The only thing I can tell you,' he concluded in an ambiguous message, 'is to take the right path.' The RCMP also determined that early in April, twenty-six *Nisei*, eight naturalized Canadians, and eight Japanese nationals attended a meeting at the home of an official of the Japanese consulate and that some Canadian-born Japanese were considering surrendering their birth certificates in order to become Japanese nationals.[24] As they received orders to leave the coast, some *Nisei* tried to hide. Ironically, 'the safest hideaway was Hastings Park itself where, among their own kind with bed and board provided, only a thorough scrutiny could spot them.'[25]

The *Nisei* considered it was inhumane for the government to separate families 'as if a live tree were torn.' Some had considered volunteering for the Civilian Labour Corps but understood they would be paid only twenty-five cents per hour. Many had already exhausted their savings. The road-camp workers had learned that, after expenses, wages were pathetically low. Kiyozo Kazuta received sixty-one cents for his first month's work and ninety-five cents for the second. From his wage of twenty-five cents per hour for an eight-hour day, seventy-five cents was deducted each day for food and he was also charged for lodging and work clothes. Ninety men employed at Decoigne complained in a widely distributed circular that after paying for board, the medical fee, and unemployment insurance, and setting aside $20 for their families, they had $5.62 per month for clothing and incidentals, provided they were able to work a full twenty-five days per month. They charged that if they could not work because of weather or illness they were not paid, and they were uncertain of their coverage under workmen's compensation. Moreover, none had heard of their families actually receiving any money. Indeed, the BCSC realized that because of deductions, road-camp workers were actually less well off than internees who made twenty cents per day all found. So intense was the camp workers' discontent that S.T. Wood, commissioner of the RCMP, repeatedly recommended reuniting families.[26]

The BCSC tried to persuade workers that they need not worry and denied that it intended to prevent 'families from being re-united,' but it was not convincing. Privately, Arthur MacNamara, associate deputy minister of labour, admitted there was no family accommodation in the work camps and suggested Japanese men should not complain as their situation was analagous to that of soldiers. Meanwhile, as the men left, women and children fretted about the future, feared that prowlers might take advantage of the absence of able-bodied men, and complained of injustice in the selection of men for the road camps.[27]

By early April some *Nisei* were so vehemently resisting evacuation to the road camps that the BCSC admitted that Japanese intransigeance created confusion. The RCMP feared a loss of prestige if it could not enforce evacuation orders. Although the BCSC did not want to detain individuals who failed to report through error or confusion, it announced it would not 'tolerate wilful disobedience' of evacuation orders. In late March it ruled that anyone who refused its orders to move would be 'detained by the RCMP.' By 10 April it had detained fifty-six Japanese for disobeying evacuation orders – and that number soon rose. Acting on legal advice, the BCSC 'detained' men rather than 'interning' them because internees could appeal and, given the informal nature of the BCSC orders, they might easily gain their release. Detainees, by contrast, could not appeal, save possibly under *habeas corpus* proceedings, but the BCSC could release them as soon as the evacuation was complete since it did not believe they were a danger to the state.[28]

Although the BCSC rejected schemes proposed by the Japanese Canadian Citizens Council[29] and the Naturalized Citizens Committee to keep families together, the council and the naturalized citizens announced they would still cooperate. A number of *Nisei* disagreed and formed the Nisei Mass Evacuation Group (NMEG). While willing as Canadians to cooperate with the evacuation order, they refused to be separated from their families and threatened to defy the evacuation order en masse.[30] They knew they did not have the support of all *Nisei* and attacked the *New Canadian* for describing them as agitators. Members of the Japanese Canadian Citizens Council, for example, believed that 'some men were gambaruing' or resisting in the mistaken hope that as internees they would not have to work. Members of the citizens council executive also understood that the NMEG was divided between those who were fighting for their rights as Canadians and those who were using the movement for other reasons. In English and Japanese, the NMEG circulated letters explaining its protest and plans 'to continue all efforts to get what we feel are our rights' as Canadians. Much to the consternation of the BCSC and the RCMP, these efforts unsettled many families who became less cooperative. Indeed, Commissioner C.H. Hill of the RCMP recommended breaking up the NMEG 'without any further delay' and concluded, after receiving evidence from 'Secret Agents and other confidential Japanese contacts,' that at least nineteen *Nisei* should be interned under the Defence of Canada Regulations. When leaders of the NMEG were abruptly shipped to Ontario road camps, the NMEG carried on with 'underground leaders,' but as one *Nisei* historian has recorded, the 'timeworn strategy – divide and conquer, and shoot the generals – appeared to have succeeded.'[31]

Some members of the NMEG believed that internment was 'the only alternative to the "Mass Evacuation."' On 25 April they went to the Immigration Detention Building in Vancouver, demanding to be interned. Commissioner Mead could not convince them they would be better off cooperating with the evacuation as he ordered the internment of seventy-seven *Nisei* and three naturalized Canadians.[32] Little more than two weeks later another group of *Nisei* failed to report for work on the Trans-Canada Highway in northern Ontario. They argued that as Canadian citizens they should have the privilege of remaining in British Columbia.

The situation at the crowded Immigration Building was tense. On 13 May about 139 who had been detained for refusing to leave or violating orders briefly created a 'rough house' and inflicted about $1200 worth of damage to walls, windows, plumbing, and window bars, and turned a hose on the guards. The BCSC let it be known unofficially that any detainees or internees might be sent to Japan after the war and prepared to remove the rioters to detention camps immediately. In the meantime, Vancouver residents attacked the federal government for leaving 'their potentially dangerous "guests" ... where they could conceivably co-operate with the Japanese raiding force.'[33]

Moving the dissidents was easier to plan than to accomplish. The continued refusal of Japanese to leave the protected area overcrowded the Immigration Building, created circumstances which could easily lead to further unrest, and posed a possible embarrassment when representatives of the Red Cross and the protecting power visited. In addition, overcrowding meant the BCSC could not arrest delinquents who knew they had little prospect of immediate incarceration. Lest Japan take reprisals against Canadians under her control, the BCSC could not use ordinary jails or penitentiaries as detention centres. All other suitable facilities were being fully used for German and Italian prisoners of war. In mid-June, space in internment camps became available and 188 *Nisei* were sent to them. Though procedural problems delayed the removal of others, by mid-July 653 Japanese had been interned, mainly for resisting evacuation orders.[34]

By that time, the NMEG had won its battle. The BCSC had accepted the NMEG demand that able-bodied men be allowed to join their families in the interior housing settlements. BCSC officials welcomed the requests of some *Nisei* and naturalized internees to join their families, since the men would be engaged in remunerative work and would save the approximately $500 annual cost per person of internment. Moreover, offering to release internees who promised to obey future BCSC orders would allow the BCSC to advise the Red Cross and the protecting power that 'we offered those persons who are incarcerated under the Commission's orders their liberty.'[35]

The BCSC closed the Immigration Building until it determined that, with the fear of internment removed, some Japanese were 'dictating terms to us' because 'they feel that we are spineless, gutless, and generally incompetent to dictate a policy and carry it out.' It then reopened the building and ordered the immediate internment of anyone disobeying its orders. Some officials thought of even stronger measures, such as removing the Canadian citizenship of those who flouted orders.[36]

The police had initially feared that many women might not cooperate with the evacuation. Interning them would embarrass the Canadian government, which had objected to Japan's internment of twenty-three Canadian women. In Vancouver, only forty-two women and sixteen children, dependents of internees, 'emphatically' refused 'to go any place other than internment, unless by force.' Some of the women 'shouted and cursed furiously' whenever anyone approached their rooms in their temporary quarters in the Immigration Building. The BCSC gradually persuaded some of them to leave for the interior settlements. Six women, five of them naturalized Canadians and the other a Japanese national, held out longer, but eventually they too went to the housing centres.[37] Their motives are unclear. They may have been trying to show loyalty to Japan by seeking internment, or, like members of the NMEG, they may have been merely protesting the evacuation.

In deciding where to place evacuees, the BCSC had to consider public opinion and security concerns as well as the well-being of the evacuees themselves. On 4 March 1942, the first official day of the BCSC's existence, Austin Taylor predicted that without government intervention it would be 'practically impossible' to move Japanese to many interior points and warned that forcing evacuees on a hostile community or imposing further restrictions on the Japanese would probably create 'an element of distrust' among them. Taylor, who thought it impossible to change the minds of interior residents who had been demanding the removal of the Japanese east of the Rocky Mountains, suggested three alternatives: expanding the road camps, establishing Japanese families on isolated crown lands where they could support themselves with farming or minor industries, or preferably using such old mining or lumbering centres as Greenwood, Kaslo, Minto, Shalath, and Lumberton, where vacant accommodation could quickly and cheaply be made habitable for 3000 males or 1000 families.

About 1500 Japanese who wished to be independent of the BCSC had the resources to do so. With its permission, they moved to various locations in the interior of British Columbia where they could work in lumbering and agriculture or live off their savings. Yet, they often encountered a hostile reception. In some cases, such as Taylor Lake, a small and isolated settlement in the Cariboo, approximately 180 individuals supported themselves by cutting pulp wood. This community attended to its 'own business' without much notice by the BCSC. The would-be independent settlers of Grand Forks in the southern interior were less successful. Local hostility meant they could enter the city only for business, and some local canners and farmers exploited them and were slow to pay wages. Thus, the BCSC had to assist them with school costs and provide some relief. At nearby Christina Lake, however, the twenty-seven families who rented a resort hotel and its cabins initially lived off their savings but later found sufficient work to become, in the words of the International Red Cross delegate, 'a truly self-supporting community.'[38]

The major self-supporting settlements were located in the Bridge River Valley at four separate sites: East Lillooet, Minto, Bridge River, and McGillivray Falls. All told, fewer than a thousand Japanese settled in this region. The BCSC had known that some Japanese could finance their own resettlement and it suspected that putting wealthy families in the housing settlements 'might create a disturbing influence by giving rise to class distinctions.' It believed that these people, 'if left alone,' could 'work out their own problems in a manner that will cause the Commission the least trouble with very little expense.' It paid their transportation costs, accepted limited responsibilities for renting sites, offered minimal assistance with schooling, reluctantly gave financial aid to those who faced 'real hardship,' and lightly supervised the communities which other Japanese enviously referred to as *kanemochi mura* (villages of the rich) whose residents seemed to have received special favours from the Canadian government. The Bridge River settlements were themselves divided into factions, which was not surprising since the overall 'boss' seemed to be Etsuji Morii. Rivals contended for leadership, people squabbled over shared rent and electricity costs, and a self-appointed labour committee tried to control access to local employment.[39]

At Lillooet, the new settlers faced white hostility. Caucasian agents had erroneously informed the Naturalized Japanese Canadian Citizens Association that the people of Lillooet were 'friendly and willing' to receive them. In fact, the Japanese were forced to settle across the Fraser River in East Lillooet. In the dry sagebrush country, the 300 evacuees built cabins without electricity or running water. The local provincial police officer allowed them into Lillooet only during daylight hours and only for business. This policy remained until 1945, when Lillooet found itself without a doctor. The Board of Trade then asked Dr Masajiro Miyazaki, who had been practising at Bridge River, to move to Lillooet, where he quickly became involved in a variety of community activities.[40]

Residents of the self-supporting settlements found work in the lumbering industry or on tomato farms. Nevertheless, the BCSC encouraged them to accept eastern placements and, to mollify the landlords, provided compensation for any rental losses.[41] On the whole, the BCSC regarded the self-supporting settlements as a success, but they were a minor part of its operations.

The road camps were a failure almost from the beginning and only a few evacuees could afford to move to self-supporting settlements. Thus, Taylor recommended moving men from the road camps to old mining and lumbering towns where they could construct housing for their families. Humphrey Mitchell, the minister of labour, agreed and authorized the BCSC to act as it saw fit, 'remembering that first consideration is the security of our own people on the coast.' Security considerations forced Taylor to yield to the protests of the Consolidated Mining and Smelting Company and to abandon plans to use Lumberton, which was located near railway and power lines serving the Kimberley mine and Trail smelter.[42]

In the old mining towns, security was not a problem, so the government ignored repeated requests from the Consolidated Mining and Smelting Company to remove Japanese from the Slocan Valley or to equip the militia with machine guns 'to make some show of resistance' against potential saboteurs. Nevertheless, BCSC representatives 'wisely consulted the local authorities and leading citizens while hinting that they had considerable power.' Opinion in the towns varied. Some communities welcomed potential customers; others were quite hostile. Within the towns themselves, there was often disagreement. At New Denver, for example, one resident recalled 'considerable difference of opinion and much hot discussion; but even those who felt disposed to oppose their coming into the town on personal grounds, began to see that the poor Japs had to go somewhere, and that they had better surrender their own prejudice and make a virtue of necessity. So the City Fathers and the Board of Trade signified their willingness to receive these unfortunate outcasts.'[43]

At the end of 1942, over half the evacuees resided in the BCSC's interior housing settlements. As the BCSC explained in its first report, the placement of an 'industrious people ... in comparative idleness in interior towns, depicts no permanent static condition but is believed to be only the frontispiece to the still unfolding story of the final relocation and rehabilitation of the whole Japanese-Canadian population.' In sum, the interior housing settlements were merely 'a step in the evacuation process and a training ground for the employment of families in the Prairies and the East.'[44]

Despite the temporary nature of the interior settlements, the BCSC sought to place 'Japanese evacuees in houses commensurate with the tradition of British fair play.' Thus, though it used tents as short-term shelters during the summer, it rejected a suggestion that women and children be housed in tents during the winter. In some towns, the BCSC easily rehabilitated old hotels and commercial buildings; at Slocan and Tashme, it had to build from scratch. Economy was a guiding principle. At Tashme, the BCSC boasted that the cost of labour and materials, excluding plumbing, was only $146 per house and at Slocan, where transportation made materials more expensive, the cost was only slightly higher. The 1100 houses the BCSC built were small, usually fourteen by twenty-eight feet, and constructed of tar paper and rough green lumber which shrank and sweated as soon as the houses were heated. A Tashme schoolgirl described her home:

Four bedrooms and kitchen
Five windows and a door
White paper on the ceilin'
Tarpaper on the floor.

In some cases, the BCSC provided materials for those who wished to improve the insulation of their dwellings, but it did not extend this program widely in order to encourage people to leave the settlements for eastern placements. Some people paid for their own improvements. In several settlements, the BCSC provided *ofuro*, the traditional Japanese community baths, but, except in older buildings which already had running water and electricity, outdoor privies and oil lamps were common. The houses were often so close to each other that even the prime minister objected, and the BCSC did not illustrate its published report with close-up pictures lest they rouse criticism and concern for fire protection. Not until a significant number of residents left for eastern Canada at the war's end was overcrowding truly relieved.[45]

As an economy measure, the BCSC had favoured facilities which would allow each family to do its own cooking. This was in contrast to the American practice of establishing mess-style dining halls in its relocation camps. Because of the lack of space and the wartime scarcity of stoves, most families had to share kitchens. Inevitably, as a Vancouver *Sun* reporter who visited Tashme in December 1943 observed, 'petty annoyances could be magnified under the unaccustomed detention of large groups of people.' Eventually the BCSC supplied additional stoves where necessary to end feuds.[46]

The BCSC believed that making each family responsible for its own meals would eliminate the cost of hiring catering staff, reduce the need for supervision, and encourage self-sufficiency. Families could buy groceries from local merchants or, in the case of Tashme, from a BCSC store. They could also grow vegetables. Representatives of the Red Cross heard complaints about the high cost of food and the scarcity of Japanese foods such as rice, but reported them without comment. Nevertheless, the BCSC was anxious to

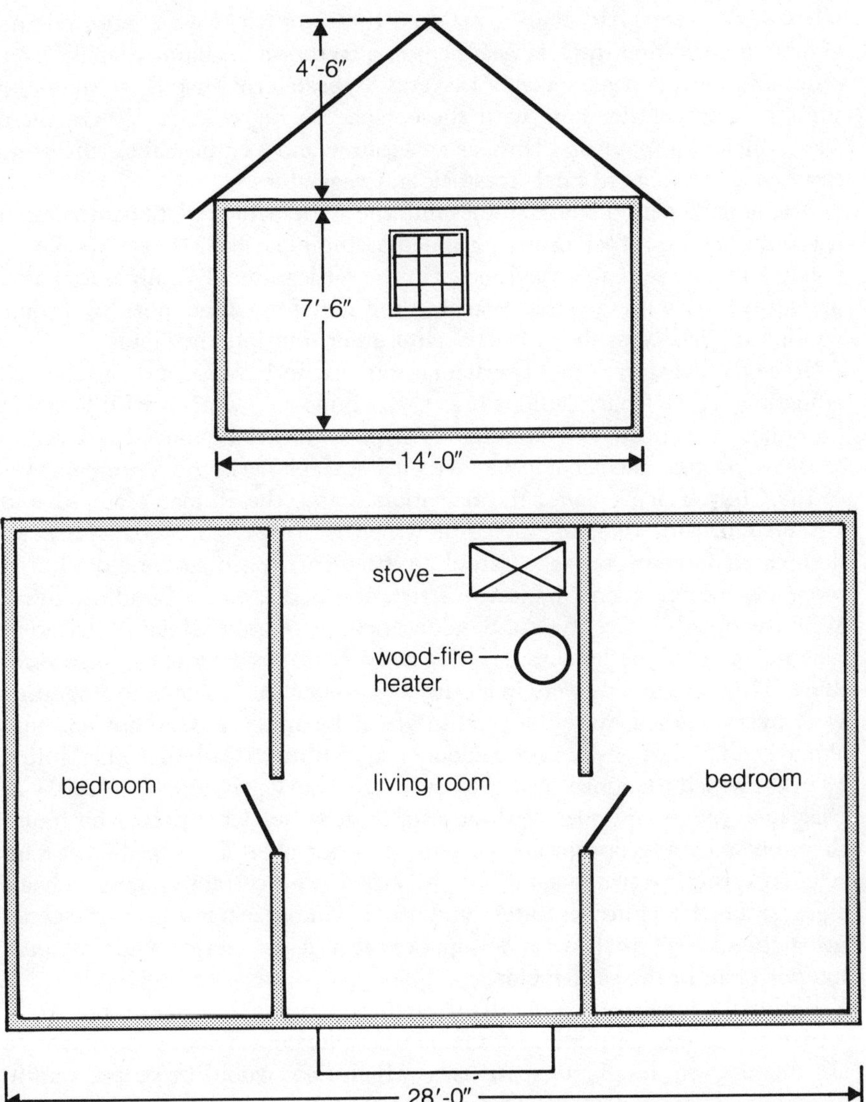

Elevation and floor plan of a standard BCSC house. DEA, file 3469–AM–40, E.L. Maag, Report on Visit to Settlements of Japanese Removed from the Defence Area on the Pacific Coast, 9–19 Jan. 1943

relieve grievances. Although it believed the complaints were only 'talking points,' it permitted the establishment of a factory at Tashme to make soya sauce and miso (a paste made of rice and soybeans used mainly in soups) to supply all the settlements with these Japanese ingredients. Where there was sufficient agricultural land, as at Tashme and Lemon Creek, the BCSC employed residents to raise livestock and vegetables.[47]

The BCSC began moving families into the settlements before construction was complete. Confusion often reigned as the BCSC lacked both a definite policy and a clear chain of authority in the settlements. By failing to match up family sizes with the space available, the BCSC forced the splitting of some families especially in the old hotels and other multiple dwellings.[48]

Some families were sent to particular settlements because of their religious affiliation. The Roman Catholic priests and nuns who worked with Japanese Catholics in Vancouver asked that their parishioners be moved as a group so their spiritual needs could be met. At Hastings Park, the representatives of the Church of England, the Salvation Army, the Roman Catholic and United churches took up the idea, which the BCSC adopted. The BCSC designated Greenwood as a Catholic settlement, Kaslo as United Church territory, Slocan as an Anglican district, and Sandon as a Buddhist town. With the possible exception of Sandon, these were not exclusive territories. The majority of the Japanese, if they actively professed a faith, were Buddhist. Thus, Buddhists were in all the settlements. At Slocan, the Anglicans were overwhelmed by the general influx of Japanese; at Greenwood, only about 120 families of the 1200 residents were Roman Catholic. The United Church, which thought it had exclusive missionary privileges in Kaslo, was chagrined by the number of Buddhists there.[49] For Christians who found themselves in an appropriate settlement – not all did – resettlement by religious group provided some social cohesion and certain practical advantages since the churches often undertook kindergarten and high-school instruction. Nevertheless, some Japanese feared the clergy might become too powerful in the settlements.

Within the Japanese community itself there was also some interest in group settlement. Some naturalized Canadians employed a Vancouver lawyer to ask the BCSC to designate locations to which they would be sent as family groups. The BCSC recognized friction between Canadian and Japanese nationals. Thus, in July it worked out a program that saw Japanese nationals gathering evacuees for Tashme and the NMEG and the Japanese Canadian Citizens Council working at Slocan.[50] Putting the last two groups together was a gamble, since the council had favoured cooperation with the evacuation and the NMEG had vigorously opposed it. Because this scheme was adopted relatively late in the evacuation process, its effects were minimal.

The movement to the interior settlements was practically complete by the end of October 1942. As of that date, 11,964 Japanese men, women, and children, or half the total Japanese population of Canada, resided in the interior housing projects. The largest, with 4776 residents, was Slocan, which really consisted of three neighbouring communities: Slocan City, Lemon Creek, and Perry Siding. The second largest, with 2584 inhabitants, was Tashme. New Denver-Rosebery had 1525 and Greenwood, Kaslo, and Sandon each had about 1000 Japanese settlers.[51]

In the interior housing settlements, the routine work was largely entrusted to evacuees hired as clerks, tradesmen, medical workers, and teachers. Finding suitable white supervisors and welfare workers for the settlements was difficult and many of the early town supervisors and welfare workers did not understand relief or the psychology of the evacuees. A white man who visited several settlements in the late summer of 1942 observed that practically every white employee of the BCSC had been an unemployed real estate or automobile salesman of English origin who delighted in 'telling how the peerage came into the family.' A United Church worker suggested that because the BCSC staff gave the appearance of being superior and did not really care for the Japanese or understand them, the people generally distrusted the BCSC. The evidence, however, is contradictory. A *Nisei* who had resided at Tashme remarked that 'the Occidental people who were in charge of the operation were far more liberal, understanding and co-operative where we were concerned than the so-called "Japanese Committee" that tried to run the place their way.'[52]

Although the settlements had much in common, including a mountainous setting, they also had distinctive characteristics. Moreover, although BCSC statistics suggest relatively stable populations, there was considerable movement in and out. From the beginning, some individuals and families left to accept outside placements either on a seasonal or permanent basis. Those who had problems in outside placements, particularly in the sugar-beet fields, could take refuge in a settlement.

Sandon, the most isolated community, was situated in a narrow, deep valley, subject to heavy snowfall and dependent on a single road and railway for communication with the outside world. Most of its residents were on relief. Nevertheless, the BCSC regarded it as one of the least troublesome communities. Since about 90 per cent of the population was Buddhist, the Buddhist priest maintained discipline. Its residents, a comparatively high percentage of them older, did not seemingly object to the lack of employment opportunities or to the difficulty of building gardens in its rocky terrain. Because of its small size and isolation, the BCSC announced plans to close Sandon in August 1944 and move its residents to other settlements.[53]

Greenwood, where about 90 per cent of the population were Canadian nationals, also had little trouble, even though a BCSC official described it as 'perhaps the least desirable of the interior towns.' Housing was mostly in rehabilitated hotels and other buildings, with an average space of only 33.5 square feet per person. Yet, when offered opportunities to move to better homes, families preferred to stay with friends. Almost as soon as they arrived, the men found work on railways and in lumbering. By the fall of 1944 a *New Canadian* correspondent reported that most family groups were self-supporting and there was a 'feeling of independence and a return to almost normal working conditions.'[54]

Kaslo, according to one BCSC report, was 'the most satisfactory settlement.' Its population, of whom about a quarter were Japanese nationals, lived in renovated stores, hotels, and office buildings. Although accommodation was crowded with as many as eight families sharing a floor of a hotel with only one kitchen and bathroom among them, a United Church lay woman who visited in the summer of 1943 marvelled at 'the wonderful community spirit' and 'spirit of self-sacrifice' among residents. That spirit was a microcosm of the whole town. Although about 115 residents, including several of Chinese origin, signed a petition against the coming of the Japanese, many white residents looked forward to helping the government solve the Japanese problem and of benefiting from new business for their economically declining city. The sympathetic editor of the local weekly newspaper reminded readers that the Japanese were 'wards of the Canadian Government' and not alien enemies, that the majority spoke English and belonged to Christian churches, but had been put 'in a real "spot" by the "war party" in Japan.'[55]

The evacuees who began arriving in mid-May were generally welcomed except by the Canadian Legion. The United Church invited the Japanese to its regular services but added a Japanese-language service and Sunday School to relieve overcrowding. The adult Japanese participated in community activities including garden shows, church socials, and the annual Remembrance Day ceremonies. The children and most of the young people also joined community activities. At the Victoria Day Sports Day, kimono-clad girls escorted the May queen; boys and girls took part in the foot races, and adults played baseball. Generally, whites and Japanese competed in sports as equals. At first, baseball teams were all Japanese but by mid-summer 1942 some Japanese teams had accepted white players. The Japanese introduced soccer to Kaslo and played in tournaments at the local golf club. Yet, integration was not quite complete; the city and the BCSC set up separate bathing beaches for whites and Japanese.[56]

Teenagers attended the public high school but did not mingle easily with their white classmates. The principal attributed the problem to their inability to speak good English. One of his students saw it differently and explained, 'In the town the Japanese never get along with the English. Always a quarrel or fight. We, the Japanese have the majority of kids (dead end kids) and always chase them away with slingshots. That's the only weapon we got. Those clumsy bunkheads (dumb in school) don't even know how to make a slingshot. However the mountie gave us hell and we had to throw our slingshots away. Although there may be the bad points there is also many good points about this "Race Hatred." Everybody seems to be a crackshot at this business of slingshots.'[57]

Though the patience and industry of the newcomers impressed the older residents of Kaslo, the Japanese were also welcome because they made Kaslo the 'livest "ghost town" in the west.' Indeed, whenever it was suggested that the Japanese might be removed from Kaslo, white residents protested for business reasons, but they had also developed a true respect for their new neighbours.[58]

Evidence of what the Japanese thought of Kaslo is scanty, but the comments of a *Nisei* brother and sister to their father are suggestive. The young lady observed that 'It can be [a] wonderful thing but community life can be disconcerting at times.' Her brother commented that 'Kaslo is all right for recreation as baseball, badminton, basketball, skating and so forth but it's just no good ... in an Educational and Economical way.' Indeed, while the young people had plenty of leisure activities, a United Church worker who visited early in 1943 warned of problems caused by young people with few opportunities for a normal home life or occupation developing 'a hoodlum type of conduct and attitude.'[59]

While Sandon, Greenwood, and Kaslo had maximum populations of about a thousand and were temporary settlements only, New Denver, on the east shore of Arrow Lake, and its satellite, Rosebery, had a population of about 1600 Japanese and became a more or less permanent refuge. In its heyday, New Denver had been a prosperous service centre for the surrounding mines, but by 1941 its population had dwindled to about 350. Although the town had debated accepting evacuees, the prime minister's office was startled to receive a letter from the New Denver branch of the Canadian Legion declaring its willingness to accept the Japanese 'in a spirit of Democratic co-operation and true Christian spirit.'[60] As at Kaslo, the Japanese participated in community activities.

New Denver, the BCSC administrative centre for the interior settlements, was also the site of the BCSC tuberculosis hospital. Its size and the presence of more than a thousand Japanese nationals may explain some of its problems. An early difficulty was a strike of construction workers. Fearing tuberculosis, workmen thought the hospital should be at a greater distance from the houses. Arriving late in the morning and quitting early, the men demanded that city water, not lake water, and firewood be delivered to their houses, which should be better ventilated and heated. When the BCSC agreed to try to remedy the problems, the men returned to work.[61]

The BCSC believed the strike was mainly over housing but thought the real problem was a small group of Japanese nationals who had been trouble-makers in road camps and who had 'the avowed intention of bucking the Commission.' Japanese residents of New Denver had different interpretations. Ryuichi Yoshida, who was working at Rosebery, recalled that the dispute was over working conditions, poor pay, and dissatisfaction with the camp supervisor, but Rosebery workers refused to join the strike because they were anxious to finish building houses for their families before winter set in. Shizuye Takashima, then a child, remembers grievances about the water supply but thought the final blow was a government decision to charge the aged and infirm $11 a month rent on their shacks and to close the bachelors' quarters. Her father claimed the strike failed because there was 'no unity in our community.' Divisions within New Denver persisted. When Japan sent gifts to residents in early 1944, New Denver was 'completely split into two factions.' Some residents welcomed the food treats and were grateful to Japan; others were insulted and upset that an enemy country would try to win their allegiance. These divisions were even more acute during the turmoil over 'voluntary repatriation' in 1945. During 1946, however, New Denver became the centre for those Japanese families who, because of age, infirmity, or other difficulties, could not be relocated easily. As of 1 January 1947 about 900 Japanese remained in New Denver. Some were tuberculosis patients and their families; a few were professionals such as Dr Paul Kumagai, a dentist, and the Reverend T. Komiya, the minister of the United Church. Still others liked the area, bought property, and remained as independent citizens.[62]

About twenty miles south of New Denver, Slocan Extension was centered on the old Slocan City, where the BCSC renovated old buildings. New settlements, with standard BCSC dwellings, were formed at the Bay and

Popoff Farms on the outskirts of town. Lemon Creek, six miles further south, began as part of Slocan administratively but eventually became a separate project. Though about 23 per cent of Slocan's population were Japanese nationals, the factionalism which disturbed New Denver was not evident.

The small white population of the Slocan area welcomed the Japanese as consumers of farm produce and came to see them as good community citizens who fenced the war memorial and erected a flag pole from which the Union Jack flew. Younger men gradually accepted work elsewhere by war's end, but many older people, whose white friends supported them, seemed anxious to settle permanently and 300 of them had to be forced to leave in November 1946 when the Department of Labour closed the settlement. Nevertheless, some people managed to stay; one *Issei* couple who opened a grocery store in 1942 operated it until their retirement in 1974.[63]

While the Kootenay settlements were based on old mining towns, Tashme was built exclusively as a housing centre on the site of the Trites Ranch, fourteen miles east of Hope. Austin Taylor, who believed it was 'the most natural proposition in our entire set-up,' expected that work constructing the Hope-Princeton highway or on Tashme's farm and sawmill would provide employment and make the community largely self-supporting. The BCSC was proud of its farm, which raised pork and produce for sale at its store, its soya and miso factories, bake shop, barber shop, and shoe repair depot. It also operated a sawmill and shingle mill and, as in other settlements, employed residents to provide normal municipal services. Thus, despite its intentions to keep jobs in the settlements to a minimum to encourage dispersal eastward, the BCSC employed about 15–20 per cent of the population.[64]

Because Tashme, nestled in a valley about a mile wide and fifteen miles long, was 'surrounded by precipitous mountain slopes closing in at each end,' it was easy to prevent residents from straying westward into the protected area of the coast. As a United Church worker later wrote, 'It is not a wonder that to us, the mountains were a constant source of beauty and wonder, a reminder of the majesty of God, but to the people who couldn't leave the valley they were a prison wall.' Though Tashme was little more than 100 miles from Vancouver, it was in many ways the most isolated of the settlements for, unlike the interior 'ghost towns,' it was, save for the BCSC, RCMP, and church workers, entirely Japanese. Of its maximum population of 2644, 795 were Japanese nationals. Indeed, some residents believed that the BCSC had deliberately placed *Issei* who it thought might be troublesome or security risks in Tashme and had made it the most restrictive of the settlements. Family groups dominated. The majority of the residents were Buddhists, but there were also about 500 Protestants and 50 Catholics.[65]

Theoretically, Tashme may have been the BCSC's ideal settlement, and its residents believed the BCSC used it as a show piece. In fact, it was one of the most troublesome. At first, some people refused to go to Tashme, the last housing centre to be settled. Some wanted to join family and friends in other settlements; others had an 'internal feeling' against a 'certain group' which had already gone there. A United Church representative who visited in early 1943 observed that 'Tashme Camp has a greater proportion of unreconcilables than any other, and they certainly spend a considerable time in thinking up ways of making life tough for the Commission.'[66]

With the exception of a large barn that was converted into one-bedroom apartments, with electricity, central heating, a community kitchen and washrooms, to house elderly families in 'the aristocratic part of town,' and a barracks-like dormitory for about ninety single men of all ages, the accommodation consisted of standard BCSC houses. Water came from standpipes; toilets, shared by four families, were outside; and oil lamps provided light. Eventually, electric light and water were extended to all buildings, but in the summer of 1945 only a quarter of the houses had inside water pipes. Tashme residents complained about their housing but their particular grievance was the monopoly of the BCSC store, its high prices, and the BCSC practice of discouraging mail-order shopping by imposing a 10 per cent service charge on money orders, charging a delivery fee, and screening orders to insure that people on maintenance did not buy luxuries. Nevertheless, in January 1943 the International Red Cross delegate thought the residents of Tashme were a 'contented people.' Former residents had bittersweet memories. A *Nisei* who spent almost four years there remarked, 'I enjoyed every day of my stay there ... Funny, I said to myself when I left there that I'll never miss a dump like Tashme but now, I miss it more than anything ... [and] think of all the friends I've made there.' By 1945, however, Tashme was in greater turmoil than most settlements because the government began sending families there in preparation for repatriation, and began moving out those who had not signed to go to Japan.

All settlement residents experienced a sense of isolation. Hideko Hyodo, who visited all the settlements as school supervisor, found it 'a great revelation' to attend an educational conference in Banff in the summer of 1943. Though she had been in the interior for only a year, she found 'much change in the outside world – the numerous activities and responsibilities that are now being taken over by women. Of course we do see something about it in the papers but when one is so removed from the scene of activity, we do not have a very good conception of the true state of affairs. Perhaps this is one of the reasons why so many of the Japanese here are so disinterested about movement from [the] evacuation towns.' Eighteen months later, a shocked teacher at Bayfarm School in Slocan reported that of 228 children in grades five and up, seventy-four did not know the name of the prime minister. He concluded, 'the results pointed to one thing – the gross ignorance of the children regarding the world at large. These are the children shut inside a huge stone wall, utterly oblivious of the gigantic change outside.'[68]

Though newspapers circulated freely, personal correspondence was censored and long-distance telephone calls required RCMP or BCSC approval. Longwave radios were sometimes returned to those who requested them but in the mountains, reception was unreliable. At Tashme, some residents secretly kept a shortwave radio, listened to broadcasts from Japan, and distributed this information in an almost daily Japanese-language circular, the *Tashme News.* The *Tashme News* reported how the Japanese navy and army were winning the war; on 7 December 1943 it commemorated the second anniversary of the war by describing Japanese victories in the Pacific, Burma, and North China. It stated that construction of a Greater East Asia Co-Prosperity Sphere had progressed, that the 'Great Asian Race' had overthrown Britain and the United States, and that its long-cherished dream was coming true. The next day's issue included the emperor's message of 8 December 1943 expressing his complete satisfaction with the recent battles, but urging the navy and air force to make greater efforts as the enemy was still trying to prevent Japan's dreams of constructing a 'New Order of the World' and creating a 'Greater Asia.' According to the *Tashme News,* U.S. naval claims of success were mere propaganda. Yet, in reporting one battle, the *Tashme News* presented conflicting views. A dispatch from Tokyo emphasized conditions favourable to the Japanese navy; a United States navy press release claimed American victories. To these reports was added a Reuter dispatch that the American navy had abandoned the operation because of heavy damages and casualties. Such news was designed to convince readers that the Japanese navy was winning and that the United States was merely releasing false propaganda.[69]

Despite access to accounts from both sides, residents of the settlements were physically isolated. They could not travel without a permit from the BCSC or the RCMP. Outside British Columbia this regulation had been relaxed in August 1943, but in British Columbia, Japanese still needed a permit to travel more than fifty miles or to leave their homes for more than thirty days. Since the only access to the settlements was usually by a single road or rail line, on each route the BCSC 'erected a suitable guard house ... staffed by uniformed Civilian Security Guards who are Special Constables of the

R.C.M. Police.' All traffic was required to report, and Japanese who could not show the proper permit could be charged with an offence. Permits were granted for those who could show cause for a journey. One RCMP officer observed, 'Death of a relative no matter how distant is the surest and most used excuse. It is always a source of amazement the number of relatives each deceased Japanese had.' Yet, delays and difficulties in getting permits caused frustration.[70]

Isolation and frustration undoubtedly contributed to an ill-defined sense of malaise. Ken Adachi, who spent part of his childhood in a settlement, observed that 'the cumulative effects of camp life were only dimly perceived – if perceived at all – by the majority of the evacuated people. Generalizations about the social and psychological consequences of camp life ... could be misleading for the evacuation obviously did not have the same effect on everyone.' A worker in a road camp near Tashme described existence in the interior towns as 'a shameful life' and rhetorically asked what young people, once filled with energy and ambition, could 'see in the dull, confined, harmful life leading to nowhere?' The *New Canadian* regularly complained of the 'shabbiness of spirit' that was developing and remarked how 'the cribbed and confined conditions' of the settlements discouraged 'the more progressive-minded and liberal-minded of evacuees.'[71]

The generational split which had appeared in the 1930s as the *Nisei* developed a political consciousness reappeared in the settlements, but conflicts also followed national lines. BCSC officials noted that 'Young Canadians, who imagined their Canadian citizenship meant something' were being 'taunted by the nationals who refer scathingly to the actions of a democratic country.' David Suzuki, a *Sansei* or third-generation schoolboy who could not speak Japanese, recalls that at Slocan, 'My peers sometimes echoed their parents' bitterness and hoped Japan would kick the hell out of the Allies. I didn't really know what war meant, but was always loudly and fiercely Canadian. As a result, I was often beaten up at school. My father and mother always encouraged me to be outspoken. Among the more reticient Nisei, this kind of brashness was resented.'[72]

In Hastings Park and in the early days of the evacuation, *Nisei* had acted as leaders but, as one of them rued, they 'flunked their responsibilities by surrendering power to Issei' who had 'neither the essential basic grounding in the Canadian point of view or manner, nor the foresight beyond tomorrow's woodpile, to provide really constructive leadership.' Some *Issei* encouraged friends and neighbours to sign for repatriation to Japan. Confident of Japan's ultimate victory, they were not troubled by small daily hardships. Perhaps because of this apparent passivity, the BCSC did not believe loyalty could be simply determined by national status. In the summer of 1943, Commissioner George Collins suggested the government was giving 'too little thought to some of the old Nationals' who, because of illiteracy, had not bothered to become naturalized but who had no 'particular feeling for Japan.' Indeed, he believed that many were 'more loyal to Canada than the Canadian-born.' He was, however, worried about the *Kika*, the *Nisei* who had been educated in Japan. He concluded, 'it is very difficult to know who is a dangerous type of Japanese and who is not, and it cannot therefore be assumed that the Nisei, or Canadian-born Japanese are loyal to Canada; the Naturalized are neutral; and the Nationals are disloyal.'[73] Questions of loyalty and generational conflicts would later come to a head in the 1945 debate on 'Voluntary Repatriation'; in the short run, most residents of the settlements were preoccupied with such basic problems as shelter, health, the education of their children, and securing an income.

In providing housing, the BCSC had been conscious of the need to satisfy the Red Cross and the protecting power. Similarly, it paid special attention to medical services. Where hospitals existed, it renovated and expanded them; in other centres it built them from scratch. The BCSC employed Japanese doctors, dentists, optometrists, and nurses as well as Occidental doctors and nurses. Residents on maintenance – that is, relief – received free medical treatment. Complaints about medical care were confined to minor grievances such as the reluctance of one doctor to make house calls. The pride of the BCSC's medical programs was its 100-bed tuberculosis sanitarium at New Denver. Indeed, one of the documents sent to Japan to demonstrate Canada's good treatment of evacuees was an illustrated Red Cross report showing the comfortable facilities there.[74]

While health care was a major concern of the BCSC, many of its wards were more worried about the education of their children. For Japanese, education is a serious matter. Normally in Canada, education is a provincial obligation, but British Columbia refused responsibility for the education of evacuee children. Thus, the BCSC found itself acting as an educational agency. In some cases its involvement was minimal. Where local school boards in Alberta and Manitoba and, in a few cases, in British Columbia admitted fee-paying Japanese students, the BCSC subsidized them. At Greenwood, where the priests and nuns who had worked with the Japanese in Vancouver accompanied their parishioners and established a school with classes for about 400 students from kindergarten through high school, the BCSC subsidized the elementary program at the rate of $10 per pupil per year. In the self-supporting settlements, the BCSC provided copies of correspondence-lesson papers and a subsidy of $5–$10 per student per year. The BCSC deliberately gave only minimal supervision to these schools lest the self-supporting communities ask for additional aid. Nevertheless, it determined that they were 'carrying on a very intelligent and worthwhile volunteer educational programme.'[75]

The main educational concern of the BCSC were the approximately 3000 children of elementary school age in the housing projects. It had recognized its educational duties almost from the beginning of the evacuation. While it seems to have had the best educational interests of the children at heart and wanted 'to make good Canadians of the Canadian born Japanese,' it did not want to make its schools too good lest it discourage families or teachers from leaving the settlements.[76]

A remarkable school system emerged. Under the close supervision of the BCSC, it was managed by Hideko Hyodo who had taught for sixteen years in BC public schools preparing Japanese students for entry into regular classes. The curriculum was reluctantly and slowly provided by the BC Department of Education, which allowed the BCSC to buy, at cost, prescribed textbooks and the lessons prepared by its Elementary Correspondence Branch for children who were unable to attend regular schools. The department refused, however, to allow individual Japanese children to enrol in its courses; it also refused to check answer papers, though it eventually provided one complete set of answers which the BCSC then mimeographed and distributed to its teachers. The correspondence lessons became teachers' guides and many teachers depended heavily on them. Shizuye Takashima commented: 'those stupid correspondence courses. We have to answer hundreds of questions ... I don't understand any of them.'[77]

Although it 'dictated the educational programme' and insisted that the schools operate exclusively in English, the BCSC left their organization 'more or less' to the Japanese whose 'keenness' for education would 'get the utmost out of the whole plan.' The BCSC expected its only real contribution would be to provide classroom space, some books and supplies, and to pay the salaries of Miss Hyodo, her principal assistant, Teruko Hidaka, and fourteen supervisors who would each organize a 'volunteer staff of Japanese High School and University students who will help in the coaching or teaching of the Japanese students.' The supervisors would be chosen from qualified teachers (of whom there were none other than Misses Hyodo and Hidaka) or from high-school and university students who had had some pedagogical training at Hastings Park. Unlike the War Relocation Authority in the United States which employed more white than Japanese teachers, Caucasians did not teach in BCSC classrooms.[78]

The BCSC expected most teachers would be volunteers, but the prospective teachers refused to work without remuneration. Since most of their pay would come back to the BCSC through savings in the maintenance allowance, the Department of Labour agreed to pay them at a rate comparable to that of road-camp workers so as to encourage them to move east where better-paying jobs were available. Most university graduates and students in the settlements refused to accept teaching assignments because of the low salaries. Thus, most of the approximately 120 teachers at any one time were a transient group of female high-school graduates and students. Many accepted placements in the east; others left to get married. Even in 1944 and 1945 many teachers lacked experience. Like all teachers, they learned on the job. To assist them the BCSC organized summer schools under the direction of instructors from the Vancouver Normal School.[79]

The BCSC readily admitted that English was the weakest subject of its students and that the children suffered from a lack of association with Canadian children of other origins. In order 'to prevent retrogression from Canadian standards' and 'to encourage development along purely Canadian lines,' the BCSC insisted that no Japanese was to be used in its classrooms. In one or two centres where the pro-Japan element was strong, the BCSC quickly prevented certain men from entering the classrooms and from trying to set up parent-teachers' associations to take over the schools. The BCSC worried about the increasing use of Japanese by the children and the existence of clandestine language schools at Tashme and Lemon Creek, but could not enforce regulations against them. Because it feared that restrictions might create 'a persecution complex,' especially among older Japanese who expected to return to Japan with their children, it simply reminded residents that the use of Japanese by the children at home and at play handicapped them in school and, if they remained in Canada, would handicap them in every aspect of life and antagonize other Canadians. The *New Canadian* urged parents to have their children practise English; some enthusiastic teachers issued detentions to pupils who spoke Japanese around the school.[80]

In 1945, as the government prepared to segregate the loyal and the disloyal – that is, those who were willing to resettle east of the Rockies and those who wished repatriation – the schools reflected the tangled loyalties of the communities they served. Teachers reported that many students awaiting repatriation seemed dispirited and developed a 'what's the use' attitude towards their studies. Many teachers were pro-Japan. These the Department of Labour transferred to Tashme, Lemon Creek, and Slocan where the other repatriates would be gathered. Since it was expected children in these settlements would go to Japan, the department decided that if parents requested it, teachers could have more freedom in using Japanese and could teach it during the last hour of the school day provided the schools also followed the regular curriculum. The department refused to allow parents to control the schools but, in the interests of general harmony, curtailed the visits to Tashme of its two Japanese supervisors who were 'extremely Canadian and Christian in outlook.'[81]

Apart from a few small experiments in trades training, the summer schools for teachers were the only post-elementary education programs undertaken by the BCSC. Unlike its American counterpart which offered a full range of studies from grade one through high-school graduation, the BCSC never seems to have considered it had any direct responsibility for high-school studies. When families asked about high school, they were apparently told, 'The Japanese people do not need, nor do they deserve higher education.' In its first published report, the BCSC merely noted that 'High School students desiring to pursue their education further are making their own arrangements.' Most high-school students in the settlements attended private schools operated by several Christian churches.[82]

The BCSC did ascertain that the High School Correspondence Branch of the provincial Department of Education would accept Japanese students at a charge of $65 (a sum that was far beyond the means of most families) for a full year's course. Students, however, could share lesson papers and then individually write provincial government exams. This self-directed instruction was far from ideal. Late in 1942, after Japanese parents asked for help, the Reverend W.R. McWilliams of the United Church suggested using former missionaries as teachers in BCSC schools. J.A. Tyrwhitt, the supervisor of interior housing projects, proposed that the missionary teachers would be most useful in operating kindergartens and supervising high-school students. The BCSC offered space, where available, heat, light, and janitorial services on condition that the schools not admit students eighteen years of age or over since they should be moving east to employment. The BCSC also favoured vocational training that would assist students in getting jobs. The BCSC expected the churches to pay for instruction, books, and supplies from their own funds or from tuition fees.[83]

The BCSC, anticipating competition among the Christian churches, arbitrarily assigned responsibilities for Tashme, Lemon Creek, and New Denver to the United Church; for Greenwood, Sandon, and New Denver, to the Catholic church; and Slocan, to the Anglicans. Except in the 'company towns' of Tashme and Lemon Creek, the BCSC could keep the churches within their assigned spheres of influence only by moral suasion.[84]

Overall, the high schools, no matter which denomination was in charge, were reasonably efficient, and provided students with an opportunity to continue their education, to prepare for advanced studies, and to enjoy constructive diversions including such typical extracurricular activities as dances, sports, clubs, concerts, and year books. Indeed, almost fifty years later, some former students remembered the 'fun' part of their high-school education. The accomplishments of the schools, despite the lack of experience or formal training of many of the teachers who were former missionaries or conscientious objectors, was undoubtedly the result of the cooperation of parents and students. Gwen Suttie, the principal of the United Church high school at New Denver, admitted that 'one reason for the undoubted success of our school was ... the almost complete lack of disciplinary problems. Education had top priority for the Japanese parents and the children themselves really wanted to come to school.' A former student of Tashme High School praised the teachers but noted, 'You've got to hand it to the kids too. They studied hard ... Education is very important.'[85]

For parents, securing an income was even more basic than educating their children. In all settlements, save Sandon, where geography limited opportunities, the BCSC hoped to make as many families as possible self-supporting so as to ease the burden on taxpayers and to help maintain morale. Men who could find work nearby in agriculture, railway maintenance, and lumbering were fortunate, for the BCSC insisted they be paid the going wage. Such outside jobs were scarce and, in spite of itself, the BCSC became a major employer. Initially, it hired many construction workers; later, it employed residents in the varied jobs of every small community, such as teachers, clerks, electricians, and janitors. A few Japanese veterans of the Canadian Expeditionary Force of the First World War acted as security guards. Cutting firewood for the settlements and for sale in the coastal cities employed 700–900 men. A variety of small projects such as dressmaking and manufacturing wooden handicrafts created work for a few. Wages were low. Outdoor workers earned twenty-two to forty cents per hour; professional and inside employees earned $30 to $75 per month, although doctors and dentists were paid more.[86] To encourage the dispersal of single employable men, the BCSC tried to keep its jobs for married men but even then it did not have sufficient jobs for everyone.

Families were expected to live off their earnings or their savings, but the BCSC provided maintenance or direct relief to any indigent person of Japanese race anywhere in Canada at a rate not above that granted locally. In British Columbia this ranged from $18.15 per month for a single person to a maximum of $55 per month for a family of seven or more. Since it provided shelter, fuel, and light to all settlement residents and clothing to indigents, the BCSC reduced the rates proportionally. The BCSC also provided a supplementary allowance to working families whose pay yielded less than the relief scale.[87]

The BCSC, however, had long known that its relief payments were probably inadequate. Both the Spanish consul and the Red Cross representative reported hearing many complaints. The BCSC recognized it had 'to be extremely careful in its treatment of Japanese, for fear of reprisals against our own nationals in the Far East,' but it did not want to alienate domestic opinion by raising rates above those paid to provincial relief recipients or veterans. It also wanted to encourage dispersal to other parts of Canada (see chapter six). When the Spanish consul continued to report complaints about insufficient maintenance, Arthur MacNamara, the associate deputy minister of labour, recommended the immediate appointment of 'some independent authority with national standing in nutritional matters' to make a full survey of the welfare and maintenance situation. If there were no basis for complaints, Canada would have no worries about Japan retaliating; if there were, it would be easier to get Canadian support for change. Thus, within the month, the cabinet approved the appointment of a royal commission under the chairmanship of Dr F.W. Jackson, the deputy minister of health and public welfare in Manitoba, to inquire into welfare and maintenance in the interior housing settlements.[88]

Given that the royal commission was announced in December 1943 just a few weeks after the Vancouver papers had been filled with news and photographs of 210 Canadian repatriates arriving home with stories of hardships in Japanese internment camps, public comment on the appointment of the commission was restrained, although Howard Green, MP, thought the establishment of such a commission was 'strange when one learns of the way Canadians have been treated under Jap control.'[89]

In all the settlements, the royal commissioners invited camp committees to submit complaints. They heard about the failure of maintenance payments to meet the high cost of food; the overcrowding of houses and their unsuitability for the severe climate; the inadequacy of fuel; the delays in supplying clothing and shoes for families on maintenance; and the lack of indoor recreational facilities, especially for children. They also heard that 'the health of the people is adversely affected by inadequate housing and insufficient food and ... has resulted in increased illness and malnutrition of children.' The commissioners, who accepted the premise that the settlements were 'a temporary means of meeting an emergency,' rejected complaints about fuel, clothing, and recreational facilities outright. They commended the general administration of the BCSC; endorsed the policy of dispersal; recommended denying maintenance to both Canadian and Japanese nationals who were single and employable; praised the provision of medical care; and supported the policy of retaining some liquid assets as a rehabilitation fund for settlement residents. To try to develop a 'yardstick' to measure conditions, the commission determined that even 'unsafe and undesirable' apartments in the settlements were equal to quarters formerly occupied by the Japanese in the Powell Street area of Vancouver. The commission concluded that conditions in the interior settlements were 'as a war-time measure, reasonably fair and adequate.' 'Reasonably fair and adequate' expressed something short of perfection. Indeed, the commission recommended continuing the practice of winterizing houses and expanding the outside placement program in order to ease overcrowding. Though it urged the Department of Labour to hire unemployables to prepare them for outside employment, it recommended consideration of a higher wage scale.[90]

The release of the Jackson Commission report in March 1944 drew little public attention. The Vancouver *Sun* and *Province* published a precis of its findings without comment. The *New Canadian* was disappointed the commission had not recommended more, but had not really expected much. Department of Labour officials were generally pleased, though George Collins, commissioner of Japanese Placement, saw pitfalls in implementing the recommendations. He noted, for example, that people did not always take advantage of better housing because of desires to stay with friends or avoid jealousy. He also reported that when the BCSC laid off skilled workers such as electricians and office clerks to encourage them to move east, other Japanese, through intimidation, prevented qualified people from accepting these essential positions. The Department of Labour, however, agreed to increase maintenance rates by 10 per cent unless there were exceptional reasons for not doing so.[91]

The Canadian government, of course, was still concerned about possible repercussions in Japan. Japan had recently cited a matter-of-fact report in *Time* magazine about the settlements to attack the 'scandalous conditions' in the camps. Significantly, both E.L. Maag of the International Red Cross and the Spanish consul approved of the Jackson Report and its implementation.[92]

In the year after the report was issued, the number of people on full or partial maintenance remained at just over 4000, or about 40 per cent of the population of the settlements. While some residents still complained that maintenance payments were too low given the high cost of food, it is noteworthy that in his June 1945 report, Maag noted 'not one single complaint about the food situation.' Rather, he remarked on the 'happy and healthy appearance of the children' and the marked improvement in conditions since his first visit in 1942.[93]

Life in the camps and settlements had often been difficult. The BCSC and the Department of Labour had tried to treat their wartime wards with reasonable fairness and adequacy, but their attitude had often seemed grudging rather than generous. Nevertheless, on leaving New Denver in September 1945, one woman told her daughter, 'All in all ... the three years have not been very hard, when you think of all the poor people who have been killed and hurt, and now the suffering in Japan.'[94] Though they had lasted longer than the BCSC had foreseen, the camps and interior settlements had served their purpose as early stages in the dispersal process for many; for others, they were a refuge from which they could eventually go to Japan.

Six

'No Japanese from the Rockies to the Sea':[1] The Dispersal and Repatriation of the Japanese Canadians

Early in January 1942 the *New Canadian* suggested that although a 'forcible exodus and dispersion' would be 'something too horrible to think up,' a carefully carried out plan might be a good thing for promoting the assimilation of the Japanese with the Occidental community.[2] A month later it observed: 'A new strange period in our history is rapidly approaching every Japanese Canadian along the British Columbia coastline. Dispersion eastward is fast becoming a reality, and we see before us the end, temporary or permanent, of the Japanese community as we have known it. Increasing numbers of young second generation are striking out on their own, leaving the compactly-knit circle of family and friends, going east to seek out a new life. Organized movements of first generation – into private industry and government employment – in other parts of Canada are about to be set in motion.'[3]

Whether they believed that relocation was inevitable and hoped that moving early would offer a better chance for re-establishment, or whether they were as fearful of bombing raids as their Caucasian neighbours,[4] the voluntary evacuees correctly anticipated government policy: Japanese who wished to remain in Canada had to resettle across the country and not return to the coast. As an interim measure, the government set up the interior housing settlements, but its goal was to disperse the Japanese across Canada and relieve what had long been 'a sore point' with British Columbia.[5] The *New Canadian* also foretold a common pattern: many *Nisei* were willing to venture east; frequently their parents were not. The reluctance of many Japanese Canadians to disperse ultimately led the Canadian government to offer them a dramatic alternative – 'voluntary repatriation' to Japan.

Because of the effectiveness of British Columbia's past propaganda about the Yellow Peril and the suspicions of all Japanese aroused by Pearl Harbor, the BCSC found 'the process of Evacuation was considerably hampered by protests from widely scattered parts of the Dominion.'[6] Shortly before the general evacuation policy was announced, Hugh Keenleyside told a United Church clergyman who wanted to place Japanese on Ontario farms that he favoured 'anything that can be done to scatter the Japanese population in Canada' but feared that 'often the men who are most in favour of scattering in theory are opposed to it in practise particularly when it takes the only sensible form, that of finding a job suitable for the man concerned.'[7] Work with the Japanese eventually brought church members and humanitarians east of the Rockies into direct contact with Japanese people for the first time and made new friends for both, but it was a slow process.

During the weeks of uncertainty after Pearl Harbor, a number of Japanese voluntarily moved to the Okanagan Valley of British Columbia and the Raymond district of southern Alberta where Japanese friends and relatives, well established in agriculture, could offer employment and shelter. Their experience anticipated the conflict between traditional hostility to the Japanese and the needs of local agriculturalists for a labour supply that many Japanese encountered later in other parts of Canada.

The approximately 750 Japanese who had been developing farms and orchards in the northern Okanagan Valley, particularly around Kelowna and Vernon since the late 1910s, were generally well accepted and integrated into the agricultural economy through such means as membership in cooperative marketing agencies.[8] Soon after Pearl Harbor, local Boards of Trade and Fruit Growers' Associations announced they would welcome coastal Japanese, under proper supervision, to work on road construction and in orchards.[9] By the end of February, an influx of approximately 2000 Japanese created considerable hostility since many wanted to purchase land and some, one municipal official complained, were arriving in new automobiles 'and acting in a very truculent manner.' The real problem, claimed the Kelowna *Courier*, was that 'Five thousand Jap settlers in the Okanagan Valley will be a threat to our lives and property now but the real menace is to our economic security after the war.' Although the Okanagan correspondent of the *New Canadian* reported that Japanese Canadians there were 'not suffering from the added racial feeling because of the war,' the mayor of Kelowna, W.A.C. Bennett, MLA, and representatives of various agricultural organizations warned that 'something drastic' would happen if 'the present alarming uncontrolled infiltration of Japanese from [the] coast' did not stop. When Ottawa announced that all Japanese would be moved inland, several Okanagan centres held mass protest meetings and a sign appeared on a Kelowna roadside: 'Coast Japs – You Are Not Wanted – Get Out.'[10]

A somewhat similar situation developed in the sugar-beet growing areas of southern Alberta. At Raymond, several hundred Japanese had lived in harmony with the rest of the community for twenty-five or more years. By mid-February 1942, a few coastal Japanese had moved into the district and the Alberta Sugar Beet Growers considered hiring Japanese labour, though not all its members liked the idea. Rumours that the federal government would send additional Japanese to southern Alberta and to the beet-growing districts of Manitoba led some prairie cities to demand that no Japanese be moved into their vicinities except under supervision and in non-competitive work.[11]

The reaction to the voluntary evacuees in the Okanagan and in Alberta presaged problems the BCSC would experience in placing all Japanese. Farmers were usually glad to have a reliable labour supply; city residents tended to be hostile to the newcomers. In Kelowna, for example, in the spring of 1943 a vigilante committee drove out a Japanese family who had stopped temporarily while waiting for accommodation to be prepared on a nearby orchard.[12] Gradually, town dwellers recognized the importance of Japanese labour and accepted them. Moreover, although the Japanese were uncertain about the duration of their stay, many became permanent settlers.

The initial hostility of Okanagan residents to receiving evacuees had helped convince the BCSC to establish the interior housing settlements; the interest of Alberta beet growers in Japanese labour led it to consider similar placements in Manitoba and Ontario. The governments of Alberta and Manitoba accepted the Japanese on the condition that the federal government assumed all financial responsibilities, including costs of welfare and education, provided supervision to prevent sabotage, and, in the case of Alberta, agreed to remove the Japanese after the war. Some prairie cities, notably Calgary, Medicine Hat, and Lethbridge, refused to accept evacuees; Edmonton reluctantly admitted a few who were joining relatives; but Winnipeg was very cooperative in accepting families. BCSC officials attributed the problem in southern Alberta to the independence of the Japanese and their relatively large numbers in a small area. In Manitoba, where the Japanese were less numerous and their work opportunities more diverse, they met less hostility and developed a greater sense of permanence.[13]

Many evacuee families were so eager to go to the beet fields where they could stay together that they regrouped themselves to meet the requirement that families include at least 80 per cent workers and number approximately six in order to fit the available housing. Disappointment awaited many. As the winter of 1942–3 approached, some families asked to go to the interior housing projects because of inadequate housing, insufficient earnings to keep them through the winter, or dissatisfaction with the farms to which the Beet Growers Association had assigned them. When the BCSC ascertained that houses were being winterized and that satisfied farmers would provide food for the winter, it sent only the few large families or those who had been unsatisfactory workers to the housing settlements. During the winter the BCSC had to provide maintenance or welfare for many beet workers, but it hoped that, with more favourable weather, the now experienced workers would earn considerably more and be less likely to require assistance in the future. The BCSC also encouraged several hundred men to leave the farms to take up wintertime forestry work and assisted young women to obtain domestic work in nearby cities. Skilled tradesmen had little problem finding additional employment to supplement family earnings.[14]

So many younger people seemed keen to move out of agricultural work into the cities that by early 1943 the Department of Labour, which had taken over the work of the BCSC, expected to have openings for additional families from the housing settlements. By that time, however, the beet fields had lost their attractiveness. In Alberta, the federal government's promise to remove the Japanese after the war meant beet work was probably only a temporary placement. Moreover, many beet workers complained that they lacked freedom to move about freely and that they were unable to earn enough to support themselves.[15] Their employers, however, were generally pleased with the 3000 Japanese Canadians working in beet production in Alberta and the 1000 toiling in Manitoba. When the growers persuaded the Department of Labour to 'freeze' the Japanese in their jobs as essential agricultural workers, the Japanese bargained for higher wages but remained, in the words of sociologist Forrest E. LaViolette, 'wards of the federal government and serfs of the soil' who were exploited by some farmers.[16]

Ontario's government initially had reservations about receiving Japanese. Then, in mid-March 1942, Premier Mitchell Hepburn, who himself employed some Japanese in his onion farm, announced his province would take 2000 Japanese nationals as road builders in northern Ontario. Late in 1942, some of the younger men returned at their own expense to the Revelstoke-Sicamous road project in British Columbia rather than spend the winter in northern Ontario. Approximately 350 men were also placed in Ontario beet fields but they too were disappointed because earnings were less than expected and Ontario rural communities were less accepting than their prairie counterparts.[17]

While agricultural placements, like road and bush work, provided some gainful employment, at the end of 1942 over half the evacuees still resided in the interior housing settlements. The BCSC had early decided that the permanent solution to Canada's Japanese problem was to disperse them in 'comparatively small groups throughout the country.' When the government transferred the responsibilities of the BCSC directly to the Department of Labour early in 1943, George Collins became the commissioner of Japanese placement. His formal title clearly indicated the goal of finding Japanese gainful employment throughout the country where they could 'be assimilated into community life in the same manner as the Chinese.' That obviously did not imply complete assimilation into Canadian society, but it did mean economic and legal integration and the scattering of the Japanese throughout Canada.[18]

To achieve its ends, the Department of Labour established placement offices in Nelson, Lethbridge, Winnipeg, Fort William, Toronto, and Montreal. These offices worked closely with the National Selective Service, a wartime agency controlling virtually all employment in Canada, to find suitable jobs. Placement officers advised employers of the need to provide equal wages and treatment for Japanese, checked to prevent exploitation, sought to provide a favourable atmosphere for Japanese in eastern communities, and worked to 'discourage absenteeism and excessive job-changing [among the Japanese] ... in order to build up their reputations as well as increase production.' The *New Canadian* agreed that *Nisei* must not allow themselves to be perceived as cheap labour or as 'six-week Japs' who did not stay on the job long enough to become useful to their employers. It instructed its readers that none of their 'obligations to our group [are] as clear and as concrete as they are in the records of our relationship with new employers' since each *Nisei* 'must consider himself as an ambassador of good will to thousands of Ontario citizens who have never met anyone of Japanese origin.'[19]

During 1943, the Department of Labour used 'every legitimate means of persuasion and propaganda' to encourage all housing settlement residents to move east. Because the Department of External Affairs had warned against forcing anyone to move lest Japan retaliate against the 140,000 British subjects in her hands and because it did not want to intern any more men than were 'absolutely necessary,' the Department of Labour generally did no

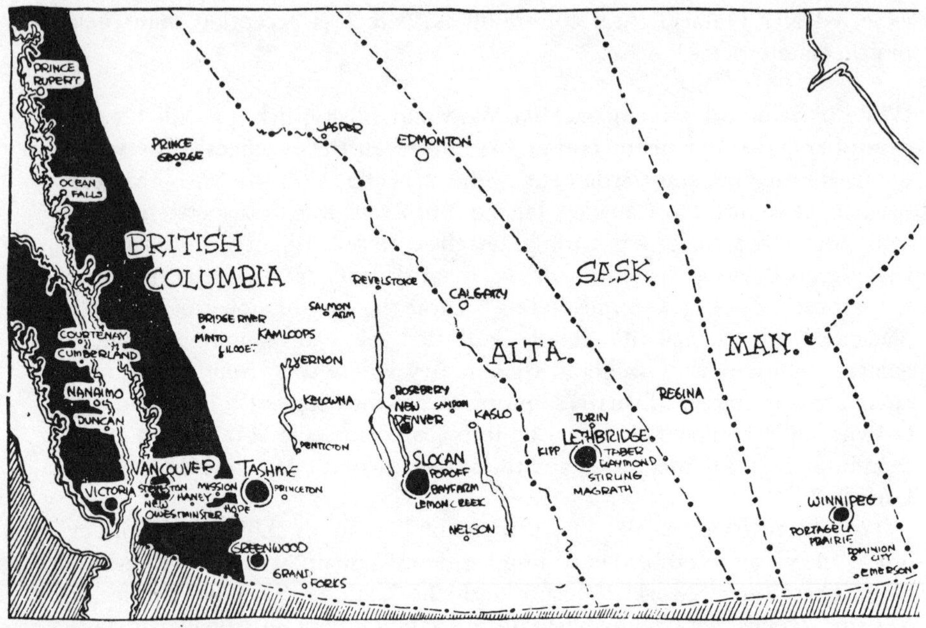

more than deny relief or employment in its projects to men who refused outside placements.[20] Despite its exasperation with able-bodied men without dependents who refused the opportunities for agricultural work in Ontario, it agreed that individual Japanese must work out their situations 'with what assistance we can render in the way of location and type of industry offered.'[21]

Thus, the Department of Labour tried to entice residents eastward by offering jobs, establishing employment registration bureaus in each settlement, paying a more generous travel allowance than that given Canadian soldiers, and publishing testimonials from satisfied eastern residents and job advertisements in the *New Canadian.* Editorially, this newspaper observed that dispersal offered 'the very real hope of a new and fresh start and the building of a firm and happier future than any we may even remotely hope for in this province.' Indeed, the department so depended on the *New Canadian* as a 'propaganda medium' that it sent Thomas Shoyama, its editor and publisher, to visit Ontario to gain first-hand information, and dispatched the Japanese-language editor, Takaichi Umezuki, on a similar mission to

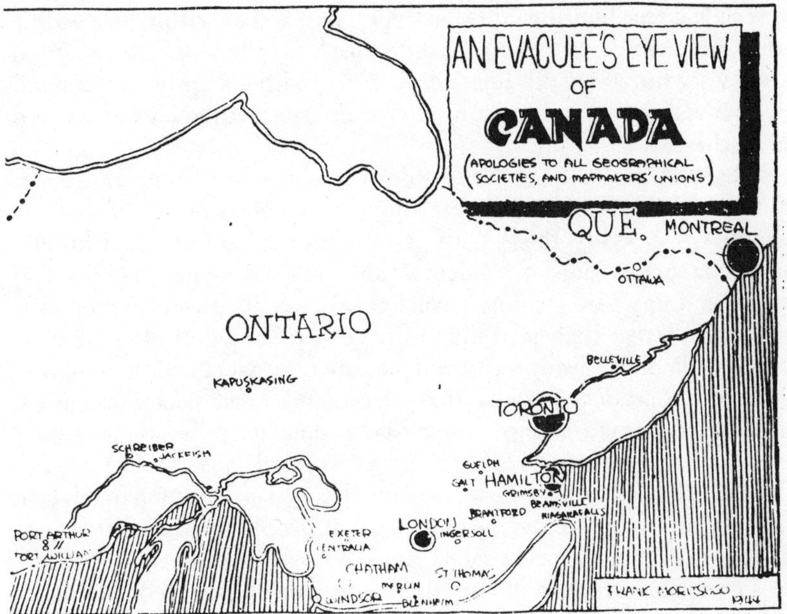

The New Canadian, Kaslo, BC, Christmas 1944

Alberta and Manitoba. Shoyama reported the advantages of eastern resettlement, but complained that the government had not officially stated that it would be permanent. In the words of the *New Canadian*, the relocation program had 'encountered a passive resistance' which 'slowed the eastward flow to a mere trickle compared with what had been expected and with what is certainly desirable.'[22]

Residents had good reasons for not wanting to leave the housing centres. Those who had recently left road camps had some money and were anxious to spend time with friends and relatives. Other feared that if conditions in the east, especially in the Ontario beet fields, were as unsatisfactory as some unhappy workers described them, they might find themselves in difficult situations without funds or permission to return to British Columbia. They also wondered what would happen when postwar demobilization reduced the demand for their labour. By 1944 the *New Canadian* could ease such concerns by referring to federal social security plans, including family allowances and house-building programs and the long-term nature of agricultural work. It also suggested that young couples employed in domestic work in the east received free housing and such high salaries that within a year they could save sufficient money to establish themselves in business. It chastised young fellows who were still 'hogtied' to their mother's apron strings and reported that visitors from the east found the housing settlements 'dead' and referred to the east as 'home.'[23]

Nevertheless, Canada east of the Rockies remained a kind of foreign country to which the young and brave might move but whose cold winters made families, especially those with small children, 'uneasy and afraid.' And, of course, many interior residents, especially older ones, had been so discouraged and upset by seemingly constant changes in government policy that the *New Canadian* suggested they were close 'to being "Indian reservation" material.' While praising improved placement services and travel allowances, the *New Canadian* warned that placement 'must become genuine "resettlement of human beings" ' and that people must be assured they would not have to seek a new refuge once the war ended. As an *Issei* veteran of the Canadian Expeditionary Force explained to a friend, 'having to relocate again is the same worry returning anew.' Such people were comforted by the security of the housing settlements and fearful of 'an unfriendly society' outside. The superintendent of the Slocan settlement reported that older Japanese were fixing up their houses and gardens since 'as long as they can eat and sleep in Slocan they are satisfied to stay here rather than leave for unknown conditions.'[24]

Meanwhile, the *New Canadian* explained somewhat obliquely that while 'no criticism could be made of Labour Department officials, the same could not be said of their understanding of human nature.' A good example concerned the efforts of Mrs C.V. Booth of the Vancouver office of the Japanese Division. Like other officials who complained of 'Japanese psychology' and who tried to 'encourage the old people to permit the young people to leave the Province,' she could not understand why parents so feared letting their young adult daughters go east. To counter such worries she proposed that she and some welfare workers would personally accompany a group of young women to the east and see them placed as domestic servants in suitable homes. After her *Nisei* confidante, Hideko Hyodo, the supervisor of schools, advised that Japanese families believed 'the responsibility for their daughters is not terminated until the time of their marriage,' Mrs Booth reminded parents that if they hoped for 'a happy and normal marriage' for their daughters they should 'remember that the young men who have the will and spirit to establish homes, will be setting up their homes, not in relocation centres but in Eastern Canada.' Although Mrs Booth hoped to take a 'large group' east, only thirty-five joined her. Five more moved late in the summer but, after concluding that 'the Japanese do not respond to mass persuasion,' Mrs Booth abandoned attempts for a large-scale movement of potential domestic servants and proposed to work with individuals.[25]

Mrs Booth learned from experience. While she did resort to 'making life not quite so pleasant' in the housing settlements to encourage single women to leave, she realized she would have to 'sell' eastern resettlement by advertising educational opportunities, offering better placements, such as work as student nurses and stenographers for young women, removing irritating travel restrictions, reuniting families, and providing temporary accommodation in small hostels in Toronto and Montreal. She also called for greater cooperation with the YWCA and church groups to facilitate the absorption of small numbers of Japanese into community life in order to avoid the congregation of Japanese 'in self-contained communities' as in British Columbia and thus reproducing a major political problem. In fact, Mrs Booth's work was eased considerably by the Co-operative Committee on Japanese Canadians which the YWCA and the women's missionary societies of four major Protestant denominations formed to assist young Japanese women in securing placements and housing in Ontario cities.[26]

While the Department of Labour used gentle suasion on young women, in November 1943 it decided that all single males between the ages of eighteen and fifty-five who were Canadian citizens by birth or naturalization would henceforth be governed by the National Selective Service Regulations which controlled the employment of all Canadians. Many single men immediately volunteered in order to have some say in the kind of job they might accept and its location. Initially, they could not accept jobs in British Columbia but, when interior lumber operators protested the loss of their labour supply, the department announced that Canadian citizens could take jobs in logging camps and other essential industries and, if they had such jobs, they would not be ordered east. In the meantime, some *Nisei* petitioned the prime minister complaining that they were being treated less favourably than Japanese nationals who were not subject to selective service and requesting deferment of the regulations until their status as citizens was clarified. Though Howard T. Pammett of the Department of Labour suggested that the restoration of certain citizenship rights, as had been done in the United States, would encourage cooperation, his superior, Arthur MacNamara, rejected the idea lest it arouse the 'Jap Haters' in the House of Commons.[27]

The *New Canadian* noted other ironies. First, the selective service program would mean that the most 'capable and productive element' of Japanese society would be moved east and would leave the 'least desirable elements' in British Columbia. Second, Japanese nationals could stay put if they wished and could appeal any grievances to the protecting power or the Red Cross. In suggesting that imposing responsibility without granting any privileges in return would cause resentment and interfere with dispersal, the *New Canadian* hinted that the occasion offered an opportunity to raise the question of the rights of Japanese Canadians as citizens. As time passed, the newspaper used other incidents, such as the refusal of Japanese Canadians in Toronto to accept a gift parcel from the Japanese Red Cross, to press for full citizenship rights.[28] Similarly, along with the Japanese Canadian Committee for Democracy (JCCD) in Toronto, it revived the campaign to allow *Nisei* to enlist in the Canadian army. Military service seemed the only route to enfranchisement. In the spring of 1944, Bill 135, the War Services Election Bill, threatened to disfranchise all Japanese in Canada, including those who had lived and voted in provinces other than British Columbia before the war, unless they had a record of service in the Canadian army.[29]

Eastward movement continued slowly but in the spring of 1944 a new pattern emerged; family groups began to move, chiefly to farms in southern Ontario. That province also offered work in trade and manufacturing and, for two *Nisei,* employment as teachers, a profession which had been almost completely closed to them in British Columbia. Jobs were plentiful and varied in Ontario since, as the *New Canadian* believed, 'the conservative nature of the people meant their strong beliefs in Christian and democratic traditions tempered racial hostility.'[30]

Yet not all Ontarians were so inclined. In the spring of 1942 the mayor of Toronto had declared that Japanese should not be allowed to enter his city because of its many war industries. Some communities such as Ottawa and the affluent Toronto suburb of Forest Hill Village actually refused to admit Japanese, even though there was a demand for Japanese female domestics. In late 1943, Toronto, which then had a Japanese population of about 700, refused to accept any more Japanese except for students and 'compassionate cases' such as family reunions.

The experiences of individual Japanese in Toronto varied. One young *Nisei* told a friend that 'people out here are so broad-minded and carefree. It's because we are treated just like any other white people.' However, another complained that 'you are more or less free to go around doing things but otherwise you are under a mental strain all the time. Whether you're on the street car or anywhere there are bound to be people in [the] crowd calling you down. You're a Jap and you're reminded every once in a while about it.' Such hostility was particularly conspicuous in smaller communities where local jealousies caused unfortunate incidents. At Ingersoll, in southwestern Ontario, a 'riot' occurred when a mob of about 200 young men, apparently jealous of Japanese boys going out with white girls, attempted to break into a residence occupied by *Nisei.* The police dispersed the mob before anything happened, detained the leaders, and advised the *Nisei* to stay off the streets at night for a while as a precaution.[31]

In Montreal, then Canada's largest city, the *Nisei* found a much friendlier reception. An early arrival told the *New Canadian* in October 1943 that it was easy to find jobs although housing, especially for families, was scarce and expensive. By early 1944 there were 240 ex-British Columbia Japanese in Montreal, of whom 178 were gainfully employed. The rest were students, housewives, and children. Though domestic service and cooking were the most common occupations, the evacuees had a variety of jobs and some established their own businesses.[32]

Resettlement in Montreal was eased by the Nisei Sponsoring Committee, a pioneering organization of church and social workers which assisted the Department of Labour in finding jobs and homes for newcomers, introducing them to community activities, and providing care in time of illness or other difficulties. According to Mrs Booth, Mrs P.S.C. Powles, an ex-missionary, had 'done more to re-establish the Nisei in Montreal than any other agency could possibly have done.' Though some young people resented Mrs Powles's 'solicitude,' Mrs Booth took her to the housing centres 'to inspire confidence in the older generation.' Together, they showed films on eastern Canada. By the summer of 1944 Montreal had become the most important single destination for relocatees, and the Franciscan Mission opened a hostel for Japanese families and individuals. Although Premier Maurice Duplessis had declared that Quebec would not take Japanese after the war, the Japanese found 'much less prejudice' in Montreal 'than in many English-speaking parts of the country.' In fact, the Montreal *Nisei* were so rapidly 'being assimilated into the Canadian stream of society' that they had no organization of their own and some young men married French-Canadian women and joined the Roman Catholic church. However, the Japanese population of Montreal at the end of 1945 was only 716.[33]

During the early months of 1946 the population rose sufficiently to permit the Japanese Standing Committee in Montreal to publish a monthly *Montreal News Bulletin* which, in a June 1946 Japanese-language item, warned readers not to visit friends who were being temporarily housed in the Farnham Hostel lest they 'give other residents in the area a bad impression that might cause the closing of the hostel.'[34] Whether growing numbers cooled the reception or whether the *Bulletin* was simply being prudent lest an apparent concentration of Japanese arouse antagonisms is not clear. In any case, the presence of so few Japanese in Montreal before 1946 reveals the limited initial effects of the dispersal program; the later increase indicates a dramatic change.

The availability of employment in British Columbia, the old problem of fear of the unknown, the reluctance of families to separate, even temporarily, and the false sense of security of the housing settlements still deterred dispersal, as did increasing uncertainty about postwar employment, resentment over attempts to deny the franchise to relocated Japanese, and the forced sale of their property at the coast.

A few days before issuing the general evacuation order, the federal government had forbidden persons of Japanese origin from buying or leasing land anywhere in Canada.[35] This policy may have been inspired by 'The White Farmers' who feared competition from displaced fishermen. In January 1942, several Fraser Valley municipalities sought provincial legislation to bar Japanese from purchasing or renting additional farm land or from sharecropping.[36] More likely Ottawa believed that evacuees would be more readily accepted if they could not become permanent residents. In fact, the policy discouraged dispersal and late in 1943 it was relaxed slightly to allow the leasing of property for productive or business purposes.[37] The basic policy, however, remained; Japanese Canadians could reasonably observe 'that the war situation is being exploited by other vested interests to rid themselves of legitimate competition.'[38]

Far more demoralizing for evacuees was order-in-council PC 469, issued in January 1943, which authorized the custodian of enemy property to liquidate the property and chattels they left behind. According to a *Nisei* historian, the sale of their property 'revealed the government's true intention of dispersing the "undesirables" to all sections of Canada' and effectively destroyed 'any hope of a large-scale return of the dispossessed to the West Coast ... With one foul stroke, the government doomed the restoration to their rightful owners the Fraser Valley farms, so painfully brought into production, or the businesses so patiently nurtured.'[39] As a Tashme resident told a friend, 'If all the things that I had left at Campbell River had been sold at normal prices I might have been in a mood to go to the east as I would then have had enough for the family's needs but they were all sold for a mere song and what we got would not be enough for anything.'[40]

Many British Columbians had favoured selling Japanese property to insure that the evacuees would never return. For months there had been calls for the sale of 'all Japanese held lands' and the dispatch of 'all Japanese whether naturalized or not' to Japan.[41] When the government announced the liquidation policy, the Vancouver *Sun* welcomed the news 'that no mass return of

Japanese after the war to the area is contemplated.' A Vancouver alderman described the policy as 'another step in getting the Japs out of our country.'[42]

Ian Mackenzie, like many other British Columbians, saw liquidating property as a means of insuring that the Japanese Canadians would never return to the coast. The decision to liquidate property also answered immediate problems, the inability of the Custodian's Office to protect the property entrusted to its care and the need to maintain production on Fraser Valley farms. A precedent had been set with the disposal of fishing vessels. In order to make the boats available for the 1942 season, the federal government set up the Japanese Fishing Vessels Disposal Committee under the chairmanship of Mr Justice Sidney Smith. The committee encouraged boat owners to negotiate directly with prospective purchasers but, when some fishermen sought 'excessive' prices for their craft, it established a 'Suggested Negotiating Price' and eventually resorted to 'Forced Sales.' Overall, however, average sale prices were 21.7 per cent above appraised values but 22.5 per cent below the owners' initial asking prices. The committee, however, could not sell 181 older and poor-quality vessels, many of which had further deteriorated while in custody, until Nelson Bros. Ltd, a fish-packing and -canning firm, bought a number of them at prices below appraised values. Understandably, many owners were dissatisfied. Indeed, in his postwar investigation of claims, Mr Justice Henry Bird admitted that the vessels had suffered 'abnormal depreciation' after delivery to the navy because of exposure to the elements and inadequate care. Bird's jurisdiction, however, did not extend to such depreciation.[43]

Problems of caring for other assets of Japanese Canadians inspired the custodian to recommend their sale. Immediately after Pearl Harbor his only concerns had been taking control of the property of internees, completing their business dealings, liquidating their assets through public tender, and trying to avoid antagonizing either public opinion or the internees. Once Ottawa decided to move all Japanese from the coast, the custodian's chief representative in Vancouver prepared 'to protect' their property other than fishing vessels and financial securities and 'then investigate control and dispose of same if this is considered advisable.' Initially, the custodian only acted on request from Japanese-Canadian property owners, but an order-in-council soon empowered him to take full control of Japanese-Canadian property within the defence zone to prevent its owners from selling it and leaving the province without paying their legitimate debts, and to prevent white persons from buying it at sacrifice prices. The custodian also suspected that Japanese might hide the proceeds of property sales from the BCSC, which expected them to draw on their capital to assist in meeting living costs.

Despite warnings of the Department of External Affairs that the custodian's enthusiasm for taking control of property might put British subjects in a worse position vis-à-vis their property and might concede to Japan 'the right to strip our missionaries of their clothing, their bibles and their rosaries,' the Custodian's Office paid little attention.[44]

The custodian, E.H. Coleman, had claimed that the Japanese Canadians were pleased that the government would care for their property and save them from exploitation by speculators. In fact, within weeks the Japanese Canadian Citizens Council (JCCC) observed that the Custodian's Office was quite unsure of procedures and, together with the Naturalized Japanese Citizens Committee, complained that the evacuation policy and the abandonment of homes, businesses, and boats imposed on them 'losses of a discriminatory nature beyond the ordinary burden of war common to all Canadians.' They sought assurances that the government would provide 'for the assessment and payment of such loss at an early date after the war is ended.'[45] Such assurances were not forthcoming.

Indeed, an internal report on the Custodian's Office in Vancouver admitted that a lack of cooperation among various government departments and agencies and the reluctance of most evacuees to register their property meant the work was not being done 'as efficiently' as possible. Moreover, the auditor commented, the storage of personal property was 'an enormous problem' with costs 'out of proportion' to its real value. Yet, he conceded the custodian had a 'duty to take all reasonable steps to ensure protection.'[46]

In an attempt to keep Fraser Valley farms in operation, the custodian encouraged berry growers and poultry farmers to make their own arrangements to lease their farms to white operators for the 1942 season. To protect them against 'local pressure to sell or lease at sacrifice prices,' all arrangements had to be approved by the Soldiers' Settlement Board whose land appraisers had already begun a survey and approximate valuation of the lands. These *ad hoc* arrangements were not satisfactory. The director of soldiers' settlement, who was not keen to acquire the land, recommended it was 'simply justice and equity to the owners' to sell the lands as quickly as possible on the basis of the recent appraisal and at the best terms possible. Although inclement weather played a role, the inexperience of the new farmers, their lack of long-term commitment to the farms, and a shortage of labour led to what the *New Canadian* regretfully described as the almost complete destruction of the Fraser Valley strawberry industry.[47]

Meanwhile, urban property also deteriorated. The custodian had temporarily allowed evacuees to make their own arrangements with lawyers, real estate agents, and others to look after their property. Of 630 properties in

Vancouver in the custodian's care in January 1943, only fifty were vacant and they were in such poor condition that, despite an acute housing shortage, city building, electrical, and health inspectors would not allow them to be occupied without extensive repairs. The custodian also feared that tenants in the Powell Street area would move as soon as better accommodation became available. In most cases, the costs of repairs and taxes were greater than the possible rent. In cases where property could earn sufficient to pay for its upkeep, the custodian decided 'it would be extremely difficult to sell a house, a store or a farm to a white man at any reasonable figure if he had no assurance that the property next door was being sold and the Japanese owners would not ultimately return and be his neighbour.'[48]

Caring for personal property such as household effects and fishing nets was particularly difficult because they had been hurriedly stored in a variety of insecure places. Thieves often ransacked the boxes and, though they stole little, they so mixed up property that it was impossible to identify its owners.[49] By 1943 it was clear that the custodian could not properly care for Japanese real estate or personal property, and Ottawa decided to sell it.

To advise on the sales of real estate, the government set up separate local committees to deal with property in greater Vancouver and with agricultural land in the Fraser Valley. Both committees were chaired by a judge and both included a single representative of the Japanese Canadians. After concurring in the recommendations of their respective committees that the property should be liquidated, both Japanese Canadians resigned their appointments. Yasutaro Yamaga of the agricultural land committee quit in disgust when the other members of the committee consistently ignored his recommendations and assigned properties a lower value than he judged appropriate.[50] Neither Yamaga nor Kishizo Kimura of the urban property committee was replaced.

In Greater Vancouver, the committee hired appraisers to establish current market values. Often it checked the appraisals itself. Sales began in July 1943 and carried on through 1945. All told, 426 properties, both commercial and residential, were sold for $936,190, which was 10 per cent more than their appraised value but 14 per cent less than their assessed value. An additional $92,293.70 worth of household goods and other belongings were sold at auction. In the Fraser Valley, partly because of geographic scattering, the committee played a less active role. There, by the end of 1946, 741 properties had been sold, chiefly to the government itself for use under the Veteran's Land Act.[51]

Once the property was sold, the custodian took charge of the proceeds. He deducted an amount to cover selling costs and, if the owner were self-supporting and not living in the interior housing settlements, it was sent to him. Residents of the housing settlements received their money in small instalments only sufficient to meet immediate living costs lest they risk all their capital in the high-stakes gambling games which were a problem in the settlements or otherwise squander it and hence have to apply for maintenance. Moreover, the Department of Labour wanted them to keep as much capital as possible for future resettlement.[52]

Some officials in the Department of External Affairs privately questioned the legality of forced liquidation but the government rejected their recommendation that no property be sold without the owner's consent unless the sale was clearly in the owner's interest. External Affairs officials also noted that unlike the United States, Canada made no distinction between property owned by her own nationals and by enemy aliens, but no one pursued the point.[53]

Though shocked and disappointed, property owners, who had understood the government had taken control of their property as 'a protective measure only,' resorted to the courts, not to strikes and sabotage, to protest. In testing the legality of 'forced liquidation,' we are, declared the *New Canadian*, 'fighting a front-line battle to uphold the principles basic to democratic tradition.' Thomas Shoyama, its editor, ascertained from Vancouver lawyers that a suit respecting the property of *Niseis* and naturalized persons had a 'good chance' of success and that one respecting Japanese nationals had a 'fair chance.' Many property owners, but not all, raised funds to launch a legal battle and helped prepare test cases for a naturalized Canadian, a Canadian-born citizen, and two Japanese nationals. The *New Canadian* chastised those who didn't contribute for taking advantage of others or for being 'nationalist-minded' and depending on Japan, through the protecting power, to represent their interests. The case was not heard in the Exchequer Court until May 1944, a delay which increased the suspicions of the *New Canadian* that 'Justice may be conveniently blinded to suit the purpose of the Government.' Once in court the case became bogged down in technicalities until 1947, when Mr Justice Thorson ruled it was outside the jurisdiction of his court.[54]

Those who depended on the protecting power fared no better. As early as the spring of 1942, Japan had inquired about property. Once the liquidation decision was announced, the Spanish consul reported that the liquidation order had 'caused much confusion in the minds of Japanese property owners and ... I am receiving almost every day protests from them.' Worried Department of External Affairs officials, fearing that compulsory liquidation would give Japan an excuse to liquidate the much more valuable Canadian property such as missions and the assets of Canadian insurance companies under its control, merely replied that liquidating property was the only way to protect owners. Most owners refused to recognize the wisdom of this. In response to a second protest, the Canadian government denied any 'persecution or discrimination against Japanese residents as compared with nationals of other Axis Powers.'[55]

Once the war ended, the Japanese Canadians complained that the custodian had not protected their property and had sold it at 'ridiculously low prices.' They sought compensation to help them begin their new lives east of the Rockies or in Japan. They had the support of Canadian friends, especially in the churches, who had been protesting the liquidation of property against its owners' wills since 1943. In the fall of 1946, the Japanese Canadian Committee for Democracy (JCCD) cooperated with the Co-operative Committee for Japanese Canadians, a Toronto-based umbrella group 'composed of representatives of returned Canadian missionaries and other persons concerned with safeguarding the maximum human rights and the freedom of loyal persons of Japanese descent during the time of war,' to survey property losses and lobby for the establishment of a claims commission and the payment of compensation. In response to this campaign, which was related to the protest against repatriation and to complaints in the press about the 'shocking manner' in which property was handled, the government in July 1947 appointed Mr Justice Henry Bird to investigate the 'claims of persons of the Japanese race who are resident in Canada' that the custodian disposed of real and personal property at less than fair market value and that personal property in his care was lost, stolen, or destroyed. The Co-operative Committee was so disappointed that Bird's mandate did not cover 'all tangible property losses arising out of the evacuation,' including losses caused by forced sales, that it briefly considered boycotting the commission. However, it decided to participate and, in association with the Japanese Canadian Citizens Association, collected, filed, and defended claims for 1300 individuals. It reluctantly accepted Bird's suggestion that in order to save time the claims must be dealt with in categories rather than individually; later, some members of the national executive of the Co-operative Committee resigned because of disagreements over this procedure.[56]

When Mr Justice Bird made his report in 1950, he agreed that in the early months of the evacuation there had been 'regrettable losses' of chattels because of inefficiencies in the Custodian's Office and that, in rural areas, property had been sold at less than market value. He recommended an 80 per cent increase in the payment to those whose property had been sold for use under the Veteran's Land Act; upward revisions of 12 to 30 per cent for fish nets, motor vehicles, and personal property; and some compensation for goods that disappeared while in the hands of the custodian. As far as the Greater Vancouver properties were concerned, he found that the custodian had sold them at fair market value and merely recommended that vendors be reimbursed for selling costs.[57]

The Co-operative Committee was disappointed, especially with regard to the Greater Vancouver properties, but realized that refusing to accept the commission's recommendations would cause further delay and additional expense and was unlikely to yield a larger award. As historian Toyo Takata explained, 'the *Issei* were too old to pursue the matter, the *Nisei* too engrossed in their current livelihood, and the issue simply faded.' It did, but not forever. In the 1980s, as a new generation matured and as Japanese Americans renewed their demands for compensation, the Japanese Canadians resumed their fight for redress. The Canadian government offered $12 million as a community fund; the National Association of Japanese Canadians sought compensation of $25,000 for each of the approximately 14,000 surviving evacuees. In the fall of 1988, the dispute was settled. The Canadian government offered $21,000 to affected individuals who were still living, the restoration of Canadian citizenship to those who had lost it, and a pardon for any person of Japanese ancestry convicted under the War Measures Act or related legislation.[58]

Discontent with property arrangements, uncertainty about their futures in eastern Canada, and the false security of life in the interior housing settlements helped thwart Canada's efforts to disperse its Japanese population across the country. Officials in Ottawa realized that if the restrictions on their activities east of the Rockies were eased, loyal Japanese Canadians might be more willing to move there. Moreover, if the federal government could demonstrate the loyalty of the Japanese Canadians, the other provinces might be more willing to accept them. Thus, in mid-March 1944 R.G. Robertson of the Department of External Affairs resurrected an earlier proposal to separate the loyal from the disloyal and to deport the latter, even though they might be Canadian-born. Robertson knew public opinion polls had revealed that Canadians favoured the deportation of Japanese nationals but would allow the Canadian-born or naturalized Canadians to remain.[59] In his memorandum for the prime minister, Robertson emphasized the need to 'remove as far as possible the aspects of racial discrimination' affecting British subjects and Canadian nationals who were personally 'guilty of no offense other than that of having Japanese ancestry.' He predicted that once all 'doubtful' cases had been carefully examined and provision made to deport the disloyal, the provinces would cooperate with the dispersal policy. The Cabinet War Committee accepted the principle, subject to clarification, about a proposed loyalty commission or tribunal which would judge doubtful cases.[60]

The Department of National Defence had already set out to ascertain the loyalties of those *Nisei* who had once indicated an interest in joining the army. When *Nisei* learned that if they were sent overseas they might not be allowed to return to Canada, some withdrew their offers to serve. Other *Nisei* were deterred by bitterness over the government's treatment of them, concerns about their dislocated families, and fears of racism in the army. Nevertheless, when the government decided in January 1945 to enlist *Nisei* as translators and interpreters to assist British forces in the Asian theatre, slightly more than one hundred volunteered to serve. Their enlistment, though not secret, was not publicized until the war was over and gave them few privileges of citizenship.[61]

In the meantime, nothing was done about determining the loyalty of the majority of the Japanese-Canadian population. Throughout 1944 and early 1945, policy often seemed vague. When British Columbia members of parliament asked about future plans, Labour Minister Humphrey Mitchell admitted that no one knew what the policy would be; the acting prime minister, J.L. Ralston, merely reminded Parliament that there were 'Canadians in Japanese hands.' At least one Labour Department official was frustrated at having to work 'in the dark' with government departments whose only consistent theme seemed to be that 'a policy of total repatriation and expatriation of all Japanese irrespective of nationality will be pursued.'[62]

Prime Minister King feared that public opinion in British Columbia might force his government to take 'an extreme position.' Ian Mackenzie had publicly declared he would 'not remain 24 hours as a member of any Government or a supporter of any Party – that ever allows them [the Japanese Canadians] back again to these British Columbia shores.' Liberal and Progressive Conservative constituency organizations were passing similar resolutions, as were such traditional anti-Japanese groups as the Native Sons, the Army and Navy Veterans, and the boards of trade. Attorney-General R.L. Maitland had declared that the Canadian-born Japanese had often been more trouble than the natives of Japan, and both major Liberal newspapers in the province favoured the repatriation of all Japanese Canadians.[63]

Even in 1943 and 1944 not all British Columbians felt this way. A few delegates at the convention of the BC Command of the Canadian Legion protested the 'Hitlerism' of a Liberal Association resolution for repatriation. The Vancouver City Council tabled a repatriation resolution when it realized it would not pass unanimously. Some groups totally opposed repatriation. The CCF warned it was not a practical solution because of international complications. The United Church joined the Vancouver Consultative Council for Co-operation in Wartime Problems and representatives of the Baptist, Roman Catholic, and Anglican churches in telling the prime minister that any proposal to expel all Japanese was 'wicked and preposterous,' and that exiling Canadians would be 'an act of indefensible tyranny and folly' and a surrender to the 'racial attitudes of Nazism.' Like many who opposed wholesale deportation, the Consultative Council and its clerical supporters favoured dispersal throughout Canada.[64] In fact, a public opinion poll in August 1944 suggested that 64.9 per cent of British Columbians favoured dispersal.[65]

Nationally, the major Christian churches favoured dispersal. More importantly, they backed up their resolutions in favour of voluntary dispersal, the enfranchisement of Japanese, and the lifting of bans on property acquisition with programs designed to educate their congregations to accept the Japanese and to find suitable positions for them. For example, in February 1943 an Anglican church newsletter asked readers to contact placement committees in Toronto or Montreal if they could put any Japanese Canadians in suitable positions in order to demonstrate Christian fellowship and possibly to convert nominal Buddhists to Christianity.[66]

Sentiments in favour of dispersal tended to coincide with the thoughts of some of the prime minister's policy advisers. Indeed, R.G. Robertson recommended that the prime minister preface his announcement of the government's policy on the Japanese Canadians with a statement that

> the government is convinced that the principles involved in the stand we are taking in the present war against persecution and intolerance and in the British traditions of justice and fair play, require that unjust persecution should not be visited on innocent persons who have lived in peace in Canada and most of whom are citizens of Canada merely because they were of a particular race. The interests of Canada must be paramount, but the Government of Canada has noted that there has not been one single case of sabotage by persons of Japanese race in this country during the war and is of the opinion that the presence of a few thousand persons of Japanese race in a country of eleven and a half million cannot possibly constitute a menace to the interests of the country. Subject therefore to the interests of the country and to strict elimination of all persons who have manifested disloyalty to Canada during the war, the Government is determined to deal justly with the remaining persons of Japanese race in Canada.[67]

Finally, on 4 August 1944 Prime Minister King announced the government's policy. He repeated Robertson's observation that no Japanese person had been charged with sabotage or disloyalty and described plans to disperse loyal Japanese throughout the country after a quasi-judicial commission examined 'the background, loyalties and attitudes of all persons of Japanese race in Canada to ascertain those who are not fit persons to be allowed to remain here.' Those deemed disloyal would be deprived of any status they might have as British subjects and would be deported to Japan as soon as 'physically possible.'[68]

The plan referred both to dispersal and repatriation. The *New Canadian* was cheered because it had always believed dispersal would mean 'permanent resettlement, rather the mere re-allocation of manpower,' but soon complained that continued restrictions east of the Rockies and the absence of details about resettlement were creating instability in the form of 'uninformed public hostility' and the 'inertia of the evacuees themselves.'[69] In fact, Department of Labour officials had been considering dispersal plans. They favoured retaining travel restrictions until dispersal was complete but permitting loyal Japanese to acquire or lease real property, except within defence areas, and enfranchisement within ten years. They concluded that the Japanese 'should be told what restrictions, if any, would be placed on them if they declared themselves loyal to Canada.'[70] In a covering note, George Collins observed that 'public sentiment' made it necessary to handle the Japanese 'differently from the other racial groups representing the countries with which we are now at War' since there was insufficient time to mount a publicity program 'to minimize or refute' charges made over the previous forty years. Officials also fretted over when to approach the provinces about accepting Japanese as permanent residents in view of a pending federal election. The Prime Minister's Office hoped that delay would provide a better idea of the number to be dispersed and allow further progress with actual relocation. The Department of Labour, however, wanted quick decisions from the provinces since the Japanese were unwilling to move without some guarantee of permanency. It also wanted to take advantage of wartime employment opportunities.[71]

The dramatic policy of repatriation had already captured the attention of the public and of the Japanese Canadians. Most commentators accepted the principle of deporting only the disloyal; an opinion poll released in January 1945 indicated that most Canadians agreed. At the coast, however, old fears and complaints died hard. The Victoria *Colonist* regurgitated prewar spy stories and rhetorically asked how any commission could 'determine the loyalty to this land of one born of enemy alien stock.' A Vancouver newspaper columnist, however, hit the mark when he suggested the agitation for repatriation had 'nothing to do with the ensign of the rising sun or the Union Jack. It has everything to do with the dollar.'[72]

Although opinion in British Columbia was far from unanimous, policy makers in Ottawa seemed to give more weight to the stereotyped views emanating from the West Coast than to the evidence of growing tolerance, at least for the Canadian-born Japanese. Thus, federal officials worked on a voluntary repatriation plan to reduce the number of cases for the proposed Loyalty Commission and for placement. 'Voluntary' was the key word since there were serious doubts about Canada's legal powers to deport naturalized citizens, native-born Canadians who had not become aliens, and individuals who had acquired Canadian domicile and therefore did not fit into the Immigration Act's precise definition of 'undesirable immigrant.' Some haste was necessary lest Japan's military reverses discourage applicants. Despite the anxiety of the Department of Labour to implement the policy, especially after the United States announced loyal Japanese Americans could return to the coast, the cabinet did not formally approve the principle of repatriation until February 1945 and deferred the appointment of a Loyalty Commission.[73]

At last, in mid-March 1945, Humphrey Mitchell, the minister of labour, simultaneously issued two posters in English and Japanese as well as advertisements in the *New Canadian* which gave Japanese Canadians two options. One announcement, addressed to all persons of Japanese racial origin in Canada, invited them to apply for voluntary repatriation. The notice warned that any who were repatriated on 'other than a voluntary basis' could not be guaranteed free passage or the right to take their assets with them. A covering letter concluded that assistance offered by the Canadian government 'will mean to many who desire repatriation, relief from unnecessary anxiety and it will allow them to plan for their future, and that of their children, along economic, social, and cultural lines which they fear may be denied them were they to remain in Canada.' Similarly, supervisors in the housing settlements were urged to impress upon their charges 'that they are being given this opportunity to assist them to rehabilitate successfully in Japan.'[74]

Certainly in British Columbia the Department of Labour stressed 'the repatriation aspect of the programme.' While British Columbians welcomed a definite dispersal program as a means of solving their 'Japanese problem,' the Vancouver *Province* reported that reactions to the dispersal plan ranged from cooperation in Saskatchewan to a point-blank 'no' from Quebec, a declaration by Premier George Drew of Ontario that the federal government must consult the provinces, and 'no comment' from several provinces. It also quoted negative editorial comment from points as far east as Saint John. These hostile responses embarrassed the federal government, which had not yet negotiated with the provinces, and temporarily led the Department of Labour to emphasize the voluntary repatriation plan and to give relocation a minimum of publicity.[75] With good reason the Reverend W.H.H. Norman, a returned missionary sympathetic to the Japanese, reported that 'the official bulletins have in many cases been interpreted in some such terms as "for God's sake go back to Japan – or else." '[76]

The second poster instructed Japanese Canadians in British Columbia who wished to 'remain in Canada [that they] should now re-establish themselves East of the Rockies as the best evidence of their intention to co-operate with the Government policy of dispersal.' The announcement warned that failure to accept employment east of the Rockies might be deemed a 'lack of co-operation' and that employment opportunities might be less favourable later. As an enticement, it noted that several thousand Japanese had already re-established themselves and that placement offices would be 'making special efforts this Spring' to open up suitable employment. The government offered free transportation for all family members and their effects as well as a placement allowance.[77] At that time, approximately 10,000 people still lived in the settlements.

Despite a warning from T.B. Pickersgill, the new commissioner of Japanese placement, that editorial comment suggesting the program was 'a means of ridding B.C. of the Japanese' would develop Japanese resistance to relocation, some BC newspapers interpreted it that way. The Vancouver *Sun*, for example, proclaimed in a headline: 'All Japanese ordered out of B.C.: East of the Rockies or Back to Japan.' The White Canada Research Committee, which had been waging a small but vocal protest against Asian immigration since 1929, emerged as the Japanese Repatriation League and circulated nationally a petition for the repatriation of 'all people of Japanese ancestry now in Canada.' More influential were the politicians. Herbert Anscomb, the provincial minister of public works, declared that 'the Japanese in British Columbia are going back to their home and we will provide the boats to take them there.' During the spring 1945 federal election campaign, both Liberal and Conservative candidates called for the removal of all Japanese, if not from Canada entirely, at least from British Columbia. For Liberals that meant challenging their party's policy. Some members of the CCF, which was usually quick to note the rights of the 'loyal Japanese' as Canadian citizens, agreed that disloyal Japanese and any who volunteered should be repatriated. However, the issue was not a major one and the Wartime

Information Board reported that nationally the press gave little publicity to the repatriation survey.[78]

The policy of 'voluntary repatriation' or dispersal hardly surprised the Japanese Canadians. In a new year's forecast, a columnist in the *New Canadian* had predicted that 1944 would see the drawing of 'certain distinctions' within the Japanese community 'between those of us who prefer to remain in Canada, in the hope of restoration and acquisition of full-fledged rights of citizenship and equality; and those who lean more strongly toward a future in Japan.' The decision, he observed, could not be made simply on lines of citizenship since many who were technically aliens wanted to become useful Canadian citizens while some who were Canadians 'were not interested in their citizenship and would welcome the opportunity to go to Japan.'[79]

Though internees at Angler sought advice from camp leaders, most Japanese Canadians said little publicly about their innermost thoughts on repatriation. When the Department of Labour asked the *Nisei* principals of their schools to report reactions to the prime minister's August announcement, several replied that their limited knowledge of Japanese made it impossible to discuss the matter with the *Issei*, that such an inquiry was 'very touchy,' would seem like 'prying into ... private affairs,' and that 'nobody wishes to express his own feeling or tell of his own plan, as nobody knows what will happen tomorrow.'[80] In any case, residents of the housing settlements were reluctant to move. Some claimed they lacked the funds to buy household effects or winter clothing. More significant was uncertainty about the permanency of relocation. Thus, some thought the implied choice of relocation or repatriation was 'extremely unreasonable.' Pickersgill denied any 'compulsion or threat' was involved, but his reply that 'people of Japanese origin are better off by going to definite employment than remaining in our interior settlements, where there are just as many uncertainties about the future, if not more,' was hardly reassuring, especially since he would make no commitments about the permanency of employment, housing, or future citizenship rights. Indeed, Pickersgill frankly told settlement residents that because of possible hostile reaction elsewhere in Canada, the government was offering generous terms to voluntary repatriates. While repatriation was its primary focus during the spring and summer of 1945, the Department of Labour pressed its eastern placement program by removing from its payroll anyone who wished to stay in Canada but rejected eastern employment.[81]

In private, individuals were quite forthcoming in their thoughts about making a decision between dispersal and repatriation. Yet, the overwhelming theme in letters intercepted by the censor was uncertainty. Was their primary loyalty to Canada or Japan? Should they stay put and hope for the best? Should they cooperate with the dispersal program and move east? How could families be kept together? No consensus emerged and, over time, individuals and families often changed their minds.

Only for those whose experience in Canada had strengthened their loyalty to Japan was there no problem. One resident of an interior settlement wrote: 'I'm looking forward to going farther East on a repatriation ship. There is simply no hope in this country of so much racial hate and prejudice. When they say "A Jap is a Jap," what more can we do except to dye our hair, skin and eyes, unless we want to be a Chinese – which I wouldn't be for a million dollars.' The wife of an internee encouraged her husband to sign for repatriation. If he promised to be loyal to Canada in order to be set free, she told a relative, he would 'be disloyal to Japan.' Some who signed for repatriation were confident of Japan's eventual victory; others were less certain. Inmates of Angler dismissed newsreels of bombing raids on Japan as Canadian propaganda. Many thought conditions in Japan could be no worse than in Canada. A *Nisei* observed: 'If Japan wins the war, the Canadians will hate us still more. If by any chance Japan loses, we may be treated as slaves ... Some think that life will be difficult if we go back to Japan. But we must remember the depression will affect this country just as bad when the war is over ... Be firm, I think it is better for the Japanese to sacrifice our lives and do our best in fulfilling our mission.'

Despite their harsh experiences, other *Issei* and *Nisei* were determined to remain Canadian. One *Issei* mused:

> When the war broke out four years ago, most of us Japanese had already pledged allegiance to Canada ... [I]t will be impossible for us to find any comfortable place in Japan. The colour of hair is different, but for more than fifty years we have been used to the climate and customs of this country. There is no other place for our children to fall back to because Canada is their birth place. In fact, they are pure Canadians. If all the Japanese will only realize that at that point it will be unnecessary for us to hesitate to say whether we are loyal or disloyal. It is clear enough for anybody to see which course we should follow and what attitude we should take.

Some *Nisei* were so proudly Canadian that in spite of prejudice they were determined to make Canada a better place. One spunky lad who settled in Ontario felt very much at home because several restaurants barred Japanese! Nevertheless, he told a friend who had signed for repatriation:

> I guess it's the devil in me that made me take the choice of coming out East. I just

couldn't give these bunch of cheap time politicians the satisfaction of seeing our spirits broken. Maybe if I did remain in Canada I may still be classed as an enemy alien but I am taking the chance that some day the white people will recognize us as Canadians ... This business of making us choose between Japan and Canada is very unfair ... And to think that some people around Vancouver want to send us back to Japan or rather deport us to spread the idea of the civilized western world. It really makes me laugh.

Others feared that by signing for repatriation they would be 'falling into the trap the government has set for us.'[82]

For many, the decision to sign was not a patriotic issue but a family or economic concern. Yet, the intercepted letters reveal that decisions were made only after agonizing thought, much consultation among family members, and midst great uncertainty that was 'almost as bad as the turbulent days of pre-evacuation when destination of folks was so uncertain.' Some signed because the chief wage earner of the family thought he was too old or too wanting in English-language skills to get work elsewhere in Canada. Some feared losing jobs they already had in British Columbia. Some expected they would be as unwanted east of the Rockies as they were in British Columbia, or doubted the opportunity to re-establish themselves because of uncertainty about jobs, the housing shortage, and the ban on purchasing property.[83] Some were simply disgusted with their life in Canada and felt the evacuation policy implied that assimilation was impossible for them. A few feared conscription into the Canadian army; others resented the treatment of veterans of the First World War as enemy aliens. Many who signed had no great desire to go to Japan. A Slocan resident wrote, 'We have suffered hardship in Slocan and presuming that we may have to suffer more by going east we signed though we have not the least desire to return to Japan.' Others signed because they had aged parents in Japan or, and this was particularly true in the case of young *Nisei*, because the rest of the family decided to go.[84]

Frequently, people signed simply because they wanted to avoid any further disruptions in their lives or wanted to remain in British Columbia as a family unit as long as they could. Many individuals who signed for repatriation, especially *Nisei*, believed that when the time came, Canada would not force them to leave. One told his girl friend that just because he had signed, she should not jump to 'conclusions and think I am actually going to Japan, as that would be the last place I'd ever want to go. After all, ... I can't hardly carry a conversation in Japanese with anyone, let alone get along with some Japanese, so why should I aggravate matters by leaving Canada.'[85]

Many, of course, did not sign for repatriation. Some were uncertain about their reception in Japan and were discouraged by reports that elderly people who had returned on exchange ships had been sent to Manchukuo. Others doubted their ability to adapt to Japanese customs or to function in the Japanese language. A few shrewd individuals, especially those who were already east of the Rockies, chose not to sign because they believed they could thus hedge their bets. They could stay in Canada but could choose to go to Japan after the war.

Residents of the interior settlements could apply for repatriation throughout the late winter and spring of 1945. To make it appear that the program was entirely voluntary, the government required RCMP officers who interviewed repatriates to read and initial a memo ordering them to exercise great care to ensure that applicants came forward voluntarily lest signatories later complain of coercion. Nevertheless, some Tashme residents formally protested to the Spanish consul that 'the signing of the declaration was more or less compulsory rather than voluntary.' Similarly, residents of the Slocan Valley told Mitchell that because the 'terms and conditions' set forth in his notice precluded 'any choice other than signing The Application for Repatriation to Japan, and facing an uncertain future of deep anxiety East of Rockies,' 'the term "voluntary" ... [was] not a true statement of expression of unaffected free will.'[86]

The interviews were so brief – experienced interviewers could handle 400 people per day – that interviewees complained they could not ask questions about the prospect of returning to British Columbia after the war or employment opportunities east of the Rockies. To facilitate the program, settlement supervisors were instructed to give their employees a paid holiday on the first day that the RCMP was present, to set up the interview room so applicants would have privacy, and to have placement officers in a separate room interview those who did not want to sign. Space limitations, however, often made privacy impossible, and residents did not want neighbours to know of decisions that often were divisive. A Tashme resident explained: 'This hubbub will result in a lot of sadness owing to parents and children not thinking alike. For instance there is one family here whose daughter has gone to the east, the father wants to go to Japan, the mother wishes to stay in this country and join the daughter in the east ... Since this investigation has started many who were friends up to yesterday find today that a great gulf has sprung up between them and do not even exchange words across it.'[87]

The Department of Labour had not planned a systematic canvass of potential repatriates east of the Rockies nor did it initially require residents of British Columbia outside the housing settlements to report if they did not intend to sign. When an unexpectedly large number did sign for repatriation, the department realized it needed to know exact numbers to make 'a reasonably even distribution across Canada of people of Japanese origin.' In Manitoba, for example, so many signed for repatriation that the Manitoba supervisor of Japanese predicted that one day there would be 'few Japanese anywhere in Canada except in parts of British Columbia and southern Ontario.' Therefore, it required all Japanese Canadians to state their intentions to the RCMP. By mid-August 1945 a total of 10,397, including 3484 dependent children, had signed. This represented 43.3 per cent of the Japanese population of Canada.[88]

Japan's surrender in August 1945 meant little immediate change in government policy, in the attitude of Canadians generally, or in the response of Japanese Canadians to dispersal. Indeed, between the end of the repatriation survey in the spring of 1945 and the end of the year, only 925 persons left the housing centres. About 125 went to the Prairies; the rest, further east. The one family who ventured to the Maritimes was greeted in New Brunswick by the same complaints they had heard in British Columbia before the war. They did not stay long. On the west coast, people were still demanding a nation-wide dispersal so British Columbia would not have 'the Japanese headache all to itself' and the deportation of all who had signed for repatriation.[89]

The need to encourage dispersal, the desire to ease restrictions on those remaining in Canada, the imminent expiry of leases on the sites of some housing settlements, and, above all, the war's end made the government anxious to begin repatriation as quickly as possible. Because no suitable ships were available, however, the first of five sailings of repatriates did not leave Vancouver until 31 May 1946. Thus, officials had ample time to work out the logistics of moving the repatriates and their effects, but even then there were last-minute hitches such as the refusal of one captain to sail from Vancouver until sufficient flannelette was provided to insure that infant repatriates were properly diapered on the voyage. The time lag also allowed repatriates to inquire about baggage allowances, exchange rates, financial assistance for re-establishment in Japan, and compensation for property and other losses resulting from the evacuation.

The delay also gave many 'voluntary repatriates' a chance to change their minds. Only 285 had sought cancellation before the surrender, a fact which led the *New Canadian* to fret that the government might conclude that the great majority of those who signed were prepared to go to Japan. Once the war ended, requests for cancellation increased dramatically. By 31 December

1945, 4720 people, the majority of whom were Canadian-born, had applied for cancellation. Their reasons varied. A handful admitted worry about going to a war-devastated Japan, but most feared an eastern placement. Many had expected they could easily withdraw their requests and had signed merely to prolong their stay in British Columbia. Others claimed distress caused by the sale of their property and that legal restrictions had temporarily confused them.[90]

Meanwhile, the Department of Labour, which was sensitive to criticism, wanted to discourage potential repatriates from changing their minds. Some incidents at Tashme illustrate this well. In September 1945 the Vancouver *Province* asked permission to send a reporter to Tashme to interview applicants for repatriation and to ask 'Why they signed for repatriation, how they feel about the atomic bomb, what did they think about the end of the war with Japan and numerous other questions.' Although T.B. Pickersgill recommended granting the request as a means of dispelling suggestions of intimidation, his superiors in Ottawa thought such interviews would be harmful and recommended instead that the editor speak to the men who were in charge of the repatriation process.[91]

The matter was soon out of the department's hands. About the same time, the United Church congregation at Tashme invited Dr J.H. Arnup, moderator of the United Church, to visit them. During the meeting residents told him why they had signed for repatriation and explained their desire to cancel their applications now that the war was over. Dr Arnup advised them to apply for cancellation as individuals. A few days later, in Edmonton, Dr Arnup told a reporter that the Canadian-born Japanese in British Columbia had signed for repatriation 'under duress' because they were told that 'unless they signed they would be sent out of the province immediately.' Pickersgill publicly denied the suggestion of duress.[92]

Privately, Pickersgill, who was particularly annoyed by Arnup's suggestion that individuals apply for cancellation, recommended that the department consider 'exercising very rigid control of public meetings' at Tashme and at least demand advance notice of such meetings. The department agreed and enforced the rule. One high-school teacher remembers how 'The Commission was furious and restricted our visitors – we had to have written permission for every visitor we might have come to Tashme and we were not to have meetings of more than 3 people. The latter we ignored.' Nevertheless, the speaker invited to address the high-school graduation ceremony the following June was specifically forbidden to speak about the atomic bomb.[93] Though the war was over, censorship still prevailed at Tashme where repatriates were being gathered. The Department of Labour was anxious to remove any stimulus to potential agitation for cancellation of applications for repatriation.

Anticipating such demands for cancellation, cabinet ministers and senior officials debated policy. Humphrey Mitchell proposed rejecting all requests for cancellation except those made by the Canadian-born before Japan's surrender on 15 August and deporting all Japanese nationals who could not satisfy the proposed Loyalty Tribunal or commission. In contrast, Norman Robertson, who diplomatically described this idea as 'rather harsher than necessary,' suggested allowing the Canadian-born to apply for cancellation before the Loyalty Tribunal was appointed and entertaining requests from others who applied before the surrender or who might suffer particular hardship. Possibly as a compromise, the cabinet agreed not to take any immediate steps to repatriate Canadian natives who had applied for cancellation before 1 September 1945 but to reject all other applications and to repatriate all Japanese interned under the Defence of Canada regulations.[94]

The warning of M.J. Coldwell, the parliamentary leader of the CCF, that he intended to seek a suspension of repatriation plans 'in the interests of Canada's reputation among the nations of the world,' reminded the government of mounting public opposition to the deportation of Canadian-born Japanese and the revocation of their nationality.[95]

Although the *New Canadian* found it necessary to urge those who were threatened with deportation to protest and 'make a determined "gambari" stand,' some Japanese had already complained. Two Slocan residents charged that the BC Security Commission had used 'false representations' to get them to sign away their Canadian nationality, but the courts dismissed their case on the technicality that the Security Commission was no longer a legal entity. The Japanese and their friends continued to use the courts, but they correctly realized the greater efficacy of political action. Since May 1945 the JCCD had been informing the public of the implications of repatriation. It joined forces with the Co-operative Committee for Japanese Canadians in arguing that the policy was contrary to the United Nations charter which pledged its members 'to encourage respect for human rights and for fundamental freedoms for all without distinction as to race, language, religion or sex.' To underscore its argument, the Co-operative Committee asked the prime minister if perhaps Canada was 'already unwittingly a party to the Nazi treatment of an innocent and highly reputable minority.'[96]

The Co-operative Committee, the *New Canadian*, and church groups urged those who wished to change their minds to deluge the government with letters stressing that their repatriation requests had not really been voluntary, that signing had simply seemed the easiest thing to do at the time. The Co-operative Committee advised letter writers to emphasize their expectation of being able to change their minds easily, their lack of desire to live in Japan, and their efforts to raise their children to be good Canadians. In the case of the Japanese-born, the committee suggested their Canadian-born children appeal to the government. Children over sixteen should stress their ability to support their parents; children under sixteen, their desire to remain in Canada. Some letters were poignant. In a widely distributed leaflet, members of the United and Anglican churches at Tashme declared: 'We their children, being as we are their hope of support for the future and feeling strongly the natural ties of blood and affection, are faced with separation from them or exile from our native land.' A ten-year-old girl told the prime minister, 'I really do not want to go to Japan. I have never seen the place and I do not want to either. I was born in B.C. and I like my country very much. I know I can't get along in Japan. My parents have done nothing bad that they have to be deported. Please let my parents stay here so that I, a Canadian born may remain also.' The children's letters were neatly handwritten; officials were less impressed by letters apparently typed by the Co-operative Committee or by printed forms.[97]

Members of the Co-operative Committee interviewed Humphrey Mitchell, Norman Robertson, and officials of the Department of Labour but got little satisfaction. The committee then decided 'to awaken the public to the seriousness of the situation.' The end of the war gave it new impetus and encouraged many Canadians, including editors of such leading Liberal newspapers as the Toronto *Star* and the Winnipeg *Free Press*, to pick up the theme that repatriation was deportation and a Nazi-like policy. As well, Canadians, especially members of the United Church, began sending letters and petitions to Ottawa expressing their opposition to the deportation plan. Most of the letters came from the Toronto area, where the Co-operative Committee was based, or from Manitoba, where it had many friends in the churches, but a few also came from coastal British Columbia.[98]

Nevertheless, loud voices from British Columbia still wanted the repatriation of some, if not all, of the Japanese Canadians. The Vancouver *Sun*, now demanding only the removal of those who had not revoked their applications by 2 September 1945, questioned 'the true loyalty of the second-guessers' who 'played both ends against the middle while waiting to see which way the cats of war would jump.' In Parliament two Liberals, Tom Reid (New Westminster) and George Cruickshank (Fraser Valley), joined the Conservative, Howard Green (Vancouver South), in claiming that 'the Japanese came to this country under a definite plan of the Japanese war lords' long before

Pearl Harbor. Reid was adamant that all Japanese should be sent to Japan; Green and Cruickshank would allow those acceptable to other provinces to remain.[99]

While civil liberties and church groups lobbied the government to permit individuals to cancel their requests for repatriation, they also knew the federal government would not change the repatriation policy unless the dispersal program was succeeding. Thus, the National Interchurch Advisory Committee invited congregations to sponsor Japanese families and assist them 'to take their places as normal Canadians in the community.' Church workers at Tashme asked members of the Student Christian Movement in Canadian universities to find places for senior high-school boys where they could work for their room and board or jobs which would allow them to attend night school. While the Christian churches organized their efforts to aid resettlement, individual Japanese often observed that 'groups such as the Jewish people opened their doors first.'[100]

The Japanese themselves also flooded the government with requests to improve the dispersal program through such practical means as increased resettlement allowances or, in the case of residents of southern Alberta, permanent residency status, enfranchisement, and the lifting of the obligation to get police permission to move or travel any distance. In Toronto, the JCCD prepared a lengthy brief noting that, in the United States, permanent relocation had been 'accomplished successfully,' while Canada had achieved 'no semblance' of it because of her failure to keep families intact, protect property, or grant citizenship rights. Yet the committee also observed that some Japanese Canadians had successfully relocated in eastern Canada, actively participated in trade unions and churches, and entered a variety of occupations including white-collar work, skilled trades, and professions which had been closed to them in British Columbia. Overall, said the committee, they had proven themselves '100% Canadian.' Thus, the committee concluded, 'Many or most of the Japanese Canadians in the East would not even think of returning to B.C. but without the assurance of the Government as to being allowed to stay East, they have not ventured to establish themselves and are still in the fluid transcient [sic] stage.'[101]

During the fall of 1945 senior bureaucrats warned of serious political embarrassment if Canada did not allow her citizens to withdraw their requests for repatriation since, under the U.S. Bill of Rights, Japanese Americans had been allowed to change their minds. Canadian officials realized of course that those who had signed for repatriation had done 'something which might leave seriously open to question where their allegiance does lie.' This argument became part of the form letters the Department of Labour used to answer petitions. The bureaucrats suggested that forming a loyalty commission or tribunal, as had been proposed in August 1944, and extending the deadline for withdrawal until 31 December 1945 might solve the problem. Their political masters, Humphrey Mitchell and Ian Mackenzie, preferred the existing program, but Prime Minister King instructed Mitchell to make a statement on requests for reviews of repatriation applications in 'pretty general' terms and to leave an opening for a review of cases where coercion was alleged or established.[102]

Thus, Mitchell announced that the government would accept applications for revocation made by Canadian-born and naturalized citizens before 2 September 1945, would review applications made by the Canadian-born after that date, and reject all applications made after 2 September by Japanese nationals. He was inexplicably silent on the fate of naturalized Canadians who applied after 2 September. In any event, 2 September 1945, the date of Japan's unconditional surrender, was the key date. As Mitchell explained, 'until the defeat of Japan the Japanese wanted to go back to their own country ... [and] we took them at their word. But when the atomic bomb cropped up, and Japan was defeated, they were prepared to change their minds. That is the problem in a nutshell.'[103]

In fact, the government had made a major concession by reconsidering the cases of the Canadian-born, a point which the *New Canadian* accepted as a step in the right direction. However, the threat of deportation still hung over most naturalized Canadians and Japanese nationals, many of whom were parents of Canadian-born children. The harshness of the policy caught public attention. A pamphlet, *Save Canadian Children and Canadian Honour*, distributed by the Vancouver Consultative Committee urged Canadians to promote 'the protection of the basic human rights of all Canadian citizens of Japanese ancestry, whether children or adults, and also of all Japanese nationals legally resident in Canada and duly observant of Canadian law.' Press comments emphasized the deportation of some 10,000 Japanese, without any real effort to explain that all had made voluntary application to be sent to Japan.[104]

Drafting legislation to implement the policy was not easy. Section 3(g) of Bill 15, the Emergency Powers Bill, which permitted the federal government to control 'the entry into Canada, exclusion and deportation, and revocation of nationality,' aroused great hostility among church and civil-liberties groups who complained it threatened 'the civil liberties not only of Japanese Canadians but of any and all Canadians.' At a time when citizenship legislation was pending, the argument was telling. A Vancouver resident, and no friend of the Japanese, suggested 'there must be a good way to deport

Cooked Tours

Vancouver Sun, 14 December 1945

Japanese and other alien enemies without enacting legislation which would sweep away the individual rights and freedoms we are supposed to enjoy as citizens of a democratic society.' Within Parliament, when opposition members referred to the 'entirely unnecessary' or 'pernicious' clause, they stressed the broad rights of citizenship.[105]

To avoid a parliamentary fight and to act before the powers for deportation under the War Measures Act expired on 31 December 1945, the Special Cabinet Committee on the Repatriation and Relocation of the Japanese implemented the deportation policy by order-in-council rather than by legislation. However, in the temporary absence of both the prime minister and Ian Mackenzie, it could not agree about who the proposed Loyalty Commission should examine or whether it should be empowered to 'denationalize and deport' native-born Canadians. The next day, after considerable discussion and warnings from Norman Robertson about policies that would be perceived as pure 'racial discrimination,' the cabinet decided the Loyalty Commission should not deal with Canadian-born Japanese. Moreover, subjecting them to possible deportation and revocation of citizenship would go beyond existing legislation.[106]

On 17 December 1945, Prime Minister King tabled three orders-in-council passed under the War Measures Act. PC 7356 was designed to meet the Department of External Affairs request that repatriates not return to Japan as Canadians, and simply declared that any deportee who had been naturalized would cease to be a British subject or Canadian national on his departure from Canada; PC 7357 provided for the appointment of a Loyalty Commission to examine doubtful cases, such as internees, among the Japanese not born in Canada. The first two were relatively straightforward, but PC 7355 authorized the minister of labour to deport Japanese nationals who had requested repatriation or who were still interned on 1 September 1945, naturalized Canadians of Japanese race who had not revoked their repatriation requests before midnight, 1 September 1945, and Canadian-born who had not revoked repatriation requests before receiving deportation orders. Wives and children under sixteen could be included in these orders. In presenting the orders-in-council, the prime minister stressed that, while the orders authorized the minister to move these people, it did not order him to deport them. To paraphrase one of Mr King's most famous statements, deportation if necessary, but not necessarily deportation! In clarifying the situation, Justice Minister Louis St Laurent explained that 'the only ones who are to be forcibly dealt with under these orders are the naturalized Canadians of the Japanese race, or Japanese nationals.' Neither King nor St Laurent had sympathy for naturalized citizens who sought to go to an enemy country during wartime. St Laurent noted that no decision had been made about the Canadian-born who wished to remain in Canada but if any action were taken, Parliament, not the cabinet alone, would legislate.[107]

The general tenor of the orders-in-council found widespread support. The Vancouver *Sun* was more concerned about the number of Japanese who were likely to remain in British Columbia than about the principles of citizenship. The Victoria *Colonist* did not distinguish between Japanese and Canadian nationals as it recounted the inassimilability of the Japanese, blamed them

The Good Samaritans

Vancouver Sun, 29 December 1945

for atrocities committed in Asia, declared they had not renounced their 'allegiance to the Japanese throne,' and concluded that their retention in Canada, particularly in British Columbia, would cause such a 'provocative situation' it would be 'in the best interests of the Japanese themselves to be deported.' Inland, the Kamloops Board of Trade demanded the deportation of all Japanese who signed for repatriation. Indeed, Attorney-General R.L. Maitland later argued that Japanese who 'still expressed a desire to return to Japan' after Japan had shelled the coast and launched incendiary balloons, were 'a menace to Canada.' Such ideas were not confined to British Columbia.

The Halifax *Herald* was oblivious to citizenship considerations when it suggested the problems of the Japanese in Canada were 'the fault of the Barbarians of the East who have committed the foulest and most monstrous crimes against humanity and civilization.' Similarly, the Toronto *Telegram* declared that 'any Japanese man who wanted to forsake Canada when he thought Hirohito and Tojo were going to win cannot be trusted to be loyal to this country and he certainly should be thrown out.'[108]

In contrast, the orders-in-council angered those who objected to policies based on race. The Toronto *Star*, which had the largest circulation of any Canadian newspaper, admonished that 'one of the crimes charged against the Nazis ... is the deportation of civilians on racial and religious grounds. This is precisely what Canada is doing in respect to her Japanese citizens.' More significant, though it does not appear to have been appreciated in Ottawa, was the comment of the Vancouver *Province*, the leading British Columbia newspaper, that Canada could not 'send some thousands of these helpless and pathetic people back to Japan ... without doing violence to the foundation of her own nationhood.' 'We cannot,' declared the newspaper, 'deport Canadian citizens without dishonoring Canada and casting doubt on the value of Canadian citizenship.'[109]

In a similar spirit, church and civil liberties groups throughout Canada again passed resolutions, wrote letters, distributed leaflets, and circulated petitions. Many letters simply referred to the need for justice and human rights, some condemned 'Nazi-like' policies, and a few called only for a delay in repatriation because of severe food shortages in Japan. Many letters followed a more or less standard form indicating they were part of an organized campaign, but a few had comments based on personal experience. In mid-February 1946 the Prime Minister's Office received ten to fifteen letters daily protesting the deportation policy and few calling for the deportation of all Japanese. In addition, throughout the spring and summer of 1946, readers of the *New Canadian* responded to its exhortations, especially to residents of the interior settlements, to apply for revocation and 'to prevent, through democratic methods, the deportation of innocent Canadian citizens and law-abiding Japanese nationals.' The campaign, the *New Canadian* argued, was not a fight just 'to stop deportation' but against laws which applied specifically to Japanese. Within the Japanese community the JCCD maintained the lead in challenging involuntary 'repatriation.' Its legal adviser, Andrew Brewin of Toronto, had earlier recommended litigation through a suitable test case. Although the JCCD was assured of the assistance of the Co-operative Committee, its difficulty was finding such a test case since most of the likely candidates were in British Columbia and were

Victoria *Daily Colonist*, 20 January 1946

reluctant to litigate, possibly because they suspected it would be difficult to find an able and sympathetic lawyer. Moreover, the Vancouver Consultative Committee warned that British Columbia judges might be subject to political pressure.[110]

The passage of the orders-in-council put a new aspect on the case. Arguing that they were *ultra vires* because the War Measures Act only allowed the deportation of aliens, Brewin had a writ issued in the Supreme Court to test their legality. Meanwhile, the Co-operative Committee continued to protest the proposed deportation as a violation of the 'fundamentals of democracy.' In addition, the Canadian Council of Churches interviewed Prime Minister King, Humphrey Mitchell, and Brooke Claxton, the minister of national health and welfare, to ask that naturalized Canadians who did not wish repatriation should be allowed to make their cases before the proposed Loyalty Commission.[111] While awaiting the Supreme Court decision, the Department of Labour did not issue repatriation orders to Canadian-born Japanese over the age of sixteen lest they resort to *habeas corpus* proceedings. The policy also allowed the minister of labour to make the politically attractive statement that he had not signed deportation orders for Canadian citizens.[112]

The Supreme Court, which heard evidence on 24–5 January 1946 presented its judgment on 20 February 1946. It was badly split. Chief Justice Rinfret and two others found the orders-in-council to be *intra vires;* the other judges had doubts about various parts. In effect, the orders were valid but there was uncertainty about the deportation of Canadian-born wives and children. The situation invited an appeal to a higher court, the Judicial Committee of the Privy Council in London. Pending the appeal, the Cabinet Committee decided to deport only those who wished to go to Japan, to continue the dispersal program, and to defer the appointment of the Loyalty Commission. The cabinet, even Ian Mackenzie, agreed.[113]

Pleased by this 'unusually encouraging news,' the *New Canadian* became increasingly confident that the government would not impose forcible deportation no matter what the Privy Council decided. Since the government was trying to abolish appeals to the Privy Council, the Co-operative Committee offered to withdraw its appeal if the government would reconsider individual cases of revocation and withdraw orders exiling Canadian citizens. Although the cabinet would not abandon its course, the Co-operative Committee, which had the legal assistance of the CCF government of Saskatchewan, was pleased with the prime minister's assurance that 'serious consideration' would be given to its representation. King, however, also recalled his government's obligation to the families of Canadians killed in the Far East, especially

Hong Kong, and the claims of St Laurent and Mackenzie that British Columbians did not want Japanese to return to the coast.[114]

British Columbian response to the Supreme Court decisions was predictable. The Vancouver *Sun* regarded the decision as a vindication of government policy; the Victoria *Colonist* wondered why the government had even questioned the validity of its own orders. In Parliament, BC members warned against using the proposed Citizenship Act to allow Japanese to evade deportation. In Victoria, Attorney-General Maitland called for the deportation of Canadian-born Japanese who had signed for repatriation. A resolution urging the deportation of all Japanese appeared too late in the legislative session to be debated but Gordon Wismer, who became attorney-general after Maitland's sudden death, urged Mackenzie to have Parliament enact legislation covering the policies laid out in the order-in-council lest the Judicial Committee rule against them on a technicality. Several Liberal constituency associations and veterans' groups shared these sentiments.[115]

In contrast, both the *Province* and the *News-Herald* praised the government for not forcing anyone to leave before the Judicial Committee ruled. Others were less sanguine about the government's intentions. The Vancouver Consultative Council asked church members to sign an open letter addressed to 'Men and Women of Japanese Origin Lawfully Residing in Canada.' The letter, which apologized for past injustices and described banishment for racial reasons as 'un-British,' was designed to reduce bitterness among the Japanese Canadians and to persuade the government that many British Columbians opposed 'the brutal deportation of thousands of innocent people.' Equally striking were protests against deportation from Caucasians in the Slocan Valley: 'The Government's present policy reminds many of us that we too, at one time from ignorance received these people in our midst with suspicion and dislike. But when we got to know them we found them to be respectable law-abiding Citizens whose living standard and decorum are equal to occidental Canadians in similar walks of life.'[116]

Opposition to the deportation orders was concentrated in the vicinities of Toronto and Winnipeg and among members of the major Protestant denominations, but it was not confined to these areas or churches. The Roman Catholic bishops of Quebec protested the injustice of restoring rights to Germans and Italians while deporting Japanese. In Montreal, several groups including the Canadian Jewish Congress, the Saint-Jean-Baptiste Society, and the YMCA formed the Montreal Committee on Canadian Citizenship / Le Comité pour la défence de la citoyenneté canadienne to oppose repatriation as 'dangerous in itself' and an attack on 'the fundamental rights of minorities' and also to collect funds for the appeal to the Privy Council.[117]

Look Who's Squawking!

Vancouver Sun, 4 March 1946

The Co-operative Committee continued to remind members of parliament that the courts were 'only concerned with the legality of the Orders,' and that Parliament was responsible for 'the moral justice of the policy.' It asked them to withdraw the orders-in-council as being 'wrong and indefensible' and 'a grave threat to the rights and liberties of Canadian citizens.' Moreover, the committee noted that 'deportation on racial grounds' had been defined as a crime against humanity. For the general public, the committee distributed 50,000 copies of a leaflet, *Our Japanese Canadians: Citizens Not Exiles,* which sketched the history of the question, summarized the arguments presented to parliamentarians, and urged people to protest to the prime minister and to contribute to the committee's legal costs.[118]

Such importunings were effective. When Department of Justice officials drafted a bill to provide for the deportation or resettlement of Japanese in Canada, other public servants immediately recognized it would arouse public and parliamentary opposition. As Norman Robertson noted, 'the government might also be open to criticism in attempting to infringe the rights of citizens.' Although Ian Mackenzie thought it 'a good bill,' the cabinet did not enact any Japanese legislation at the 1946 session.[119]

Meanwhile, the case against the deportation orders proceeded through the courts until 2 December 1946, when the Judicial Committee, one of whose members was Sir Lyman Duff, a former chief justice of the Supreme Court of Canada, ruled that 'none of the Orders-in-Council is in any respect *ultra vires*' and dismissed the appeal. In short, the Canadian government had the right to deport Canadian citizens.[120]

Canadians at the time were unusually conscious of citizenship; the first Citizenship Act was due to come into effect on 1 January 1947. Many editors urged the government to cancel the orders as acts of racial discrimination which contradicted the new concept of Canadian citizenship. Even the Vancouver *Sun* suggested the orders should apply only to ex-aliens 'who repented of seeking Canadian citizenship during the period Japan was winning the War.' It shared the view of the *Province* that 'Canada has a new Citizenship Act which aims, and quite properly, to give a new prestige to Canadian citizenship. But the act is futile and meaningless while citizenship is subject to revocation on frivolous grounds like that of racial origin.'[121]

Responding in part to public opinion, the cabinet revoked all of the orders-in-council of 15 December 1945 save for an amendment to one that provided for voluntary repatriation. Individuals who wished to go to Japan could still receive financial aid, but no one would be deported. The cabinet decision was unanimous but King recorded that St Laurent had 'fought strongly and

DUAL PERSONALITY

Vancouver Sun, 3 December 1946

bravely for deporting all who could be deported including some Canadian citizens' lest, in the future, the Japanese demand the same rights as other Canadians. Ian Mackenzie was unhappy but admitted the government could probably not get support for a deportation policy. The other cabinet members accepted the prime minister's arguments that it 'would be a crime' to repatriate well-behaved Japanese, that people were now trying to foster good-will and peace and 'would probably raise a real issue' that would embarrass the Liberal party. Even British Columbians, he observed, had changed their minds. Yet, the press release of 24 January 1947 which announced the cancellation of the orders-in-council was not completely gracious. It noted that 'the separation of those whose continued presence would be undesirable in Canada has been accomplished on a voluntary basis.' Nevertheless, the *New Canadian* greeted the announcement as 'welcome news indeed.' Though some British Columbians still suspected the loyalties of the Japanese, the provincial government found little fault with the decision provided the Japanese were kept away from the coast and out of the fishing industry. The

Prime Minister's Office noted neither newspaper items nor letters favouring retention of the deportation policy.[122] The government had successfully gauged public opinion.

The change in public opinion only partially explains the cabinet decision. By the end of 1946 the Department of Labour reported that the voluntary movement of 3964 repatriates to Japan and the dispersal program had been so successful that instead of about 9500 Japanese in Housing Projects 'who resisted all efforts to relocate them and whose attitudes were uncertain,' there were now only about 1000. Such small numbers, the department decided, did not warrant forcible deportation.[123]

Indeed, throughout most of 1946 the department had been encouraging dispersal, but the legal uncertainties about repatriation discouraged dispersal especially when families were divided on the question. In Slocan, for example, where many probable repatriates had been gathered to await transportation, *Issei* petitioned the Canadian government for compensation for property losses so they would be able to re-establish themselves in Japan, but most young people were 'desperately against going to Japan.' Some girls secretly applied for cancellation; others looked for husbands in the belief that their parents would allow them to stay if they were married.

Yet family loyalties were strong. Many young people who had withdrawn their own applications for repatriation refused to leave British Columbia as long as their parents were subject to deportation. The *New Canadian* counselled them to move east 'since fear of the concentration of Japanese in B.C. is undoubtedly a large factor behind the pressure to deport a large section of these people.' The Department of Labour agreed. 'After consideration at the top level,' the department accepted Pickersgill's advice that paying railway fares to the east for deportable Japanese whose children wanted to stay in Canada was cheaper than maintenance grants and meant the Japanese would be out of British Columbia if the courts ruled the deportation orders invalid. Those who moved were still 'subject to deportation,' but were advised that 'their conduct and attitude' would be considered in any subsequent review. Only single Japanese nationals or families composed entirely of Japanese nationals who had signed for repatriation were not encouraged to go east.[124]

The Department of Labour also made movement relatively easy. It opened hostels providing temporary accommodation in Farnham, Que., Moose Jaw, Sask., Transcona, Man., and in northern Ontario. The *New Canadian* commended the hostels as a means of speeding up dispersal, allowing families to move together and to negotiate directly with prospective employers, but it reported that the hostels reminded some of Hastings Park. Nevertheless, over half of those who moved east in 1946 used the hostels temporarily.[125]

In the spring of 1946 the eastward trickle of Japanese Canadians had begun to grow 'into a steady stream' During the year, 4700 left British Columbia. About a quarter settled on the Prairies, chiefly in Alberta, the remainder went to eastern Canada, primarily Ontario. Agriculture, especially the raising of sugar beets, continued to provide the main employment on the Prairies; in the east opportunities were more diverse, although the Department of Labour concentrated on placements on farms and with pulp and paper companies. Pickersgill claimed the movement was the result of a 'growing realization on the part of the Japanese that it is not in their own interest to congregate in one section of the country.' The *New Canadian* tactfully credited the changes to Department of Labour polices that had made relocation more attractive, including promises to relax wartime restrictions, and Pickersgill's persistent work.[126] It might also have mentioned the policy of requiring men laid off from BC sawmills to go east if jobs were available, even though their families might not be able to join them immediately.

Nevertheless, small groups were recalcitrant. When 400 persons in Slocan who were judged relocatable refused to move east, the department denied them permission to take jobs in British Columbia, did not provide schools for their children, and warned they might be sent out on twelve hours' notice. Such pressure made many families so anxious to leave they found housing for themselves. Other families, described by the *New Canadian* as *Gambari*, said they would move only if forced, that they preferred repatriation, or that they doubted the determination of the Department of Labour in making them move since good jobs were plentiful in British Columbia. By December 1946, however, only a dozen families remained in Slocan and they were preparing the site for transfer to the War Assets Corporation for disposal.[127] By the end of 1946 only about a thousand people remained in the interior housing projects, and most of them were invalids or unemployables and their dependents who were to be housed in the one surviving settlement, New Denver. British Columbia, which had once had 95 per cent of Canada's Japanese population, now had only 33 per cent, and they were widely dispersed throughout the interior. The Department of Labour concluded that 'for all practical purposes, movement eastward from British Columbia is complete except for isolated individual families and single persons.'[128]

The Department of Labour also assisted those who wished to leave southern Alberta for eastern points. The possibility that they might be forced to leave, the continuation of travel restrictions, the belief that they could not buy land, less than ideal working conditions, and hostility to their presence, particularly in Lethbridge, led some evacuees to leave Alberta in 1946 and 1947. The total number of Japanese in Alberta, however, remained fairly constant since some from British Columbia replaced those moving east. In 1948 the Alberta government agreed to allow the Japanese there to remain and, after a two-year transition, to accept full responsibility, including costs of welfare and education, for its new citizens.[129]

While the evacuees were moving east in 1946, the federal government was devising means to insure they would not return to the Pacific coast. In the spring of 1946 the Department of Justice drafted legislation to provide for the 'resettlement of Displaced Persons of the Japanese Race.' The bill denied the Japanese the right to return to the coast, allowed the minister of labour to govern their movement within Canada, provided arrangements whereby each province would be expected to accept a quota of Japanese, and permitted Ottawa to move Japanese for whom no resettlement arrangements had been made 'to some part of Canada not within the geographical limits of any province,' presumably Yukon and the Northwest Territories.[130] Because of flaws in the original draft, the Department of Justice prepared another version providing the necessary administrative authority, but the Department of Labour, aware of increasing concern about citizenship rights, rejected this second draft which claimed that 'all persons of the Japanese race' had been removed from the coast for security reasons because some of them 'manifested sympathy with or support of Japan.' The department, fearing 'a critical debate' over the claim, recommended as a 'safe course,' the continuation of its controls over movement for another year or two and legislation enabling the custodian of enemy property to complete the liquidation of Japanese property.[131]

Thus, on 24 January 1947, while announcing the cancellation of the deportation orders, King outlined plans to remedy injustices committed in the sale of Japanese property and to revoke most special controls other than restrictions relating to their movement and the denial of fishing licences. In April the government lifted all controls on the movement of Japanese except in British Columbia. In the course of the debate on the extension of the Emergency Powers Act (which had replaced the War Measures Act) to 31 March 1948, Ross Thatcher, a CCF member of parliament from Saskatchewan, proposed lifting all restrictions. In arguing against this, the atavistic BC Liberal and Conservative members claimed their province's security was still at stake because if Japan rose again, the Japanese would dispossess others, especially veterans, and regain their prominence in the fisheries and forestry. Thatcher's amendment was overwhelmingly defeated.[132]

Protesting that legal barriers on their movement were inconsistent with the new Canadian Citizenship Act, leaders of the Japanese community publicly suggested that few Japanese were likely to return to the coast. Many had quickly made new lives and friends for themselves in Ontario and Quebec. As one Montreal resident wrote to a white friend from Tashme, 'As far as the Japanese returning back to Vancouver, I doubt very much that they will. Most of us are making a new start in life so I don't think we care to move again although I'm sure [the] majority of us would like to see our "home town" again.' Nevertheless, the *New Canadian* admitted that individuals who were not satisfactorily resettled might desire to return to the coast.[133]

Public opinion in British Columbia was gradually changing. Although various patriotic organizations and Liberal and Conservative constituency associations at the coast and in the Okanagan Valley protested the return of the Japanese, not everyone agreed. The Vancouver *News-Herald* tellingly questioned the worth of military security as an excuse for keeping the Japanese away from the coast given 'Japan's present helpless state.' Students at the University of British Columbia called on the university administration to facilitate the attendance of Japanese students and the Burrard Young Conservatives favoured the 'unrestricted movement' of Japanese in Canada. One reason for the change in attitude was undoubtedly the increasing belief that the Japanese would not return to the coast. A public opinion poll in Vancouver showed that although in March 1946, 54 per cent of those polled thought the Japanese would return, in June 1947 only 27.5 per cent thought this way.[134]

When the federal cabinet considered renewing restrictions on the Japanese in early 1948 it was aware of the changing mood in British Columbia, the likelihood that few Japanese would return to the coast, and the prospect that another 500 would soon move from the interior to eastern points. The cabinet, however, was concerned about the political impact of ending the restrictions on the Japanese. Premier Byron Johnson, the Liberal leader of the Coalition government in British Columbia, and all of the province's Liberal MPS had warned of 'great trouble,' including the loss of by-elections in Yale and Vancouver-Centre (the latter caused by the elevation of Ian Mackenzie to the Senate), if the orders were lifted. The prime minister endorsed the liberal principle of minority rights but wondered if Canada wanted to protect 'the minority consituted by a handful of Japanese, or was it the minority constituted by the entire population of British Columbia' as represented by their members of parliament. He feared losing the by-elections and other BC seats at the next general election. Only Justice Minister J.L. Ilsley opposed continuing the orders.[135]

Meanwhile, the Department of Labour decided it needed to control the Japanese for another year lest a considerable number of them move into coastal British Columbia or the Okanagan Valley. Thus, on 15 March 1948 Humphrey Mitchell, the minister of labour, presented the legislation controlling the movement of Japanese to Parliament, but he stressed that the authority would expire on 1 April 1949. When Thatcher proposed that the order expire on 1 April 1948, both Tom Reid (Liberal, New Westminster) and George Pearkes (Progressive Conservative, Nanaimo) hinted that whites might take revenge on returning Japanese. The debate, however, was devoid of most of the emotional rhetoric of the past. Nevertheless, by a vote of 73 to 23, the Commons defeated Thatcher's amendment and accepted Mitchell's recommendation that the Japanese not be allowed to move about in British Columbia or reside at the coast without ministerial permits.[136]

The best evidence of the new mood in British Columbia and the atavism of MPS such as Reid and Pearkes was the angry response to this decision. The Vancouver *Sun*, long the opponent of the Japanese, refrained from editorial comment but Elmore Philpott, one of its editorial-page columnists, congratulated Angus MacInnis (CCF, Vancouver East) for defending the return of the Japanese and contended that 'the substantial majority of all people in British Columbia believe that all Canadians should have the right to live their lives on a basis of fair play.' Later, after a Canadian of Japanese ancestry was jailed for visiting his birthplace without a permit, the *News-Herald* repeated an earlier allegation that Canada had no reason to be smug about Jim Crow laws in the United States. By early 1949 there was ample evidence that even those who had been most hostile to the Japanese had changed their minds. Assured that few would return to the industry, the United Fishermen and Allied Workers Union expressed no opposition to the return of the Japanese. The Associated Boards of Trade of the Fraser Valley, after a heated debate, defeated a resolution opposing the return of the Japanese.[137]

Further proof of the changing situation came early in 1949 when the British Columbia legislature, without dissent, enfranchised Japanese Canadians. To a significant extent, the dispersal policy was responsible for the relative ease with which this barrier to full citizenship was lifted. As the Vancouver *Sun* explained, 'Seven years have brought a radical change in the situation. The Japanese themselves are scattered all across Canada, instead of being congested in a special area around Vancouver. They are willing and anxious to be Canadian, owing this country their first loyalty.' As the orders barring the Japanese from the coast expired, the coastal press took little notice apart from reporting the statement of Toshi Tanaka, the secretary of the Japanese Canadian Citizens Association, that some coastal employers still practiced discrimination and that few Japanese were likely to return to the coast because they had been absorbed into the economies and social life of their new Canadian homes. Indeed, though *Nisei* found life in the east to be difficult at first, many undoubtedly agreed with the Toronto professional man who later concluded that ' "Going East" was certainly advantageous.' The Toronto *Star* in 1949 correctly observed that the success of the dispersal program was 'in no small measure due to the stoic, patient character of the Japanese people and to the co-operation given them by other provinces and by socially minded groups of citizens everywhere.'[138]

While the majority of Japanese Canadians moved east of the Rockies, a total of 3964 individuals went to Japan. Of these, 1355 were Japanese nationals; 630, naturalized Canadians; and 1979, Canadian-born of whom one-third were under the age of sixteen.[139] The repatriation program – and after January 1947 it was truly a voluntary repatriation program – continued until September 1947 when the Canadian government, which had been criticized for providing 'free tourist trips,' announced it would no longer provide free passage and financial aid even for repatriates whose luggage had been examined by the RCMP and shipped to the west coast. No doubt those *Nisei* who were going to Japan only because of filial duty were pleased with the decision.[140]

A number of *Nisei* who had gone to Japan with their families had already expressed a wish to return to Canada as had some who had been stranded there by the outbreak of war. Legally, Canadian-born Japanese, except for those repatriated during the war, were admissible to Canada under the Immigration Act though some doubt existed about those who had been forced to serve in the Japanese armed forces. The Japanese Canadian Citizens Association secured permission for a few strandees and repatriates to return but, on the advice of Hugh Keenleyside, did not press the issue until all the restrictions on Japanese in Canada had been lifted.[141]

By the end of 1949, 174 repatriates had returned to Canada but they were not entirely welcome. The *Sun* asked, 'What kind of shuttle service do they think the country's running?' The number increased slightly after the withdrawal of the Allied Occupation in 1951 and the end of the Korean War in 1953 reduced opportunities for work with the American forces. Although parents still expected their eldest sons to remain in Japan to sustain the household and care for them in their old age, they were less reluctant to let their other Canadian-born children return to Canada. In Mio, the 'America Village' in Wakayama Prefecture and source of many emigrants, the Mio-

Canada Liaison Association which was organized in 1950 contacted former Mio residents in Toronto. By 1961 the Toronto branch had arranged employment for 120 returnees as contract labour on nearby mushroom farms. Canadian relatives provided passage money for other returnees. Yet not all Japanese Canadians were hospitably inclined. One complained to the National Japanese Canadian Citizens Association that 'those who abandoned this country some years ago are shamelessly coming back to this country. When I consider that these people resisted the Canadian government in the internment camp during the war and went to Japan, given an allowance of $200 each, I cannot help but wonder why I had to apply myself to such unprofitable work as growing white radishes for six years.'[142]

In Japan, the repatriates had a difficult time. The appalling destruction of the cities, levelled by fleets of American B-29 bombers, shocked them. The governmental system was in chaos, housing was so short that two or three families often occupied a single house, and, despite government controls, food was scarce and the black market flourished. One *Nisei* wrote to a Canadian friend, 'it wasn't so much the food or the conditions of Japan, but the disappointed look on everyone's face, the cry of complaint, disgusting remarks and the feeling of the Niseis, that made such an ugly scene ... We could taste the bitterness of the disasters of war, especially after putting eyes on so many homeless orphans, foodless, clotheless, begging for food and money; staggering on street sides, sleeping on the cold ground.'[143]

The food problem had greeted the repatriates at the reception centre near Yokohama when they first arrived. Bread, made of a mixture of barley, wheat, rice polishings, and potatoes, was 'so tough and distasteful that even a dog would not eat it.' Many young people became more anxious to return to Canada. Families who were fortunate enough to have relatives in the countryside fled to farms where food was more widely available but even there, Kōnosuku Nishikihama recalled, 'there was no salt nor sugar. The best supper dish was a big bowl of cooked wheat and rice in a ratio of 4 to 1. We usually ate steamed sweet potatoes ... I closed my eyes and swallowed.' Repatriates, who had been advised by the *New Canadian* to take goods rather than cash to Japan, often bartered their belongings for basic food.[144]

Many *Nisei* found their limited knowledge of the Japanese language caused difficulties in school or in finding employment. Learning to read Japanese with its 'lines and curves going this way and that' was a problem. Those who were fluent in English and Japanese, however, found themselves in such great demand as translators and interpreters that companies offered them special bonuses, much to the chagrin of other Japanese. Even these fortunate few were bothered by differences in customs and way of life. One repatriate wrote that his 'daughter who received [an] education up to the tenth grade in Canada could not read and write Japanese, nor could she bear sitting on the floor even for five minutes; she could not even get married to a farmer because she had no experience in farming.' The clash of cultures, of course, was sharpest in rural areas where people were bound tightly by tradition and convention. Such reports did not encourage those awaiting passage to Japan.[145]

The story was not entirely dismal. In Mio, over 300 repatriates had a significant impact. English words flourished, fashionable western clothes attracted attention, and repatriated children performed tap dances for school entertainments. Though assimilation was not such a problem, the repatriates in Mio suffered the same severe living conditions as others. Friends and relatives in Canada were not permitted to remit money until 1949 but they did send cloth, yarn, and other goods which could be sold on the black market. Earning a living was also a problem. To create their own jobs, repatriates in 1947 founded the Mio Fishing Industry Company, but they lacked a good knowledge of the Kii Channel fishing grounds and could not easily work with local labour. The company went bankrupt in 1952.[146]

The Canadian repatriates were also frustrated by the complete failure of the Japanese government to recognize their problems. Labouring under the scrutiny of the American Occupation, the administration had too many problems to worry about a few thousand Canadian returnees, particularly since it had to provide for soldiers and civilians still scattered through the remnants of the empire and the prison camps of the victors. Since Japan had no diplomatic relations with countries with which it had not yet signed peace treaties, the repatriation of Japanese from Manchuria, Korea, China, and Southeast Asia created great public concern.[147] The newspapers were full of articles on the millions yet to be repatriated; they had little space or sympathy for the Japanese Canadians. Indeed, neighbours sometimes blamed the Canadian repatriates for the air raids that had destroyed much of the country.

Initially, the bureaucrats of Japan's Repatriation Bureau refused to consider the Canadians as repatriates since they had returned voluntarily and not as refugees. Moreover, whereas refugees had often fled with only the poor clothing on their backs, the Canadians had arrived 'dressed like gentlemen' and carrying plenty of baggage. In 1947 the Ministry of Foreign Affairs publicly noted that none of the estimated 23,000 Japanese still in Canada seemed subject to restrictions.[148] The observation was not quite true but it suggested that the government of Japan wondered why the Japanese Canadians had come home.

Faced with an official stonewall, *Issei* and *Nisei* repatriates organized the

National Federation of Repatriates from Canada and petitioned Tokyo for recognition of their status as war repatriates so they might receive compensation for their war losses. They did not associate themselves with the general organization of repatriates because their losses had resulted from the *outbreak* of the war rather than from Japan's ultimate defeat. Though a government inquiry into their status found no evidence of involuntary repatriation, the Repatriation Allowance Act of 1957 included them and provided a small grant-in-aid.

This token gesture did not satisfy everyone. Calling on their status as former Canadians, in 1960 and 1961 branches of the federation appealed to the Canadian embassy in Tokyo for financial compensation for the 'hardships caused by the War' and 'the unavoidable circumstances of our repatriation.' Even though the petitioners claimed that many repatriates had 'died from poverty and malnutrition' and that financial distress had consigned the survivors to a living standard 25 per cent below that in Canada, embassy officials were not impressed since the repatriates appeared not to be 'badly off in terms of Japanese standards of living.'[150]

The loyalties of these repatriates were certainly tangled. At the same time as they were petitioning Canada, they were seeking compensation from Japan under Article 14(a) 2 of the Japanese Peace Treaty of 1951, which provided that 'each of the Allied Powers shall have the right to seize, retain, liquidate or otherwise dispose of all property, rights and interests' of Japan and its nationals. Thus, *Issei* who were dispossessed by the Canadian government and repatriated to Japan sought compensation because Tokyo had acquiesced to the appropriation of their property as part of the reparations to be paid to Canada. The search for compensation became a political and judicial one in Japan. In 1960 Take and Fujimoto Akiyama, two Japanese nationals, went to court to seek compensation for bank accounts which the Canadian custodian of enemy property told them they had forfeited when they were repatriated in 1943. In what became known as the 'Canada Decision,' the Tokyo High Court in 1965 decided they were entitled to compensation even though no legislation provided for it. On appeal in 1968, the Supreme Court of Japan dismissed the case on the grounds that both victims and the nation should equally bear the losses caused by the assignment of overseas property for reparations. In the meantime, however, the Japanese government had set up a commission of inquiry which eventually suggested that the state pay compensation as a special measure even though it had no legal responsibility for the repatriate's losses. As a result, in 1967 Japan's Parliament, the Diet, passed the Law Relating to Special Allowances for Repatriates.[151]

The Japanese public, it must be noted, was sharply critical of this legislation. Many who had suffered losses and hardships during the war could not understand why repatriates should receive special treatment or why tax money should be spent for this purpose.[152] The repatriates thus found themselves welcomed neither in Japan nor in Canada. Ironically, the repatriation question had made Canadians, both Japanese and Caucasian, more conscious of the value of Canadian citizenship.

Seven

Behind the Barbed-Wire Fence: Internees and POWs in Japan, Japanese-Controlled Territory, and Canada

Along with the tens of thousands of British, American, Australian, and Dutch soldiers captured in Asia, the Canadian soldiers taken at Hong Kong became part of the labour supply available to Japan. As was its right under international law, Japan could make use of soldiers and non-commissioned officers as workers, and it did so, eventually moving substantial numbers to Japan for work in mines or shipyards. Interned civilians there were held under guard, their primary struggles being to survive on inadequate rations and in the face of disease. Both POWs and civilian internees in Japan endured abysmal conditions. In Canada, where no Japanese POWs were held, the government did intern a substantial number of Japanese Canadians behind the barbed-wire fences of Angler Camp in northern Ontario. Their material conditions were better than those borne by Canadians in Japan, but confinement sat no better on them.

Before the fires at Pearl Harbor had been brought under control, the RCMP had arrested thirty-eight Japanese suspected of subversive intentions.[1] Included were a Japanese-language school teacher in New Westminster, a staff member from each of the three Japanese newspapers in British Columbia, a Buddhist priest, a doctor in Vancouver, the secretary of the Fishermen's Cooperative in Steveston, a tomato farmer, and a businessman. The arrested men all claimed to be puzzled by their incarceration; Canadian authorities told them only that they were 'inscrutable' and security risks. Yasutaro Yamaga, a successful *Issei* farmer and a leading figure in the Fraser Valley town of Haney, in fact considered many of those picked up to be pro-Canadian.[2] Tokikazu Tanaka, the teacher, claimed four years later that he had never understood his arrest – there was nothing 'dangerous' about him and he had in fact been 'contributing to Canada's national policy by educating children to become good Canadian citizens.'[3]

The reasons for the arrests and the evidence that lay behind them remain completely unclear. The weaknesses of RCMP intelligence about the Japanese Canadians have already been noted, and the files on these arrests, almost a half century after the fact, remain closed to researchers.

Many more Japanese Canadians were soon in internment. By June 1942 the authorities had cracked down on the Nisei Mass Evacuation Group and others who had continued to resist the British Columbia Security Commission's evacuation orders. In that month, 188 *Nisei* were sent to Angler, Ontario. By mid-July, the number of internees held there had reached 653.

Internment was different from evacuation, a fact that has become confused or forgotten in recent histories and in the Canadian press. The Japanese Canadians who were moved to the BC interior were not held behind barbed wire by armed guards and, though subject to strict controls and less than favourable conditions, they could move with relative freedom. Those in work camps had some freedoms restricted, though in specified circumstances they too could, for example, leave British Columbia to take employment in Ontario. The internees at Angler, in contrast, were held under armed military guard, their liberty severely constrained, their uniform dress prescribed.

Angler was no holiday resort. Located deep in the Lake Superior bush country on a railway line far from any town, the camp held between 400 and 800 men of whom most were Mass Evacuation Group resisters. Others were interned for violating BCSC regulations such as leaving road camps to visit their families without passes or for causing disruptions in the work camps. Still others had been interned because they supported Japan in the war or had sought internment to demonstrate their loyalty to Japan.[4] As one Japanese national explained, 'as an old soldier of Japan, as a loyal Japanese,' he had to seek internment even though it might force him to commit suicide.[5] Such internees were intensely patriotic and wrote of their determination not 'to bring shame to the great *Yamato* race which is now advancing so boldly in the cause of the Co-Prosperity Sphere for East Asia.'[6] One internee, Takeo Nakano, who did not share this view, wrote of the 'substantial number' who 'believed absolutely in Japan's eventual victory and expected personal postwar compensation from a defeated Canada.'[7] Another internee told his wife that he was 'a true Japanese' and wanted to protest 'the hairy beasts' [foreigners'] racial discrimination.' He and his comrades 'obstinately' resisted efforts to make them seek outside employment.[8] Such *Gambariya* regarded the bright red circle on the back of their uniform shirts not as a target for their guards, but as 'the rising sun of the Japanese flag.' Many decorated the red circle with patriotic slogans such as *hakko-ichii* (the whole world under one roof) and *giyo-hoko* (make courageous sacrifices for the state). They also drilled in military order under the direction of an aged veteran of the Russo-Japanese war.[9] Some Japanese nationals, however, treated such actions with disdain. 'Ecstatic are the wearers,' wrote Nakano in a *haiku* of those who flaunted their red-circled shirts, 'But what a fine target.'[10]

Even by 1945 when it was evident that Japan's defeat was already inevitable, some *Gambariya* doubted that the United States navy had landed in the Philippine Islands. How, one asked himself, could the Americans 'be marching as if they were marching in an uninhabited island, without any resistance from Japanese soldiers?' At the end of May when this same internee read in a Canadian newspaper that Tokyo had been completely burnt out by B-29 bomber raids, he recorded that 'such a thing cannot happen.'[11] Some *Issei* internees even refused to believe the news of Japan's surrender in August 1945. This, they said, must be a fabrication to calm the white masses.[12]

The Canadian government was aware of the divided loyalties of the Angler internees, but seemed to give a higher priority to the well-being of Japanese nationals since they could – and did – protest to the protecting power and the International Red Cross. Those protests sometimes caused difficulty. In 1943, for example, the Department of External Affairs was obliged to deny Japanese government allegations that sentries at Angler had fired on internees, had threatened to shoot men who did not line up for roll call within ten minutes, and that one sentry had 'pointed his bayonet at [a] Japanese internee to urge him to work, and wounded him in [the] hip.' Such charges were completely false, Ottawa said, and, moreover, indicated 'the deception of the Japanese authorities in learning of the basically good treatment extended to Japanese in Canada.'[13] The Canadian authorities did recognize the rights of internees by arranging for them to receive a gift of special foods from the Japanese government and by granting requests for more rice, green vegetables, and curry powder and less potatoes, cheese, and bread.[14]

In fact, the meals at Angler were good, one internee even describing them as 'the best kind in the world.'[15] As a result, Ottawa faced problems persuading internees to leave the camp for agricultural work because conditions were 'too good.' One man, quoted by a Department of Labour official, said, 'Why should I leave here, the Government is looking after the folks for me, while they are doing this I can eat the best of food and all I want of it ... Then I can go to my bunk and read and sleep till the next meal comes around. Then too we have our moving picture shows, baseball games, tennis courts, recreation halls, etc., why this has been one grand holiday, I could never afford to pay for it myself.'[16] There was almost certainly an ironic cast to that statement that the official missed. The reality of the internees' life, as Nakano noted, was 'that we were not free to do what we wanted to do.'[17] Moreover, like the residents of the settlements in the BC interior, mail was censored, so much so that sometimes only fragments made it through the screening.[18]

The BCSC's intent was to arrange jobs for internees so they could 'resume productive employment.'[19] Physically fit men generally were forbidden to return to British Columbia but, in line with its dispersal policy, the BCSC would move families east if internees accepted work there. Some *Nisei* accepted. As one explained, he was a Canadian and willing to cooperate in return for reunion with his family.[20] Whereas at the end of 1942, 758 men were in internment, by the following September only 448 remained. At the end of the war, however, Angler still held 425 internees.[21]

Clearly, the plan to disperse all internees who were not security risks had failed. In the autumn of 1943, despite some reservations about being able to distinguish between the 'harmless' and the 'dangerous,' officials agreed to release the harmless to useful employment and to remove them from *Gambariya* influences at Angler.[22] Although some 150 younger men indicated their desire to accept employment, many subsequently changed their minds, probably because of pressures from their parents or threats from within the camp.[23] Takeo Nakano, who was older than most held at Angler, remembered that when he decided to leave late in 1943, one 'true *gambariya* diehard' cursed him as 'a traitor to Japan' for wanting to take work that would help Canada's war effort. Some internees, of course, looked 'forward to being under the JAPANESE government.'[24]

Japan's defeat did not immediately bring an end to the internment. While the majority of those still at Angler in January 1946 were prepared to indicate a desire to stay in Canada or to be repatriated, a total of 128 remained completely defiant to the end, refusing even to indicate their choice to Ottawa; of these, seventy-four were Japanese nationals, twenty-one were naturalized Canadians, and thirty-three were *Nisei*.[25] Some of the latter in fact asserted that since they were 'deprived of their rights as Canadian citizens,' it was up to the Canadian government to decide their fate.[26] That toughness of spirit, that conviction that their rights had been violated, was wholly admirable.

The attack on Pearl Harbor inevitably put Canadian and other Allied citizens in Japan and Japanese-occupied territories at risk. The majority of Canadian citizens in East Asia were missionaries sponsored by Canadian organizations or, in a few cases, affiliated with American and other foreign religious groups. Other Canadians were employees of such agencies as the Chinese Maritime Customs, or of British and Canadian shipping companies and other commercial organizations. As far as the Canadian government knew, 534 Canadian citizens, including twenty merchant seamen, lived in Japan or areas under Japanese control including occupied China and Korea.[27] However, the total number of Canadians in East Asia was probably closer to a thousand. Canadians abroad did not have to report to the Canadian government and there were a number of individuals who subsequently claimed Canadian status through family or business connections.

In Japan, the outbreak of war brought little immediate change in the living conditions of many Canadians. For example, Ernest Bott, a missionary and a teacher of English at Waseda University, was warned not to meet his classes on 9 December 1941 for fear of 'extreme patriots,' but, unlike most male enemy nationals, he was not interned. His wife Edith, an English teacher at the Women's Higher Normal School in Tokyo, continued her classes until the end of the year, when all foreigners were forbidden to teach in government schools. Other female missionaries remained in their homes under 'a sort of informal house arrest,' free to leave if they reported to the policeman on duty.[28] The aged missionary teacher, Agnes Coates, a staunch friend of Japan and the Japanese, told her children in Canada that she was in no danger: 'they take good care of their aged in Japan and especially those who have been "sensei," surely you need not worry about my being well looked after, especially as I am in a position not to be financially indebted to them, and am able to see that they receive proper "O Bei" [bribes] in various ways for favours done me.'[29] Another missionary, Sybil Courtice, dean of the Toyo Eiwa Girls' School, and her colleague Miss F.G. Hamilton, who had been principal until the Japanese government forced the appointment of a Japanese in 1938, had their salaries paid by Toyo Eiwa's board of directors after remittances from Canada ceased with the outbreak of war.[30]

Some missionaries were arrested as early as 9 December. Father Adélard Desbiens, one of three French-Canadian Catholic priests arrested that day, wrote that he had been well treated at Nagasaki, where he was first arrested, 'not so well' at Yokohama, and 'badly' at Yamakita, where he remained until war's end. The accounts of Fathers G. Aubry and Gabriel-Marie Couture were much the same, although they were at Nagasaki and Kobe and at Sendai and Urawa, respectively.[31] Four months after Pearl Harbor, the Vatican signed a concordat with Japan which tended to secure more lenient treatment in Japan for Catholic missionaries than for Protestants. Throughout Japanese-controlled territory, however, Roman Catholic missionaries received treatment as varied as that of Protestants or POWs.

According to an official statement of policy issued on 30 January 1942, the main purposes for interning enemy civilians were to prevent them from carrying out intelligence activities and to protect them. To this end, camps would be located to make escape impossible, and the police would keep close watch and punish internees who failed to carry out instructions. Mail was censored but religious freedom was guaranteed. The Japanese promised equal treatment to internees, protection of their health, fair supplies of food on a rational plan, and special treatment for the sick.[32]

At that time, the government of Japan knew that Japanese civilians, including a few in Canada, had been interned in Allied countries and that Japanese Canadians and Japanese Americans were living in extremely tenuous circumstances. The Ministry of Foreign Affairs, in particular, urged that enemy nationals be treated with care lest ill-treatment rebound against Japanese abroad or be used by the Allies as an excuse for anti-Japanese propaganda.[33] The civil authorities in Tokyo obviously realized that Allied citizens in their control were as much hostages as the Japanese nationals in Allied hands.

In fact, most enemy alien civilians in Japan had limited freedom until September 1942. Then, perhaps in retaliation for the evacuation of Japanese from the Pacific coasts of the United States and Canada and the internment of others, almost all enemy aliens in Japan were interned. Restrictions, wrote one Canadian missionary, 'were greater than for the first six months of war for there had to be some way of retaliation found for treatment of Japanese in America and elsewhere.'[34]

However, the Japanese authorities were inconsistent. One internee noted, 'Several old women were left in their homes, while others just as old and frail were put into the camp; and there seems to [have] been no particular reason why a number of able-bodied younger women were allowed their freedom. It does not seem to have depended on personal attitudes either, for some of the most pro-Japanese were among those interned.'[35] Nevertheless, Margaret Armstrong of the United Church's Women's Missionary Society remained at liberty, possibly because she had become a Japanese citizen in 1940 (a very rare occurrence in a racially conscious nation) and had lived so long in Toyama that she had become an institution.[36] Similarly, some Roman Catholic nuns were interned in their own convents. Although their freedom of movement was so curtailed they had no contact with Japanese members of their own orders, they did have access to their gardens and had no major problems with food.

Most internees in camps endured an inadequate and unbalanced diet. For example, Sybil Courtice, who was repatriated in 1943, stated that while staff from a Tokyo restaurant prepared food at her camp, 'the majority of internees felt that their general health suffered because of an abnormal diet.' A colleague concurred while noting the need to remonstrate against Japanese friends who insisted on sending in food despite their own wants. The Japanese government had prescribed a weekly ration per internee of 1050 grams of rice, 3400 grams of bread, 450 grams of meat, 1050 grams of fish, 2700 grams of vegetables, 200 grams of flour, 150 grams of butter, 200 grams of oil, 300 grams of eggs, 130 grams of sugar, 450 grams of fruit, and 600 grams of milk.[37] Late in 1942, Japanese radio announced a reduction to a daily allowance of 400 grams of bread, 10 grams of meat, 140 grams of fish, 100 grams each of potatoes and vegetables, 400 millilitres of milk, and one egg. In addition, said the propaganda broadcast, each internee received 300 grams of sugar and 900 grams of butter cheese monthly, and 'at tea time fruits and pastries were supplied.'[38] Had it been provided, that ration, while small for North Americans, would have maintained life and health; unfortunately, it was not. While there were sufficient carbohydrates such as bread, there was always a serious shortage of vegetables.

After the first camp, Sendai, which housed both men and women, was closed in December 1942, most of its residents were transferred to Sumire Camp at Tokyo. Later, male internees were sent to Urawa.[39] While Miss Courtice admitted that conditions at Sumire were crowded – an average of about 45 square feet per person as sleeping room plus an average of about 25 square feet per person in public space such as the dining room, laundry, recreation room, and chapel – sanitation and medical care was satisfactory.[40] One of her associates, Catherine Greenbank, remarked on how Japanese friends seemed 'very much embarrassed. They showed great sympathy and made known generally their disapproval. Some felt because it was "war" it was the natural thing. They were taught that they must not sympathize or show their interest in us but many braved the unpleasantness and showed kindness in any way they could. Camp officials were very kind and considerate.' One Roman Catholic nun agreed that conditions were satisfactory and officials 'as kind as possible'; another complained of the absence of beds, of inadequate medical facilities, poor sanitation, and the 'suspicious' and 'rude' nature of the Japanese in charge.[41]

Individual expectations and experiences undoubtedly coloured impressions of camps in Japan as they did the perceptions of Canadians confined elsewhere in the Japanese empire. Nevertheless, it is clear that conditions did vary greatly from camp to camp and from time to time. A Department of External Affairs analysis of questionnaires completed by *Gripsholm* repatriates concluded:

> The treatment which the Japanese accorded those detained by them varied considerably from one district to another and from one camp to another. On the whole, there are few stories of deliberate brutality. The Gendamerie [*sic*] or police are invariably reported as being rude or purposely unpleasant. The other officials Army, Consular officers etc. are said by some to be indifferent, by others to be kind, on such rare occasions as the internees had any contact with them, the civilians are reported as being on the whole, kind and considerate. Referring to the police, one man says, 'they were at least very disagreeable to several internees when they were not openly harsh, taking occasion of the smallest offence to scold or abuse.'[42]

Outside Japan itself conditions were especially varied and food, or rather the lack of it, loomed even larger in the lives of the Canadian civilians than it did in Japan.

Initially, Japanese authorities in the Philippines were not quite sure what to do with the approximately fifty Canadians there. Within a few days, however, except for infants and their mothers, the infirm, and the elderly, the Canadians were among approximately 4000 American, British, and Dutch internees in a camp set up on the campus of Santo Tomas University in Manila. The Canadians' reports on their diet vary. One couple, whose daughter was ten years old when they were released after two years in camp, reported that 'the food ration for adults was two meals a day: one about 11 consisting of a tablespoonful of cornmeal, the milk of one coconut for every 10 people, some synthetic coffee and every other day a teaspoonful of sugar. The second meal about 4.30 was made up of a vegetable hash or peanut loaf, most of which was rice, one banana, some synthetic tea and a small amount of rice. Once a week there was a very small meat ration, water-buffalo meat entirely fatless. Children had three meals a day and one egg daily.'[43] Even though they received a gift of a dozen eggs every week from their former house-boy, their daughter maintained her weight but she did not grow. A sadder story concerned a Dutch-born veteran of the Canadian Expeditionary Force who was interned with his ailing wife and four Canadian-born children. They had no money apart from gifts from a fellow internee and a small amount the girls could earn baby sitting. As a consequence, the father of the family lost seventy pounds in less than two years. Inexplicably, the family was not repatriated on the *Gripsholm* and their fate is unknown.[44]

In contrast, a childless couple, who were repatriated, reported that their diet, though monotonous, provided about 1800 calories per day and those with money could patronize Filipino fruit and vegetable vendors who came to the camp daily, an internee-run restaurant which served hotcakes, sausage, vegetables, and eggs, and the camp canteen which sold staples and some meat and eggs. They also described how internees organized medical, educational, religious, and recreational services and maintained a high level of morale despite physical difficulties. After their release they wrote in a circular letter to friends:

> You wouldn't have liked it – neither did we. Leaving comfortable homes; crowding into rooms containing from 15 to 60: sleeping on hard beds; eating off tin plates; standing in line for food, showers, toilets and absolute lack of privacy were some of our problems. ... [Nevertheless] ... we had the Japs buffaloed by our cheerfulness and acceptance of the inevitable. They just couldn't understand our attitude towards our work and play. They probably expected us to protest and cause trouble over certain restrictions and decisions – but what good would that have done us? As it was, we probably gained more leniency and were left much more to our own devices. We can't give the Japs credit for our treatment, but we can be thankful that they left us alone and permitted us to do our own purchasing and governing.[45]

While the Japanese at Santo Tomas were generally indifferent towards their internees, some drunken Japanese officers brutally tortured and murdered two French-Canadian missionaries on the southern island of Mindanao. According to testimony provided by an American missionary, in August 1942 local authorities informed the two priests that if they voluntarily went to the Davao internment camp, they 'would not be worried in any way.' En route to the camp, the missionaries stopped for the night at Lagtingan where the mayor's wife invited them to dinner. Following the custom of the country, the other guests kissed the hands of the Canadian priests. This provoked the Japanese officers who, later that night, got drunk and struck the missionaries on the head with rifles and chairs. During several hours of torture the officers tore the skin off the missionaries' feet, forced them to march, and, finally, bayoneted them and threw their bodies in the river.[46]

Another murder of Canadian missionaries occurred in China. As in the Philippines, it seems to have been an isolated incident following a perceived insult to local Japanese officers. As a gesture of thanks, three Canadian Jesuits who had been operating a school at Fenghshien in Hsuchow invited some Chinese benefactors and a few Chinese puppet government officials to a dinner at their mission. Unfortunately, they did not invite the Japanese adviser to the local government who was so angered that he had the three priests detained by the gendarmerie that very night and charged them with 'scattering anti-Japanese propaganda and with connivance with Chinese guerillas in acts inimical to Japan.' A German missionary brought the incident to the attention of the Japanese commander who, after investigating, ordered their release. That night, 18 March 1943, the local Japanese adviser called on the Canadian priests to sign a confession. When they refused, he ordered them taken to military headquarters where they were shot dead. Their bodies were removed to the mission compound, and it was announced that Communist troops had entered the city and killed them. Concerned about possible consequences for other missionaries, the superior of the Jesuit Mission refused to supply the names of the individuals concerned and specifically asked that no inquiries be made of the Japanese authorities. The Canadian government, realizing that other missionaries were hostages, honoured the request. It asked the Swiss, as the protecting power, to try to secure more details but 'on no account' to 'approach the Japanese authorities for information.'[47]

In China, about 300 Canadians were caught behind enemy lines. The majority were missionaries, including about 200 Catholic priests, brothers, and nuns, twenty-eight United Church missionaries, sixty-eight members of the interdenominational China Inland Mission, and two Anglicans.[48] At first, enemy nationals could stay in their own homes subject to restrictions, though funds were frozen except for very limited withdrawals from bank accounts. Like other enemy aliens in China they had to wear red arm bands, in their case bearing the Chinese characters 'Tud Chi' meaning Canadian.[49]

The treatment accorded Canadians and other enemy aliens in China varied greatly, especially during the first year of the Pacific war. In February 1942 the Board of Foreign Missions of the United Church reported that Canadian missionaries in China and Korea were well 'and in their own homes and not interfered with except that they are restricted in their movements.'[50] In Peking they had the freedom of the city but in Tientsin and most other places they were confined to certain parts of the cities, usually the international quarter. The Jesuits at Suchow had to remain within their compound walls. Some missionary sisters in Canton, however, were left virtually at liberty and continued to run their schools and good works, but an Anglican nurse at Kweiteh was arrested as a prisoner of war.[51] On 8 December 1941 at Cheeloo University Hospital, Tsinan, the Japanese military ordered missionaries to discontinue their clinics, confiscated radios, and looted library books, office equipment, and scientific apparatus. On 16 January 1942 the authorities ordered the missionaries to shut their hospital but permitted the staff to remain in their own homes until 1 April 1942, when the missionaries were ordered to concentrate in one corner of the campus in preparation for repatriation.[52]

Some missionaries were obliged to move to larger cities on or near the coast. Most were in Shanghai. 'Within these cities,' one Canadian report observed, 'they were allowed to reside and come and go freely [and] ... for the most part to continue their activities.' Nevertheless, the gendarmerie arrested individual missionaries 'generally on unknown or indefinite charges, or for the purpose of exacting information. ... Their experiences varied from a few hours' detention to several months, and from more or less harmless questioning to severe torture.'[53]

The variations in treatment were not surprising. Dr A.E. Armstrong of the United Church's Board of Foreign Missions told a correspondent in late March 1942, 'as you know from experience in North Honan, the Japanese military do not have specific instructions from headquarters' on the treatment of missionaries. 'That is to say, each Commander is on his own and does as he likes,'[54] a recurring refrain. Ottawa tended to the same view, blaming abuses on the military authorities but generally believing in the 'good intentions' of the Foreign Office at Tokyo.[55]

Beginning in Shanghai in November 1942, Japanese authorities began interning most enemy nationals. According to rumour and a press campaign, this 'was a case of reprisal measures against the internment and the bad treatment accorded to Japanese nationals in the United States, Canada and India.'[56] A Canadian missionary later wrote, 'the reason given was always the internment of Japanese in America.'[57] When Britain, through the Swiss government, inquired about internees' living conditions, Japan replied that while internment in special centres had been necessary 'to prevent espionage in occupied China,' she had created civil assembly centres, rather than internment camps, along the lines of camps created in the United States, Canada, and elsewhere so families could stay together.[58] Indeed, a Canadian repatriated from Shanghai remarked on how the Japanese were reluctant 'to use the word "interned" or "camp" and insisted on the term "civil assembly centre."' However, when told of the rations provided to Japanese in North America, camp officials admitted 'they could not furnish similar rations if they wanted to do so as they had been at war for five years in China and have neither the provisions nor the money to obtain them.'[59] In some instances, people were given advance notice of their move to camps and could take luggage, including beds, bedding, a chair, food, money, books, and medicine with them. Their houses were then sealed but there was much looting.[60]

Conditions within the camps in China varied. The camp at Weihsien in

Shantung was housed in what had been an American Presbyterian Mission School. Its residents included about fifty Canadians, missionary priests, professors, nurses, doctors, and their families, as well as some twenty Canadian children who had been attending the China Inland Mission schools at Chefoo and who were moved there in August 1943. One repatriate attributed the 'kinder attitude' of the guards at Chefoo to the presence of many small schoolchildren.[61] At Weihsien, camp residents organized a school and, with the assistance of the Swiss consul, even ran Oxford university-entrance examinations. Medical personnel among them organized a hospital and maintained good health among the inmates despite insufficient medicine, poor sanitation, and inadequate food. Many repatriates commented favourably on the quality and quantity of bread available, thanks in part to the presence of a baker in their midst, but observed that otherwise the food was 'of poor quality what there was of it' and complained of a bad-tempered issuing officer who sometimes deliberately withheld vegetables until they rotted. Further humiliations were guards who acted as 'lords over servants' and commonly resorted to 'face-slapping.'[62]

At Footung Civil Assembly Centre, where about 1080 men were housed in warehouses abandoned as a fire hazard in 1929 by the British American Tobacco Company, the commander expressed 'complete indifference to the welfare of internees' in what he regarded as a 'punishment camp.' Food generally was 'fair according to oriental standards, but these both in quantity and quality were insufficient for occidentals.' As time passed, the quality of the diet declined. Red Cross supplies brought the average daily caloric intake, but not that of vitamins and calcium, up to adequate levels. Given the presence of many missionary doctors in Footung, the quality of medical care was high but serious illnesses brought on by nutritional deficiencies had to be treated without proper medicine or equipment.[63]

Although missionaries were present in almost all the camps, their concentration seems to have been greater in some. One Japanese camp commandant, a Christian, regarded himself 'as having been divinely placed in this largely missionary camp to soften the hard blows of war for his fellow Christians.'[64] Such a situation was unusual but the missionaries, possibly because of their dispositions and training, seem to have borne the hardships of incarceration better than other internees. One Roman Catholic priest, interned at Peking, noted an initial bigotry and tension between Catholics and Protestants in the camp but boasted that when 'the rest of the camp ... saw the Fathers take the heaviest of the work and the sisters usually the dirtiest, ignorance gave way to admiration.'[65] A Canadian priest shipped from Suchow to internment in Shanghai in mid-1943 wrote that even in camp, 'we enjoyed relative freedom. We had our books and our leisure, the joys and comforts of the communal life in a religious setting.'[66]

The reports of other internees suggests that that priest either had an unusually sunny outlook or a unique experience. Certainly his situation contrasted sharply with the circumstances of seven Canadian men who had the misfortune to be arrested in Shanghai without notice on 5 November 1942. These seven were taken to the Haiphong Road internment camp where, with 339 other Allied nationals, they found themselves in severely overcrowded quarters and facing steadily declining rations. They were required to bow to Japanese personnel 'whenever seen,' but far worse than their physical circumstances or this humiliation was doubt about their future. Japanese authorities claimed they were political prisoners held for military reasons. Indeed, most camps were nominally under Japanese civilian authority, but military guards were posted at each one and it 'was well known that the whole organization was dominated by the all-powerful and omnipresent gendarmerie, and took orders from them.'[67] Particularly in a camp such as Haiphong, the control of the camp by the gendarmerie, a Japanese equivalent of the Gestapo, created 'an ever-present feeling of uncertainty regarding individual personal safety and/or treatment.' One Canadian, a political scientist and missionary, noted, 'the Colonel in charge had a kindly spirit, but we were constantly subject to questioning & removal by the gendarmerie.' Inmates, who had no idea of why they had been classified as 'political prisoners,' believed they were 'somewhat in the nature of hostages on whom the wrath of the Japanese military may be vented when reverses occur or when bombings take a toll of Japanese civilians in occupied China or Japan.'[68]

The Canadian government's main source of information about these camps were the reports of the *Gripsholm* repatriates in the fall of 1943. For those who were not repatriated, conditions worsened. In the fall of 1944, the Red Cross reported that 199 Canadians interned in Shanghai were in acute circumstances because, for six months, Japan had prevented Switzerland, the protecting power, from distributing Canadian government funds to allow internees to purchase a few necessities from the camp canteen and had intimidated uninterned friends from sending in comfort parcels. Even those with money suffered; inflation was severe. In 1943 Canada had allocated $7 per person to provide a small hamper of comforts as a Christmas gift to Canadian prisoners of war. A year later, the Red Cross advised that that sum would buy only a small box of candy and indicated that a sum of $40 to $60 was required for a hamper consisting of a small tin of powdered milk, a pound-and-a-half of bacon, a pound each of cheese, sugar, and oats, a half pound of sweets, and a quarter pound each of tea and egg powder. Reporting that the health of Canadian civilians had so deteriorated that 'their position might be called desperate,' the Red Cross recommended extending the Christmas gift program to them.[69]

Conditions in Shanghai were bad; at Stanley Camp in Hong Kong they were horrible. Approximately 2500 enemy nationals were incarcerated there, including about sixty-two Canadians, some of whom, such as some missionary sisters, had been lumped in with the British. Most internees at Stanley Camp had been rounded up without warning a few days after the fall of Hong Kong and had been marched through the city to filthy, verminous, and unventilated rooms in third-class hotels where they were locked up without food or water for twenty-four hours. Two weeks later, after subsisting on a diet of rice and water supplemented by whatever they could buy from hawkers, they were again marched through the city carrying their few belongings, and were taken by boat to Stanley Camp, where they had an average of 41 square feet of space each.[70] There was little furniture. One Canadian woman wrote: 'the room our family [of eight] was thrust into was knee-high in filth, contained not one window pane and not a stick of furniture, and the floor on which we had to sleep was of stone, dirty and cold. We made window panes out of tin and cardboard, impromptu beds with stone blocks and padded iron railings, little stools and tables out of wood we found lying around, and thus we lived from day to day, à la Robinson Crusoe, only he never saw a gendarme!' Such treatment, Anthony Eden, the British foreign secretary, told the British Parliament in March 1942, was 'carefully calculated to humiliate' Europeans and Americans.[71]

For the inmates of Stanley Camp, however, food, not prestige or space, was the greatest problem. Despite Red Cross parcels and gifts from friends outside the camp, it was never satisfactory. In August 1943 the chairman of the Malnutrition Medical Board in the camp reported that:

> The rations provided by the authorities were, in every way, inadequate and unsuitable ... [After] ... some improvement during the summer of 1942 [when] ... daily calories for the third quarter rose to over 2000, with 60 gms. protein ... there was slow steady deterioration (the average for the year being 1855) and the average for the first seven months of 1943 was 1611 calories with 48 gms. of protein. Nor was the quality satisfactory. The rice, the staple food (8 oz. per day) was 'polished' and of poor quality; the meat predominantly water-buffalo beef; much of the fish Pacific Conger Eel and much of the vegetable, Chinese 'water spinach'; all articles of a kind and quality not usually considered fit for human consumption.'[72]

Less scientifically but more graphically, one repatriate reported that 'the daily diet consists of one cup of boiled rice in the morning, one at noon and in the evening a cup of beans mixed with water buffalo meat – about one and a half ounces, or eel meat.'[73] Another indicated that the rice was usually of 'a poor grade, sometimes just sweepings.'[74] Not surprisingly, weight losses were heavy; one medical report indicated that by mid-1943 the average weight loss for fit men was 19.5 per cent of their normal body weight. Deficiency diseases such as beri-beri reached epidemic proportions. Between January and June 1943 the camp hospital treated 1103 cases of nutritional diseases.[75]

As in Shanghai, the inmates of Stanley Camp feared the gendarmerie. A young Canadian woman who had resided in Hong Kong for twenty years described the Japanese camp commandants as sympathetic and cooperative but explained they could do little as they 'were mere servants of the Gendarmerie & Civil Authorities in Hong Kong.' She concluded that 'Stanley Prison – the official prison of the Hong Kong Japanese Gendarmerie is reminiscent of the proverbial Bastille, in similar days of terror and Bloodshed & the voice of Humanity calls for an immediate & full enquiry after the welfare of our fellow human-being[s] who are *at this moment* the pitiful victims of a brutal, bloodthirsty, unreasoning Oriental Gestapo.'[76]

An additional complication for the Canadians in Stanley Camp was 'dissension' in their ranks and morale that was 'none too good.' Some Canadians believed the British camp leader was 'playing into the hands of the Japanese.' With his permission and that of the Japanese authorities, the Canadians met to elect their own leader and to discuss repatriation strategy. When one Canadian argued that repatriation 'was bound up with the presence of Canadian troops in Hong Kong ... and that it would be selfish to leave without them and have them open to reprisals when the Japanese left Canada,' Father C.B. Murphy, the newly elected Canadian leader, told the self-appointed hostage that, while he had sympathy for the troops, they were military prisoners not civilian internees. The time allotted for the meeting elapsed while the Canadians were still debating whether or not they should appeal for repatriation directly to Japanese authorities or work through the British camp leader. External Affairs officials, who later questioned the repatriates, concluded that the camp was 'full of cliques and factions,' and that the only thing on which all repatriates agreed was that the food was bad and likely to get worse.[77]

Fortunately, many Canadians, apparently including all who had been incarcerated in Stanley Camp, were repatriated late in 1943. Indeed, in Japan proper, one Japanese account indicates there were only ten Canadian civilians left in two of the twenty-two camps in Japan.[78] At the Japanese surrender in August 1945, the first senior Canadian officer to reach Tokyo ascertained there were thirty-nine male and forty female Canadians in Chinese camps.[79] This figure was almost certainly lower than the total remaining even after the repatriation voyages of 1942 and 1943. What happened to the others is unclear. Although many were harassed by the Japanese army and gendarmerie, few were killed or tortured. Some Canadian internees in China were well treated depending on the officers in charge of their camp, but virtually all suffered from malnutrition and disease and some died as a result.

However bad their situation, the Canadian civilian internees, like the Japanese Canadians held at Angler, could at least look forward to the possibility of repatriation.[80] In June 1942, thanks to the efforts of the U.S. government,[81] a Japanese ship carried hundreds of Allied nationals, largely but not exclusively diplomats, their dependents, and other officials, to Port Elizabeth, South Africa, where they were exchanged for Japanese officials repatriated from North America.[82] Nineteen government officials and fifty-one others, including fourteen United Church missionaries, returned to Canada on this first repatriation voyage.[83]

One repatriate from Korea recalled that missionaries there were first told that repatriation was voluntary, 'but we were not long in realizing that all foreigners in Korea were "being sent" home. All of us were called to the Provincial Police Department to signify our willingness.'[84] Elsewhere, the selection process was generally either capricious or so random that not even determined missionary efforts to make the lists succeeded with the Japanese.[85] When these first repatriates returned to Canada, the *United Church Observer* noted that journalists were disappointed because the repatriates 'had no atrocities to report.'[86] In fact, government and church officials had warned repatriates to say little lest they cause difficulties for those still in Japanese hands.[87] Even so, some returnees undertook lecture tours or talked with the press, dwelling on the harsh conditions in the internment camps, and suggesting that they 'wouldn't trust a Jap.'[88]

A second exchange of non-official civilians took place in September and October 1943. Again, the United States arranged matters and Canada had to accept whatever space was available. This time sixty-one Canadian residents of Japanese origin were exchanged for some 210 Canadians from Japan and Japanese-controlled territories. No one seemed to know how the Canadians were chosen but medical or compassionate grounds were of little or no significance.[89] In Japan, the government seemed anxious to get rid of French-Canadian Catholic missionaries but, because the missionaries had refused repatriation before the war, because it feared upsetting the Canadian public if the majority of repatriates were Catholic, and because of its concern for internees in Hong Kong, the Canadian government was anxious to give priority to women and children.[90] For a variety of reasons, the repatriation voyages of June 1942 and the fall of 1943 were the only expeditions of their kind. Even then, not all wanted to be repatriated and, by the spring of 1946, some of those who had been repatriated were seeking permission to return to Japan and China.[91]

Although Canada's primary concern was repatriating her citizens who were under Japanese control, she was also anxious to be rid of Japanese internees at Angler. The Japanese Canadians, all male and all but one interned at Angler, were selected by the Spanish consul, acting as Japan's protecting power in Canada. The repatriates agreed to give up all rights and privileges of Canadian nationality, to take only a small amount of money and limited baggage to Japan, and to permit the custodian of enemy property to liquidate any remaining assets and to hold the proceeds until the end of the war. Moreover, Japan had to agree to accept them.

That only sixty-one Japanese Canadians (of over 200 Angler inmates who sought repatriation) were exchanged was a result of space shortages on board the Swedish ship *Gripsholm,* which carried the repatriates. Had Ottawa had its way, all of those who wanted repatriation would have been sent; indeed, so eager was the Canadian government that it did not even exercise its right to forbid repatriation for males of military age.[92]

Arranging the *Gripsholm* exchange was a tedious process, a diplomatic exercise carried out through intermediaries. Although Canada was anxious for further transfers, the exercise was not repeated. Japan halted Commonwealth exchanges because Australia had declared pearl divers to be security risks; Tokyo also rejected further exchanges with the United States because of its concern about conditions at an American 'segregation' centre for 'disloyal' Japanese Americans and because of American attacks on Japanese hospital ships.[93]

As it was, both sides used the exchanges for such propaganda purposes as they could. The Department of External Affairs urged that the repatriates from Angler be given tobacco and other comforts, and it even suggested that visits to canteens be arranged so that souvenirs could be purchased.[94] Similarly, there was surprise among Canadian officials that, as one reported, 'The Canadian repatriates ... look[ed] healthier and better dressed than we had imagined that they would.' Presumably they too had been fattened up prior to their release (and the sea voyage on the *Gripsholm* must also have speeded recovery). Even so, one Canadian official noted, 'Every one of them expressed a thorough detestation of the Japanese.'[95] So much for propaganda.

As Brigadier R.S. Malone noted, civilian internees in Japan were treated far better than prisoners of war. Between January 1943 and April 1944, 1183 Canadian enlisted men (and one medical officer) were shipped to Japan in four separate drafts for forced labour, mainly in coal and iron mines. 'They gave us a physical test,' one sergeant remembered. 'They lined us all up on one side of the road, and if you were able to make it to the other side of the road, you were able to go on the draft.'[96] If conditions were bad in Hong Kong, they were far, far worse on board the ships to Japan and worse still in Japan itself. 'We were forced to work regardless,' one Royal Rifles sergeant said, 'if you could stand up you had to go. And in those circumstances, the food was barely enough to keep one alive.'[97]

The first draft, about 500 Canadians, went to the Nippon Kokan shipyards at Kawasaki. Other groups were at Yokohama, at Omine, sixty miles from Nagasaki, and at Oyama; still others worked in coal mines at Taira, Shinagawa, and Sendai. At Sendai, one Winnipeg soldier remembered, 'You worked in the mine fourteen days in a row ... Everybody was given a quota of coal to do ... Everybody had to produce their quota of coal, everybody was kept down there until the slowest group was finished.'[98]

Much the worst of the camps in Japan was at Niigata. The 'hell hole'[99] had such bad conditions that the camp staff was said to have been punished by the Japanese authorities 'long before the surrender' and some, the Canadian authorities were told, 'served sentences of a year in Civil Gaol.'[100] POWS generally described camp commandants as 'brutal' – although at Omori, Tokyo, Canadians considered that they were fairly treated.[101]

The Swiss legation, the Canadian protecting power in Japan from mid-1942 onwards, repeatedly tried to find out as much as it could on the condition of the POWS, and the Foreign Ministry seemed sympathetic to its efforts. In August 1943 the *Gaimushō* wrote to the POW Information Bureau to note the efforts of the Swiss and to add that the Japanese minister to the Vatican had reported that 'one of the reasons the Canadian government had not returned evacuees to their homes is the lack of information received about the Canadian soldiers captured at Hong Kong.' This, the Foreign Ministry said without conviction, was clearly an excuse; still, more information could be provided. The bureau responded much the way officials do in every country. The Japanese government had provided all facilities possible for the POWS and responded to all inquiries about their health and safety. In other words, rather than complaining, the Canadians should be 'grateful for our efforts.'[102]

The Swiss also reported that the POWs at Yokohama received the same pay as corresponding Japanese ranks (a POW sergeant reported that he was paid 3 yen, 6 sen for one month's work, or about 30 cents Canadian!)[103] and received slightly more food than Japanese depot troops, rations that were less in quantity than those intended for combat units.[104] The Japanese undoubtedly considered that they had done more than was required in giving the POWs more plentiful rations than their own soldiers received (although it is possible, indeed probable, that the Swiss were fooled by the Japanese authorities); after the war, the victors would take a contrary view.

At Niigata, the International Red Cross in May 1944 reported that camp authorities had been unable to issue full rations during the previous winter, and the POWs, unaccustomed to the diet, suffered intestinal troubles. Camp leaders (in the presence of their guards, the IRC said) suggested the food was now better than it had been. That was unlikely, the Red Cross noted, since the poor state of health enabled only a small percentage of POWs to work.[105] At another camp, in early 1944, where the daily food ration was only 13 ounces with one teaspoonful of meat a month, starvation killed POWs at the rate of one a day.[106]

The conditions became even more terrible and the food worse as American submarines cut the Japanese sea lanes and the conquered territories that had exported rice and foodstuffs to Japan were liberated or cut off. 'In the morning,' a corporal recollected, 'we got approximately eight ounces of boiled rice. Green tea. And they gave us sourdough buns ... made out of barley flour ... the mainstay of our lunch.' At noon, lunch would consist of the bun, 'soya sauce and water,' and 'lots of green tea. After we finished the tea, we'd eat the tea leaves because it was food.' 'I, personally, was starving to death,' a corporal from Quebec remembered. Occasionally, Red Cross parcels reached the prisoners, one for eight to seventeen men. 'That was after the Japs had taken out the sugar, the chocolate, anything that they wanted for themselves,' one private claimed. What was left, a corporal stated, was 'a can of bully beef, or a can of milk, you had to divide between seventeen men.' Scarce as Red Cross parcels were, the physical condition of the prisoners rose or fell depending on their availability. One bandsman saw his weight drop to 'about eighty-five, ninety pounds. Now, I'm small of stature,' he said, 'and my normal weight was about a hundred and thirty pounds. So I held my weight between eighty-five and ninety, which is not too bad, considering men of over two hundred pounds were holding the same weight.'[107]

Pathetic as their rations were, the POWs may have been better off than Japanese civilians in the final stages of the war. A Japanese survey of the

POW camp at Osaka in 1945 declared that POWs received as much food as Japanese soldiers and more than twice as much as civilians: rice and wheat – 705 grams/day for POWs, 705 grams for Japanese soldiers, and 330 grams for civilians; meat and fish – 35 grams/day for POWs, 40 grams for soldiers, and 10 grams for civilians. The Japanese calculated that POWs and soldiers received 3000 calories a day, a calculation that Canadian evidence suggests was grossly inflated, while civilians subsisted on only 1400.[108]

By mid-1945 even the POWs, cut off from news and information as they were, knew that the war was reaching its climax. The prisoners at Kawasaki regularly saw American B-29 bombers flying overhead, and at least one Tokyo fire bomb raid came close to the camp. Then on 6 and 9 August the United States Army Air Force dropped atomic bombs on Hiroshima and Nagasaki. A company sergeant major at Omine remembered that when the Nagasaki bomb went off sixty miles away, 'we all thought it must have been three hundred, four hundred, five hundred B-29s.' Few of the Canadian POWs had any doubt that the decision to drop the atomic bombs was the correct one. One held at Yokohama argued that the war might have lasted two or three years more without the A-bomb. 'I feel they saved thousands of lives by dropping the atomic bomb.'

Another private held in the POW camp at Sendai recollected that 'We had an idea the end was coming. We could tell, just by the way they were acting ... All of a sudden work was called off. They called us out on the parade square' and the Japanese camp commandant 'told us the war was over. And with that, he turned around ... disappeared out the gate, and we never saw him again.'[109]

In all, 136 Canadians died in the POW cages in Japan; 128 Canadians died in the Hong Kong prison compounds, in addition to the four Grenadiers shot in their abortive escape attempt. This was a death rate of 27 per cent of those captured when Hong Kong fell on Christmas Day, 1941, appallingly high when compared to the 4 per cent rate among Canadian POWs in German camps in World War II.[110] Other countries' POWs had similarly high death rates in Japanese custody.

For some Canadians in Japanese hands, death came slowly from starvation and disease; for others death resulted from beatings and atrocities – the Canadian authorities had a partial list of nine POWs who died in Japan or en route there as a result of beatings; an additional eight pages of names listed other POWs in Hong Kong and Japan who had been beaten or otherwise abused by their captors.[111] In all, more Canadians died as prisoners of war than in the Hong Kong battle itself.

As it had at Hong Kong, the Canadian government moved quickly to gather the information necessary to prosecute those responsible for the maltreatment of its soldiers.[112] Under Lt-Col. J.O.F.H. Orr, before the war the crown prosecutor in Vancouver, the Canadian War Crimes Liaison detachment in Japan prosecuted twenty-five defendants in six common trials and twenty-five more in individual trials between the early summer of 1946 and May 1947. Forty-nine of those charged, a group that included civilian guards, medical orderlies, soldiers, and officers, were found guilty and one was acquitted. Sentences ranged from one year's imprisonment to death. An additional twenty-six Japanese, prosecuted by the British or the Americans, were stated to be 'cases in which Canada is interested' – that is, affidavits from Canadians formed part of the prosecution's case.[113]

A small Canadian team, headed by Brigadier Malone who had been attached to General Douglas MacArthur's staff after service in Europe, arrived in Japan just after the surrender to improvise immediate care for the surviving Canadian POWS.[114] With the cooperation of the American forces, Malone collected the POWS, sending the seriously ill to hospital ships in Tokyo Bay and the more fit to Manila, where Canadian rehabilitation and medical teams had already been dispatched. After a period of rest and recuperation – according to Malone, the freed POWS needed to be 'rehabilitated a bit before they saw their families ... They all needed proper food, medical care and psychiatric counselling, time to adjust to freedom and to catch up to date again with a world which had changed'[115] – the survivors of the Hong Kong force came back to Winnipeg and Quebec City and fifty more towns across Canada. More than a quarter of the soldiers who had left Vancouver in October 1941 for what they expected to be 'garrison duty' in Hong Kong had failed to return home.

The Japanese surrender did not end the problems of the Hong Kong survivors. Many suffered permanent psychological scars from their prison experiences. Virtually all were plagued by intestinal parasites. A 1947 survey of 553 Winnipeg Grenadiers found that 72 per cent still had parasites – whipworm, hookworm, and threadworm. In addition, every returned veteran suffered from avitaminosis, a blanket term covering all vitamin deficiency diseases. Paraesthesia of the extremities was common, optic atrophy affected 15 per cent, and the life expectancy of the survivors was ten to fifteen years below the Canadian national average. A further medical study, done for the Canadian government in 1963, found the Hong Kong veterans to have a death rate 23 per cent higher than that of other Canadian veterans and, the researchers noted, 'an abnormally high death rate from coronary artery ... disease.'[116] The effects of long imprisonment and inadequate rations and medical care were profound indeed.

Once the war was over, the Canadian missionaries who had remained in Japan, mainly Dominicans and Franciscans, tried to resume their lives. They suffered from the same shortages of food, fuel, and consumer goods as Japanese civilians, and they had also to regain their orders' properties, seized during the war by the Japanese government, repair them, and resume contacts with Christians in the community. Some were dependent on relief funds arranged by the Canadian government. E. Herbert Norman, head of the Canadian Liaison Mission in Japan, reported in September 1946 that 'Living conditions for Canadians in Japan are far from easy or pleasant. The Japanese government has been held much more strictly to account in supplying extra rations that foreigners are entitled to buy from the Japanese stores. In many localities such supplies are unavailable, or very scarce, or of poor quality.' Then Norman added that two distributions of Red Cross supplies had been made in the last two months. So difficult was Japan's condition one year after V-J Day that Red Cross parcels still were needed to keep foreigners healthy.[117] The Japanese civilians, without access to such supplies, had to wait for the return of prosperity.

The Canadian experience in Japanese hands, therefore, can only be described as mixed. Most civilian internees in Japan and Japanese-controlled territory were reasonably well treated, although food and medicine shortages were severe. Many of the military prisoners of war, in contrast, had to bear substantial abuse immediately after capture at Hong Kong and in their POW camps in Hong Kong and in Japan, and all suffered severely from shortages of food and medicines wherever they were held. The Japanese Canadians who were interned at Angler had also lost their freedom but had none of these other problems.

Eight

Conclusion

The war years were a time of tragedy for Canadians, Japanese Canadians, and Japanese alike. The Canadian government, whatever the contemporary and sometimes compelling justifications for its actions against the Japanese Canadians, nonetheless behaved in ways that seemed to belie its claim to be fighting on behalf of freedom and democracy. But, then, few in Canada before the war had viewed the Japanese Canadians as full citizens. In British Columbia, with rare exceptions, they did not even have that most fundamental of rights, the franchise. During the war Canada made few distinctions between those Japanese Canadians who were citizens by birth or naturalization and those who were Japanese nationals and, hence, enemy aliens. The Imperial Japanese government, for its part, was not unduly hampered by the rhetoric of democracy and acted with brutal indifference to the treatment inflicted by the military on prisoners of war and, to a somewhat lesser extent, on civilian internees, all of whom, of course, were enemy aliens. The story of Canadians and Japanese during the Second World War is one of prejudice, misunderstanding, and cruelty. Multiple wrongs can never make a right and there were plenty of wrongs on both sides.

The war brought long-simmering events to the boil. In British Columbia, the racist dislike and economic fear of the Japanese Canadians escalated towards panic as the army and navy of Imperial Japan swept over the Pacific in the days and weeks after the attack on Pearl Harbor. As a result of this panic and plans for public demonstrations against the Japanese Canadians, the Canadian government caved in to racist fears and to the opinions of journalists and amateur strategists who over-estimated Japan's threat to the west coast of North America and under-estimated the enormous logistical difficulties Japanese forces would face in crossing the Pacific. The consequence was the order that all persons of Japanese racial origin must leave the coast.

Nevertheless, it must be remembered that military commanders and leaders of all political stripes on the coast were unanimous in demanding the removal of the Japanese on both military and public safety grounds. That unanimity carried weight in Ottawa, especially with Ian Mackenzie relaying the voice of his province in the highest quarters of the government and Mackenzie King vividly remembering the anti-Japanese riot of 1907. In retrospect, the RCMP and the chiefs of staff in the capital who remained calm and counselled against the evacuation of the Japanese Canadians were correct. Unfortunately, after two-and-a-half years of disasters to Allied arms and just weeks after assurances about the impregnability of Pearl Harbor and Singapore, politicians were sceptical of the claims of generals, admirals, and air marshals that Japan could not attack North America. And, of course, no one in Ottawa ever took the RCMP's intelligence-gathering skills seriously.

Moreover, democratic governments are elected by the people, must respond to them in war as well as in peace, and must maintain law and order. Mackenzie King's Liberal government had the dual responsibility of listening to demands for action from British Columbia and protecting the Japanese Canadians from attacks by their white compatriots. The former could be done; the latter may well have been impossible in February 1942, given the shortage of trained troops everywhere in Canada. Had Japan launched any kind of an attack on the Pacific coast, even a hit-and-run raid, something that senior Allied military planners considered possible until well into 1943, Canada could not have guaranteed the safety of the Japanese Canadians. Moreover, the reliability of the police and of militia battalions raised in British Columbia would have been questionable if their frightened and angry relatives and friends were attacking Japanese Canadians. Given the anti-Japanese sentiments evident east of the Rockies, Active Service Force units were unlikely to have been any more reliable. Paradoxical as it seems, the Japanese Canadians were subjected to the hardships of the evacuation as much for their own protection, and, by implication, the protection of Canadians in Japanese hands in Hong Kong and elsewhere, as for any other reason.

Critics of the government's actions must remember that almost no one in British Columbia or elsewhere in Canada opposed the evacuation. Not until the war was nearly over and the government used dubious means to encourage the repatriation of Canadian Japanese did a significant groundswell of opposition develop, particularly among Christian churches and civil liberties groups. In the end, the government yielded to this chorus of complaint and abandoned the repatriation program, even though the courts ruled it valid.

The virtually unanimous public support for evacuation in 1942 does not excuse the bungling with which it was carried out. The BCSC and its successor, the Department of Labour, were always well intentioned, especially when the Department of External Affairs reminded them of Canadians held by the Japanese. But, in devising such policies as sending able-bodied men to work camps and separating them from their families, the BCSC was obviously inspired more by the desire to get the Japanese Canadians out of sight and out of mind than by humanitarian instincts. Similarly, the government approved the seizure of Japanese-Canadian property for the sake of administrative convenience and granted such niggardly compensation that many Japanese Canadians rightly concluded they had been robbed.

Yet, contrary to a popular and persistent perception in Canada, only about 800 Japanese Canadians were actually interned. They included some ardent supporters of Imperial Japan and the most vociferous opponents of the evacuation and the separation of families. These internees – less than 10 per cent of the adult males in the Japanese Canadian community – were placed under military guard in northern Ontario. The remaining 22,000 or so Japanese Canadians were evacuated inland, most to be housed at least temporarily in rough accommodation in the BC interior or on prairie sugar-beet farms. The circumstances of wartime Canada demanded stringent economy and, in the interior housing settlements and on the beet farms, the Japanese Canadians received little more than the bare necessities of shelter and education. Because of the importance Ottawa accorded to the International Red Cross and to Japan's protecting power in Canada, and because of the obvious implications for Canadians held by the Japanese, the Canadian government did ensure that its wards received good food and health care.

At the same time, many Japanese-Canadian men found themselves doing 'voluntary' labour in work camps. In their situation, the concept of voluntarism must have appeared akin to compulsion. Yet, unlike most Canadians in Japanese hands, Japanese Canadians were able to leave the work camps, the interior housing settlements, and even the Angler internment camp to take employment east of British Columbia. Their reception varied. Farmers welcomed their labour; merchants in declining BC mining towns enjoyed their trade; residents of more prosperous communities from Kelowna to Toronto tended to be hostile. Yet, wherever the Japanese Canadians resettled, over time they earned full acceptance into the community at large.

Those Japanese Canadians who were born in Canada or who had become naturalized suffered particularly cruel blows during the war. Their faith in Canadian democracy was sorely tested. The wish of some to serve in the armed forces was denied until almost the end of the war. They had to absorb the same shock of evacuation and, in some cases, internment that faced Japanese nationals in Canada, as well as the whole crisis over repatriation which splintered the community and families. Moreover, unlike Japanese nationals, they could not easily appeal to the International Red Cross or the protecting power. Without question, the *Nisei,* Canadian citizens by birth, merited much better treatment than they received. Their loyalty to Canada was severely tried but, with rare exception, never faltered. They proved to be more aware of the rights and obligations of citizenship than those who discriminated against them on the basis of race alone.

Perhaps the most incomprehensible aspect of the treatment of the Japanese Canadians concerned repatriation. The government applied strong pressure, and the Japanese-Canadian community was torn by the strain. Many wanted to go to Japan because they could not bear the way they had been treated in Canada; others, as stories and attitudes expressed in the *Tashme News* and in intercepted letters reveal, wanted to go because their loyalties lay there; still others were dragged along unwillingly by family ties. The evacuation of the Japanese Canadians from the west coast can be explained as a tragic consequence of war; the Canadian government's efforts to repatriate the Japanese Canadians, however, smack of vengeance unworthy of a democratic government.

The Canadian government and the Canadian people treated the Japanese Canadians, most of whom were British subjects, very harshly during the war. Nonetheless, the evacuees and internees, no matter what their citizenship, unquestionably were better treated than Canadian soldiers and civilians in Japanese hands. The survivors of the debacle at Hong Kong had the misfortune to fall under the control of an authoritarian military regime that, operating under a different code of behaviour from most Western armies, beat, overworked, and starved its captives. Few in Japan concerned themselves with the plight of the POWs; few today seem aware of their country's past actions. Canadian civilians, mostly missionaries, in Japan were usually better treated, but they suffered severely from the same food and medicine shortages endured by the people of Japan. Even then, some Japanese civilians dipped into their own meagre supplies to bring gift packages to interned Canadian friends. The Canadians who had the misfortune to be caught in Japanese-controlled territory endured a variety of experiences ranging from kind consideration at the hands of some of their captors to brutal torture. All suffered from severe food shortages.

Canada's concern for Canadian POWs and civilians under Japanese control and fears of reprisals against them, not altruism, shaped her policy to evacuees and internees. The Japanese Canadians and the Canadians in Japan were mutual hostages. The *Gaimushō* understood the rules but the surviving records suggest that the military, increasingly a law unto itself under the government of General Hideki Tojo, did not play the game. While the

Japanese press sporadically referred to the wartime sufferings of Japanese abroad, the army saw POWs as men who had dishonoured themselves by surrendering and demonstrated little concern for their countrymen overseas.

In sum, Japan loomed far larger in the eyes of the Canadian government than Canada did to the generals and admirals who controlled the government in Tokyo. Given the different forms of government and the disparities in power, that was inevitable. Ottawa, moreover, was also hostage to the Canadian public. Just as the King government could not treat the Japanese Canadians too badly for fear of reprisals against Canadians in Japan, so it could not treat them too well lest it alienate Canadians whose tolerance in wartime was, perhaps, less than usual. The well-entrenched prejudices of the Canadian public, stimulated by Japan's aggression, by atrocities committed on Allied troops, and by wartime propaganda, allowed for precious few distinctions between Canadian citizens of Japanese origin and Japanese nationals.

The taking of hostages is as old as warfare, as contemporary as today's newspaper. War forced both Canada and Japan into the hostage business. For neither government was it a welcome enterprise, but it was the Japanese in Canada and the Canadians in Japan and Japanese-occupied territory who paid the price as mutual hostages.

Notes

PREFACE

1 Forrest E. LaViolette, *The Canadian Japanese and World War II: A Social and Psychological Account* (Toronto 1948)
2 Ken Adachi, *The Enemy That Never Was: A History of the Japanese Canadians* (Toronto 1976)
3 W. Peter Ward, *White Canada Forever: Popular Attitudes and Public Policy Toward Orientals in British Columbia* (Montreal 1978). For a full review of the early studies on the Japanese in Canada see Patricia E. Roy, ' "White Canada Forever": Two Generations of Studies,' *Canadian Ethnic Studies* xi (1979): 97–101.
4 Ann Gomer Sunahara, *The Politics of Racism* (Toronto 1981)
5 Joy Kogawa, *Obasan* (Toronto 1981)
6 Muriel Kitagawa, *This is My Own: Letters to Wes and Other Writings on Japanese Canadians, 1941–1948*, ed. Roy Miki (Vancouver 1985)
7 Takeo Ujo Nakano with Leatrice Nakano, *Within the Barbed Wire Fence* (Toronto 1980)
8 Barry Broadfoot, *Years of Sorrow, Years of Shame* (Toronto 1977)

CHAPTER 1 The *Imin* and Canadians

1 According to official Japanese passport records, 181 Japanese who left for Canada in 1891 were the first Japanese immigrants to Canada (see table 1). About 100 of them worked briefly in the coal mine at Cumberland on Vancouver Island. At least one died of starvation and others fled home to Japan. Yasutaro Yamaga, ed., *Henē Nōkai Shi* [A History of the Haney Agricultural Association] (Beamsville, Ont. 1963), 10
2 Statistics suggest that emigration absorbed only 2.5 per cent of the natural

increase in the Japanese population in the years 1865–1945. See *Gaimushō* [Ministry of Foreign Affairs], Emigration Section, *Warera ga Kokumin no Kaigai Hatten* [Expansion of Our People Overseas], *Shiryō-hen* [Sources and Documents] (Tokyo 1971), 137.

3 Minoru Tōgō, *Nihon Shokumin Ron* [On Japanese Colonization Overseas] (Tokyo 1906), 291

4 An emigration section established in the *Gaimushō* in 1891 did not survive the departure from office of Takeaki Enomoto, the minister of foreign affairs, in 1892. After retiring, Enomoto contributed to the establishment of the Colonization Society. See *Shokumin Kyōkai Hōkoku* [Reports of the Colonization Society], 1893–1903, nos. 1–100 (Tokyo; reprinted 1986–7).

5 Naomasa Oshimoto, 'Imin Toriatsukai Kikan no Hensen' [Transition of Agencies Dealing with Emigrants], *Kaigai Ijū Jigyō Dan Jūnen Shi* [A Ten-Year History of the Japan International Cooperation Agency] (Tokyo 1973), 4; Alan Takeo Moriyama, *Imingaisha: Japanese Emigration Companies and Hawaii, 1894–1908* (Honolulu 1985), 32

6 See Toraji Iriye, *Hōjin Kaigai Hatten Shi* [A History of Japanese Overseas Expansion] (Tokyo 1942, reprinted 1981), 107ff; Moriyama, *Imingaisha*, passim; Tomonori Ishikawa, 'Nihon Shutsu-Imin Shi ni Okeru Imingaisha to Keiyaku-Imin' [The Place of Emigration Companies and Contract Emigrants in the History of Japanese Emigration], *Ryūkyū Daigaku Kiyō* [Ryukyu University Bulletin] 14 (1970): 19ff.

7 Mitsuru Shimpo, *Ishi o Mote Owaruru Gotoku* [As Though Driven Away with Stones] (Toronto 1975), 14

8 Rintaro Hayashi, *Kuroshio no Hate ni* [At the End of the Black Current] (Tokyo 1974), 42, 49

9 Vancouver *Daily News-Advertiser*, 19 July 1893

10 [Reports of the Colonization Society], no. 14, 1894

11 On British Columbians' views of Chinese immigrants see Patricia E. Roy, *A White Man's Province: British Columbia Politicians and Chinese and Japanese Immigrants, 1858–1914* (Vancouver 1989). For an example of the consulate's statements see Vancouver *World*, 24 March 1897.

12 On emigration generally see Tomonori Ishikawa, 'Tōkei Yori Mita Nihon Shutsu Imin' [Japanese Emigration Viewed Through Statistics], *Chiri Kagaku* [Geographical Science] 11, 14, 19 (1969–72); Yasuo Wakatsuki and Jōji Suzuki, *Kaigai Ijū Seisaku Shi Ron* [A History of Overseas Migration Policy] (Tokyo 1975). Audrey Kobayashi, a geographer at McGill University, is undertaking a major study of Japanese emigration to Canada. Her essay, 'Social Consequences of Regional Diversity Among Japanese Immigrants to Canada: A Preliminary Review,' in K. Victor Ujimoto and Josephine Naidoo,

Asian Canadians: Contemporary Issues, Selections from the Proceedings of the Asian Canadian Symposium VII, June 1986, introduces this work.

13 *Ritsumeikan Daigaku Jinbun Kagaku Kenkyūsho Kiyō* [Bulletin of the Research Institute for Cultural Sciences, Ritsumeikan University] 14 (1964). This is a special issue on Kotō.

14 On Mio, see Teiichiro Fujita, 'Tokugawa Jidai no Mio Mura – Amerika Mura no Zenshi' [Mio Village in the Tokugawa Period – Prehistory of America Village], *Wakayama no Kenkyū* [Studies on Wakayama] 3 (1978): 69–83; Tadashi Fukutake, *Amerika Mura* [America Village] (Tokyo 1953); Shigeharu Koyama, *Waga Rūtsu: Amerika Mura* [My Roots: America Village] (Kyoto 1984), and 'Kanada Imin no Mura: Wakayama-ken Amerika Mura kara' [A Village of Emigrants to Canada: America Village in Wakayama], *Rekishi Kōron* [Opinions on History] 1 (1979): 128–35.

15 Yasuo Wakatsuki, 'Japanese Emigration to the United States, 1866–1924: A Monograph,' *Perspectives in American History* 12 (1979): 497–8

16 Emigrants required 80 to 100 yen, a substantial sum when the average farm labourer's wage was 7 to 9 yen per month. See Takamitsu Ōkawahira, *Nihon Imin Ron* [On Japanese Immigration] (Tokyo 1905), 51–2; Moriyama, *Imingaisha,* 84–6. See also Yasuo Wakatsuki, 'America Imin Tashutsu Chiku no Yōin Bunseki' [Analysis of Primary Factors in the Regions with High Emigration Levels to the United States], *Tamagawa Daigaku Nōgakubu Kenkyū Hōkoku* [Bulletin of the Faculty of Agriculture, Tamagawa University] 19 (1979): 123, and 'Japanese Emigration to the United States,' 515.

17 Yamaga, ed., *Henē Nōkai Shi,* 20; Tairiku Nippō Sha, ed., *Kanada Dōbō Hatten Shi* [A History of Fellow Countrymen in Canada] (Vancouver 1909), quoted in Shimpo, *Ishi o Mote Owaruru Gotoku,* 21

18 See Fukutake, *Amerika Mura;* Masao Gamō, *Umi o Watatta Nihon no Mura* [The Japanese Village that Crossed the Ocean] (Tokyo 1962).

19 See Masaaki Kodama, 'Dekasegi-Imin no Jittai' [Actual Conditions of Sojourner Emigrants], *Hiroshimi-shi Kōbunshokan Kiyō* [Bulletin, Public Archives of Hiroshima City] 3 (1980), 31ff; Kodama, 'Imingaisha no Jittai' [Actual Conditions of Emigration Companies], *Shigaku Kenkyū* [Studies in Historiography] (Oct. 1980), 459ff; and Kodama, 'Meiji-ki Amerika Gasshūkoku e no Nihonjin Imin' [Japanese Emigrants to the United States in the Meiji Era], *Shakaikeizai-shigaku* [Studies in Socio-Economic History] 47 (1981): 73ff.

20 Those educated in Japan, the *Kika Nisei,* had Japanese personalities and temperaments. Their English was usually less fluent than that of other *Nisei,* and they were often closer to their parents' generation than their own and had difficulty readjusting to Canadian society when they returned from their schooling.

21 Canada, Royal Commission on Chinese and Japanee Immigration, *Report* (Ottawa 1902), 40
22 At the turn of the century, Tomey Homma, a boarding-house keeper in Vancouver, challenged the right of British Columbia to deny him, a naturalized British subject, the right to vote. His case went to the ultimate court of appeal, the Judicial Committee of the Privy Council in London, England, which ruled against him. For further details see Patricia E. Roy, 'Citizens Without Votes: East Asians in British Columbia,' in Jorgen Dahlie and Tissa Fernando, eds., *Ethnicity, Power & Politics in Canada* (Toronto 1981), 153–4.
23 NGB, vol. 40-2, no. 1732, Nosse to Hayashi, 29 March 1907
24 WLP, 149111, Nosse to governor general, 17 May 1897
25 Kamloops *Sentinel*, 30 July 1901
26 WLP, 34238, Shimizu to Laurier, 7 Aug. 1899; Vancouver *Province*, 20 April 1900
27 Royal Commission on Chinese and Japanese Immigation, *Report*, 40
28 *Katsudō no Nihon* [Active Japan] 4 (Oct. 1906): 1–3
29 See Ōkawahira, *Nihon Imin Ron*, passim; Minoru Tōgō, *Nihon Shokumin Ron* [On Japanese Colonization Overseas] (Tokyo 1906).
30 NGB, vol. 39-7, no. 1235, Morikawa to Hayashi, 28 Nov. 1906
31 NGB, vol. 39-2, nos 1227, 1228, Nosse to Saionji, 2, 3 Sept. 1906. Earlier correspondence between Nosse and Laurier can be found in DEA, vol. 727, *Report by the Honourable Rodolphe Lemieux, K.C., Minister of Labour, of His Mission to Japan* (Ottawa 1908).
32 Vancouver *Daily Province*, 4 June 1907; Vancouver *Semi-Weekly World*, 23 July 1907
33 The most detailed published account of the riot is Howard Sugimoto, *Japanese Immigration, the Vancouver Riots, and Canadian Diplomacy* (New York 1978). For an extended analysis of its causes and consequences see Roy, *A White Man's Province*, ch. 8.
34 Royal Commission on Losses Sustained by the Japanese Population of Vancouver, BC, *Report* (Ottawa 1908), 53–4; King to Richard Jebb, 30 Dec. 1907, WLMK, 6148-50
35 NGB, vol. 40-3, no. 1758, Morikawa to Hayashi, 24 Sept. 1907
36 NGB, vol. 40-3, no. 1752, Ishii to Hayashi, 17 Sept. 1907
37 NGB, vol. 40-3, no. 1758, Morikawa to Hayashi, 24 Sept. 1907
38 NGB, vol. 40-3, no. 1796, Nosse to Hayashi, 22 Dec. 1907
39 NGB, vol. 40-3, no. 1780, Komura to Hayashi, 7 Nov. 1907; ibid., Nosse to Hayashi, 21 Oct. 1907
40 Ibid., Nosse to Hayashi, 21 Oct. 1907, and no. 2200, Hayashi to Genro and cabinet, 29 Nov. 1907
41 On the Lemieux mission see Robert J. Gowen, 'Canada's Relations with Japan,

1895–1922' (University of Chicago, PHD dissertation, 1966), 142ff; Kunihiro Haraguchi, 'Nihon Kanada Kankei no Ichi-kōsatsu – Rumyū Kyōyaku Kaitei Mondai' [On Canada-Japan Relations – Revision of the Lemieux Agreement] *Kokusai Seiji* [*International Politics*] 58 (1977): 45ff; Masako Iino and Hiroko Takamura, 'Bankūbā Bōdō kara Rumyū Kyōyaku e' [From the Vancouver Riot to the Lemieux Agreement], *Tsuda Juku Daigaku Kiyō* [Tsuda Review] 14 (1982): 41ff.

42 Four classes were eligible for admission to Canada: 1) returning residents and their families; 2) persons engaged by Japanese residents in Canada for domestic service; 3) contract labourers; and 4) contract labourers to work on Japanese agricultural holdings. The total of (2) and (4) was limited to 400. On the negotiations see DEA, vol. 727, *Report by the Hon. Rodolphe Lemieux*.

43 NGB, vol. 40-3, no. 2200, Hayashi to Genro and cabinet minister, 29 Nov. 1907

44 NA, Grey Papers, Laurier to Grey, 5 Dec. 1907

45 GK, 'Eiryō Kanada ni okeru Honpō-jin Tokō-seigen oyobi Haiseki Ikken' [Concerning Entrance Restriction and Exclusion of Japanese in British Canada], 3-8-2-20, vol. 9, Shimizu to Hayashi, 27 May 1908

46 For a slightly fuller account of the 'picture bride' system which, of course, conformed to the Japanese tradition of arranged marriages see C.H. Young and H.R.Y. Reid, *The Japanese Canadians* (Toronto 1938), 15n.

47 PP, vol. 16, McBride to Martin Burrell, 15 Jan. 1913; ibid., Burrell to McBride, 21 Dec. 1912; HCD, 3 April 1913, 1050; Nanaimo *Free Press*, 1 April 1914

48 NGB, Taisho 2-1, Nakamura to Makino, 1 March 1913

49 C.J. Woodsworth, *Canada and the Orient* (Toronto 1941), 253. The manuscript was completed in 1938 but publication was delayed.

50 A.R. Stone and Sybil Courtice, *Witnesses of the Way in Japan* (Toronto [c 1935]), 5

51 *The Sisters of the Holy Names of Jesus and Mary in Basutoland and in Japan* (Montreal 1941), 8

52 Hugh L. Keenleyside, *Memoirs of Hugh Keenleyside*, I: *Hammer the Golden Day* (Toronto 1981), 316

53 Woodsworth, *Canada and the Orient*, 353

54 See Masako Iino, 'Japanese Immigration and Canada-Japan Relations in the 1930s,' in J. Carlsen and J.-M. Lacroix, eds., *Canadian Society and Culture in Times of Economic Depression* (Ottawa 1987), 52.

55 *Sun*, 15 April 1919

56 BCARS, Attorney-General's Records, file 1918-17-2060, John Oliver to Arthur Meighen, 13 June 1921. Copies of resolutions opposing the renewal of the alliance may be found in NA, Arthur Meighen Papers, vol. 130.

57 John Nelson, 'Will Canada be Yellow?' *Maclean's*, 15 Oct. 1931, 16. For details

of the 1921 election and the associated propaganda see Patricia E. Roy, 'The "Oriental Menace" in British Columbia,' in S.M. Trofimenkoff, ed., *The Twenties in Western Canada* (Ottawa 1972), 243–58.

58 KD, 7 Nov. 1922

59 KD, 24 Feb., 10 and 19 March 1923; WLMK, C61567, Ohta to King, 10 April 1923, and Ohta to J.E. Robb, 22 Aug. 1923

60 BC Legislative Assembly, *Report on Oriental Activities* (Victoria 1927), 9

61 DCER, 'Extracts from Minutes of Imperial Conference, 1926,' IV, 100

62 WLMK, C612168-70, Interview between the prime minister and the Japanese consul general, Mr Matsunaga, 2 April 1925

63 KD, 25 May 1928

64 GK, 'Kakkoku ni okeru Hainichi Kankei Zakken, Kanada no Bu, Rumyū Kyōshō Dai-ni-ji Kaitei Kankei' [Miscellaneous Items Concerning Exclusion of Japanese in Various Countries, Section on Canada, Concerning the Second Revision of the Lemieux Agreement], J110, J/X1-B2-1, vol. 3

65 Sohō Tokutomi, *Yamato Minzoku no Seikaku* [Aware, the Yamato Race!] (Tokyo 1928), 1ff

66 Nobuya Bamba, 'Jūzoku Riron kara Rentai Riron e' [From the Theory of Subordination to the Theory of Solidarity], *Sekai* [World] (Oct. 1979), 160; Klaus Pringsheim, *Neighbors Across the Pacific* (Westport, Conn. 1983), 31ff

67 GK, 'Kakkoku ni okeru,' J110, J/X1-B2, Fukuma to Shidehara, 22 Nov. 1929

68 *Province*, 25 Sept. 1931; DEA, D1 series, vol. 16, file 8409, Memo for Dr Skelton, 3 March 1938. On the decline of anti-Asian sentiment in British Columbia see Patricia E. Roy, 'The Illusion of Toleration: White Opinion of Asians in British Columbia, 1929–37,' in K. Victor Ujimoto and Gordon Hirabayashi, eds., *Visible Minorities and Multiculturalism: Asians in Canada* (Toronto 1980), 81–91.

69 Nihon Shokumin Kyōkai [Association for Japanese Colonization], *Kōki Nisen-Roppyaku-Nen Kaigai Dōbō Daihyō o Mukaete* [Welcoming Fellow Japanese Abroad in the 2600th Year of the Imperial Reign] (Tokyo 1941), 1. Cf Takumushō and Gaimushō, *Kigen Nisen-Roppyaku-Nen Dai-Ikkai Zaigai Dōbō Daihyōsha Kaigi Gijiroku* [The Proceedings of the First Conference of Delegates of Fellow Japanese Abroad in the 2600th Year of the Imperial Reign] (Tokyo 1940).

70 Ibid., 165

71 DImm, vol. 86, file 9309/16, Keenleyside to F.C. Blair, 5 April 1938; ibid., Board of Review (Immigration), Interim Report and Supplement, 14 May 1938; Board of Review (Immigration), *Report* (Ottawa 1939)

72 Vancouver *Sun*, 17 January 1938

73 *Sun*, 10 Feb. 1938. See also HCD, 1 Feb. 1938, 68; *British Columbia in the Canadian Confederation* (Victoria 1938), 353.

74 HCD, 9 March 1938, 1161–2; *Province*, 24 March 1938; DEA, G1 series, file 799-25, [Max Wershof] to Loring Christie, 31 March 1938; KD, 10, 11, and 24 May 1938

75 KD, 22 March 1938 and 31 January 1939; WLMK, C122612-6, R. Randolph Bruce to Skelton, 13 Dec. 1938, and to King, 16 Dec. 1938

76 WLMK, C210489-99, 'Confidential Report to Council on the Oriental Problem in Canada,' [30 Aug. 1938]

77 KD, 26 Aug. 1938 and 30 Jan. 1939; WLMK, C122862, Memorandum of conference, W.L.M. King with T.D. Pattullo, 10 Jan. 1939; DEA, G1 series, file 799-25, secretary of state for dominion affairs to secretary of state for external affairs, 25 Jan. 1939

78 *Province*, 25 July, 7 Jan., and 24 Feb. 1940; DEA, G1 series, file 212-39C, S. Tomii to Skelton, 28 June 1940

79 *Province*, 16 Aug. 1940

CHAPTER 2 The Approach of War in the Pacific

1 Rekishigaku Kenkyūkai [Society for the Study of History], ed., *Taiheiyō Sensō Shi* [History of the Pacific War] (Tokyo 1971), I, 234

2 Bōei-chō Bōei Kenshūjo Senshi-bu [History Department, Institute of Defense, Defense Agency, Tokyo; hereafter cited as Institute of Defense], *Daihonei Rikugunbu* [Army Section, Imperial Headquarters] (Tokyo 1967), I, 261

3 Japanese Consul in Mokden, cited in Institute of Defense, *Daihonei Kaigunbu Daitōa Sensō Kaisenkeii* [Navy Section, Imperial Headquarters and Details of the War in Greater East Asia] (Tokyo 1979), I, 48

4 Shigetarō Shimada, 'Daitōa Sensō ni itaru Kaiko' ['Memoirs on the Processes Leading to the Pacific War'] cited in ibid., I, 62

5 The best study is Christopher Thorne, *The Limits of Foreign Policy: The West, the League and the Far Eastern Crisis of 1931–33* (New York 1973).

6 On the Sino-Japanese War see Rekishigaku Kenkyūkai, ed., *Taiheyō Sensō Shi*, II and III (Tokyo 1971–2).

7 Ibid., I, 327

8 *Daihonei Rikugunbu*, I, 251

9 *Daihonei Rikugunbu*, I, 112

10 *Daihonei Rikugunbu*, I, 396

11 Chihiro Hosoya, ed., *Nichiei Kankei Shi, 1927–1949* [History of Anglo-Japanese Relations, 1927–1940] (Tokyo 1982), 85. The London Naval Treaty of 1930 extended the 5:5:3 ratio of capital ships agreed at the Washington Conference of 1922 to smaller vessels and continued the freeze on capital ship construc-

tion until 1935. Many in the Japanese navy were furious at this development, considering it an insult and a treaty that could limit Japanese freedom in East Asia and the Pacific.

12 See Christopher Thorne, *Allies of a Kind: The United States, Britain, and the War Against Japan, 1941–45* (Oxford 1978), 33, which argues Japan was more hostile to the United Kingdom than the United States.

13 *Daihonei Rikugunbu*, I, 383, 396

14 Katsumi Usui, *Chūgoku o meguru Kindai Nippon no Gaikō* [Modern Japanese Diplomacy on China] (Tokyo 1983), 162

15 Ibid., 171–2; Rekishigaku Kenkyūkai, ed., *Taiheiyō Sensō Shi*, III, 240

16 *Daihonei Rikugunbu*, II, 139–44

17 Nobuya Bamba, 'Jūzoku Riron kara Rentai Riron e' ['From the Theory of Subordination to the Theory of Solidarity'], *Sekai* (Oct. 1979), 160

18 DCER, V, 313ff

19 C.P. Stacey, *Canada and the Age of Conflict*, II: *1921–1948* (Toronto 1981), 162

20 *Kokumin*, 28 July 1935; *Osaka Mainichi*, 31 May 1935

21 DCER, V, 715ff; Stacey, *Canada and the Age of Conflict*, II, 191–3

22 GK, documents on files J-1-1-0, X1-B1, X1-B2, J-1-2-0, J2-6

23 DEA, vol. 723, file 64, 'Re Mr Robertson's Note ...' 19 Aug. 1939; Skelton memo for prime minister, 15 July 1941

24 Ibid., vol. 805, file 571, Robertson memo for prime minister, 15 July 1941

25 On strategic metals exports see ibid., vol. 111, docs. on file 714, and KD, 7 Sept. 1940. Trade data is from *Canada Yearbooks*, 1902, 1931, 1942, 1943–4.

26 DEA, vol. 805, file 571, Robertson memo to prime minister, 15 July 1941

27 CWC, 23 April, 1 May 1941; KD, 28 April 1941; Klaus Pringsheim, *Neighbors Across the Pacific* (Westport, Conn. 1983), 51

28 On Canada-Japan relations generally see Michael G. Fry, 'The Development of Canada's Relations with Japan, 1919–1947,' in Keith A.J. Hay, ed., *Canadian Perspectives on Economic Relations With Japan* (Montreal 1980), 7ff.

29 Chilliwack *Progress*, 1 June 1904, quoted in Patricia E. Roy, *A White Man's Province: British Columbia Politicians and Chinese and Japanese Immigrants* (Vancouver 1989), chap. VII

30 Roger Sarty, ' "There Will Be Trouble in the North Pacific": The Defence of British Columbia in the Early Twentieth Century,' *BC Studies*, 61 (spring 1984), 11

31 Ibid., 12

32 DND, Mf C5853, NSS 1023-18-1, G.J. Desbarats to undersecretary of state for external affairs, 11 July 1917

33 Sarty, 'There Will Be Trouble,' 26

34 W.A.B. Douglas, 'The RCAF and the Defence of the Pacific Coast, 1939–45,'

unpublished paper presented at the Canadian Committee on the History of the Second World War Conference, 1981, note 16

35 Ibid., 28

36 On this scenario, see, for example, Beaverbrook Library, London, D. Lloyd George Papers, file F/9/3/30, governor general to Churchill, transmitting Borden to Lloyd George, 1 April 1921; file F/25/1/41, Hankey to Lloyd George, 15 June 1921. We are indebted to Professor John Saywell for these references.

37 DCER, III, 340–1

38 R.H. Roy, *For Most Conspicuous Bravery: A Biography of Major-General George R. Pearkes, V.C., through Two World Wars* (Vancouver 1977), 100

39 UCA, Board of Foreign Missions, Japan Mission, box 5, file 91, E.C. Hennigar to Dr Arnup, 11 Feb. 1938

40 DND, Mf C5853, NSS 1023-18-2, G.A. Youle to commander, Esquimalt, 25 Oct. 1932

41 DCER, V, 337

42 J.L. Granatstein, 'The "Man of Secrets" in Canada, 1934,' *Dalhousie Review* 51 (1971–2): 504ff

43 DEA, vol. 721, file 47, Loring Christie memorandum, 'The Defence of Canada,' 3 Feb. 1936

44 James Eayrs, *In Defence of Canada,* II: *Appeasement and Rearmament* (Toronto 1965), 213ff, prints most of the military appreciation.

45 C.P. Stacey, *Six Years of War* (Ottawa 1955), 7ff

46 DEA, vol. 817, file 662, 'The Fixed Defences of Juan de Fuca Strait,' 12 Jan. 1938

47 DND, HQS5199-B, 'A Review of Canada's Position With Respect to Defence,' July 1938

48 See T.M. Hunter, 'Coast Defence in British Columbia, 1939–41: Attitudes and Realities,' *BC Studies* 28 (winter 1975–6), 3–28.

49 W.A.B. Douglas, *The Creation of a National Air Force:* II: *The Official History of the Royal Canadian Air Force* (Toronto 1986), 401

50 DEA, vol. 721, file 47, Joint Staff Committee assessment, 6 July 1938, att. to Ian Mackenzie to Mackenzie King, 10 Jan. 1938

51 Douglas, *Creation of a National Air Force,* II, 401

52 KD, 6 Sept. 1939

53 James Eayrs, *In Defence of Canada,* I: *From the Great War to the Great Depression* (Toronto 1965), 71ff

54 S.W. Dziuban, *Military Relations Between the United States and Canada, 1939–45* (Washington 1959), 3

55 Cited in Eayrs, *In Defence of Canada,* II, 177

55 Cited in ibid., 177

56 KD, 5 March 1937
57 DEA, vol. 744, file 163, 'Canada and the United States: Security Measures Against Air Attack,' 29 April 1935
58 KD, 31 July 1936
59 DCER, V, 265
60 Eayrs, *In Defence of Canada,* II, 179, citing the Canadian minister to the United States after a 1940 conversation with Roosevelt
61 See David Remley, 'The Latent Fear: Canadian-American Relations and Early Proposals for a Highway to Alaska,' and Robin Fisher, 'T.D. Pattullo and the British Columbia to Alaska Highway,' in Kenneth Coates, ed., *The Alaska Highway* (Vancouver 1985), 1ff.
62 C.P. Stacey, *Arms, Men and Governments: The War Policies of Canada 1939–1945* (Ottawa 1970), 96–7
63 Eayrs, *In Defence of Canada,* II, 180
64 On concern for Canadian neutrality see also USNA, Records of Foreign Service Posts, RG 84 C8, box 1490, vol. 4, Memorandum of interview with Col. H.D.G. Crerar, 14 March 1938.
65 The Canadian reports are in WLMK, ff C112709ff. See also Eayrs, *In Defence of Canada,* II, 180–2.
66 Ibid.; Dziuban, *Military Relations,* 3
67 See WLMK, Memo, Gen. T.V. Anderson to minister of national defence, 23 Nov. 1938, ff C112879ff.
68 Ibid., Gen. Anderson memorandum, 'Visit to Washington,' 23 Nov. 1938, f C112881
69 J.L. Granatstein, *Canada's War: The Politics of the Mackenzie King Government, 1939–45* (Toronto 1975), 115
70 DEA, vol. 781, file 394, 'An Outline Synopsis ...' 17 June 1940
71 Stacey, *Arms,* 344–6, lists the recommendations of the PJBD.
72 USNA, RG 59, PJBD Records, box 2, 'Joint Canadian-United States Basic Defense Plan – 1940,' 10 Oct. 1940
73 Stacey, *Arms,* 349ff
74 DND, vol. 11764, file PC 010-9, Memorandum, district war plans officer to commandant, 28 March 1941
75 KD, 26 July 1940; CWC, 26 July 1940
76 Stacey, *Six Years,* 166–7; Douglas, *Creation of a National Air Force,* II, 402; WLMK, King to Pattullo, 21 Aug. 1940, ff 248359-60
77 DND, Mf C8366, file HQS8613, 'Appreciation, Defence of Pacific Coast of Canada,' 18 Nov. 1941
78 *Tokyo Asahi,* 26 Sept. 1940. Many comments in the Japanese press on the

Ogdensburg Agreement were reported to Ottawa. See DEA, vol. 2789, file 703-40, McGreer to Ottawa, 9 Sept. 1940.

79 *Osaka Asahi*, 7 March 1941

80 *Tokyo Asahi*, 20 Aug. 1940

81 Ibid., 26, 27 Sept. 1940

82 Robert Keyserlingk, ' "Agents Within the Gates": The Search for Nazi Subversives in Canada during World War II,' CHR 66 (June 1985): 224

83 George V, ch. 2, s. 6

84 DEA, vol. 1964, file 855E, Robertson to Skelton, 28 Aug. 1939 and att. letter, S.T. Wood to Lapointe, 26 Aug. 1939. See J.L. Granatstein, *A Man of Influence: Norman A. Robertson and Canadian Statecraft, 1929–68* (Ottawa 1981), 83–4

85 Granatstein, *Man of Influence*, 86

86 NA, N.A. Robertson Papers, vol. 13, file 164, 'Statistics of Internment,' 3 Jan. 1941. The total figures are in Keyserlingk, 'Agents Within the Gates,' 239.

87 Ramsay Cook, 'Canadian Freedom in Wartime, 1939–1945,' in W.H. Heick and Roger Graham, eds., *His Own Man* (Montreal 1974), 45

88 *Tairiku Nippō*, 15 May, 12 July, 13 Sept. 1941; Misturu Shimpo, *Ishi o Mote Owaruru Gotoku* [As Though Driven Away With Stones] (Toronto 1975), 180

89 *Tokyo Asahi*, 5 Oct. 1940

90 WLMK, Keenleyside memorandum, nd [c. 14 March 1938], ff C129321ff

91 CVA, Mayor's correspondence 1940, Minutes of meeting, 1 Oct. 1940

92 CWC, 8 Oct. 1940

93 BCARS, Halford Wilson Papers, Wilson to Finance Committee, Vancouver City Council, 24 Sept. 1940

94 EAR, file 263-38, Wismer to Col. LaFlèche, 8 Oct. 1940; CWC, Pattullo to King, 23 Sept. 1940

95 KD, 26 Sept. 1940

96 DEA, vol. 2007, file 1939-212, pt I, Keenleyside to Skelton, 28 Sept. 1940

97 CWC, 1, 3 Oct. 1940; PCO, vol. 1, file C-10-3, Keenleyside to King, 2 Dec. 1940

98 Ibid., Report and Recommendations of the Special Committee on Orientals in British Columbia, Dec. 1940

99 DHist, file 169.012(D2), Stockwell to secretary, DND, 10 Oct. 1940

100 EAR, file 1552-40C, King to S. Yoshizawa, 1 Feb. 1941

101 See Patricia Roy, 'The Soldiers Canada Didn't Want: Her Chinese and Japanese Citizens,' CHR 59 (Sept. 1978): 341ff; Roy Ito, *We Went to War* (Stittsville, Ont. 1984), 107ff.

102 The committee members included H.F. Angus of the University of British

Columbia, who was sympathetic to the Japanese Canadians; Col. Macgregor Macintosh, MLA, who was not; and Lt-Col. A.W. Sparling of the army and F.J. Mead of the RCMP. On divisions in the community see Ken Adachi, *The Enemy That Never Was* (Toronto 1976), 192; *Tairiku Nippō*, 9 Jan. 1941.

103 *Tairiku Nippō*, 14 Oct., 5 Dec. 1941; Adachi, *Enemy*, 231; *Province*, 6 Dec. 1941

104 DEA, Acc. 83-4/259, box 115, file 1698-A-40, Minutes, 25 July 1941

105 Ibid., Report and Recommendations, App. A, 28 July 1941

106 The RCN already had a plan for this. See ibid., 'Statement of Case, Joint Services Committee,' nd [summer 1941].

107 Ibid., Memorandum for Mr Robertson, 21 Oct. 1941. But see London's views: EAR, file 28-C(s), secretary of state for dominion affairs to prime minister, 23 Oct. 1941.

108 DEA, vol. 2453, file I-25, intercepted and translated telegram, foreign minister to Vancouver, 22 Feb. 1940

109 Hugh L. Keenleyside, *Memoirs of Hugh Keenleyside*, I: *Hammer the Golden Day* (Toronto 1981), 430. For examples see HCD, 28 April 1933, 4423, and 1 April 1938, 1968.

110 DND, vol. 11917, file 5-1-128 1938-9, RCMP Report, 13 Jan. 1938

111 DEA, vol. 2007, RCMP Report, 29 July 1941; DND, Mf C5853, NSS 1023-18-2, naval staff officer, Esquimalt, to director, Naval Intelligence and Plans, 9 Feb. 1938

112 Ibid., Staff Officer (Intelligence) Report, 10 March 1937

113 C.E. Hope and W.K. Earle, 'The Oriental Threat,' *Maclean's* (1 May 1933); HCD, 28 April 1933, 4747; Ottawa *Citizen* and *Journal*, 29 April 1933

114 Institute of Defense, *Hokutō-hōmen Kaigun Sakusen* [Naval Operations in the Northeastern Pacific] (Tokyo 1969), 27

115 Akira Yamaki, 'Beikoku-tsū no Nakazawa Tasuku Chūjō o Shinobu' [Recollections of Vice Admiral Tasuku Nakazawa as an Authority on U.S. Affairs] in *Tsuisō Kaigun-chūjō Nakazawa Tasuku Kankō-kai* [Private Group Publishing the Recollections of Vice Admiral Tasuku Nakazawa] (Tokyo 1978), 58–9

116 *Hokutō-hōmen Kaigun Sakusen*, 27, 241–4

117 Yamaki, 'Beikoku-tsu,' 58; Ichiro Yokoyama, 'Beikoku ni okeru Nakazawa-san' [Nakazawa in the U..S.], in *Tsuisō Kaigun-chūjō Nakazawa*, 64

118 There was a naval attaché with the mission in Ottawa. The UK Naval Intelligence believed him part of the 'Japanese intelligence system on the American continent.' See DND, Mf C5855, NSS 1023-18-1, 'Annual Report on the Imperial Japanese Navy for 1938,' 4 April 1938.

119 On propaganda effects in Japan see *Taiheiyō Sensō Shi*, I, 327.

120 Copy in UBC, Pitt Meadows Japanese Farmers Association Records, 1 Oct. 1937
121 Letter in ibid. See also Adachi, *Enemy*, 184–5.
122 See, for example, UBC, Angus MacInnis Papers, box 54a, file 8, MacInnis to Canadian Japanese Association, 11 Dec. 1937, and ibid., file 12, MacInnis to T. Umezuki, 18 April 1939; DND, Mf C5853, NSS 1023-18-2, naval staff officer, Esquimalt, to director, Naval Intelligence and Operations, 9 Feb. 1938; NA, J.W. Dafoe Papers, H.F. Angus to Dafoe, 15 Oct. 1940; and Angus, 'The Effect of the War on Oriental Minorities in Canada,' *Canadian Journal of Economics and Political Science* 7 (Nov. 1941): 508. For examples of the anti-Japanese campaign see Thomas Socknat, *Witness Against War: Pacifism in Canada 1900–45* (Toronto 1987), 168, and UBC, A.M. Stephen Scrapbook, with its pamphlets and reports.
123 DEA, file 729-31, 'Extract from Report on Japanese Activities,' 10 March 1937
124 DImm, vol. 86, file 9309/16, C.H. Hill to commissioner, RCMP, 25 Aug. 1938
125 See KD, 8 March 1939; DEA, vol. 2960, file 11, 'Far Eastern Conflict,' 18 Jan. 1938; Harvard University, Pierrepont Moffat Papers, Memos 4, 12, 22 Oct. 1940 and 24 July 1941. See also DCER, VIII, esp. 1202ff.
126 E. Ouchi, ed., *'Til We See the Light of Day* (Vernon, BC, nd [1982?]), 70. The first editor left to join the English-language *Manchurian Daily News*. On the Chinese-Canadian anti-Japanese campaign see UBC, *Chinese Times*, for example, translations for 16, 19 Oct. 1937, 7 Jan. 1938. See also Harry Con et al., *From China to Canada* (Toronto 1982), 188ff.
127 *Tairiku Nippō*, 19 Jan. 1940
128 S.R. Elliot, *Scarlet to Green: A History of Intelligence in the Canadian Army 1903–63* (Toronto 1981), 74
129 DEA, vol. 2007, file 1939-212, pt 2, 'Report on the State of Intelligence on the Pacific Coast with Particular Reference to the Problem of the Japanese Minority,' 27 July 1941; DND, vol. 11913, 'Japanese' file, Cmdr Hart to R.B.C. Mundy, 21 Aug. 1940; RCMP, Declassified Records, 'Japanese Activities in British Columbia,' June 1942. This BSC report was alarmist in tone and less than well informed.
130 'Report on the State of Intelligence'
131 The best account is Wesley Wark, 'Cryptographic Innocence: The Origins of Signals Intelligence in Canada in World War II,' *Journal of Contemporary History* (spring, 1987). For an example of the use to which intercepts could be put see CWC, 8 Oct. 1940.
132 DEA, vol. 2453, file 1-25, foreign minister to Vancouver, 22 Feb. 1940; Robertson to Christie, 14 March 1940

133 Elliot, *Scarlet to Green*, 373
134 Wark, 'Cryptographic Innocence'
135 Elliot, *Scarlet to Green*, 463–4
136 DND, Declassified Examination Unit Files, Memo for chairman, Supervisory Committee, 15 Aug. 1941; Lt C.H. Little memo, 18 April 1942; Examination Unit history, chap. VI, 1ff
137 DEA, vol. 2007, file 1939-212, pt I, Keenleyside to Angus, 28 June 1940. Angus agreed: 'There may be unreliable elements among the Japanese here. I do not know and doubt if anyone knows.' Dafoe Papers, Angus to Dafoe, 15 Oct. 1940
138 See Keyserlingk, 'Agents Within the Gates,' 216–17; Reg Whitaker, 'Official Repression of Communism during World War II,' *Labour/Le Travail*, no. 17 (spring 1986).
139 Elliot, *Scarlet to Green*, chap. 3
140 DND, vol. 3864, file NSS 1023-18-2, Memo, F/L Wynd to senior air staff officer, 24 June 1940; DImm, vol. 86, file 9309/15 and /16, F.C. Blair memo, 21 March 1938, and F.W. Taylor to commissioner, RCMP, 31 May 1938
141 DND, vol. 3864, file NSS 1023-18-2, 'Extract from Report on Japanese Activities on the West Coast of Canada,' 10 March 1937; ibid., Mf C5853, file NSS 1023-18-2
142 DHist, file 322.009(D358), Col. LaFlèche to F.C. Blair, 15 June 1938
143 DND, vol. 11917, file 5-1-128 1938–9, RCMP report, 3 June 1938; ibid., vol. 11913, 'Japanese' file, 'Vancouver' [an agent] to Cmdr Hart, 30 June, 13 July 1940; ibid., vol. 2730, file HQS 5199X, Gen. Crerar–Commissioner Wood correspondence, 2 Aug. 1940ff; DEA, vol. 2007, file 1939-212, pt II, RCMP report, 29 July 1941; Ann Sunahara, *The Politics of Racism* (Toronto 1981), 23
144 Sunahara, *Politics of Racism*, 23; Muriel Kitagawa, *This is My Own: Letters to Wes and Other Writings on Japanese Canadians, 1941–1948*, ed. Roy Miki (Vancouver 1985), 98-9
145 PCO, vol. 1, file C-10-3, Wismer to LàFleche, 8 Oct. 1940; UBC, J.W. deB. Farris Papers, box 6, G.G. McGeer to E. Lapointe, 2 July 1940
146 DEA, vol. 2007, file 1939-212, pt II, 'Report on the State of Intelligence'
147 Cited in John Saywell, 'Canadian Political Dynamics and Canada-Japan Relations: Retrospect and Prospect,' 26, published in Japanese in *Kokusai Seiji* [International Politics] (May 1985), 121-3. See Peter Ward, *White Canada Forever* (Montreal 1978), 145.
148 CVA, Mayor's Correspondence 1940, Report of Meeting 'to discuss Certain Aspects of Civil Security ...,' 1 Oct. 1940; DEA, file 263-38, R.R. Tait to Keenleyside, 28 Oct. 1940; RCMP, vol. 3564, file G-19-2-24, Tait to commissioner, 28 Oct. 1940

149 DND, vol. 2725, file HQS 5199-W-1a, 'Joint Canada-U.S. Basic Defence Plan–1940,' 10 Oct. 1940

150 Ibid., vol. 3864, file NSS 1023-18-2, Robertson to Col. Maclachlan, 14 Aug. 1941; ibid., vol. 2730, file HQS 5199X, 'Memorandum of the Joint Services Committee, Pacific Coast, on the Subject of Dealing with Persons of Japanese Origin in the Event of an Emergency,' 20 Sept. 1941

151 Ibid. See also documents in ibid., vol. 2688, file HQS 5199-1.

152 Cited in Sunahara, *Politics of Racism*, 19

153 RCMP, vol. 3564, file C-11-19-3, adjutant general to district officers commanding, 21 June 1939

154 IMP, vol. 32, file X-52, Committee report, 9 Feb. 1939; ibid., Heeney to Mackenzie, 6 Feb. 1939, and chief of the general staff to Mackenzie, 3 Sept. 1938

155 DND, vol. 2730, 'Memorandum of the Joint Services Committee,' 20 Sept. 1941

156 Ibid., vol. 2688, file HQS 5199, Crerar memo, 14 Aug. 1941

157 EAR, file 28-C(S), Massey to King, 28 Feb. 1941

158 This telegram was likely shown to Prime Minister Churchill. See his *Second World War* (Boston 1951), III, 736, for his reaction.

159 CWC, 5 March 1941

160 On how the information likely reached London see Ruth Harris, 'The "Magic" Leak of 1941 and Japanese–American Relations,' *Pacific Historical Review* 50 (1981): 83. On Magic see Ronald Lewin, *The American Magic* (New York 1982), 44ff.

161 Ibid., 45–6

162 USNA, General Records of the Department of the Navy, RG 80, 'Magic' Documents, box 56, Tokyo to Washington, 30 Jan. and 15 Feb. 1941; Los Angeles to Tokyo, 9 May 1941; Tokyo to Vancouver, March 1941. See also USNA, Records of the National Security Agency, RG 457, 'Magic' Documents, SRH018, SRDJ nos. 1233-4, 1246-9, 1370, 1525, Vancouver to Tokyo, 7, 14 July, 11, 19 Aug. 1939. See Greg Johnson's doctoral paper 'Mackenzie King and the Cancer in the Pacific,' York University, 1984.

163 The importance of these telegrams has been challenged in the U.S. House of Representatives. Testimony is reprinted in Lt-Col. J. Herzig, 'Japanese Americans and "Magic,"' *Rikka* 10 (winter 1984): 2ff. This assault in no way affects the Canadian material.

164 DEA, vol. 2411, file 102-MP-40, 'Activities of Japanese Diplomatic and Consular Officers,' remains almost completely closed.

165 WLMK, 'Notes on a War-time Intelligence Service,' 27 Nov. 1939, ff C257903ff

CHAPTER 3 Canadians in Hong Kong and Japan

1 See, however, Mackenzie King's account of a conversation with the Japanese minister to Canada, 7 September 1940. J.W. Pickersgill, *The Mackenzie King Record,* I: *1939–44* (Toronto 1960), 149
2 UCA, R. Gordon Struthers Papers, box 1, Mathieson to 'Dear Friend,' 6 Dec. 1937
3 Munroe Scott, *McClure: The China Years* (Toronto 1977), 224
4 DEA, vol. 1866, file 226D, Shanghai to Foreign Office, 28 Nov. 1939
5 Alvyn J. Austin, *Saving China: Canadian Missionaries in the Middle Kingdom, 1888–1959* (Toronto 1986), 255–7
6 See, eg, Stephen Endicott, *James G. Endicott: Rebel Out of China* (Toronto 1980), 143.
7 UCA, Board of Foreign Missions, Honan, box 10, file 167, G.K. King to Dr Armstrong, 18 June 1941
8 Ibid., file 159, account of events, nd [late 1939]
9 Ibid., South China Mission, box 3, file 62, Dr Cockfield to Dr Arnup, 12 Sept. 1939
10 For example, *United Church Observer,* 15 Nov. 1939, 1, 30. Cf DCER, VIII, 1141
11 DEA, vol. 1866, file 226A, 'Canadian Interests in China 1937–1939,' 26 Sept. 1939
12 DCER, VIII, 1128, 1141
13 UCA, Board of Foreign Missions, Japan, box 5, file 91, E.C. Hennigar to Dr Arnup, 11 Feb. 1938
14 EAR, file 861-40C, consul-general, Keijo, to Canadian chargé, Tokyo, 9 Dec. 1940
15 DCER, VIII, 1149
16 EAR, file 861-40C, chargé, Tokyo to Ottawa, 15 Sept. 1941 and following
17 UCA, Board of Foreign Missions, Japan, box 5, file 97, H. Outerbridge to Dr Arnup, 19 Dec. 1939
18 Ibid., box 6, file 116, A.P. McKenzie to Dr Arnup, 22 April 1941
19 DCER, VIII, 1142–3. See also Hugh L. Keenleyside, *Memoirs of Hugh Keenleyside,* II: *On the Bridge of Time* (Toronto 1982), 160–2.
20 *The Sisters of the Holy Name of Jesus and Mary in Basutoland and Japan* (Montreal 1941), 65
21 DCER, VIII, 1144
22 UCA, Harper Coates Family Papers, box 1, file 14, Coates to children, 20 Oct. 1941
23 DCER, VIII, 1147, 1152
24 Ibid., 1154ff

25 Ibid., 1149
26 Protestants had families while the Catholic missionaries only had to worry about themselves, or so remembered Père Maurice Marcel Lamarche, SJ. Interview conducted on our behalf by Ms Sylvie Beaudreau in Montreal, Feb. 1987
27 EAR, file 861-40C, chargé, Tokyo to Ottawa, 15 Sept. 1941 and following
28 Ibid., 'The British Precedent in Taking Retaliatory Measures Against Japanese Nationals,' nd, attached to memo, 20 Oct. 1941
29 Ibid., 'On the Advisability for the Canadian Government to take Retaliatory Measures Against Japanese Nationals,' 20 Oct. 1941
30 DCER, VIII, 1169
31 DND, vol. 772, file 349, memorandum, 13 Aug. 1940
32 Ted Ferguson, *The Desperate Siege: The Battle of Hong Kong* (Toronto 1980), 5
33 W.S. Churchill, *The Second World War*, III: *The Grand Alliance* (Toronto 1950), 177
34 Oliver Lindsay, *The Lasting Honour* (London 1978), 1
35 Ibid., 3; Ferguson, *Desperate Siege*, 5–6. In those views, Grasett sounded almost exactly as did his peers. The best account is John W. Dower, *War Without Mercy: Race and Power in the Pacific War* (New York 1986), 98ff.
36 This telegram and others between Canada and Britain are collected in PRO, Dominions Office Records, DO 114/111, 66ff.
37 C.P. Stacey, *Six Years of War* (Ottawa 1955), 441–2. This section is based on Stacey and all unreferenced quotations are from his exemplary account.
38 S.R. Elliot, *Scarlet to Green* (Toronto 1981), 375
39 On the Royal Rifles of Canada see *The Royal Rifles of Canada in Hong Kong–1941–1945* (Sherbrooke, Que. 1980) especially part I.
40 Lindsay, *Lasting Honour*, 10
41 Elliot, *Scarlet to Green*, 375
42 Ferguson, *Desperate Siege*, ix
43 Institute of Defense, *Hon Kon Chōsa Sakusen* [Hong Kong and Changsha Operations] (Tokyo 1971), 13
44 Ibid., 4, 13
45 Ibid.
46 Institute of Defense, *Daihonei Rikugunbu* [Army Section, Imperial Headquarters] (Tokyo 1967), I, 100
47 *Hon Kon Chōsa Sakunen*, 18
48 Ibid., 39–40, 56–61
49 Ibid., 48–9, 79–80
50 DEA, Acc. 83-84/259, box 160, file 2670-A-40, 'Extracts from the Diary of Rifleman Sydney Skelton'

51 *Hon Kon Chōsa Sakusen*, 208–11
52 DEA, box 160, file 2670-A-40, Skelton Diary, gives ample testimony to the presence of fifth columnists.
53 *Royal Rifles*, 48
54 Daniel Dancocks, *In Enemy Hands* (Edmonton 1983), 223
55 *Hon Kon Chōsa Sakunen*, 241–3
56 Stacey, *Six Years of War*, 481
57 *Hon Kon Chōsa Sakusen*, 320
58 DEA, Acc. 83-84/259, box 230, file 4464-D-40, 'Report by Miss Anna Mae Waters, nurse with the Canadian Forces at Hong Kong, as given on board the S.S. *Gripsholm*,' Nov. 1943
59 Ferguson, *Desperate Siege*, 211. See DEA, Acc. 83-84/259, box 160, file 2670-D-40, Canadian Postal Censorship memoranda, 10, 20, 27, 30 March 1942.
60 R.J. Pritchard and Sonia Zaide, eds., *The Tokyo War Crimes Trials* (New York 1981), vol. VI, 13114–17
61 DEA, Acc. 83-84/259, box 160, file 2670-D-40, Mr Duff's report on Hong Kong, nd
62 HCD, 16 March 1942
63 DEA, vol. 2089, file AR 23/2, pt 7, 'Notes on a Talk Given by Dr. Marcel Junod,' 21 June 1946
64 Junpei Shinobu, 'Daitōa Sensō to Horyo-toriatsukai Mondai,' *Gaikō Jihō* 102 (May 1942): 3
65 L. Friedman, ed., *The Law of War: A Documentary History* (New York 1972), vol. II, 1078
66 *Yomiuri Hōchi*, 9 Nov. 1944
67 Kazunobu Shinozaki, 'Furyo 210,000' [210,000 POWS], *Jikyoku Jihō* (April 1942), cited in Yoshio Chaen, *Daitōa Senka Gaichi Furyo Shūyōjo* [Overseas Prisoners' Camps During the Greater East Asia War] (Tokyo 1987), 97
68 *Tokyo Asahi*, 18 March, 13 May 1942
69 Dancocks, *In Enemy Hands*, 225
70 Ibid., 228–9
71 Pritchard and Zaide, eds., *Tokyo War Crimes Trials*, vol. VI, 13122
72 USNA, RG 218, Records of the Joint Chiefs of Staff, pt I: 1942–45, The Pacific Theatre, reel 1, Elmer Davis to Adm. Leahy, 24 Dec. 1943, f A102782
73 An account of conditions in late January 1942 is in DEA, Acc. 83-84/259, box 160, file 2670-A-40, 'Report on Events ... by Sub-Lieut. Proulx.'
74 Ibid., box 175, file 2998-D-40, pt 2, 'Interim Report on First Visit to Prisoners of War Camps ... in Hong Kong'
75 Ibid., box 160, file 2670-A-40C, press release, 'Conditions at Hong Kong,' 12

July 1942, based on information from the British protecting power, Argentina. See the account of a Red Cross visit to a POW camp in Martin Booth's novel, *Hiroshima Joe* (London 1986), 169–71, and PRO, Cabinet Records, Cab 66/22, W.P. (42) 82, 14 Feb. 1942, where the question of giving publicity to maltreatment of POWS was raised in Churchill's War Cabinet and with Canada. Significantly, Ottawa advised caution, the minister of national defence clearly preferring to withhold all comment. See ibid., C. Ritchie to Sir E. Machtig, 14 Feb. 1942.

76 DND, Mf C5338, file HQS 9050-17-3, War Office to Foreign Office, nd [late 1942]

77 DEA, Acc. 83-84/259, box 160, file 2670-A-40, minister in China to secretary of state for external affairs, 24 July 1943

78 Records of the Joint Chiefs of Staff, pt 1, reel 1, JCS504, 'Japanese Atrocities–Reports by Escaped Prisoners,' 17 Sept. 1943, ff A74066ff

79 'Hong Kong Vets Raise an Awkward Question,' Toronto *Globe and Mail*, 15 Aug. 1987

80 *Royal Rifles*, 172–3

81 DEA, Acc. 83-84/259, box 160, file 2670-A-40, Interrogation Report No. SKP/5/44, 20 Oct. 1944

82 Ibid., 'Note as to the Activities of Mr Zindel–CICR Delegate in Hong Kong During the Month of March 1943'

83 Ibid., box 175, file 2998-D-40, pt 2, 'Conditions in Hong Kong PW Camps,' 4 July 1943

84 Yoshio Chaen, *Dai-Nippon Teikoku Naichi Furyo Shūyōjo* [Imperial Japanese Domestic Prisoners' Camps] (Tokyo 1986), 76

85 Pritchard and Zaide, eds., *Tokyo War Crimes Trials*, vol. VI, 13140

86 DEA, Acc. 84-85/019, vol. 248, file 8767-40, F.J. Mead to E.H. Coleman, 27 Sept. 1945. The account in Roy Ito, *We Went to War* (Stittsville, Ont. 1984), 269, is slightly incorrect.

87 Affidavits are on DHist, file 163.009(D41), 'Investigation of War Crimes, Jan 44/Sep 46.' See also DEA, Acc. 84-85/019, vol. 248, file 8767-40, E.R. Hopkins to deputy minister, 22 March 1946.

88 DEA, Acc. 84-85/019, vol. 248, file 8767-40, Memorandum for acting secretary of state for external affairs, 15 May 1946

89 Ibid.

90 Ibid., and extract from letter from minister of justice, 24 May 1946

91 Ibid., L.B. Pearson to L. St Laurent, 18 Dec. 1946; DHist, file 113.3A1013(1), 'Final Report, War Crimes Investigation Section, Directorate of Administration, Army Headquarters, 30 Aug 47.' See also Ito, *We Went to War*, 269ff,

which is again incorrect. Ito suggests Inouye came to Hong Kong in 1944, but there are depositions by POWs citing beatings by Inouye in 1943. DHist, file 163.009(D41), 'Investigation of War Crimes'

92 DEA, Acc. 84-85/019, vol. 248, file 593(D8), 'Notes of Conversations with Officers Going to Districts to Assist AJAGS in Preparation of Depositions from Repatriates,' 8 Jan. 1946

93 On Canadian war-crimes organization for Tokyo and Hong Kong trials see Maj. W.P. McClemont, 'War Crimes Trials,' *Canadian Army Journal* 1 (July 1947): 16ff, and DCER, XII, 290ff.

94 DHist, file 593(D8), 'Notes of Conversations,' 8 Jan. 1946; ibid., 'Final Report'

95 Dancocks, *In Enemy Hands*, 239–40

CHAPTER 4 The Decision to Evacuate

1 *Colonist* and *Province*, 9 Dec. 1941

2 CWC, 7 Dec. 1941; KD, 7 Dec. 1941

3 *News-Herald*, 4 Dec. 1941

4 EAR, file 3464-B-40C, F.J. Hume to King, 9 Dec. 1941; RCMP, vol. 3564, C.H. Hill to commissioner, 8 and 9 Dec. 1941; NC, 12 Dec. 1941

5 BCARS, Halford Wilson Papers, Tsutae Sato to J.W. Cornett, 11 Jan. 1941. A school at Haney, however, adopted a textbook approved by the California State Department of Education.

6 RCMP, vol. 3564, officer commanding 'E' division to commissioner, 3 Dec. 1941, and Upton, Memorandum, 24 Jan. 1942; WLMK, C249449, H.L. Keenleyside, Memorandum, 6 Feb. 1942. In the summer of 1942 the federal cabinet authorized the expenditure of $80,000 to meet claims for damage to vessels and equipment. PC 3737, 5 May 1942

7 RCMP, vol. 3564, Mead to commissioner, 26 Dec. 1941, and Hill to commissioner, 11 Dec. 1941; Rintarō Hayashi, *Kuroshio no Hate ni* [Beyond the Black Current] (Tokyo 1974), 156–62

8 *Province*, 18 Dec. 1941

9 For example, WLMK, 271142, Vernon and District Japanese Community to King, 9 Dec. 1941; WLMK, 264101-2, T. Mitsui, president, Japanese Branch of the Canadian Legion, to King, 10 Dec. 1941; NC, 12 Dec. 1941; *Tairiku Nippō*, 12 July 1941; Mitsuru Shimpo, *Ishi o Mote Owaruru Gotoku* [As Though Driven Away With Stones] (Toronto 1975), 180; *Province*, 8 and 15 Dec. 1941; *News-Herald*, 24 Dec. 1941

10 DEA, G2 series, vol. 2935, file 2817-A-40, Angus Macdonald to King, 16 Dec. 1941; DHist 181.009 (D5546), L.F. Stevenson to secretary, Department of National Defence for Air, 2 Jan. 1942; RCMP, vol. 3564, file C11-19-2-24, R.O.

Alexander to chief of general staff (CGS), 30 Dec. 1941; CEP, vol. 2, file 16, G.W. McPherson, Memoranda of 18 and 21 Dec. 1941

11 *Province*, 19 and 29 Dec. 1941

12 DEA, vol. 3004, file 3464-H-40C, K. Stuart to Keenleyside, 26 Dec. 1941; RCMP, vol. 3564, file C11-19-2-24, Hill to commissioner, 20 Dec. 1941; ibid., J.R. Radford, circular, 20 Dec. 1941; *Colonist*, 23, 30 Dec. 1941; DEA, vol. 2798, file 773-B1-40, vol. 1, Victoria Kiwanis Club, Resolution, 30 Dec. 1941

13 CWC, 29 Dec. 1941

14 RCMP, vol. 3564, file C-11-2-24, Wood to commissioner, 3 Jan. 1942; DEA, G1 series, file 263-38, Hume to King, 2 Jan. 1941

15 DEA, G1 series, file 263-38, Robertson to John Hart, 3 Jan. 1942; IMP, vol. 24, Robertson to Mackenzie, 5 Jan. 1942

16 DEA, vol. 2798, file 773-B-1-40, J.G. Turgeon to King, 6 Jan. 1942; ibid., Ira Dilworth to H.F. Angus, 6 Jan. 1942; ibid., Dilworth to Gladstone Murray, 6 Jan. 1942; RCMP, vol. 3564, file 11-19-1-24, G. Upton, Report, 6 Jan. 1942; ibid., Ashton quoted in O.J. Wales to Maurice Bernier, 7 Jan. 1942; *Province*, 8 Jan. 1942; WLMK, J1, vol. 330, H.T. Matson to King, 12 Jan. 1942; *Colonist*, 6 Jan. 1942

17 *Sun*, 5 Jan. 1942; *Times*, 7 Jan. 1941; *News-Herald*, 7 Jan. 1942. See also Elaine Bernard, 'A University at War: Japanese Canadians at UBC During World War II,' *BC Studies* 35 (autumn 1977): 36–55.

18 DLab, vol. 174, meeting to Consider Questions Concerned with Canadian Japanese and Japanese Nationals in British Columbia, 8 Jan. 1942

19 DHist, 193.009 (D3), Monthly Appreciation, 15 Jan. 1942

20 DHist, 112.11 (DIA), vol. 3, General M.A. Pope to CGS, 11 Dec. 1941 and 21 Jan. 1942; W.A.B. Douglas, *The Creation of a National Air Force*, II: *The Official History of the Royal Canadian Air Force* (Toronto 1986), 353; PRO, Cabinet Records, Cab 122/43, CPS (42) 42, 17 Dec. 1941; DHist, 112.3M2 (D495), Field Marshall J.G. Dill to General George Marshall, 20 Feb. 1942; DEA, vol. 2946, file 3050-N-40, Keenleyside to Beaudry, 16 Feb. 1942

21 See Douglas, *Creation*, 404ff. Aware of this, the United States tried to take operational control of the Canadian forces under the terms of the ABC-22 defence plan negotiated earlier in 1941, an effort that Ottawa successfully resisted. DHist, 112.11 (DIA), vol. 3, General S.D. Embick to Pope, 14 Jan. 1942; ibid., Pope to CGS, 16 Jan. 1942

22 DHist 193.009 (03), Joint Service Committee Pacific Coast, Minutes, 9 Jan. 1942

23 DND, reel C8340, file HQS, Pope to CGS, 13 Jan. 1942

24 Maurice Pope, *Soldiers and Politicians* (Toronto 1962), 177; Escott Reid, 'The Conscience of a Diplomat: A Personal Statement,' *Queen's Quarterly* 74 (win-

ter 1967): 587–9; Hugh L. Keenleyside, *Memoirs of Hugh Keenleyside,* II: *On the Bridge of Time* (Toronto 1982), 173. The conference also agreed that Canadian nationals of Japanese racial origin should be allowed to volunteer for service in the Canadian army and be called up under the National Resources Mobilization Act. In both cases they would serve outside British Columbia. Support for the proposal was lukewarm; the standing committee opposed it and Mackenzie would not press it. The prime minister agreed and the idea was dropped. See Patricia E. Roy, 'The Soldiers Canada Didn't Want,' CHR 59 (Sept. 1978): 349.

25 IMP, vol. 32, Minutes of Meeting, 8 Jan. 1942; ibid., Mackenzie to King, 10 Jan. 1942

26 IMP, vol. 32, Mackenzie to Hart, 15 Jan. 1942

27 WLMK, J1 series, vol. 326, handwritten note on Keenleyside to King, 13 Jan. 1942; IMP, vol. 32, press release, 14 Jan. 1942; IMP, vol. 24, B.M. Stewart to Mackenzie, 26 Jan. 1942

28 *Province,* 14, 15 Jan. 1942; NC, 16 Jan. 1942; *Sun,* 14 Jan. 1942

29 DLab, vol. 174, Mackenzie to B.M. Stewart, 23 Jan. 1942; IMP, vol. 32, Mackenzie to Robertson, 28 Jan. 1942

30 *News-Herald,* 31 Jan. 1942; DLab, vol. 174, J.H. McVety to MacNamara, 28 Jan. 1942; ibid., Major H.C. Bray to director, military operations and intelligence, 29 Jan. 1942

31 DND, reel C8369, file 8704, Joint Service Committee, Pacific Coast, Minutes, 30 Jan. 1942; DHist 193.009 (D3), R.O. Alexander to secretary, Chief of Staff Committee, 13 Feb. 1942; DND, reel C8366, file HQS 8613, Pope to Alexander, 16 Feb. 1942

32 HCD, 29 Jan. 1942, 151–6

33 HCD, 2 Feb. 1942, 266–7

34 British Columbia, Legislative Assembly, *Votes and Proceedings,* 12 Feb. 1942; *Sun,* 3 Feb. 1942

35 *Sun,* 13, 14, 16, 17, and 23 Feb. 1942. The Victoria *Times* also carried dispatches from Hutchison, but they were usually shorter and less dramatic. See also an article by Grant Dexter, *Sun,* 17 Feb. 1942.

36 WLMK, 279332-6, A. McGavin to King, 20 Feb. 1942. The advertisement appeared in the *Times,* 17 Feb. 1942.

37 EAR, file 3464-B-40C, W.C. Nichol to Keenleyside, 9 Feb. 1942; *Province,* 17 Feb. 1942

38 IMP, vol. 24, Vancouver City Council Resolution, 9 Feb. 1942, with J.W. Cornett to Ralston, 10 Feb. 1942; BCARS, Wilson Papers, Resolution of Vancouver City Council, 16 Feb. 1942; DLab, vol. 655, M.F. Hunter to each

city and municipality in British Columbia, 14 Feb. 1942. A file of these petitions may be found in DEA, vol. 2798, file 773-E-40.

39 DEA, vol. 2798, file 733-B-1-40, J.A. Macdonald to King, 17 Feb. 1942

40 WLMK, 288847-9, W.C. Woodward to King, 11 Feb. 1942; *Sun*, 16 Feb. 1942; IMP, vol. 32, T.W.S. Parsons to R.L. Maitland, 17 Feb. 1942; *Colonist*, 21 Feb. 1942; New Westminster *British Columbian*, 21 Feb. 1942

41 WLMK, J1 series, vol. 330, R.W. Mayhew to King, 12 Feb. 1942; BCARS, Wilson Papers, Report of Meeting, 12 Feb. 1942; IMP, vol. 24, S. Mussallem to Mackenzie, 21 Feb. 1942

42 KD, 19 Feb. 1942

43 *Province*, 25 Feb. 1942; *News-Herald*, 21 Feb. 1942; *Times*, 19 Feb. 1942; IMP, vol. 24, Hugh Dalton to Mackenzie, 27 Feb. 1942

44 DLab, vol. 174, Olaf Hanson et al. to King, 21 Feb. 1942; IMP, vol. 25, C.M. Gregg to Mackenzie, 17 Feb. 1942; WLMK, J2 series, vol. 295, Charles Wing to A.W. Neill, 19 Feb. 1942

45 IMP, vol. 25, B.O. Moxon to Mackenzie, 20 Feb. 1942; *Province*, 20 Feb. 1942; BCSC, vol. 2, file 50, Citizens Defence Committee, circular [21 Feb. 1942]; ibid., M.C. Robinson to Major-General H.F.G. Letson, 24 Feb. 1942; WLMK, J4 series, vol. 361, David McKee to members, 25 Feb. 1942

46 BCSC, vol. 2, file 50, J. Price to speaker and members of parliament, 21 Feb. 1942; ibid., Price to Grant McNeil, 25 Feb. 1942; DLab, vol. 655, Hubert Savage to 'Dear Sir,' 24 Feb. 1942, and J.V. Johnston to King, 26 Feb. 1942

47 RCMP, vol. 3563, file C-19-2-9, vol. 1, Mackenzie to Ralston, 23 Feb. 1942; IMP, vol. 25, Mackenzie to St Laurent, 24 Feb. 1942

48 NA, J.L. Ralston Papers, vol. 77, Chiefs of Staff, Appreciation, 19 Feb. 1942, and Notes for Speech, 24 Feb. 1942

49 Ibid., vol. 72, secret session file statement; ibid., R.B. Hanson to King, 20 Feb. 1942. According to the prime minister, tough questioning from members angry about the inadequate defences of British Columbia had persuaded Ralston and his officers to bend. KD, 20 Feb. 1942

50 *Sun*, 23 Feb. 1942; KD, 23 and 24 Feb. 1942; WLMK, C249460-2, A.D.P. Heeney to King, 25 Feb. 1942

51 The PJBD minutes for 10–11 November 1941 are in WLMK, vol. 320, f 3370. The fullest account of the coordination attempts after 7 December 1941 is in Gregory Johnson, 'North Pacific Triangle? The Impact of the Far East on Canada and its Relations with the United States and Great Britain, 1937–48' (PHD thesis, York University, 1989), 246–50.

52 *Colonist*, 27 Feb. 1942. See also Nanaimo *Free Press*, 26 Feb. 1942, and *Columbian*, 28 Feb. 1942. *Times*, 2 March 1942; *Colonist*, 3 March 1942; *Province*, 2

March 1942; DLab, vol. 655, Canadian Legion, Mission to King, 2 March 1942

53 Muriel Kitagawa, *This Is My Own: Letters to Wes and Other Writings on Japanese Canadians, 1941–1948* (Vancouver 1985), 6

54 NC, 26 Jan. 1942; *Asahi*, 6 and 28 Feb., 15, 23, and 24 March 1942

55 NC, 26 Jan. and 27 Feb. 1942; DEA, Acc. 84-4/259, vol. 223, file 4166-40, V.C. Best to Keenleyside, 23 Feb. 1942

56 *Province*, 11 and 18 March 1942; *Colonist*, 17 March 1942

57 *Sun*, 20 March 1942

58 *Sun*, 13 March 1942. See also C.P. Stacey, *Six Years of War* (Ottawa 1955), 170.

59 *Sun*, 21 and 24 March 1942

60 *Sun*, 26 March 1942; *Province*, 26 March 1942

61 *Sun*, 4 April 1942; *Province*, 4 April 1942

62 KD, 19 May 1942

63 DHist, 112.11 (DIA), vol. 3, Memo, General J.C. Murchie to minister, 13 March 1942; DHist, 193.009 (D6), Captain F. Houghton to CGS, 28 April 1942, enclosing Appreciation of the Situation as at 1st April 1942

64 Stacey, *Six Years of War*, 172

65 PCO, series 18, vol. 14, file W29-1, First Meeting of Pacific Command, 1 April 1942

66 H.P. Willmott, *The Barrier and the Javelin* (Annapolis 1983), chap. 3

67 DND, vol. 11764, file PC 010-9-18, Memorandum, 7 July 1942, with Commander A.H. Reed to commanding officer, Pacific Coast, 11 July 1942

68 KD, 3 June 1942

69 J.J. Stephan, *Hawaii Under the Rising Sun* (Honolulu 1984), chs. 6–7

70 USNA, RG 218, Records of the US Joint Chiefs of Staff, Mf reel 10, f 39322ff, Combined Chiefs of Staff paper, 'Probable Maximum Scale of Attack on West Coast of North America,' CCS 127, 29 Nov. 1942; ibid., CCS 127/3, Aug. 1943. Stacey, *Six Years of War*, ch. XV

71 DND, vol. 11764, file PC 010-9-4, Minutes of meeting of members of the PJBD and Joint Chiefs of Staff, 3 July 1943

72 Douglas, *Creation*, 424

73 Ibid., 427; C.P. Stacey, *Arms, Men and Government: The War Policies of Canada, 1939–1945* (Ottawa 1970), 133

74 RCMP, vol. 3567, file C3129-1-4, vol. 1, Robertson to S.T. Wood, 9 March 1942; *Sun*, 10 March 1942; *Province*, 11 March 1942; WLMK, C249463, C.N. Senior to Mackenzie, 10 March 1942

75 BCSC, vol. 2, file 40, Mackenzie to Taylor, 16 March 1942

76 Cowichan *Leader*, 6 April 1942; Comox District *Free Press*, 2 April 1942; Comox *Argus*, 26 March 1942

77 *The Federationist,* 19 March 1942; *News-Herald,* 31 March, 11 and 12 Aug. 1942; *Province,* 4 and 20 April 1942

78 DLab, vol. 175, Minutes of meeting of British Columbia MPS in the office of Humphrey Mitchell, 21 July 1942; *Province,* 30 July 1942; WLMK, J4 series, vol. 361, King, Memorandum, 25 Sept. 1942

79 *Sun,* 6 and 9 Jan. 1943; *Province,* 6 and 7 Jan. 1943; *News-Herald,* 7 Jan. 1943; IMP, vol. 25, W.E. Payne to Mackenzie, 11 Jan. 1943, and Mackenzie to Payne, 20 Jan. 1943

80 KD, 19 Feb. 1942

CHAPTER 5 In Temporary Quarters: The Experiences of the Evacuees

1 EAR, file 3464-J-40, draft memo for the prime minister, nd [c 24 Feb. 1942]; CWC, 26 Feb. 1942; RCMP, vol. 3563, Wood to St Laurent, 26 Feb. 1942; KD, 27 Feb. 1942

2 BCSC, vol. 1, file 1, W.A. Eastwood to E.L. Boultbee, 9 Oct. 1942; BCSC, vol. 7, file 163, Welfare Committee minutes, 28 Oct. 1942; IMP, vol. 24, R.R. Burns to Mackenzie, 10 Sept. 1942; BCARS, Mrs J.W. Awmack Collection, W. McBride, 'Tashme,' 25 March 1947, and unsigned letter, c 1945

3 BCSC, vol. 7, file 163, Minutes of the Advisory Board, 23 April 1942; NC, 3 Jan. 1943

4 *Province,* 2 March 1942

5 BCSC, vol. 10, file 305, Robertson to MacNamara, 11 April 1942; vol. 16, file 605, Robertson to Taylor, 25 July 1942, and A. Rive, conversation with BCSC, Vancouver, 1 June 1942; BCSC, vol. 15, file 605(2), Pedro E. Schwartz, Report, 27 July 1942; DLab, vol. 657, MacNamara to Pickersgill, 12 Feb. 1945. In October 1945, as part of the repatriation program, officials checked files to determine which Canadian nationals had sought advice or assistance from the protecting power. BCSC, vol. 14, file 600, Pickersgill to MacNamara, 30 Oct. 1945

6 NA, Secretary of State Records, H4 series, vol. 811, Robertson to MacNamara, 5 June 1942; WLMK, J1 series, vol. 355, Spanish consul, Montreal, to secretary of state for external affairs, 20 Oct. 1942, and Robertson to Spanish consul, 27 Oct. 1942; DEA, Acc. 83-84/259, vol. 3004, file 3464-B-40, pt 2. Quotations from Japanese publications, May 1943, in Report of Directorate of Military Intelligence, 8 Feb. 1944

7 Shimpo, *Ishi o Mote,* 188; NC, March 1942, passim; Hayashi, *Kuroshio no Hate ni,* 175–6

8 BCSC, vol. 7, file 163, Minutes of Advisory Board, 13 March 1942; Jun Kabayama, *Onchō-ki* [An Account of Grace] (Tokyo 1971), 128–9; UBC, Kōnosuke

Nishikihama, *Omoide no Ki* [Reminiscences], 1977, 14–15, UBC, Yamaga Collection, vol. 3, file 4, Yasutarō Yamaga, 'Owaruru Mamani [Being Driven Away], unpublished memoir

9 Nishikihama, *Omoide no Ki,* 10. Several accounts appear in Barry Broadfoot, *Years of Sorrow, Years of Shame* (Toronto 1977), 86–96. See also David Breen and Kenneth Coates, *Vancouver's Fair: An Administrative and Political History of the Pacific National Exhibition* (Vancouver 1982), 96ff.

10 BCSC, vol. 7, file 163, Minutes of Advisory Board, 23 April 1942; BCSC, *Removal of Japanese from Protected Areas, March 4, 1942 to October 31, 1942* (Vancouver 1942), 8; Ken Adachi, *The Enemy That Never Was* (Toronto 1976), p. 248; Muriel Kitagawa, *This Is My Own: Letters to Wes and Other Writings on Japanese Canadians* (Vancouver 1985), 15; Broadfoot, *Years of Sorrow,* 87; BCSC, vol. 15, file 605(2), Pedro E. Schwartz, Report of Inspection Tour of Japanese Camps and Settlements, 27 July 1942, and Taylor to MacNamara, 26 Aug. 1942; BCSC, vol. 7, file 150, T.W.S. Parsons to Taylor, 4 March 1942

11 Kiyozo Kazuta quoted in Gordon G. Nakayama, *Issei* (Toronto 1984), 173

12 BCSC, vol. 15, file 605(2), Rev. Yoshio Ono et al. to International Red Cross representative, 10 June 1942; BCSC, vol. 16, file 612, C.G. MacNeil to Mead, 16 March 1942, and file 614, Denis Murphy to Taylor, 4 April 1942; BCSC, vol. 7, file 163, Minutes of Advisory Committee, 23 April 1942. Adachi, *Enemy,* 244–5, paints a very unflattering picture of Morii. See also Rolf Knight and Maya Koizumi, *A Man of Our Times: The Life History of a Japanese-Canadian Fisherman* (Vancouver 1976), 59–61 and 79–80. The RCMP had known that at least some Japanese Canadians distrusted Morii. DND, reel C8365, HQS 8613, R.L. Cadiz to B.R. Gibson, 3 Dec. 1941

13 BCSC, vol. 11, file 500, W.S. McRae, Report, c July 1942

14 BCSC, *Removal,* 9

15 BCSC, vol. 13, file 513, Miss Sugihara to C.V. Booth, 2 Oct. 1945; Shizuye Takashima, *A Child in Prison Camp* (Montreal 1971), np

16 IMP, vol. 32, J.E. Read, Memo, 12 Jan. 1942, and Mackenzie to King, 10 Jan. 1942

17 Take Akiyama, 'Memoir,' (in the possession of Masako Iino); IMP, vol. 32, MacNamara to Mitchell, 19 Feb. 1942; UBC, Kantaro Kadota Collection, box 4, file 6, Kiyozo Kazuta, untitled note

18 WLMK, 287616-20, Spanish consul, Montreal, to secretary of state for external affairs, 20 Oct. 1942; N.A. Robertson to Spanish consul, 27 Oct. 1942; DEA, vol. 30004, file 3464-B-40 pt 2, secretary of state for external affairs to Canadian minister, Washington, 17 Nov. 1942

19 IMP, vol. 32, Parsons to R.L. Maitland, 17 Feb. 1942, and Maitland to Mackenzie, 19 Feb. 1942

20 BCSC, vol. 8, file 201, Japanese Movement, Pacific Coast, Week Ending 25 June 1942; Department of Labour, *Report on the Administration of Japanese Affairs in Canada, 1942–1944* (Ottawa 1944), 13

21 WLMK, C220372, Journal of Discussions, Permanent Joint Board on Defence, 26–27 May 1942; DHist, 314.009 (D17), acting minister of national defence to Mitchell, 1 June 1942; DND, reel C5394, HQS, 7236-56, extract from minutes, Joint Chiefs of Staff, 4 July 1942. Operators of tourist facilities in the Rocky Mountains were also unhappy about the presence of Japanese workers in National Parks. NA, Parks Canada Records, vol. 175, file Y165, director, Lands, Parks and Forests Branch, to J. Wardle, 20 March 1942, and T.A. Crerar to J.I. Brewster, 18 March 1942. We are indebted to Frances Woodward for this reference.

22 BCSC, vol. 15, file 605(2), Taylor to MacNamara, 26 Aug. 1942, and Schwartz, Report, 27 July 1942; IMP, vol. 24, K. Tanaka to BCSC, 26 May 1942; BCARS, Department of Highways Records (GR1585), file 554-3, R.M. Corning to J.M. Miers, 27 Jan. 1943

23 BCSC, vol. 2, file 53, J.A.J. Illington, Vernon Detachment, RCMP, Report, 18 May 1942; N.W. Willett to BCSC, 26 Oct. 1942; Supt. E.C.P. Salt, RCMP, Report, 27 May 1942; BCSC, vol. 9, file 208, Jasper Detachment, RCMP, Report, 7 March 1942; secretary of state, H4 series, vol. 811, Robertson to consul general of Spain, 27 Oct. 1942; DLab, vol. 171, Wardle to MacNamara, 30 July 1942

24 BCSC, vol. 14, file 600, H.H. Wrong to consul general of Spain, 22 March 1943; BCSC, vol. 2, file 53, Eastwood, Memo, 13 July 1942; NC, 9 March 1942; Knight and Koizumi, *A Man*, 77; Takeo Ujo Nakano with Leatrice Nakano, *Within the Barbed Wire Fence: A Japanese Man's Account of His Internment in Canada* (Toronto 1980), 16

25 BCSC, vol. 3, file 66, Mead to MacNamara, 31 March 1942; Nisei Mass Evacuation Group to Taylor, 15 April 1942; Secretary of State, H4 series, vol. 811, K.T. Shoyama to Keenleyside, 25 March 1942; BCSC, vol. 2, file 53, Wendell B. Shaw, Report, 30 Sept. 1942, and C.H. Hill to BCSC, 11 April 1942; IMP, vol. 24, RCMP, Record of Conversation between Kondo and Ottawa, 24 March 1942

26 Toyo Takata, *Nikkei Legacy* (Toronto 1983), 130

27 Hayashi, *Kuroshio no Hate ni*, 167; BCSC, vol. 3, file 66, letter, 28 Feb. 1942; Kazuta, untitled note; BCSC, vol. 2, file 53, Decoigne Work Camp No. 2 to All Concerned, 5 July 1942; IMP, vol. 24, Mead to MacNamara, 3 June 1942; EAR, file 3464-J-40C, Wood to Keenleyside, 1 May 1942, and Wood to St Laurent, 5 June 1942

28 BCSC, vol. 3, file 66, Mead to 'Vagon,' 5 March 1942; NC, 4 April 1942; EAR,

file 3464-J-40C, MacNamara to Keenleyside, 11 May 1942; BCSC, vol. 7, file 144, letters to Taylor, 20 and 21 April 1942

29 EAR, file 3464-J-40C, Wood to Keenleyside, 13 April 1942; BCSC, vol. 2, file 53, Taylor to OC, RCMP, Vancouver, 8 April 1942; Taylor to T.B. Caulkin et al., 10 April 1942; Taylor, Order no. 5, 27 March 1942; St Laurent, Order for Detention, 21 April and 5 May 1942; Mead to OC, RCMP, Vancouver, 25 April and 5 May 1942

30 This new group had been formed by some of the leaders of the Japanese Canadian Citizens League, an organization founded by *Nisei,* in 1936 to seek rights of Canadian citizenship. The Naturalized Citizens Committee was also a new body. For details see Adachi, *Enemy,* 160–4 and 239–47.

31 BCSC, vol. 3, file 66, NMEG to Taylor, 15 April 1942

32 BCSC, vol. 2, file 53, NMEG to All Concerned, 5 May 1952, and Hill to BCSC, 8 May 1942; JCCA, vol. 1, Vancouver Minute Book, 13 May 1942; BCSC, vol. 3, file 66, NMEG to *Nisei,* 17 April 1942, and L.S. [?] to Mead, 2 May 1942; Takata, *Nikkei Legacy,* 129

33 BCSC, vol. 3, file 79, NMEG to Taylor, 11 June 1942, and vol. 2, file 53, Hill to commissioner, RCMP, 28 April 1942

34 BCSC, vol. 8, file 199, F.W. Taylor to A.C. Taylor, 18 May 1942; BCSC, vol. 2, file 53, Shirras to Kemp et al., 14 May 1942; *News-Herald,* 15 May 1942

35 BCSC, vol. 2, file 53, Mead to MacNamara, 1 and 4 June 1942; undersecretary of state for external affairs to BCSC, 28 May 1942; MacNamara to Taylor, 29 May and 26 June 1942; A.H.L. Mellor to MacNamara, 20 July 1942; *Province,* 17 June 1942

36 BCSC, vol. 3, file 79, NMEG to Taylor, 4 June 1942; M. Ayakawa et al. to Mead, 5 July 1942; Mellor to MacNamara, 4 July 1942; BCSC, vol. 2, file 53, Mead to OC, E Division, RCMP, 1 Aug. 1942

37 BCSC, vol. 2, file 53, Taylor to Mead, 31 July 1942; DEA, Acc 83-84/259, vol. 3004, file 3464-B-40, pt 2, Upton to commander, E Division, RCMP, 10 Aug. 1942, and Mead to Rive, 19 Aug. 1942

38 RCMP, vol. 3563, Wood to St Laurent, 3 March 1942; DEA, Acc 83-84/259, box 174, file 2998-B-40, King to Canadian minister to Argentine, 18 March 1942; DEA, vol. 3004, file 3464-J-40, MacNamara to Read, 4 May 1943

39 DLab, vol. 174, Taylor to Mackenzie, 4 March 1942, and Mackenzie to Taylor, 5 March 1942; BCSC, vol. 2, file 31, S.G. Blaylock to Taylor, 16 March 1942; BCSC, vol. 7, file 63, Minutes, 13 March 1942; *Cranbrook Courier,* 19 March 1942

40 WLMK, 272307-13, Blaylock to King, 5 Sept. 1942, and N.A. Robertson to

Blaylock, 11 Dec. 1942; DLab, vol. 176, Blaylock to C.D. Howe et al., 31 July 1942, and Mead to MacNamara, 4 Aug. 1942; BCARS, J.C. Harris Papers, box 3, file 3, J.C. Harris, 'Notes and Memories of the Coming of the Japanese to the Slocan Lake Country 1942,' New Denver, 28 March 1944

41 BCSC, vol. 34, file 2201, Japanese Movement, 30 Nov. 1942; UCA, PamFC106, J3J2, 'Memo re Japanese in the Interior,' [1943]; DEA, Acc. 83-84/259, vol. 201, file 3464-AN-40C, E.L. Maag, 'Japanese Settlements. Inspection Tour ... June 16th ... June 28th, 1945'

42 BCSC, *Removal of Japanese,* 11; BCSC, vol. 4, file 128, Eastwood to W.A. MacBrayne, 20 Aug. 1942; Nishikihama, *Omoide no Ki,* 10; Kitagawa, *This Is My Own,* 13; BCSC, vol. 4, file 127, W.A. MacBrayne, Bi-Monthly Reports, 30 April and 16 June 1943

43 BCSC, vol. 4, file 128, 'Lillooet Self Supporting Project,' nd, and MacBrayne to Eastwood, 24 Oct. 1942; Takata, *Nikkei Legacy,* 125; Nakayama, *Issei,* 152. See also Masajiro Miyazaki, *My Sixty Years in Canada* (Lillooet 1973).

44 BCSC, vol. 34, file 2201, Japanese Activity ... 30th June, 1943

45 BCSC, vol. 4, file 128, MacNamara to Taylor, 13 July 1942; RCMP, vol. 3564, file C-11-19-2-9, vol. 4, S.T. Wood to MacNamara, 28 Nov. 1942; BCSC, vol. 15, file 606, H.T. Pammett, 'Memorandum re Proposal for Reorganization of the British Columbia Security Commission,' 3 Dec. 1942; BCSC, Administration, 48

46 BCSC, vol. 20, file 700, Taylor to MacNamara, 6 July 1942; BCSC, vol. 7, file 163, Advisory Board minutes, 4 Sept. 1942; BCSC, vol. 15, file 605(2), Pedro E. Schwartz, Report of Inspection Tour, July 1942; EAR, file 3464-J-4, King to Mitchell, 26 Aug. 1942; BCSC, vol. 8, file 202, MacNamara to Eastwood, 30 Sept. 1942; Jeanine Tsuyuki, 'A Tashme House,' *Tales from Tashme,* May 1943. The BCSC did borrow tents from the United States army to provide short-term housing. At Slocan, construction delays meant that some families were living in tents which had either no stoves or makeshift ones as late as November. BCSC, vol. 7, file 144, D.A. Deeks, RCMP, Slocan, Report, 1 Nov. 1942. The problem was short-lived.

47 F.E. LaViolette, *The Canadian Japanese and World War II* (Toronto 1948), 100; UCA, 'Memo re Japanese in the Interior,' [1943], *Sun,* 22 Dec. 1943

48 BCSC, vol. 22, file 800, R.L. Webb to Taylor, 29 March 1942; BCSC, vol. 7, file 144, W.T. Bannan to Eastwood, 7 May 1942; BCSC, vol. 15, file 605, Taylor to MacNamara, 24 July 1942; Department of Labour, *Administration,* 14

49 BCSC, vol. 1, file 1, J.A. Tyrwhitt to Eastwood, 6 July 1942, and vol. 7, file 144, Dr C.L. Hodge, Report, 1 June 1942

50 DLab, vol. 174, W.M. Duke to Mackenzie, 3 March 1942; BCSC, vol. 7, file

163, Meeting of the Joint Committee of the Christian Churches, 8 April 1942; DEA, Acc. 83-84/259, vol. 201, file 3469-AM-40, Scott, Memorandum, 18 Feb. 1943; Maag, Report, 1943; BCSC, vol. 10, file 305, W.P. Bunt to Shirras, 22 May 1942

51 WLMK, 282078-80, Paul D. Murphy, 'Memo on Japanese Evacuation,' 2 May 1942; BCSC, vol. 10, file 305, Welfare Committee Minutes, 1 May 1942; BCSC, vol. 3, file 79, Eastwood to DesBrisay et al., 16 July 1942

52 BCSC, vol. 3, file 79, Japanese Movement ... 31 October 1942

53 BCSC, vol. 34, file 2201, Japanese Movement ... 30 November 1942; and Japanese Activity ... 30 June 1943; Maag, Report, Jan. 1943; DEA, Acc. 83-84/259, vol. 201, file 3469-AM-40, Scott, Report, 3 Feb. 1943

54 BCSC, vol. 34, file 2201, Eastwood, Report, 8 March 1942; BCSC, vol. 7, file 144, Report on Greenwood Leases, 26 Oct. 1943; Scott, Report, 18 Feb. 1943; NC, 2 Sept. 1944

55 BCSC, vol. 34, file 2201, Japanese Movement ... 31 December 1942; DLab, vol. 3004, intercepted letter, 5 Nov. 1943; *Kootenaian,* 19 March and 30 April 1942. About 115 residents of Kaslo, including several of Chinese origin, did sign a petition against the coming of the Japanese. BCARS, PP (GR1222), vol. 163, file 5, R.E. Green to Maitland, 29 April 1942

56 WLMK, J1 series, vol. 323, F. McGibbon to W.K. Esling, 20 June 1942; information on activities in Kaslo is from the *Kootenaian,* 1942–5, passim.

57 NC, 4 March 1944; DLab, vol. 1527, intercepted letter, 10 April 1944

58 *Kootenaian,* 28 May 1942 and 1943–5, passim

59 UBC, Tanaka Collection, box 16, file 1, letters, 18 Feb. and 25 Jan. 1945; UCA, 'Memo re Japanese in the Interior' [1943]

60 BCSC, *Removal of Japanese,* 22. On New Denver's early history see Cole Harris, 'Industry and the Good Life Around Idaho Peak,' CHR 66 (Sept. 1985): 315–43; DLab, vol. 655, W.J. Turnbull to MacNamara, 27 Oct. 1942.

61 BCSC, vol. 34, file 2201, W.A. Eastwood, Report, 8 March 1943

62 DEA, Acc. 83-84/259, vol. 3004, file 3464-B-40, pt 2, Boultbee to F.P. Bernard, 29 Oct. 1942; BCSC, vol. 34, file 2201, Japanese Movement ... 30 November 1942; Knight and Koizumi, *A Man of Our Times,* 77–8; Takashima, *A Child in Prison Camp,* np; DLab, vol. 1527, intercepted letter, 31 Jan. 1944; Gwen Suttie, 'With the Nisei in New Denver,' *British Columbia Historical News* 5 (Feb. 1972): 24

63 *Arrow Lakes News,* 15 July 1943; BCSC, vol. 22, file 800, Slocan Bi-Monthly Reports, 22 April and 19 July 1943, and S.N. Ross to MacNamara, 12 March 1946; BCSC, vol. 4, file 203, Colin Clifford, Slocan District Board of Trade to W.G.C. Lansckail, Nelson Board of Trade, 2 Dec. 1943; Adachi, *Enemy,* 339–40; Nakayama, *Issei,* 196

64 BCSC, vol. 12, file 500, Taylor to MacNamara, 6 July 1942; BCSC, vol. 34, file

2201, Japanese Activities ... 30th January 1943; BCSC, vol. 4, file 127, Collins to MacNamara, 12 Nov. 1943

65 BCSC, *Removal of Japanese,* 26; BCARS, Awmack Collection, draft speech, nd; EAR, file 3469-AM-40, Maag, Report, Jan. 1943

66 Takata, *Nikkei Legacy,* 135; BCSC, vol. 3, file 79, letter to Eastwood, 19 Oct. 1942; UCA, 'Memo re Japanese in the Interior,' [1943]

67 Scott, Report, 1 March 1943; Maag, Reports, Jan. 1943 and June 1945; BCSC, vol. 14, file 600, Schwartz to undersecretary of state for external affairs, 4 Jan. 1943; UBC, W.N. Sage Papers, box 47, letter to M. Sage, 25 Oct. 1946

68 BCSC, vol. 14, file 516, Hide Hyodo to C.V. Booth, 2 July 1943, and vol. 13, file 315, Bayfarm School Report, 1 March 1945

69 DLab, vol. 165, MacNamara to Eastwood, 18 Dec. 1942; UBC, *Tashme News,* 14 Oct.–31 Dec. 1943, passim. In 1935 the Japan Broadcasting Association, a government-funded and -controlled enterprise, began shortwave broadcasts under the auspices of the Foreign and Communications ministries. Reception was not always clear in British Columbia.

70 Department of Labour, *Administration,* 33; Knight and Koizumi, *A Man of Our Times,* 78–9; UBC, Margaret Sage Hayward Papers, draft article, 'Japanese Tashme'; BCARS, Awmack Collection, McBride, 'Tashme,' March 1947

71 Adachi, *Enemy,* 271; NC 3 April, 1 May, and 30 Oct. 1943

72 BCS, vol. 7, file 163, Maintenance Advisory Committee, Minutes, 24 Nov. 1942; David Suzuki, *Metamorphosis: Stages in a Life* (Toronto 1987), 73–4

73 NC, 13 Feb. 1943; DLab, vol. 1527, intercepted letter, 29 Feb. 1944; DLab, vol. 655, Collins to MacNamara, 10 Aug. 1943

74 Maag, Report, Jan. 1943; GK, A 700 9-11-1-10-2, 'Daitōa Sensō Kankei Ikken: Kōsenkoku-kan Tekikokujin oyobi Furyo Toriatsukai-buri Kankei: Nyū Denbā Shisatsu Hōkoku (1945)' [On the War of Greater East Asia: Concerning the Treatment of Enemy Aliens and the POWs between Belligerent Nations and Various Problems: Report of Inspection at New Denver (1945)]

75 BCSC, vol. 13, file 503, Booth to Eastwood, 17 March 1943; Eastwood to Booth, 8 July 1943, and MacNamara to Collins, 27 July 1943

76 Cf Ann Gomer Sunahara, *Politics of Racism* (Toronto 1981), 97; BCSC, vol. 7, file 163, Maintenance Advisory Committee, Minutes, 24 Nov. 1942; BCSC, vol. 13, file 503, Collins to MacNamara, 2 Aug. 1943; IMP, vol. 24, Mitchell to Mackenzie, 21 Aug. 1942.

77 Takashima, *A Child in Prison Camp,* np

78 BCSC, vol. 12, file 500, Tyrwhitt to Eastwood, 8 Nov. 1942, Tyrwhitt to F.B. Pearce, 24 Sept. 1942, and Tyrwhitt to all supervisors, 6 Oct. 142; Thomas James, *Exile Within: The Schooling of Japanese Americans, 1942–1945* (Cambridge, MA 1987), 43

79 BCSC, vol. 13, file 500, Taylor to MacNamara, 27 Oct. 1942 and file 503,

MacNamara to Taylor, 1 Dec. 1942, and Pammett to MacNamara, 4 Feb. 1943; NC, 22 Jan. 1944. Although the loyalty of all would-be teachers was investigated through RCMP records, the three who had written or received 'somewhat subversive' letters were reprimanded, not dismissed. BCSC, vol. 13, file 503, Booth to Eastwood, 17 March 1943

80 Department of Labour, *Administration,* 15–16; BCSC, vol. 13, file 503, Booth to Eastwood, 17 March 1943; Booth, 'Education,' Sept.-Oct. 1943; Collins to MacNamara, 6 Dec. 1943; MacNamara to Collins, 13 Dec. 1943; M. Fujita to education supervisor, Tashme, 3 March 1944; vol. 12, file 500, Tyrwhitt to Eastwood, 8 Nov. 1942; NC, 19 Feb. 1944

81 BCSC, vol. 13, file 513, M. Sugiura to Booth, 2 Oct. 1945; file 514, MacNamara to Pickersgill, 18 Aug. 1945, Booth, Report, 30 July 1945; vol. 17, file 630, Pammett, Report, 10 July 1945; BCARS BC, High School Correspondence Branch Records, N.F. Bowman to E.E. Lucas, 2 July 1945; DLab, vol. 657, Pammett to Booth, 6 Feb. 1945

82 BCSC, vol. 1, file 20, Boultbee to Collins, 10 Aug. 1943; Takashima, *A Child in Prison Camp,* np; Broadfoot, *Years of Sorrow,* 251; BCSC, *Removal of Japanese,* 15

83 BCSC, vol. 23, file 500, Tyrwhitt to Hyodo, 3 Dec. 1942 and file 503, MacNamara to Collins, 7 Aug. 1943, and Collins to MacNamara, 2 Aug. 1943

84 BCSC, vol. 13, file 503, Collins to MacNamara, 10 Aug. 1943, and Collins to MacNamara, 2 Aug. 1943; BCSC, vol. 1, file 20, Collins to MacNamara, 17 Aug. 1943

85 UBC, Yamaga Collection, box 3, file 9, Yamaga 'Owaruru Mamani,' unpublished memoir; Suttie, 'With the Nisei,' 20; Broadfoot, *Years of Sorrow,* 246 and 251

86 Department of Labour, *Administration,* 10–13

87 BCSC, vol. 7, file 163, minutes of meeting, 1 May 1942

88 BCSC, vol. 7, file 163, Maintenance Advisory Committee, Minutes, 14 Sept. 1942; vol. 15, file 606, MacNamara to Collins, 18 and 29 Dec. 1943, and Minister of Labour to F.W. Jackson, 6 Dec. 1943

89 *Sun,* 21 Dec. 1943. See also *News-Herald,* 23 Dec. 1943

90 Royal Commission to Enquire into the Provisions Made for the Welfare and Maintenance of Persons of the Japanese Race Resident in Settlements in the Province of British Columbia, *Report* (Ottawa 1944)

91 *Sun* and *Province,* 20 March 1944; NC, 15 Jan. and 25 March 1944; BCSC, vol. 15, file 606, Collins to MacNamara, 2 May 1944; MacNamara to Collins, 11 May 1944, and Collins to supervisors, 22 May 1944

92 *Time,* 21 Feb. 1944; DEA, vol. 3209, file 5353-G-40C, high commissioner, London, to secretary of state for external affairs, 22 March 1944; EAR, file

3464-A4-40C, Maag to Department of External Affairs, 11 April 1944, and Robertson to Schwartz, 27 June 1944

93 Department of Labour, *Administration*, 18; BCSC, vol. 17, file 630, Pammett, Report, 10 July 1945; DEA, Acc. 83-84/259, file 3464-AN-40C, Maag, Report, June 1945

94 Takashima, *A Child in Prison Camp*, np

CHAPTER 6 'No Japanese from the Rockies to the Sea'

1 BCARS, C.N. Senior Papers, box 1, Ian Mackenzie, Speech to Vancouver Centre Liberal Nominating Convention, 18 Sept. 1944; *Province*, 19 Sept. 1944

2 NC, 5 Jan. 1942

3 NC, 4 Feb. 1942

4 Muriel Kitagawa, *This is My Own: Letters to Wes and Other Writings on Japanese Canadians, 1941–1948*, ed. Roy Miki (Vancouver 1985), 85

5 BCSC, vol. 4, file 128, MacNamara to Taylor, 13 July 1942

6 BC Security Commission, *Report on the Removal of Japanese from Protected Areas, March 4, 1942 to October 31, 1942* (Vancouver 1942), 9

7 EAR, file 3464-G-40, Keenleyside to the Rev. G. Dorey, 17 Feb. 1942

8 DLab, vol. 174, W.A.C. Bennett to Ian Mackenzie, 2 March 1942; Vernon *News*, 8 Jan. 1942

9 A collection of such requests may be found in IMP, vol. 25.

10 Ibid., vol. 42, clerk, Municipal Council, Kelowna, to Mackenzie, 18 Feb. 1942; Kelowna *Courier*, 12 March 1942; NC, 25 Feb. 1942; IMP, vol. 25, W.A.C. Bennett et al. to A.C. Taylor, 28 Feb. 1942

11 David Iwaasa, *Canadian Japanese in Southern Alberta, 1905–1945* (New York 1978) [first published 1972], 64ff. See also Howard Palmer, 'Patterns of Racism: Attitudes Towards Chinese and Japanese in Alberta 1920–1950,' *Histoire sociale/Social History* 25 (May 1980): 148–54; *Province*, 15 April 1942.

12 BCSC, vol. 7, file 178, W.A. Eastwood to George Collins, 13 May 1943

13 DLab, vol. 170, William Aberhart to A. MacNamara, 17 March 1942; Aberhart to King, 27 March 1942; Taylor to John Bracken, 31 March 1942; BCSC, vol. 2, file 40, Bracken to MacNamara, 25 March 1942; BCSC, vol. 16, file 610, R.C. Brown to Eastwood, 8 Sept. 1942; DLab, vol. 178, Eastwood, 'Japanese Activity and Placements throughout Canada, period ending 30th September 1943'; F.E. LaViolette, *The Canadian Japanese and World War II* (Toronto 1948), 121

14 BCSC, vol. 8, file 203, John Shirras to C.E. Raham, 24 April 1942; Take Akiyama's 'Memoir' (unpublished mss in the possession of Masako Iino); DLab, vol. 170, Taylor to MacNamara, 29 Aug. 1942; BCSC, vol. 3, file 79,

Eastwood to MacNamara, 16 Feb. 1943; BCSC, vol. 34, file 2201, 'Japanese Movement – Pacific Coast ... June 30th, 1943'

15 BCSC, vol. 34, file 2201, Eastwood, Report, 8 March 1943, and 'Japanese Movement – Pacific Coast ... April 30th 1943'

16 Department of Labour, *Report on the Administration of Japanese Affairs in Canada, 1942–1944* (Ottawa 1944), 37; Department of Labour, *Report on the Re-establishment of Japanese in Canada, 1944–1946* (Ottawa 1947), 67; NC, 16 Feb., 6 May 1944, 28 April 1945; LaViolette, *Canadian Japanese*, 126

17 *News-Herald*, 19 March 1942; BCSC, vol. 34, file 2201, 'Japanese Movement ... October 31, 1944' and 'Japanese Movement, November 30th 1942'

18 BCSC, vol. 5, file 606, Pammett, 'Memorandum re Reorganization,' 3 Dec. 1942

19 DEA, vol. 3209, file 5353-G-40, vol. 1, Pammett, 'Re: Placement of Japanese in Self Sustained Employment,' 11 April 1944; NC, 7 and 21 Aug. 1944

20 In one case, a young man who rejected several requests to leave Slocan and accept employment in Port Arthur, Ont., was sentenced to six months in prison. The local RCMP officer reported that 'this was the nature of a test case, and should have a certain beneficial effect on others of his kind.' The Department of External Affairs quickly reminded the Department of Labour that imposing compulsory labour on Japanese risked complaints from Japan. BCSC, vol. 7, file 213, RCMP, New Denver, Report, 10 May 1943; DEA, Acc. 83-4/259, vol. 3004, file 3464-B-40, undersecretary of state for external affairs to MacNamara, 22 May 1943

21 BCSC, vol. 8, file 201, MacNamara to Collins, 14 May 1943; BCSC, vol. 10, file 325, Eastwood to W.W. Brereton, 31 July 1943; BCSC, vol. 3, file 79, Eastwood to G.E. Trueman and G. Pipher, 1 Dec. 44; BCSC, vol. 34, file 2201, 'Japanese Movement ... December 31st 1942.'

One exasperated official of the Department of External Affairs suggested that the settlements could be turned into internment camps since the Japanese 'are already interning most of our people.' He suggested allowing people to leave the camps if they accepted employment elsewhere but proposed that otherwise, the government abandon the dispersal policy and indefinitely support the Japanese 'in comparative idleness.' DEA, vol. 3001, file 3464-B-40, pt 2, S.M. S[cott], Memorandum, Policy Toward Japanese in Canada, 5 April 1943

22 NC, 6 March, 17 July, and 28 Aug. 1943; BCSC, vol. 34, file 22011, 'Japanese Movement ... December 31st 1942'

23 NC, 6 Feb. and 16 Oct. 1943, 15 Jan., 12 Feb., 8 April, 12 Aug., and 2 Sept. 1944; BCSC, vol. 22, file 813, D.A. Deeks, RCMP, Slocan, Report, 31 March 1943; UBC, Wakabayashi Collection, box 20

24 NC, 23 Jan. and 17 April 1943, 25 March 1944; BCSC, vol. 22, file 500, F.G. Skinner, Report, 22 April 1943; DLab, vol. 1527, intercepted letter, 28 July 1944

25 NC, 1 May and 16 Oct. 1943; BCSC, vol. 34, file 2201, 'Japanese Movement ... 30th April 1943'; BCSC, vol. 12, file 501, Booth to Hyodo, 15 April 1943, and Hyodo to Booth, 17 April 1943; BCSC, vol. 10, file 327, Booth to Trueman, 7 Aug. 1943, and Booth, 'Relocation and Rehabilitation of Japanese in Eastern Canada,' 2 June 1943

26 BCSC, vol. 10, file 327, Booth, 'Relocation,' 24 June 1943, and Booth to Trueman, 7 Aug. 1943; CCJC, vol. 2, 'Record of the Work of the Co-operative Committee on Japanese Canadians, June 1943 to September 1949'

27 NC, 6 and 13 Nov., 11 Dec. 1943; DEA, vol. 3004, file 3464-B-40, pt 2, 'The Natural Born Canadians of Japanese Origin and the Naturalized Canadians of Japanese Origin of Lemon Creek' to King, 4 Dec. 1943; DLab, vol. 639, Pammett to MacNamara, 9 Dec. 1943, and MacNamara to Pammett, nd

28 NC, K.W., 'Mountain Hermitage,' 6, 13, 20, and 27 Nov. 1943, 29 Jan. 1944, and passim

29 For details see Patricia E. Roy, 'The Soldiers Canada Didn't Want: Her Chinese and Japanese Citizens,' CHR 59 (1978): 353–4, and 'Citizens Without Votes: East Asians in British Columbia,' in Jorgen Dahlie and Tissa Fernando, eds., *Ethnicity, Power & Politics in Canada* (Toronto 1981), 161–3.

30 NC, 15 April, 9 and 16 Sept. 1944

31 *Province,* 23 April 1942; Adachi, *Enemy,* 287; DLab, intercepted letters, 27 Sept., 22 Oct., and 13 Nov. 1944

32 NC, 16 Oct. 1943, 19 Feb. 1944

33 BCSC, vol. 10, file 327, Booth, 'Relocation and Rehabilitation,' 24 June 1943; NC, 8 July 1943, 17 June 1944, and 31 March 1945; *News-Herald,* 17 March 1945; JCCA, JCCD, vol. 2, file 6, Kenzie Tanaka to Michael Hoshino, 14 Dec. 1945; BCSC, vol. 10, file 313, D. Mactavish, Report, 31 Dec. 1945; *Report on Re-establishment,* 20

34 *Montreal News Bulletin* 1 (4) (June 1946)

35 The only exception were annual residential leases approved by the attorney-general of the province in which they were located.

36 IMP, vol. 25, 'The White Farmers of the District of the Fraser Valley, Petition re Japanese' [Jan. 1942]

37 DLab, vol. 178, Mitchell to St Laurent, 10 Nov. 1943, and St Laurent to Mitchell, 20 Dec. 1943; CWC, 5 July 1945

38 NC, 23 Jan. 1942

39 Toyo Takata, *Nikkei Legacy* (Toronto 1983), 141

40 DLab, vol. 1528, intercepted letter, 30 May 1945

41 DEA, vol. 3464-B-40, pt 2, Memo on meeting of 30 June 1943; DEA, Acc. 83-84/259, file 3464-V-40, S. Mussalem to King, 22 Sept. 1942; Maple Ridge-Pitt Meadows *Gazette,* 13 March 1942; IMP, vol. 25, H.E. Beyer to King, 22 Dec. 1942

42 *Sun,* 26 Jan. 1943; *Province,* 8 Feb. 1943. The custodian's observation that the liquidation might not prevent the Japanese Canadians from re-establishing themselves after the war was consigned to back pages. *Province,* 11 Feb. 1943

43 IMP, vol. 19, 'Report of Japanese Fishing Vessels Disposal Committee,' Dec. 1942; Royal Commission on Japanese, Claims, 'Report,' 6 April 1950

44 CEP, vol. 2, file 16, G.W. McPherson to P.S. Ross & Sons, 20 Dec. 1944; McPherson to custodian, 21 Dec. 1942; [McPherson], Situation as Regards Persons of Japanese Race [March 1942]; DEA, vol. 3121, file 4606-C-13-40, E.H. Coleman to secretary of state, 16 March 1942; Coleman to Varcoe, 19 March 1942; Read to Varcoe, 18 March 1942; Read to undersecretary of state for external affairs, 19 March 1942; BCSC, vol. 7, file 163, Minutes of Advisory Board, 13 March 1942

45 DEA, vol. 2121, file 4606-C-13-40, Coleman to secretary of state, 16 March 1942; JCCA, vol. 1, Minute Book, Vancouver, 2 April 1942; WLMK, 272258, E.C. Banno and B. Hisaoka to King, 16 April 1942

46 CEP, vol. 2, file 16, C.L. Drewry to undersecretary of state, 26 June 1942

47 IMP, vol. 25, Crerar to Mackenzie, 27 April 1952; G. Murchison to T. Crerar, 22 April and 8 Sept. 1942; NC, 27 Feb. and 6 March 1943, quoted in Kimiaki Nakashima, 'Economic Aspects of Japanese Evacuation from the Canadian Pacific Coast,' (MA thesis, McGill University, 1946), 39–40

48 CEP, vol. 2, file 16, C.L. Drewry, Report to the Undersecretary of State Regarding the Japanese Evacuation Section of the Office of the Custodian at Vancouver, BC, 26 June 1942; IMP, vol. 24, McPherson to Coleman, 5 Jan. 1943; CEP, vol. 2, file 11, McPherson to Miss Ireland, 28 July 1944; IMP, vol. 25, McPherson to Coleman, 9 Dec. 1942, and Coleman to secretary of state [Dec. 1942]

49 CEP, vol. 2, file 15, P.S. Ross & Sons, Report on Japanese Evacuation Section of the Custodian's Office, Vancouver, 20 Oct. 1943; file 11, McPherson to Miss Ireland, 28 July 1944. From time to time, the custodian's staff sent property to owners who requested it and paid the cost, but this policy, at least for residents of the interior settlements, was discontinued because of the lack of storage space there.

50 UBC, Yasutaro Yamaga, '1942-nen Kaisen Tōji no Shimbun oyobi Kansō' [Newspapers and Thoughts on Wartime Movement (1942)]

51 CVA, Advisory Committee on Japanese Properties, H.S. Durkee, Report, 30 June 1945; BCSC, vol. 35, file 2203, Memo to cabinet, 3 March 1947

52 DEA, vol. 3121, file 4606-C-13-40, Collins to MacNamara, 3 Feb. 1943; BCSC, vol. 15, file 606, Mitchell to McLarty, 22 Dec. 1943
53 DEA, vol. 3121, file 4606-C-14-40, H.F. Angus to Robertson, 13 March 1943; NA, Laurent Beaudry Papers, vol. 6, file 105, 'BMM,' Memo, 28 May 1943; DLab, vol. 177, Mitchell to McLarty, 20 Jan. 1943
54 BCSC, vol. 4, file 217, quoted in Sgt J.K. Barnes, RCMP, Report, 9 April 1943; NC, 20 Feb., 10 April, and 24 July 1943 and 30 May 1944; Adachi, *Enemy*, 322–3; Ann Gomer Sunahara, *The Politics of Racism* (Toronto 1981), 109
55 DEA, vol. 3004, file 3464-C-40C, Schwartz to Robertson, 27 May 1942; Beaudry Papers, vol. 6, file 105, quoted in Schwartz to Robertson, 10 March 1943; DEA, vol. 2121, file 4606-C-13-40, Schwartz to Robertson, 1 May 1943; A. Rive to Robertson, 7 June 1943; Undersecretary of state for external affairs to Schwartz, 12 July 1943; DEA, Acc 83-84/259, vol. 201, file 3464-AD-40C, Rive to Schwartz, 8 April 1944
56 BCSC, vol. 34, file 2201, Taichi Ukitsu to King, Feb. 1946; BCSC, vol. 6, file 622, R. Shirakawa to T.B. Pickersgill, 9 April 1945; DEA, vol. 2798, file 773-B-1-40, Rev. W.H.H. Norman to King, 4 March 1943, and M.A.B. to Robertson, 20 July 1943; Toronto *Star*, 15 May 1947; Toronto *Globe and Mail*, 14 May 1947; Calgary *Herald*, 30 Jan. 1947; *News-Herald*, 12 May 1947; Royal Commission on Japanese Claims, *Report*; JCCA, vol. 2, 'Statement to Claimants re Origin, Nature and Work of the Co-operative Committee on Japanese Canadians,' April 1950; JCCA, vol. 1, file 8, Report of Discussions between Mr Andrew Brewin and delegates, 2 Sept. 1947; JCCA, Minutes, 1949, passim
57 Royal Commission on Japanese Claims, *Report*, passim
58 JCCA, 'Statement,' April 1950; Takata, *Nikkei Legacy*, 149
59 A Gallup Poll released in mid-February 1944 indicated that 80 per cent of Canadians favoured repatriating Japanese who were not Canadian citizens but only 33 per cent thought Canadian citizens of Japanese origin should be returned to Japan. *Province*, 16 Feb. 1944. A Canadian Institute of Public Opinion poll released two months earlier had indicated that 53 per cent of Canadians favoured repatriation of the Japanese. *Province*, 22 Dec. 1943
60 WLMK, C249497-500, R.G. Robertson to King, 27 March 1944; CWC, 19 April 1944
61 For details see Roy, 'The Soldiers Canada Didn't Want,' 354–5.
62 HCD, 5 May 1944, 2667–93; DLab, vol. 639, A.H. Brown, Memorandum, 20 July 1944
63 EAR, file 104-(S)-1, R.G. Robertson to N.A. Robertson, 12 June 1944; IMP, vol. 9, speech to Dominion Command, Canadian Legion, Vancouver, 5 June 1944; *Province*, 28 March 1944; *Times*, 29 June 1944; *Sun*, 8 July 1944
64 *News-Herald*, 3 June 1944; *Province*, 5 June 1944; 'C.C.F. Views on the Japanese

Question,' (Vancouver: CCF, BC Section, June 1943); WLMK, 308236-40, N.F. Black et al. to King, 28 May 1944

65 *Province,* 16 Aug. 1944

66 WLMK, C249524ff, representatives of the Church of England et al. to King, 27 June 1944. For a brief discussion of the franchise question see Roy, 'Citizens Without Votes,' 151–71. For examples of church educational material see Constance Chapell, *Second Pioneers: A Story of the Evacuation and Resettlement of a Japanese-Canadian Family* (Toronto 1944); Norman F. Black, *Minority Problems in Canada* (np, 1944); R.N. Savory, 'Japanese Canadians,' *Canada and Christendom* 8 (Feb. 1943): 7.

67 EAR, file 104-(S)-1, R.G. Robertson to N.A. Robertson, 12 July 1944

68 HCD, 4 Aug. 1944, 5915–17

69 NC, 12 Aug. and 23 Sept. 1944, 24 Feb. 1945

70 BCSC, vol. 16, file 622, Eastwood to Collins, 29 Aug. 1944, and Collins to MacNamara, 2 Sept. 1944

71 BCSC, vol. 16, file 622, Collins to MacNamara, 2 Sept. 1944; Brown to MacNamara, 6 Sept. 1944; Brown to Mitchell, 5 Sept. 1944; Pickersgill to MacNamara, 22 Feb. 1945; MacNamara to Pickersgill, 27 Feb. 1945

72 *Times,* 17 Jan. 1945; *Colonist,* 17 Aug. 1944; Barry Mather, *News-Herald,* 14 Oct. 1944

73 EAR, file 104-(S)-1, R.G. R[obertson], Memorandum, 20 March 1945; DLab, vol. 639, MacNamara to N.A. Robertson, 23 Oct. 1944; WLMK, C249561–3, N.A. Robertson to King, 21 Dec. 1944; DLab, vol. 639, Mitchell, Memorandum, 2 Feb. 1945; DLab, vol. 657, A.D.P. Heeney to Mitchell, 5 Feb. 1945; PCO, series 16, vol. 2, Cabinet Conclusions, 2 February 1945. At the specific request of the prime minister, the cabinet also agreed to seek to have Japan reimburse Canada for the costs of repatriation.

74 DEA, vol. 3004, file 3464-B-40, N.A. Robertson to L.B. Pearson, 30 March 1945; BCSC, vol. 16, file 622, Pickersgill to MacNamara, 19 March 1945; T.B. Pickersgill, Notice to All Persons of Japanese Racial Origin Now Resident in British Columbia, 12 March 1945

75 *Sun,* 16 March 1945; *Times,* 17 March 1945; *Province,* 17, 19, and 20 March 1945; *News-Herald,* 20 March 1945

76 DLab, vol. 658, T.B. Pickersgill to 'Dear Sir or Madam,' March 1945; BCSC, vol. 6, Pickersgill to D.C. Archibald et al., 14 March 1945; BCSC, vol. 22, Pickersgill to D. MacTavish, 19 March 1945; Rev. W.H.H. Norman, *What About the Japanese Canadians?* (Vancouver 1945), 23

77 T.B. Pickersgill, Notice to All Persons of Japanese Racial Origin Now Resident in British Columbia, 12 March 1945

78 BCSC, vol. 16, file 622, Pickersgill to editors, 15 March 1945; *Sun,* 16 March 1945; *News-Herald,* 9 April 1945; IMP, vol. 24, Mackenzie to S.W. Mulholland, 4 April 145; C.E. Hope, circular letter, 2 Oct. 1945; *Province,* 26 April 1945; Wartime Information Board, *Survey,* no. 66, 30 June 1945

79 K.W., 'Mountain Hermitage,' NC, 8 Jan. 1944

80 UBC, Tokikazu Tanaka Collection, Nisshi [Diary and News], 5 May 1945; BCSC, vol. 17, file 625, M. Nagai to C.V. Booth, and T. Sugiura to Booth, 2 Oct. 1944; DLab, vol. 1527, intercepted letter, 6 Aug. 1944; DLab, vol. 1528, intercepted letter, 10 May 1945

81 NC, 14 July 1945; DLab, vol. 657, T. Isozaki et al., Slocan Central Committee to Mitchell, 28 March 1945; BCSC, vol. 16, file 622, Pickersgill to R. Shirakawa, 5 and 10 April and 15 May 1945, and Pickersgill to MacNamara, 28 March 1945. Pickersgill's comments are corroborated in a report from 'Hakkōkai,' a Japanese patriotic society at Bayfarm, Slocan, 7 April 1945.

82 DLab, vol. 1527, intercepted letter, 3 Dec. 1944; DLab, vol. 1528, intercepted letters, 2 and 17 July 1945; confidential interview, Vancouver, Aug. 1986

83 DLab, vol. 1527, intercepted letter, 6 Aug. 1944; DLab, vol. 1528, intercepted letter, 10 May 1945; interview with a repatriate, winter 1987; DLab, vol. 1529, intercepted letter, 15 April 1945

84 DLab, vol. 1528, intercepted letters, 14 May and 21 July 1945

85 DLab, vol. 1528, intercepted letter, 12 May 1945

86 BCSC, vol. 16, C.K. Gray to All Members & Special Constables Engaged in Japanese Repatriation, 4 April 1945; JCCA, vol. 2, file 2, Japanese Committee, Tashme to E.L. Maag, 18 June 1945; DLab, vol. 658, Japanese Committee of Slocan Valley District to Mitchell, 16 April 1945

87 BCSC, vol. 16, file 622, Pickersgill to McTavish, 26 June 1945, and Pickersgill to supervisors, 6 April 1945; interview, Kazue Nishidera, Tokyo; DLab, 1528, intercepted letter, 30 May 1945

88 DLab, vol. 658, Pickersgill, circular, June 1945; BCSC, vol. 16, file 622, Pickersgill to MacNamara, 28 March 1945, and F.L. Ernst to Pickersgill, 16 May 1945; WLMK, C249590–1, R.G. Robertson to King, 23 April 1945; DLab, vol. 6457, 'Re Voluntary Repatriation Survey,' c. 30 Sept. 1945

89 *Report on Re-establishment,* 17 and 20; Sydney *Post-Record,* 29 Aug. 1945; *Sun,* 14 Aug. 1945; *Province,* 22 March 1946

90 DLab, vol. 1527, Pickersgill to MacNamara, 6 and 13 Oct. 1945, and 'Reasons for Requests for Cancellation of Requests for Repatriation as of October 15th 1945'

91 BCSC, vol. 16, file 622, Pickersgill to MacNamara, 22 Sept. 1945; A.H. Brown to Pickersgill, 25 Sept. 1945

92 *News-Herald*, 29 Sept. 1945; *Province*, 29 Sept. 1945
93 BCSC, vol. 16, file 622, Pickersgill to MacNamara, 1 Oct. 1945, and Brown to Pickersgill, 4 Oct. 1945; Mrs J.W. Awmack, Memorandum, June 1989
94 EAR, file 104-(S)-1, N.A. Robertson to King, 31 Aug. 1945; DLab, vol. 639, Minutes of Special Cabinet Committee, 12 Sept. 1945
95 DLab, vol. 659, Coldwell to St Laurent, 15 Oct. 1945
96 NC, 26 Sept. 1945; DLab, vol. 659, Pickersgill to MacNamara, 24 July 1945; JCCA, Executive Meeting Minutes, 15 May 1945; DLab, vol. 657, Co-operative Committee on Japanese Canadians to King, 25 July 1945
97 WLMK, J2 series, vol. 472, The Christians of Tashme to the Prime Minister of Canada and To Whom It May Concern, 18 Nov. 1945; WLMK, 373711, L. Sato to King, 22 March 1946
98 JCCA, vol. 2, 'Record of the Work of the Co-operative Committee on Japanese Canadians, June 1943 to September 1947'; WLMK, C249600-6, R.G. Robertson to H.H. Wrong, 24 Oct. 1945
99 HCD, 22 Nov. 1945, 2414, and 17 Dec. 1945, 3704; *Sun*, 23 Nov. 1945
100 Edith Fowke, 'Japanese Canadians,' *Canadian Forum*, Jan. 1946, 232; WLMK, 344496, Rev. W.W. Judd to King, 11 Dec. 1945; CCJC, vol. 3, 'A Church Sponsored Plan for Japanese Canadians,' c. Oct. 1945; BCARS, Mrs J.W. Awmack Collection, W.J. Williams and Winnifred McBride to secretary of SCM, 12 Feb. 1946, and letter, 16 Dec. 1963; BCSC, vol. 10, file 313, D. McTavish, Report, 31 Dec. 1945
101 WLMK, C249761ff, Petition, 2 Jan. 1946; WLMK, 366682 with Angus MacInnis to King, 23 May 1946; CCJC, vol. 1, Japanese Canadian Committee on Democracy, Brief, Oct. 1945
102 DLab, vol. 657, Pickersgill to Rev. J.H. Arnup, 24 Oct. 1945; MacNamara to J.A. Gillett, 16 Nov. 1945; DLab, vol. 660, Pickersgill to MacNamara, 30 Oct. 1945
103 WLMK, C249600-6, R.G. Robertson to Wrong, 24 Nov. 1945; C194894-6, Robertson to J.W. Pickersgill, 10 Nov. 1945; C3250125, R.G. Robertson to King, 28 Nov. 1945; DLab, vol. 639, Minutes of meeting of Special Committee of Cabinet, 5 Nov. 1945; PCO, J-25-1, A.D.P. Heeney to B.F. Wood, 20 Nov. 1945; HCD, 22 Nov. 1945, 240542
104 NC, 24 Nov. 1945; *Save Canadian Children and Canadian Honour* (Vancouver 1945); WLMK, C350125, R.G. Robertson to King, 28 Nov. 1945
105 NC, 3 Nov. 1945; WLMK, J2 series, vol. 472, Mrs M.E. Croy to King, 28 Nov. 1945; WLMK, 344908, Watson Kirkconnell, vice-president Baptist Federation of Canada, to J.L. Ilsley, 7 Nov. 1945; HCD, 23 Nov. 1945, 2454–63, and 4 Dec. 1945, 2929–3050, passim

106 WLMK, C249641, Heeney to King, 12 Dec. 1945, and C249646-7, Heeney to King, 13 Dec. 1945; PCO, J-25-1, Minutes of Special Committee of the Cabinet to Consider the Repatriation and Relocation of Persons of Japanese Race in Canada, 7 Dec. 1945; WLMK, C249649, P.M. Anderson to R.G. Robertson, 7 Dec. 1945; WLMK, C194892–3, N.A. Robertson to King, 14 Dec. 1945; PCO, series 16, vol. 3, Cabinet Conclusion, 15 Dec. 1945; DLab, vol. 639, Heeney to Mitchell, 17 Dec. 1945.

Robertson also suggested that racial discrimination could be avoided by requiring other enemy aliens or naturalized Canadians who had been detained under the Defence of Canada regulations to appear before the Loyalty Commission.

107 HCD, 17 Dec. 1945, 3696–8

108 *Sun*, 19 and 29 Dec. 1945; *Colonist*, 22 and 24 Nov. and 29 Dec. 1945; 26 Jan. 1946; Kamloops *Sentinel*, 16 Jan. 1946; Halifax *Herald* quoted in Toronto *Star*, 17 Dec. 1945; *Telegram*, 14 Jan. 1946; *Province*, 5 Jan. 1946; *Times*, 25 Jan. 1946

109 *Star*, 22 Dec. 1945; *Province*, 28 and 29 Dec. 1945

110 NC, 22 Dec. 1945, 12 Jan. and 9 Feb. 1946; JCCA, Executive Meeting Minutes, 29 Nov. and 21 Dec. 1945; JCCA, vol. 2, file 7, Kinzie Tanaka to Fred Shiga, 13 Dec. 1945. In Ontario, only 142 Japanese had sought repatriation and the JCCD did not know how many had asked to cancel. Moreover, the most likely test cases had some handicap such as 'a weakness in personality' or poor English skills. JCCA, vol. 2, file 7, G.E. Trueman to K. Tanaka, 14 Dec. 1945

111 NA, Andrew Brewin Papers, vol. 1, Brewin to St Laurent, 24 Dec. 1945; WLMK, C194934–9, F.P. Varcoe, Memorandum, 4 Jan. 1946; WLMK, 362519, Donalda Macmillan to King, 11 Jan. 1945; DLab, vol. 657, Delegation of Canadian Council of Churches, Meeting with W.L.M. King, H. Mitchell, and B. Claxton, 17 Jan. 1946; KD, 17 Jan. 1946

112 DLab, vol. 659, MacNamara to Varcoe, 12 Feb. 1946; BCSC, vol. 17, file 629, Pickersgill to A.H. Brown, 12 Jan. 1946

113 A copy of the judgment may be found in DLab, vol. 659; DLab, vol. 639, Mitchell to St Laurent, 23 Feb. 1946; WLMK, C194949–50, N.A. Robertson to King, 27 Feb. 1946; BCSC, vol. 34, file 2201, Heeney to cabinet, 27 Feb. 1946; PCO, series 16, vol. 14, Cabinet Conclusions, 6 March 1946; DLab, vol. 658, press release, 13 March 1946. A useful summary of the court proceedings may be found in Ken Adachi, *The Enemy That Never Was* (Toronto 1976), 311–17.

114 NC, 16 March, 6 July, and 7 Dec. 1946; WLMK, C294947–8, R.G. Robertson to King, 22 Feb. 1946; EAR, file 50076-40, 'Deportation of Persons of Japanese

Race,' 3 March 1946; JCCA, vol. 2, file 1, Meeting with prime minister, 26 March 1946; WLMK, C194959, Minutes of a Meeting Concerning the Problem of Japanese in Canada, 26 March 1946

115 *Sun*, 20 Feb. 1946; *Colonist*, 21 Feb. and 9 April 1946; DLab, vol. 659, Maitland to Mitchell, 20 Feb. 1946; *Province*, 9 and 10 April 1946; IMP, vol. 24, G.S. Wismer to Mackenzie, 6 May 1946

116 *Province*, 22 March 1946; *News-Herald*, 21 Feb. 1946; DLab, vol. 660, E.N. Ross et al. to Mitchell, 12 March 1946; BCSC, vol. 34, file 2201, Taichi Ukita to King, Feb. 1946; BCARS, Awmack Collection, J. MacLachlan to 'Dear Sir,' 27 March 1946

117 Many letters and petitions may be found in WLMK, J1 series, vols. 400 and 401; WLMK, 367094-5, Albini Lafortune to King, 4 March 1946; DLab, vol. 655, press release, 6 May 1946.

118 JCCA, vol. 3, Co-operative Committee on Japanese Canadians, Memorandum for the House of Commons and the Senate of Canada on the Orders-in-Council, PC 7355, 7356, and 7357 re the Deportation of Canadians of Japanese Racial Origin, April 1946; *Our Japanese Canadians: Citizens Not Exiles* (Toronto, April 1946)

119 DLab, vol. 661, A.H. Brown to MacNamara, 30 April 1946; N.A. Robertson to B.F. Wood, 7 May 1946, and Mackenzie to Mitchell, 7 May 1946. The draft bill included a clause, apparently inserted by Justice Minister St Laurent himself, that would have required anyone claiming he was not subject to the bill to prove he was not Japanese. Brown to MacNamara, 30 April 1946

120 Privy Council Appeal no. 58 of 1946, The Co-operative Committee on Japanese Canadians and another v. The Attorney-General of Canada and another from The Supreme Court of Canada, 2 Dec. 1946

121 Montreal *Daily Star*, 4 Dec. 1946; Ottawa *Evening Citizen*, 3 Dec. 1946; *Globe and Mail*, 4 Dec. 1946; Toronto *Star*, 3 Dec. 1946; Calgary *Albertan*, 5 Dec. 1946; Lethbridge *Herald*, 13 Dec. 1946; *Province*, 3 Dec. 1946; *Sun*, 3 Dec. 1946

122 KD, 22 Jan. 1947; press release, 24 Jan. 1947; NC, 1 Feb. 1947; *Colonist*, 4 Dec. 1946; DLab, vol. 657, J.E. Eckman to Mitchell, 14 Dec. 1946; WLMK, 30330977, West Burnaby Liberal Association to King, 31 Jan. 1947; WLMK, C249641, R.G. Robertson to King, 1 Feb. 1947

123 Department of Labour, *Report on the Re-establishment*, 15; DLab, vol. 639, 'Recommendations of the Department of Labour to the Cabinet Committee on Japanese Problems,' [c. 15 Dec. 1946]; WLMK, C194389, 'Secret Memorandum to Cabinet, Report from Committee on Japanese Problems,' 13 Jan. 1947

124 NC, 2 March, 6 April, and 8 June 1946; DLab, vol. 658, MacNamara to

Pickersgill, 9 May 1946; WLMK, C194967, N.A. Robertson to King, 1 May 1946

125 WLMK, C174961, R.G. Robertson to King, 20 April 1946; NC, 15 June and 13 July 146; *Report on Re-establishment,* 18

126 NC, 4 May, 7 and 14 Sept. 1946; *Report on Re-establishment,* 18

127 BCSC, vol. 22, file 800, Brown to MacNamara, 28 Sept. 1946; J.F. McKinnon to MacNamara, 16 Oct. 1946; NC, 12 Oct. 1946

128 PCO, J-25-1, R.G. Robertson to King, 3 Dec. 1946; Memo to Cabinet Committee on Japanese Problems, 11 Dec. 1946. The most significant group of non-cooperators were about thirty Japanese nationals who had been interned for resisting evacuation and refusing to take self-sustaining employment. They were placed in the Moose Jaw hostel with their dependents, including some adult *Nisei,* but refused placement. Some demanded to be returned to British Columbia; others asked to be deported. The Department of Labour would not yield and in August 1947 it stopped providing food and forced three *Issei* who were unfit for labour to return to New Denver. About thirty-five stayed put to demand compensation for property losses and the lifting of restrictions on the movement of Japanese in Canada until July 1948, when the government sent in the sheriff and forced them out. The *Gambari* were an exception and their rebellion, noted the *Nisei* historian Ken Adachi, 'was a lonely, hopeless act' that won them no sympathy from other evacuees. PCO, J-25-1, Memo to the Cabinet Committee on Japanese Problems, 11 Dec. 1946; DLab, vol. 639, Reommendations of the Department of Labour to Cabinet Committee on Japanese Problems [c. 18 Dec. 1946]; Adachi, *Enemy,* 343

129 NC, 22 Feb. 1947; DLab, vol. 639, Mitchell to E.C. Manning, 15 Jan. 1948. See also PC 589, 17 Jan. 1948

130 DLab, vol. 661, Brown to MacNamara, 30 April 1946, and vol. 639, 'Memorandum to Sub-Committee of Cabinet on Japanese Affairs,' 15 July 1946

131 DLab, vol. 639, Recommendations of the Department of Labour to Cabinet Committee on Japanese Problems [c. 15 Dec. 1946]; PCO, J-25-1, 'Draft Bill for Information of Cabinet Committee on Japanese Problems' [11 Dec. 1946]

132 PCO, J-25-1, Prime Minister's Office, press release, 24 Jan. 1947; HCD, 22 and 23 April 1947, 2312–79

133 *News-Herald,* 5 Feb. 1947; UBC, W.N. Sage Collection, unsigned to M. Sage, 21 Nov. 1946; NC, 11 Jan. 1947

134 *News-Herald,* 22 Nov. 1946, 21 Feb. and 28 April 1947; *Province,* 4 June 1947

135 DLab, vol. 649, Privy Council Office, Memorandum, 10 Jan. 1948; WLMK, 195009, R.G. Robertson to King, 15 Jan. 1948; KD, 3 Feb. 1948. King's recollection of liberal principles may have been inspired by J.W. Pickersgill, a senior member of his staff, future Liberal cabinet minister, and brother of

T.B. Pickersgill, who held that the restrictions on Japanese movement were a 'flagrant violation of nearly every fundamental Liberal principle and deeply obnoxious to hundreds and indeed thousands of the best Liberals in the country.' Since 'everyone knows the orders must be repealed sooner or later,' he argued that immediate action would mean anti-Japanese sentiment would be largely gone by the time of the by-elections, 'whereas those who feel fundamental Liberal principles have been betrayed are not so likely to forget.' Pickersgill commended the suggestion of C.N. Senior, the former secretary of Ian Mackenzie, that the government take advantage of the temporary absence of a BC representative from the cabinet to let the order excluding the Japanese from coastal British Columbia lapse. WLMK, C195016-8, J.W. Pickersgill, Memorandum, 12 Feb. 1948; WLMK, 401090, C.N. Senior to King, 7 Feb. 1948

136 HCD, 15 March 1948, 2216–2242

137 *News-Herald*, 17 and 19 March, 12 April, and 9 Nov. 1948; *Sun*, 11, 17, 18, 22, and 25 March 1949

138 *Sun*, 11 March 1949; *Province*, 1 April 1949; DLab, vol. 655, Booth to Brown, 14 April 1949; BCARS, Awmack Collection, letter, 16 Dec. 1963; Toronto *Star*, 31 March 1949. See also Adachi, *Enemy*, 361–2, and for a contrary view, Sunahara, *Politics of Racism*, 165–8.

139 DEA, Acc 84-85/019, vol. 737, file 9890-40, Memorandum for file, 10 May 1952

140 BCSC, vol. 18, file 629, Pammett to MacKinnon, 10 June 1947; press release, 5 Sept. 1947; Trueman to MacKinnon, 13 Sept. 1947

141 BCSC, vol. 34, file 2201, L.B. Pearson to A.L. Jolliffe, 16 June 1947; JCCA, vol. 2, file 27, National Executive Meeting, Minutes, 16 June and 12 July 1948, and JCCA Committee on Future Projects, Meeting, 9 June 1949

142 *Sun*, 1 March 1949; UBC, Nishikihama, 'Omoide no Ki' [Memoirs] (1977); Shigeharu Koyama, 'Mio Kanada Renraku Kyōkai 20 yūyonen no Ayumi,' [Over Twenty Years of the Mio-Canada Liaison Association], 90 (in the possession of Shigeharu Koyama); NC, 9 Feb. and 12 Oct. 1946; Hoshikazu Yoshida, interview cited in Shigeharu Koyama, *Waga Rūtsu America-mura* [My Roots in the American Village] (Tokyo 1984)

143 BCARS, Awmack Collection, letter, 8 March 1947

144 UBC, JCCA Collection, box 8, file 123, 'Omoide no Ki' [Memoirs] (1977); DEA, Acc 84-85/019, vol. 85, file 3363-D-40, pt 1, Oscar Orr, 'Report on Arrival of Japanese Repatriates from Canada,' 20 June 1946; Shigeharu Koyama, 'Mio Kanada Renraku Kyōkai 20 yūyonen no Ayumi'

145 UBC, W.N. Sage Collection, box 47, letter to M. Sage, 26 July 1948; Kazue Nishidera, Tokyo, interview, 2 Feb. 1987; Shigeo Matsushita, interview, 16 Jan. 1987; JCCA, vol. 10, file 4, letter

146 Koyama, 'Mio Kanada Renraku Kyōkai,' pt 1; Minoru Kuno, Mio, interview, 3 Aug. 1987; Nishikihama, 'Omoide no Ki'

147 An estimated 6,614,000 Japanese nationals were abroad at the end of the war.

148 GK, K'-0001-6-0219, Ministry of Foreign Affairs, 'Report,' 7 Aug. 1947; Nishikihama, 'Omoide no Ki'

149 Kōseishō Hikiage-engo-kyoku [Repatriation Bureau, Ministry of Welfare], ed., *Zoku-zoku Hikiage-engo no Kiroku* [Sequel to the Sequel of the Record of the Repatriation Bureau] (Tokyo 1963)

150 DEA, vol. 3005, file 3463-V-40, W.F. Bull to secretary of state for external affairs, 21 Nov. 1960; Takejiro Ode to Bull, 31 Oct. 1960; M. Matsumiya et al. to Bull, c. 10 July 1961; Bull to undersecretary of state for external affairs, 14 July 1961

151 [Akiyama Collection, Tokyo], O.J. Ceappy to Fujimoto Akiyama, 3 Nov. 1959; D.J. Sinclair to Akiyama, 3 Sept. 1952

152 *Hanrei Jihō*, no. 538, 1 Jan. 1969, 6; *Yomiuri*, 9 July 1965; *Asahi*, 16 Dec. 1965; *Mainichi*, 18 Sept. 1966

CHAPTER 7 Behind the Barbed-Wire Fence

1 Statistics on the number arrested differ. Ken Adachi, *The Enemy That Never Was* (Toronto 1976), and Ann Sunahara, *The Politics of Racism* (Toronto 1981), list thirty-eight; other Japanese-Canadian sources list thirty-nine or forty-eight.

2 UBC, Yamaga Collection, box 2-1, '1942-nen Kaisen Tōji no Shimbun oyobi Kansō' [Newspapers and Thoughts on Wartime Movement in 1942]

3 UBC, Tokikazu Tanaka Collection, box 16-6, 'Nisshi' [Diary and News], 7 Dec. 1945

4 Takeo Ujo Nakano, *Within the Barbed Wire Fence* (Toronto 1980), 66

5 BCSC, vol. 2, file 53, Cpl Kilmer to E Division, RCMP, 22 Sept. 1942

6 DLab, vol. 1527, intercepted letter, 10 May 1944

7 Nakano, *Barbed Wire Fence*, 66

8 DLab, vol. 1527, intercepted letter, 20 Dec. 1943

9 Mitsuru Shimpo, *Ishi o Mote Owaruru Gotoku* [As Though Driven Away With Stones] (Toronto 1975), 215

10 Nakano, *Barbed Wire Fence*, 56

11 Tanaka, 'Nisshi,' 18, 21 Jan., 31 May, 18 June 1945

12 Yamaga Collection, box 3, file 11, 'Owaruru Mamani'

13 DEA, Acc. 83-84/259, vol. 201, file 3464-AD-40C, secretary of state for external affairs to Canadian ambassador in Washington, 14 June 1944

14 BCSC, vol. 15, file 605, S.M. Scott to Spanish consul-general, 5 Feb. 1943

15 Tanaka, 'Nisshi,' 7 Oct. 1945
16 BCSC, vol. 2, file 53, C.H. Halonen to Eastwood, 8 June 1944
17 Nakano, *Barbed Wire Fence*, 61
18 Interview with Kazue Nishidera, Tokyo, 23 Jan. 1987
19 BCSC, vol. 3, file 79, 'Japanese Movement ... October 31, 1942'
20 Ibid., vol. 2, file 53, MacNamara to Eastwood, 24 Dec. 1942, and letter to BCSC, 4 Dec. 1942
21 Ibid., vol. 34, file 2201, 'Japanese Movement ... December 31, 1942'; ibid., vol. 4, file 203, H.T. Pammett, 'Notes on Meeting of 27 September 1943'; DLab, *Report on the Re-establishment of Japanese in Canada, 1944–46* (Ottawa 1947), 10
22 BCSC, vol. 4, file 203, 'Notes on Meeting of 27 September 1943'
23 DLab, *Re-establishment*, 10
24 Nakano, *Barbed Wire Fence*, 93ff; DLab, vol. 1527, intercepted letter, 8 Sept. 1944
25 BCSC, vol. 3, file 53A, MacNamara to Pickersgill, 8 Jan. 1946
26 Ibid., Cpl Lambie Report, 15 Jan. 1946. For Canadian policy towards repatriation see DCER, X, 1119ff.
27 DEA, Acc. 83-84/268, box 246, file F4925-40, certificate, 18 March 1946; DCER, VIII, 1148. In Japan itself, the Canadian legation reported shortly before Pearl Harbor that there were 177 Canadians: 56 Roman Catholic priests, 52 nuns, 48 Protestant missionaries and teachers, and 21 others including 9 women, 8 men, and 4 children. Some of these Canadians may have returned to Canada shortly before Pearl Harbor. Canadian government statistics did not include Japanese Canadians who were in Japan for schooling or visits; the Canadian legation in Tokyo apparently considered them as Japanese nationals.
28 UCA, Board of Foreign Missions, Japan, box 6, file 137a, Bott Questionnaire, nd; Howard Norman, 'One Hundred Years in Japan'
29 UCA, Harper Coates Family Papers, box 1, file 14, Coates to Willson Coates, 25 Jan. 1942. Coates remained in Japan until her death, at the age of eighty-one, on 30 June 1945. As a symbol of her efforts to bring about a better understanding between East and West, she had asked that her ashes be scattered at sea at the 180th meridian. DEA, vol. 2948, file 3051-40, pt 2, Swiss legation, Tokyo, to E.H. Norman, 1 Nov. 1945
30 Tōyō Eiwa Jogakuin Hyakunen Shi Hensan Jikkō-iinkai, ed., *Tōyō Eiwa Jogakuin Hyakunen Shi* [A Centennial History of Tōyō Eiwa Girls' School] (1984), 328–32. Hamilton was repatriated in mid-1942.
31 DEA, vol. 2945, file 3050-C-40, data cards
32 GK, file A7009-11-1, Yokuryū Tekikokujin Toriatsukai Yōkō,' [Outline of the

Treatment of Interned Enemy Nationals,] 30 Jan. 1942 [prepared in Ministry of Home Affairs]

33 Documents in DEA, vol. 2945, file 3050-C-40

34 UCA, Japan Mission Fellowship Papers, box 6, file 137a, *Japan Mission Bulletin* 6 (1 Oct. 1942)

35 DEA, Acc. 83-84/259, box 230, file 4464-D-40, 'Sumire Camp,' account by Sybil Courtice [Dec. 1943]

36 Norman, 'One Hundred Years in Japan'

37 GK, file A7009-11-1

38 DEA, Acc. 83-84/259, box 173, file 2978-40, Memorandum, 7 Dec. 1942

39 Ibid., box 230, file 4464-D-40, *Gripsholm* Repatriates' Report No. A.1 [Dec. 1943]

40 Ibid., 'Sumire Camp' [Dec. 1943]

41 Ibid., Acc. 84-85/226, vol. 7, file 2864-B-40, pts 3 and 4, *Gripsholm* questionnaires, Dec. 1943

42 Ibid., vol. 3113, file 4464-D-40, *Gripsholm* Repatriates' Report No. A.8

43 Ibid., G2 series, vol. 3113, file 4464-D-40, pt 1, 'Mrs Stone's account of her trip from N[ew] Y[ork] to Montreal with the *Gripsholm* Party, December 4, 1943'

44 Ibid., J.C. Klasson, *Gripsholm* repatriate, on internment conditions in Manila, Nov. 1943

45 Ibid., Seno and B.G. Ryan to 'Dear Friends,' Dec. 1943

46 Ibid., vol. 2946, file 20-12-41, pt 2, enclosure with C.J. King to Seminary and Novitiate for Home and Foreign Missions, 9 June 1944. Another French-Canadian missionary lost his life on 8 February 1945 when the Japanese attacked the National Psychopathic Hospital where he had been admitted at the request of the commanding officer of the Los Banos Internment Camp. Ibid., vol. 2947, file 3050-N-40, D. Lacuna to Whom It May Concern, 16 Nov. 1945

47 Ibid., vol. 2947, file 3050-P-40, enclosure with Victor W. Odlum to W.L.M. King, 21 Jan. 1944, and undersecretary of state for external affairs to the judge advocate general, 17 March 1944

48 Alvyn J. Austin, *Saving China: Canadian Missionaries in the Middle Kingdom, 1888–1959* (Toronto 1986), 275–6; UCA, Board of Foreign Missions, General Correspondence, box 14, file 285, 'Missionaries Now in Enemy Territory,' 12 Dec. 1941

49 DEA, Acc. 84-85/226, vol. 7, file 2864-B-40, pt 4, Gripsholm questionnaire

50 Board of Foreign Missions, Korea, box 5, file 129, Dr Armstrong to Mrs Fraser, 2 Feb. 1942

51 Austin, *Saving China*, 276 and 283ff
52 Board of Foreign Missions, Honan, box 11, file 176, Report of Cheloo University Hospital, 1 July 1941 to 15 Jan. 1942; Report of Cheloo University Work 1941–2
53 Ibid., box 11, file 181, 'Report Concerning Protestant Christian Missionary Work in China, June 1942–September 1943'
54 Ibid., box 11, file 174, Dr Armstrong to Mrs Faris, 27 March 1942
55 DEA, Acc. 83-84/259, box 201, file 3464-AD-40, N. Robertson to C. Vining, 5 Nov. 1942
56 DImm, vol. 54, file 2217-1, Canadian minister in Washington to prime minister, 4 Dec. 1942
57 Herbert F. Thomson, 'Experiences in Occupied China,' *McGill News*, 26 (winter 1944): 16
58 DEA, G2 series, vol. 3112, file 4464-40, pt 1
59 Ibid., vol. 3113, file 4464-D-40
60 Ibid., *Gripsholm* Repatriates' Report No. A.1., Dec. 1943
61 Ibid., file 4464-D-40, *Gripsholm* Repatriates' Report, No. A.8; ibid., Acc. 84-85/226, box 6, file 2864-B-40, pt 3, Gripsholm questionnaire
62 Ibid., vol. 3113, file 4464-D-10, *Gripsholm* Repatriates' Report, No. A.8; UCA, Struthers Papers, box 2, G.K. King to 'Dear Friends,' 14 Dec. 1943; Austin, *Saving China*, 279–80
63 DEA, G2 series, Acc. 84-85/226, vol. 6, file 2864-B-40, pt 2, *Gripsholm* questionnaire; ibid., Acc. 83-84/259, box 230, file 4464-D-40, 'Footung Civil Assembly Centre,' Nov. 1943
64 Norman Cliff, *Courtyard of the Happy Way* (Evesham, Engl. 1977), 61
65 Grant Maxwell, *Assignment in Chekiang: 71 Canadians in China, 1902–1954* (Scarborough, Ont. 1982), 121
66 Jacques Langlais, *Les Jesuites du Québec en Chine, 1918–1955* (Québec 1979), 69
67 DEA, G2 series, vol. 3112, file 4464-D-40, *Gripsholm* Repatriates' Report
68 Ibid., vol. 3113, file 4464-D-40, pt 1, 'Haiphong Road Internment Camp, Shanghai,' received by External Affairs from Herbert Norman, 7 Dec. 1943; ibid., Acc. 84-85/226, vol. 7, file 2864-B-40, pt 3, *Gripsholm* questionnaire
69 Ibid., vol. 3111, file 4462-40, N.A. Robertson to secretary, Treasury Board, 14 Nov. 1944
70 *Gripsholm* Repatriates' Report, No. A.1; Albert Best of the United Church wrote a very similar report of the round-up at Hong Kong.
71 DEA, G2 series, Acc. 84-85/226, vol. 7, file 2864-B-40, pt 4, *Gripsholm* questionnaire; ibid., Acc. 83-84/259, box 201, file 2670-D-40, high commissioner in Britain to secretary of state for external affairs, 25 March 1942
72 Ibid., vol. 3113, file 4464-D-40, pt 1, F.C. Oppen, 'Conditions Prevailing in Stanley Internment Camp, January 1942 to September 1943'

73 Ibid., pt 2, J. Howe to officer commanding, E Division, RCMP, 18 Dec. 1943, conveying information given by his sister, a repatriate

74 UCA, Albert Best Papers, box 1, file 8, account [mid-1942]

75 Oppen, 'Conditions'; DEA, Acc. 83-84/259, box 230, file 4464-D-40, 'Inward Telegram,' 30 Oct. 1943, App. II

76 DEA, G2 series, Acc. 84-85/226, vol. 7, file 2864-B-40, pt 4, *Gripsholm* questionnaire

77 Ibid., vol. 3113, file 4464-D-40C, A. R[ive] to Malcolm MacDonald, 11 Dec. 1943; ibid, file 44464-D-40, Minutes of first Canadian meeting, 9 Sept. 1942

78 Yoshio Chaen, *Dai-Nippon Teikoku Naichi Furyo Shūyōjo* [Imperial Japanese Domestic Prisoners Camps] (Tokyo 1986), 19–30

79 Richard S. Malone, *A World in Flames, 1944–45: A Portrait of War*, Part II (Toronto 1984), 260

80 On repatriation see DImm, vols. 53 and 54, file 2217-2, and DEA, vol. 2931, file 2864-40, and vol. 3112, file 4464-40.

81 On American repatriation efforts see F. Scott Corbett, *Quiet Passages: The Exchange of Civilians between the United States and Japan during the Second World War* (Kent, Ohio 1987), chap. V.

82 Best Papers, box 1, file 8, account [mid-1942]

83 Board of Foreign Missions, General Correspondence, box 15, file 323, 'Repatriated Missionaries'

84 Ibid., Report of Foreign Missions, Korea Mission, box 5, file 127, 'Report of the Interim Committee of the Korea Mission ... August, 1942'

85 Austin, *Saving China*, 281–2

86 *United Church Observer*, 1 Nov. 1942, 7, 30

87 UCA, Margaret Brown Papers, box 1, file 9, Brown to friends, 29 Aug. 1942; Board of Foreign Missions, General Correspondence, box 15, file 320, Dr Armstrong to Mrs Martin, 29 July 1942; DImm, vol. 53, file 2217-1, King to Canadian minister, Washington, 22 Aug. 1942

88 For example, Salmon Arm *Observer*, 1 April 1943; Penticton *Herald*, 16 Dec. 1943; Kelowna *Courier*, 3 Feb. 1944

89 DEA, vol. 3112, file 4464-40, pt 5, S.M. S[cott], conversation with Herbert Norman on his return with the Gripsholm, 4 Dec. 1943

90 DImm, vol. 54, file 2217-2, King to secretary of state for dominion affairs, 17 Sept. 1942; DEA, vol. 3112, file 4464-40, pt 1, A.V. R[ive] to N.A. Robertson, 10 Oct. 1942, and memo for the prime minister, 3 Oct. 1942

91 Ibid., vol. 2945, file 3050-C-40, Memo for Mr Wershof, 24 Jan. 1945; ibid., Acc. 83-84/259, file 3050-G-40, M.L. Wershof to L. Beaudry, 10 May 1946

92 DEA, vol. 3112, file 4464-40, Ottawa to Canadian minister, Washington, 8 June 1943; DLab, vol. 658, Robertson to Wood, 10 June 1943

93 DEA, Acc. 84-85/226, vol. 8, file 4464-40C, Memo, 1 Feb. 1945

94 DLab, vol. 657, Confidential memo, July 1943; DEA, vol. 3209, file 5353-G-40C, Rive to undersecretary, 27 July 1943
95 DEA, vol. 3113, file 4464-D-40, 'Mrs Stone's account,' 4 Dec. 1943
96 Daniel Dancocks, *In Enemy Hands* (Edmonton 1983), 248
97 *The Royal Rifles of Canada in Hong Kong–1941–1945* (Sherbrooke, Que. 1980), 322
98 Dancocks, *In Enemy Hands,* 250–1
99 Malone, *World in Flames,* 260
100 DHist, file 593(D8), 'Notes of Conversations with Officers Going to Districts to Assist AJAGS in Preparation of Depositions from Repatriates,' 8 Jan. 1946
101 Malone, *World in Flames,* 261
102 GK, file A7009-11-2-1, Suzuki to Hamada, 31 Aug. 1943, and reply, 3 Sept. 1943
103 *Royal Rifles,* 324
104 DEA, Acc. 83-84/259, box 175, file 2998-D-40, pt II, 'Report on Conditions of Canadian Prisoners of War and Civilian Internees in Japan,' nd [mid-1943]
105 Ibid., 'Report on Visit Made on 9th May 1944'
106 *Royal Rifles,* 331
107 Ibid., 254–6
108 Yoshio Chaen, *Daitōa Senka Gaichi Furyo Shūyōjo* [Overseas Prisoners Camps During the Greater East Asia War] (Tokyo 1987), 108
109 Dancocks, *In Enemy Hands,* 270–1
110 'Hong Kong Vets Raise an Awkward Question,' Toronto *Globe and Mail,* 15 Aug. 1987
111 DHist, file 593(D8), 'Notes of Conversations'
112 See S.R. Elliot, *Scarlet to Green* (Toronto 1981), 500
113 DHist, file 113.3A1013(1), 'Final Report, War Crimes Investigation Section,' 30 Aug. 1947
114 For Canadian and Allied planning on repatriation of POWS and internees see DCER, X, 1201ff.
115 Malone, *World in Flames,* 247ff
116 Carl Vincent, *No Reason Why* (Stittsville, Ont. 1981), 239ff
117 DCER, XII, 287–9, 350–2

Select Bibliography of Manuscript Sources

BEAVERBROOK LIBRARY, LONDON

Lloyd George Papers

BRITISH COLUMBIA ARCHIVES AND RECORDS SERVICE, VICTORIA

Attorney-General's Records
Mrs J.W. Awmack Collection
BC High School Correspondence Branch Records
Department of Highways Records
Premiers' Papers
C.N. Senior Papers
Halford Wilson Papers

DEPARTMENT OF EXTERNAL AFFAIRS, OTTAWA

Records

DIRECTORATE OF HISTORY, NATIONAL DEFENCE HEADQUARTERS, OTTAWA

Records

DIPLOMATIC RECORD ARCHIVES, TOKYO

Gaimushō Kiroku [Documents of the Diplomatic Record Archives, Ministry of Foreign Affairs, Tokyo]

HARVARD UNIVERSITY, BOSTON

Pierrepont Moffat Papers

NATIONAL ARCHIVES OF CANADA, OTTAWA

Government Records
British Columbia Security Commission Records
Office of the Custodian of Enemy Property Records
Department of External Affairs Records
Department of Immigration Records
Department of Labour Records
Department of National Defence Records
Parks Canada Records
Privy Council Office Records
Royal Canadian Mounted Police Records
Secretary of State Records

Private Papers
Laurent Beaudry Papers
Andrew Brewin Papers
J.W. Dafoe Papers
Grey Papers
Japanese Canadian Citizens' Association Records
W.L. Mackenzie King Papers and Diary
Wilfrid Laurier Papers
Ian Mackenzie Papers
Arthur Meighen Papers
J.L. Ralston Papers
Norman Robertson Papers

PUBLIC RECORD OFFICE, LONDON
Cabinet Records
Dominions Office Records
Foreign Office Records

UNITED CHURCH ARCHIVES, TORONTO
Albert Best Papers
Board of Foreign Missions Records
Margaret Brown Papers
Harper Coates Family Papers
Japan Mission Fellowship Papers
R. Gordon Struthers Papers

UNITED STATES NATIONAL ARCHIVES, WASHINGTON

Department of the Navy General Records
Foreign Service Posts Records
Joint Chiefs of Staff Records
National Security Agency Records
Permanent Joint Board on Defence Records

UNIVERSITY OF BRITISH COLUMBIA SPECIAL COLLECTIONS, VANCOUVER

J.W. de B. Farris Papers
Japanese Canadian Research Collection [includes Kadota, Nishikihama, Oyagi, Wakabayashi and Yamaga collections]
Angus MacInnis Records
National Japanese-Canadian Citizens Association Records
Pitt Meadows Japanese Farmers Association Records
W.N. Sage Papers
A.M. Stephen Scrapbooks

VANCOUVER CITY ARCHIVES, VANCOUVER

Advisory Committee on Japanese Properties Records
Mayors' Correspondence

Index